Becoming Visible

Women's Presence in Late Nineteenth-Century America

45 DQR STUDIES IN LITERATURE

Series Editors

C.C. Barfoot - A.J. Hoenselaars
W.M. Verhoeven

Becoming Visible

Women's Presence in Late Nineteenth-Century America

Edited by
Janet Floyd, Alison Easton,
R. J. Ellis and Lindsey Traub

Amsterdam - New York, NY 2010

Cover photo: Mother Jones leads a protest march down Main Street, Trinidad, Colorado, during the 1903 coal miners' strike.

Cover design: Aart Jan Bergshoeff

The paper on which this book is printed meets the requirements of 'ISO 9706: 1994, Information and documentation - Paper for documents - Requirements for permanence'.

ISBN: 978-90-420-2977-4
E-Book ISBN: 978-90-420-2978-1
©Editions Rodopi B.V., Amsterdam - New York, NY 2010
Printed in The Netherlands

CONTENTS

vi

LIST OF ILLUSTRATIONS

ACKNOWLEDGEMENTS

This volume began in June 2005 at King's College London with a colloquium, "Visible Women: American Women and Public Space 1865-1910", and the editors would like to begin by thanking all those who attended, including those participants who have written essays for this volume, for their contribution to our thinking about the presence of women in post-Civil War American life. The colloquium was funded by the American Embassy in London, the British Association of American Studies, and the Department of American Studies at King's College London. Our thanks for that support. It was organized under the auspices of the Society for the Study of American Women Writers and it is a pleasure to acknowledge the part that Karen Kilcup played in setting up, in 1993, the British branch of the Society. Finally, we would like to thank those who have helped us to prepare this volume: we owe a special debt of gratitude to Anna Luker who has taken such care in getting the manuscript ready for publication, and we are also grateful to Susan Forsyth for her assistance.

Introduction: Becoming Visible

Alison Easton, R.J. Ellis, Janet Floyd,
and Lindsey Traub

The over-arching contention of this collection of interdisciplinary essays is straightforward: the later decades of the nineteenth century in America – the immediate postbellum period, the Gilded Age, and the Progressive Era – were a time of critical change in the cultural visibility of women, whether it was a visibility attained by them, granted to them, or contested by them. During this period, economic and social changes, still profoundly inflected by matters of gender, class and race, saw women making new kinds of appearances throughout American society. Often highly controversial, these changes were recorded across and within a wide range of cultural artifacts, events and texts. In this process, women were not always visible to each other, nor to state institutions, hegemonic forces, or subsequent historiography, but their motivations, activities, and understandings were essential to shaping, at various levels, the character of their present society and the nation's future.

This collection therefore advances a range of perspectives on the complex ways in which American women were seen during this period and asks how, when and where they became more culturally visible (as opposed to merely present). The essays included here consider women with a public profile, those only intermittently "seen", and those who became invisible to later generations. By exploring the appearances of immigrant women, women of the working class, Native American, African American, and white middle-class women, we can show how, across the USA, it was fundamentally women who drove this change forward, in groups and as individuals.

The editors and contributors to this volume particularly want to understand women's presence in nineteenth-century American society and culture in terms other than the traditional polarities of inside/outside and private/public, since these dichotomizing frames simply do not fit the complexities of what was happening. Much power and consequence were invested in those binarized concepts; their rhetorical organization of space appeared central to both social recognition and personal freedom. They were generated as much by economic structures of advanced industrial capitalism and the racist social structures of segregation as by the patriarchal thinking that had given birth to liberal notions of the public and private spheres, yet they certainly did not constitute the norm for most women, even though such ideological mystifications still materially affected their lives.[1] Given that the hegemonic powers of these decades – patriarchal, capitalist, white supremacist – determined how "public" and "private" were defined, the distinction between these poles was used to establish and perpetuate social divisions (in labor and in living) that served the vested interests of the economically and racially powerful, and to occlude or deny the interests of those with less power, little power, or no power (most women, peoples of color, the working class). Consequently, the binarized terms "public" and "private" were far from transparent or static in the nineteenth century; they were not extant concrete realities but rather, as Mary Ryan puts it, "cultural constructions imposed on a complex world".[2]

What has proved remarkable, in retrospect, is how difficult any quest to move consistently beyond these polarities becomes and how these binaries re-impose themselves, if sometimes only by implication. This is perhaps a sign of how much power accrues in sustaining the socio-cultural organization that these binaries sought (and seek) to naturalize. In Deleuze's words, "It is wrong to say that the binary machine exists only for reasons of convenience ... the

---

[1] See Carole Pateman, "Feminist Critiques of the Public/ Private Dichotomy", in *The Disorder of Women: Democracy, Feminism and Political Theory*, Oxford: Polity Press, 1989, and Elizabeth Maddock Dillon, *The Gender of Freedom: Fictions of Liberalism and the Literary Public Sphere*, Stanford, CA: Stanford UP, 2004.

[2] Mary P. Ryan, *Women in Public: Between Banners and Ballots, 1825-1880*, Baltimore, MD: Johns Hopkins UP, 1990, 6.

binary machine is an important component of apparatuses of power".[3] Indeed, these binaries kept on reasserting themselves even as we tried to arrive at a title for our collection. For example, the first title we considered, "Stepping Out", seemed to offer us a lot (not least with its suggestion of a gathering of pace), yet it also somehow imputed a point of departure and an inside/outside taxonomy that we were trying to break away from, and about which we were uneasy – both generally and particularly. Generally, we were uneasy because we were aware that the strident discursive representations enshrined in these binaries were in themselves signs of tension and contradictions in the hegemonic project of establishing a "within" and a "without". Particularly, we were uneasy because we aimed to propose that such an inside/outside modeling came under increasing challenge in the decades upon which we focus, and because the phrase "stepping out" paradoxically confirmed the existence of within/without binaries even in the very process of suggesting some sort of exit was being attempted. It seemed to us that this constituted a signal problem (if the pun can be forgiven).

Facing these difficulties over articulating a more complex and dynamic model of spatialization, one possible recourse was to turn to the field of (post)colonial studies, which has needed to wrestle with similar problems over inside/outside polarizations (as our use of parenthesis intends to suggest), and to expositions, for example, by Gloria Anzaldúa, Mary Louise Pratt, and Doris Sommer, which seek to emphasize the complex ways in which asymmetries of power and their all too real pains and costs complicate the necessary attempt (which we, analogously, are attempting) to break free of binary demarcations – in the (post)colonial instance, ones principally defined by nation states.[4] In this process, the focus of such studies often falls on tortuous, exciting, dangerous, transitional penumbras, such as borderlands, diasporas and liminal fields. American capitalist "free marketplaces", like borders or diasporas, it can be argued, were and

---

[3] Gilles Deleuze, *Dialogues II*, trans. Hugh Tomlinson, Barbara Habberjam and Eliot Ross, London: Continuum International, 2006, 16.

[4] See Gloria Anzaldúa, *Borderlands/La Frontera: The New Mestiza*, San Francisco, CA: Aunt Lute Books, 1987; Mary Louise Pratt, *Imperial Eyes: Studies in Travel Writing and Transculturation*, London: Routledge, 1992; and Doris Sommer, *Bilingual Aesthetics: A New Sentimental Education*, Durham, NC: Duke UP, 2004.

are spaces both transactional and transitional, both abstract and concrete. Already contradictory in their very formulation (like the term, "nation state"), they have been fields of both open personal, cultural and financial opportunity – albeit always already highly qualified and even circumscribed – and of substantial risk and danger, whether a financial, labor, marriage or some other market be the term in question. In such exciting but also enfiladed places of exchange, the "tri-partite cross-fire" of gender, race and class, in Maya Angelou's brilliant phrase, constitutes the danger, and therefore very precise co-ordinates need stipulating when representing these fire-zones and their high risks.[5]

Offering this analogy with the highly contested field of (post)colonial theory obviously ends up, however, as at best partial and flawed, though conveying how inside/outside binaries cannot hold. Focusing instead on visibility has provided us with another, ultimately better way to try to elude conventional ways of thinking about both conceptions of and experiences of the public, and has allowed us to investigate afresh who or what determined what was public, what forces drove shifts in the status and meaning of particular spaces, and what helped dissolve these distinctions. Our approach has been to ask about modes of visibility within multiple publics and spaces – sometimes traditional, sometimes new, sometimes hybrid, sometimes liminal, and always complex – in which, in some sense or other, women were seen or experienced themselves as looked at, noted, recognized, deplored, feted. Clearly there were degrees of invisibility as well as of visibility, or of invisibility within visibility, yet some women's exceptional visibility – the extravagant presence of the opera singer, the endangered exposure of working-class radical campaigners or the physical and legal resistance of a black woman forcibly ejected from the ladies' car – has much to tell us about the situations of those less visible.

Visibility was many things for women at this period: dreadful, triumphant; opportune, limiting; dangerous, liberating; acclaimed, humiliating; pleasurable, painful; exceptional, normal; ambiguous. Being visible was not good in and of itself. Much hinged on who saw whom or who surveyed whom, whether those eyes belonged to people

---

[5] Maya Angelou, *I Know Why the Caged Bird Sings*, New York: Random House, 1969, 231.

and forces more powerful than the woman herself, and whether they were capable of understanding, engagement, fair treatment, compassion. Furthermore, there must have always been a layering of visibility – to use the concept explored in this volume by Margaret Walsh. Women would be at one and the same time visible in different ways and in differing degrees to various social groups and agencies.

Many of the contributors to this volume have explored the particular spaces in which women became visible, moved and acted, and these were numerous, disparate and, crucially, not always obviously public. Some locations – for example, streets, public buildings, factories, the houses of the poor and the well-to-do, social and political gatherings, public meetings, national celebrations, theatrical stages, parks, streets, parlors and kitchens, hotels and holiday resorts, railroads, high mountains, the far West, newspapers, campaign writings, memoirs, fictions – might be understood as public or private according to the different circumstances of their use. We have asked in these essays about access and about the means by which women entered these spaces, and when they chose to step into them or when, without volition, they found themselves positioned in them. How were spaces marked by women as their own? How did spaces mark women?

For some women, it was a matter of crisscrossing the borders between a public visibility and a private life that might be imagined as invisible or, at any rate, differently visible. Others, claiming a special or elite status in bold, brave ways, presented themselves as moving with more apparent freedom in and out of diffuse public spaces, crossing boundaries without dissonance, making intimate connections between public and family life, and enjoying a visibility – even if it still had to be negotiated. During the late nineteenth century, without doubt, women had the power to change a place by stepping into it. They purposefully both altered public spaces physically to make room for women, and redefined or transformed ideological spaces that had significance for the nation as a whole.

Such movements made the calibration of self and identity and the management of body and performance crucially important to individual women; but these were not only individual challenges. There is a striking sense of the collective in the lives and actions of the women studied in this volume. If they were acting in association with other women (and sometimes with men), or acting alone, still they operated with an awareness that their situation was never purely personal. Furthermore, their work suggests a sense of change and difference happening in and around them, and an awareness of reshaping (or attempting to reshape) their world and not just themselves. They had what Janet Zandy identifies in this volume as an "alternative Bildung", a sense of the different dynamic of their activity that became particularly noticeable by the end of the century. Contributors in this volume have turned to a wide range of historical, cultural and material cultural texts as well as literary texts (some mainstream and iconic, others little known then or now) that reflect women's appearances in these spaces, represent the inner processes by which they dealt with their increasing visibility, and record or explore their developing understandings of these changes.

The book begins with a section that explores the changing dimensions of public and private. Anne Boylan's essay opens the discussion with an analysis of the way in which the activities of certain women's organizations shaped their own visibility through creating or altering public spaces, and how class and race shaped these interventions. She reveals the ways in which these women's involvement in creating landmark public buildings and memorials and their need and demand for safer streets, shopping areas and transportation burgeoned in this period. The multiform and prevalent discourse of the separate spheres ideology has tended to obscure the view – for later generations – of much that women were actually doing, where they were to be seen and how they felt about the social, cultural and economic forces operating among them. This shaping and reshaping of public space and public life made for new and different visibilities in the postbellum period, deeply impressive in certain ways, even when only partially effective or mixed in its results.

Janet Zandy's spirited account of the lives of three "dangerous working-class women" is a timely exposition of the power of some women to go well beyond their allotted spheres to become highly visible, inspirational leaders of men and women in the tumultuous world of labor activism. Again we find women on the streets. Though Boylan's middle-class and Zandy's working-class women inhabited profoundly different sectors of this society and had very different politics, both authors here are concerned with women working for change in association with others, the individual "I" inseparable from a collective "we", stepping out and reshaping ideological spaces if not always the physical, economic, political and social ones. Boylan asks about levels of public effectiveness in her subjects' actions; Zandy shows how her subjects' radical resistance to economic injustice and to the dire oppressions of industrial capitalist system was met with violence that drove overlapping generations of activists to keep on traveling, organizing, marching, speaking in public, demonstrating, and writing.

Garment workers, the women who sewed for wages at home and in various kinds of factories, were representative of the debased system of manufacturing that Zandy's activists identified and sought to remedy. Instead of being out in the streets, these women were to be found in the contract shop and in the kitchen, performing the so-called outside work that took place in interior spaces, doing work deemed suitable for working women (though challenging to middle-class notions of female respectability), and leading to a gender-segregated, unskilled sector emerging in larger factories. Theirs was the most visible form of working-class women's lives, exposed (to mixed responses) as it was by contemporary journalists, investigators, reformers and state regulators. Margaret Walsh, writing about the needle trades, develops a concept of "layered visibility" out of these circumstances. The value and significance attached to such women shifted according to separate circles within which they lived and worked: their ethnic community, their employers and the male co-workers who had that "insider knowledge" that Zandy identifies as key to her radical women activists who knew, accepted and respected them. We can also locate this group of partially visible women within Jay Kleinberg's overview of women's remunerated work patterns generally. Her rigorous analysis of the data of women's employment over the period is the foundation of a subtle interpretation of the significance of the relative visibility of their occupations. Thus, though working outside their own homes, a large proportion of working women – and, of those, predominantly African American and Native American women – were employed "invisibly", in other people's homes or in the unvisited isolation imposed by agricultural labor. They were consequently also invisible in the period's developing employment legislation. Kleinberg shows how concepts of public and private came to have different meanings: being public evolved into the recognition of women and their work spaces in the economic sphere, together with becoming a subject of public policy and increasing state regulation, whereas "private" indicated an invisibility of women in places where it advantaged hegemonic forces to ignore them. She shows exactly why applying the public/private binary is so dangerous.

Where segregation was the dominant social, economic, political and legal structure organizing public space and private lives, visibility was primarily dangerous, but was consequently also politically urgent. Unwelcome publicity and gross misrepresentation, writes Mia Bay, discouraged African American women, especially in the South, from visible protest against endemic sexual and racial violence. Navigating such dangerous spaces was extraordinarily difficult. Sticking out in a sexually and racially charged public space could mean physical brutality and death – when transport, shop, street, office, newspapers, even the home itself were not inviolate. Bay describes how Ida B. Wells, teacher, journalist and activist, turned her own physical experience of gendered racism to powerful effect, after she protested her removal from the ladies' car on the (then unsegregated) Ohio and Southwestern railroad. Her refusal of silence, her changing from a culture of dissemblance to public engagement, her intellectual and practical challenge to white supremacism on behalf of her collective community led on to her national campaign against lynching and the increasingly active visibility of women in the sexualized politics of Jim Crow.

To conclude the first part of this collection, Alison Easton explores two reformist, indeed utopian, attempts to ameliorate actual conditions or re-imagine community. Annie Adams Fields as charity organizer and Sarah Orne Jewett as fiction writer were public women who reflected in different ways on public behavior in the space of the home. Far removed from marches, platform speeches and dangers from mobs and state forces, they were nonetheless deeply concerned with the material and personal repercussions of America's advanced industrial capitalist economy on people's material circumstances and intersocial relations. The act of visiting, whether for charitable or social purposes, became a crucial move to challenge and offset the distinction between public and private created by current forms of capitalism. Home and its inhabitants, invisible and often neglected, were made visible and attended to, with interacting across classes making them mutually visible. Whatever its limitations (and they were considerable), this was a positive, connective stepping out.

Part II of this book, "Stepping Out: Bodies, Spaces, and the Cultural Representation of Visibility", deals with the individual experience of visibility, the part this plays in identity and in social acceptability and social power, the complex modalities of this embodiment, the acts of (self-)presentation and representation of women's bodies, public performances and the dressing of bodies, and the subjective processes of personhood. All the essays in this section focus on or have recourse to written texts, fictional and autobiographical, that represent, explore and negotiate these issues.

Lindsey Traub argues that Louisa May Alcott's domestic realism, including *Little Women* (1868) explores the simultaneous subjective processes of self-surveillance and self-construction that enable women to sustain and even to control their visibility. In a series of novels in the early part of this period (1864-73), Alcott developed narrative strategies that accommodate her growing understanding of the significance of visibility and its relation to agency and cultural change for white, middle-class girls in transition to womanhood. The deliberately elusive internal evidence of color and class in Emma Dunham Kelley's novels of 1891 and 1894, R.J. Ellis then argues, has distracted critics from the more interesting attention her writing pays to her young protagonists' visibility, their reading of appearance, the play of identity in leisure spaces, and the act of self-scrutiny in public. These young women, like Alcott's earlier in this period, are liminally positioned, and must strike a careful balance between conformity and distinctiveness, between pleasure and propriety, between desire and respectability and a contemporary shifting of definitions in each of these arenas. The centrality of performance in Kelley's novels signals the way in which performativity infuses many cultural spaces, including the summer resort, the donning of fashion and even, or, rather, of course, church-going. The behavior and interactions of Kelley's young women reveal how the new woman, of whatever color, must learn the visible codes and dialects of paradigm-shifting consumer culture that cross class and ethnicity.

But perhaps no woman's body was more insistently visible and open to unmediated observation than that of the female singer, as Janet Floyd suggests. She acts within a totally public space. Popular though she was, however, uncertainties still persisted in perceptions of the singer. The relationships between the "gift" and its body, voice and self-identity, between the singer, her inner self, and her power over her audience raised multiple questions of female agency and power. Yet the association of the singer's voice with volume, space, freedom and natural expression made this also a figure that might be mobilized in the imagination of broader themes of national health and identity. The quality of American cultural, political and personal life, in a period of diminishing hostility to women's public performance, is also central to Henry James' novel, *The Bostonians* (1886). Peter Rawlings proposes that it is the philosophical (Lockean and Hobbesian) underpinning of its preoccupation with visibility, seeing and being seen that raises a caveat, through James' equivocal narration, around the "liberatory imperatives" of increased publicity and visibility for women. Redefining visibility, James finds it to be a horror, and he reacts against what he sees as a miscegenation of public and private spheres in his contemporary America. James traces the painful journey of Verena Tarrant from unselfconsciousness and high visibility to subjectivity, intimacy and the subsequent surrender of her public persona to domestic seclusion.

Narcissa Owen, on the other hand, was a public woman claiming agency in national affairs, a modern version of the Cherokee Beloved Woman but also one who, in writing for multiple audiences, intended to redefine American womanhood for all. Karen Kilcup explores Owen's *Memoirs* (1907) and the fundamental imbrication of public and private spaces effected by her autobiography's transitive discourse. Owen's public visibility varies in this work, but she performs and recounts a subjectivity that involves both public-sphere recognition and private self-authorizing. This is someone who is socially mobile and culturally multiple in her identities, and she negotiates public power and femininity in a new way for a Native American woman. To conclude this part of the collection, Shirley Foster analyses the self-presentation and representation of other end-of-the-century elite women, this time all white – three notable American women travelers. All socially powerful – Nelly Bly, journalist and circumnavigator, May French-Sheldon, explorer and Fanny Bullock Workman, mountaineer – had to respond to what Foster calls the "challenging disparity between conventional images of the female body and corporeal freedom" by consciously and ingeniously adapting, without abandoning or openly challenging, the material limits and cultural constraints of femininity, to achieve their own record-breaking goals. Though traveling to remote places in which they could not be materially visible to Americans, they also engineered a textual presence for themselves in the public press. Here they deployed their privileged social status, their bodies and their ability to negotiate hegemonic discourses of the group to which they belong, in order to eliminate restricting domestic responsibilities and effect an innovative visibility.

The final section of this book both considers how – as the nineteenth century closed and the twentieth century opened – the issue of visibility remained urgent, and begins to explore how addressing such issues at this pivotal time needed to confront a moment of seeming fracture with the past. Considering this development in representations of visibility necessarily starts to take our volume's attention away from the nineteenth century and into the twentieth, and in a sense beyond our book's boundaries. But this moment demands attention, so we have included two essays that in their different ways are particularly concerned with the changes that appeared, to those living at that period, to mark decisively the end of nineteenth-century culture. Clearly, as we have seen in the other essays in this volume, the nation had been undergoing fundamental transformations throughout the last third of the century, but the two essays in this closing section look at the point where a chasm seems to have opened up between the familiar and the new, between past and present – a sense of absolute discontinuity that generated feelings of crisis, confusion, danger and profound unease, though also, in the case of some excluded groups, a sense of rising opportunity. Timothy Hickman's essay directly addresses the concept of modernity as crisis, and how various commentators at the time sought to define this, especially those who saw the dissolution of gender-specific spheres (even though in actuality gender segregation persisted, only in different spaces) as a marker of distinction in turn-of-the-century life. Technological developments were the other key marker. Hickman singles out Frances Willard, the feminist and temperance activist, as one who interpreted this experience of modernity as opportunity, looking for what would encourage, empower and release women. Hickman encapsulates this in her enthusiasm for the bicycle: the female body ensconced on new technology, safely emerging from a previous confinement, newly mobile (rather than simply nomadic), crossing borders and traveling towards new horizons. Interestingly, in a less strategically two-faced way than Foster's women travelers and in a more abstracted, political argument than Narcissa Owen's memoirs, Willard uses "feminine" qualities and behaviors to construct her argument for stepping out into a wider world.

Susan Harris' essay also deals with the emergent sense of profound crisis, as her subjects recoiled from the imperialist co-option and misuse of that cherished fusion of Christian, familial and democratic ideals which throughout most of the century had animated reform work (in civic, philanthropic and women's rights activities) and given an identity to the women involved that spoke also to their sense of the nation. Harris' subjects are politically active women, campaigners against the Philippine-American war. In a number of essays in this book we see women attempting in various ways to think for the nation as a whole as well as specifically for the oppressed and disadvantaged or for themselves as individuals, and we see them grappling – courageously, constructively, sometimes heroically – with the dangers and opportunities of their changing visibility. In Harris' essay, as her subjects are forced to change the nature of their civil engagement, the old world was finally left behind and women took a further new step into visibility.

As you read these essays, you will discover that, occasionally and sometimes noteworthily, well-established ideas of public/private, inside/outside binaries remerge or are still deployed, though always, we believe, in more complicated forms or ways. We are not unhappy about such re-emergences: after all, the nineteenth-century state, business world, and social culture deployed these concepts constantly. We believe, however, that this collection, *Becoming Visible*, by shifting the main focus to women's economic, social, political, and cultural visibility in the United States' postbellum decades and by emphasizing movement, change and continued evolution, as embodied in the choice of our initial word in our title (*Becoming*), has found valuable new ways to reveal and understand the complex redefining of women's role, place and being at this period. We hope you agree.

PART I

THE CHANGING GEOGRAPHY OF PUBLIC AND PRIVATE

CLAIMING VISIBILITY: WOMEN IN PUBLIC / PUBLIC WOMEN IN THE UNITED STATES, 1865-1910

ANNE M. BOYLAN

It is not hard to find women in public, let alone public women, in nineteenth-century America. Women were present and visible in many different public arenas ranging from the halls of Congress to the marketplace to the courtroom, the theater, the lecture stage, and, by the last third of the century, the polling place. Yet for a long time historians and literary scholars had difficulty seeing them, because nineteenth-century gender ideology reserved spaces termed "public" for men and reserved the epithet "public woman" for prostitutes and women who seemed to transgress gender boundaries in the most flagrant ways. Moreover, this gender ideology was everywhere – in novels and advice books, magazines and schoolbooks, as well as newspapers and political speeches; it dominated the texts that historians first examined. Because the ideology appeared to depict "public women" as the only visible women in the era, scholars assumed that respectable women were invisible. Indeed, a gender ideology of spheres and realms and public/private separation was so ubiquitous in nineteenth-century texts that scholars devoted considerable effort to parsing and elucidating that ideology; eventually, however, they noticed the now-obvious presence of many different kinds of women in public spaces and began to ask how Americans reconciled women's public presence with the dominant gender ideology of their era.[1]

---

[1] See Anne L. Kuhn, *The Mother's Role in Childhood Education: New England Concepts, 1830-1860*, New Haven, CT: Yale UP, 1947; Barbara Welter, "The Cult of True Womanhood, 1820-1860", *American Quarterly*, XVIII/2 (Summer 1966), 151-74. For two important critiques of the historiography, see Linda Kerber, "Separate Spheres, Female Worlds, Women's Place: The Rhetoric of Women's History", *Journal of American History*, LXXV/1 (June 1988), 9-39; and Cathy N. Davidson,

In *The Origins of Women's Activism*, I examined this issue by studying the era during which the gender ideology of spheres first emerged, and chronicling a particularly clear example of women's public activism: the formation of woman-run voluntary societies.[2] Some women collected money for charitable or missionary enterprises; others ran large urban welfare programs for orphans, poor working women, or indigent elderly women; still others pooled the resources of working women – either African American or white – in mutual assistance programs. And, by the 1830s in Northern cities, abolitionist and moral reform organizations had come into being – expressing radical critiques of social institutions such as slavery and prostitution. By 1840, New York and Boston alone had over seventy-five such organized groups; free women of all backgrounds – black and white, Catholic and Protestant – formed and ran such associations. Among white Protestant associations, an appreciable number sought and won legal incorporation, in the process constituting themselves as rights-bearing collective entities, public bodies entitled to sue in court, own property, borrow and invest money, indenture children, secure shares of tax revenues, and in general behave like free adult citizens.[3]

Women's associations proliferated at precisely the same time that the ideology of spheres emerged to shape public conversations about nineteenth-century gender rules. The two developments were simultaneous, not sequential. Moreover, women themselves were active participants in creating and sustaining the ideology of spheres. And with the exception of a few early objections (during the years 1800 to 1810), few men criticized or opposed this new departure in women's activities. It was the rare public commentator, minister, or political figure who upbraided women's groups for their insouciance or saw associational work as conflicting with women's family

---

"No More Separate Spheres!", *American Literature*, LXX/3 (September 1998), 443-63. For some recent theoretical perspectives, see Joan W. Scott and Debra Keates, *Going Public: Feminism and the Shifting Boundaries of the Private Sphere*, Urbana: U of Illinois P, 2004.

[2] Anne M. Boylan, *The Origins of Women's Activism: New York and Boston, 1797-1840*, Chapel Hill: U of North Carolina P, 2002.

[3] See *ibid.*, and Nancy A. Hewitt, *Women's Activism and Social Change: Rochester, New York, 1822-1872*, Ithaca, NY: Cornell UP, 1984 and Lori D. Ginzberg, *Women and the Work of Benevolence: Morality, Politics, and Class in Nineteenth-century America*, New Haven, CT: Yale UP, 1990.

responsibilities. Yet the typical woman leader of such organizations was married, in her thirties or forties, and still involved in child-rearing or even child-bearing. Women leaders ran to meetings in between bearing, birthing or weaning babies, tending sick toddlers, and mourning dead children and family members. Neither women nor ministers nor politicians viewed these activities as outside the proper sphere of womanly behavior, even though the work often demanded many hours of weekly labor and bore more than a passing resemblance to the work that male merchants and managers performed. When individual women did comment on the nature of their voluntary careers, only rarely did they exhibit any concern that their associational work might conflict with family labor. During the 1820s, for instance, a Boston minister's wife noted in her diary how two members of her husband's congregation, on successive Sundays, offered opposite comments on her involvement in women's organizations. The first asked her "with a tone and manner which gave peculiar emphasis" to the question, how she could "go out so much ... and be engaged in so many charitable societies, without neglecting [her] family". The second, however, criticized her for "doing so little in a public way, and confining myself so much to my family". For herself, this minister's wife decided that if she were properly organized and worked hard, she could "redeem much time from [her family] for more public duties".[4]

The language this woman used is telling. Her voluntary society labors were "public duties", in part because she was a minister's wife, in part because she performed them for the benefit of others. Her comments serve as a reminder that the terms "public" and "private" were not transparent or static in the nineteenth century. Instead, their usage changed continually. As this woman's experience underlines, terms such as "public" and "private" seldom described concrete lived realities. Instead, they encompassed continually shifting concepts with blurred and ever-moving boundaries.

The chameleon-like qualities of terms such as "public" and "private", or "home" and "work", underscore the extent to which nineteenth-century dichotomies were fluid, certainly more so than historical actors made them appear. This fluidity can be seen in the

---

[4] Benjamin B. Wisner, *Memoirs of the Late Mrs Susan Huntington of Boston, Massachusetts*, Boston, MA: Crocker and Brewster, 1836, 120-22.

intermeshing of family and public worlds in daily life. Middle-class family life facilitated public work, both for women and for men. New Yorker Joanna Bethune articulated this point when she commented: "I cannot well attend to my duties ... & to my societies unless I am [living] in a quiet place". Conversely, public work might take place within family precincts, as Catherine Allgor has reminded us.[5] Because Margaret Bayard Smith's skills as a hostess complemented her husband's important position as a newspaper editor, their genteel parlor in Washington City was the site of much political wheeling and dealing. And of course, many a woman's voluntary society meetings took place in just such a parlor.

At the same time, the fuzziness of the boundaries of spheres did not keep anyone from wielding the language of spheres as a weapon against unpopular ideas and activities. In the antebellum era, when one finds members of a women's organization chastised for stepping outside woman's sphere, it is a sure bet that the reprimand is aimed at what the organization advocated and represented. The principle of women acting collectively for particular purposes – even when those actions involved acquiring charters of incorporation, holding property in the group's name, or seeking political favors – was seldom challenged. Instead, critics wielded ideas about spheres and inappropriate public activity selectively, and exclusively against women and organizations that advocated unpopular causes, such as abolition.[6]

To be visible in the antebellum era, then, could be a positive or a negative for women who ran voluntary associations. They might find themselves lavishly praised for their self-sacrifice or roundly denounced for the cause they espoused. Furthermore, not all antebellum women's groups equally visible, nor visible in the same arenas. In the white press, for example, black women's groups were placed in the spotlight only as subjects of racist caricature. The black and abolitionist presses covered the activities of African American women's groups, but black newspapers were scarce and published

---

[5] Bethune, quoted in Boylan, *The Origins of Women's Activism*, 110; see also Catherine Allgor, *Parlor Politics: In Which the Women of Washington Help Build a City and a Government*, Charlottesville: UP of Virginia, 2000.
[6] Ginzberg, *Women and the Work of Benevolence*, 67-97; Boylan, *The Origins of Women's Activism*, 158-66.

only intermittently until Frederick Douglass and Mary Ann Shadd Cary succeeded in establishing *The North Star* and the *Provincial Freeman* in 1847 and 1854 respectively. Catholic lay women's groups were especially imperceptible. Nuns, not lay women, represented Catholic womanhood to nineteenth-century non-Catholics – and were either admired or targeted for attacks, including dangerous physical attacks on convents (such as the 1834 convent-burning in Charlestown, Massachusetts).[7]

Such an attack served as a reminder that public visibility could be dangerous. The 1830s witnessed a number of similar events when groups of women found themselves endangered because of what they symbolized or advocated. Attacks on integrated female anti-slavery society meetings constituted another such reminder, as did the brothel riots that occurred in New York and other cities. In these instances, some women in public could be treated like public women. But only some women had to worry that they would be attacked as they met to undertake collective activities. No one bothered the missionary or orphanage society's assembly, even when it convened at a hotel or theatre. But as individuals, traveling to and from meetings, women of all backgrounds could find city streets and public spaces to be places of personal danger, whether from thieves, counterfeiters, rowdy clerks, jostling crowds, or sexual predators. Indeed, part of the impetus behind the formation of Female Moral Reform Societies was the perception among middle-class white urban migrants that cities were sinks of iniquity where moral as well as personal corruption was commonplace. When moral reform societies created the only national women's voluntary association of this era – the American Female Moral Reform Society – they sought to re-appropriate public space in order to make it safe for women like themselves.[8]

---

[7] Carol K. Coburn and Martha Smith, *Spirited Lives: How Nuns Shaped Catholic Culture and American Life, 1836-1920*, Chapel Hill: U of North Carolina P, 1999; Maureen Fitzgerald, *Habits of Compassion: Irish Catholic Nuns and the Origins of New York's Welfare System, 1830-1920*, Chapel Hill: U of North Carolina P, 2006, 21-23.

[8] Mary P. Ryan, *Women in Public: Between Banners and Ballots, 1825-1880*, Baltimore, MD: Johns Hopkins UP, 100-102; Patricia Cline Cohen, *The Murder of Helen Jewett*, New York: Random House, 1998, 82-86; Kathleen Brown, "The History of Women in the United States to 1865", in *Women's History in Global Perspective*, ed. Bonnie G. Smith, Urbana: U of Illinois P, 2005, II, 238-80.

After 1865, the impetus for creating safe streets came from many sources, including owners of the new department stores seeking to soothe the anxieties of female customers and members of women's clubs and associations. Among the striking changes occurring in the decades between 1865 and 1910 was the new and different visibility, in a variety of settings, of women from various racial, ethnic and religious backgrounds. As paid laborers in urban commercial, service, and industrial economies, as rural agricultural workers and as professionals, women workers were now accounted for in the federal census. (In taking the 1850 census, the US government had recorded the "Profession, Occupation, or Trade" only of each free "Male Person over 15 years of age".) Women were also visible in new leisure spaces created by a growing consumer culture – dance halls and amusement parks, nickelodeon shows and movies. In the new palaces of consumption and "ladies' miles" shopping districts, too, as individuals and in groups, many women took the freedom of parts of the city for granted as they went about their daily routines.

Americans' public panic about the "working girl", and the dual meanings they gave that term, date from the post-Civil War years. The term acquired dual meanings (and largely replaced the term "public woman") precisely because women's increasingly visible presence on city streets and in urban spaces, along with young single women's participation in new forms of economic and sexual exchange – what they termed "dating" and "treating" – seemed to suggest a worrying independence, especially independence from masculine control. By 1910, despite the lingering power of the imagery of masculine and feminine spheres, women and men increasingly inhabited the same spaces on city streets, in department stores, office buildings, restaurants and theaters, subways and railways, and amusement parks. Scrutinize almost any photograph of the streets of New York, San Francisco, Minneapolis, or New Orleans in 1910 and one sees men, women, and children mingling and seemingly enjoying equal access to the available spaces.[9]

---

[9] See Kathy Peiss, *Cheap Amusements: Working Women and Leisure in Turn-of-the-century New York*, Philadelphia, PA: Temple UP, 1986; Lynn Y. Weiner, *From Working Girl to Working Mother: The Female Labor Force in the United States, 1920-1980*, Chapel Hill: U of North Carolina P, 1985; John T. Kasson, *Rudeness and Civility: Manners in Nineteenth-century Urban America*, New York: Hill and Wang, 1990; Lewis Erenberg, *Steppin' Out: New York Nightlife and the Transformation of*

Of all these new forms of visibility, perhaps the most noteworthy were those that emerged from women's own concrete actions, particularly through creating or altering public physical spaces. There are a number of ways to explore this process, including examining how the presence of groups of working girls made city streets look different, or how the creation of boarding-house neighborhoods enabled young women to experiment sexually in anonymous public spaces.[10] But I want to focus on the vigorous efforts of women's voluntary associations, especially the national organizations that grew phenomenally after 1865. The presence and actions of these new groups fundamentally reshaped town and city geographies, public spaces, and transportation practices. A few examples illustrate the number and striking variety of new national organizations: the Young Women's Christian Association (YWCA, 1870); the Woman's Christian Temperance Union (WCTU, 1874); the National American Woman Suffrage Association (1890), which united two groups initially founded in 1869; the General Federation of Women's Clubs (1892); the National Council of Jewish Women (1893); the National Association of Colored Women (1896); and the Women's Trade Union League (1903). Church women's missionary societies rivaled these groups in numbers; the Woman's Convention of the Black Baptist Church, founded in 1900, could claim to represent nearly a million Baptist women by 1903, a million and a half by 1907. And during the 1890s, women's patriotic and hereditary societies arrived in droves; at the national level, three quickly took center stage – the National Society of Colonial Dames (1891); the Daughters of the American Revolution (1892); and the United Daughters of the Confederacy (1894).[11] Some of these patriotic associations undertook

American Culture, 1890-1930, Westport, CT: Greenwood Press, 1981. Sharon E. Wood, in her book *The Freedom of the Streets: Work, Citizenship, and Sexuality in a Gilded Age City*, Chapel Hill: U of North Carolina P, 2005, argues, however, that snapshot portraits were deceptive: working women met intransigent male resistance when they sought to alter the "sexual politics of the streets".

[10] See Joanne Meyerowitz, *Women Adrift: Independent Wage Earners in Chicago, 1880-1930*, Chicago: U of Chicago P, 1988; Elizabeth Clement, *Trick or Treat: Courting Couples, Charity Girls, Prostitutes and the Making of Modern Heterosexuality in New York City, 1900-1945*, Chapel Hill: U of North Carolina P, 2006.

[11] See Francesca Morgan, *Women and Patriotism in Jim Crow America*, Chapel Hill: U of North Carolina P, 2005, 19-55; Evelyn Brooks Higginbotham, *Righteous*

the heavy labor of building and preserving monuments of various sorts, including memorials to the Civil War dead and the establishment of heritage museums and historic houses. Finally, some women's groups took new approaches to political activism during the era, especially in pursuit of full suffrage. The massive organizing campaigns for state, local, and national suffrage assumed many forms, but all involved significant efforts to remake traditionally masculine spaces.[12]

These three developments – the reshaping of downtowns and city landscapes, monument-building, and the efforts of organized suffragists to claim a place in politics – offer especially clear examples of how collections of women shaped their own visibility in the 1865-1910 era. The developments were interrelated, and because they were, they raised additional issues about what visibility would mean, including questions about what safety and danger for women in public spaces would look like. And they raised questions about which women could claim safety and protection as they went about their work for their associations.

Women's organizations reshaped public spaces in a variety of ways, most obviously by locating large woman-owned and woman-oriented buildings in the heart of downtown business and shopping districts. Even before settlement houses arrived, cities such as Chicago and Boston were home to physical spaces that established a visible female presence in busy urban downtowns. In Boston, there were model lodging houses and protective living spaces designed by middle-class women for working-class women, including the Hemenway, a model lodging house run by Bertha Hazard, and the Harriet Tubman House, created by the black branch of the WCTU (the Harriet Tubman Crusaders). The latter offered safe haven for black women, middle-class and working, who could not stay in college dorms or find a respectable rooming house. In Chicago, the YWCA

Discontent: The Women's Movement in the Black Baptist Church, 1880-1920, Cambridge, MA: Harvard UP, 1993, 150-64; see also Anastatia Sims, *The Power of Femininity in the New South: Women's Organizations and Politics in North Carolina, 1880-1930*, Columbia: U of South Carolina P, 1997, 15-19; Anne Firor Scott, *The Southern Lady: From Pedestal to Politics, 1830-1930*, Chicago: U of Chicago P, 1970, 135-42.

[12] Eleanor Flexner, *Century of Struggle: The Woman's Rights Movement in the United States*, Cambridge, MA: Harvard UP, 1959.

opened a formidable boarding home building on Michigan Avenue in 1895, offering a "home in every sense of the word" for women arriving in a "city of strangers". In 1888, a federal report counted fifteen YWCA homes in large cities; in addition, it counted twenty-four non-profit organized boarding homes. The numbers increased markedly by 1900. Most were projects of local clubs, churches, and synagogues; a few were run by individual entrepreneurs; and some were founded by gender-mixed organizations such as the Salvation Army and the Traveler's Aid Society. All bore signs, plaques, or banners announcing their presence. For the national WCTU's leadership, the decision to build a temperance Temple came when, after nine years of using the Young Men's Christian Association's downtown Chicago spaces for their meetings, the women were told they were no longer welcome. Soon, they hired the renowned architectural firm of Burnham and Root to design a twelve-storey building at the corner of LaSalle and Monroe Streets, in the middle of the financial district. At the cornerstone-laying ceremony in 1890, two-thousand children paraded through the Loop chanting "saloons, saloons, saloons must go!" Chicagoans noticed. In addition to housing the WCTU's national offices, the Temple was home to its newspaper, *The Union Signal*, and to its many reform-related labors. When Frances Willard died in 1898, her body lay in state at the Temple as thousands of WCTU members filed past.[13]

Edifices such as the WCTU Temple, the YWCA building, and the Harriet Tubman House reshaped their neighborhoods. As Sarah Deutsch has argued in her insightful analysis of Boston's Women's Educational and Industrial Union (WEIU), the WEIU "did not pick the spot for their [first] building randomly, but placed it in the heart of the male-dominated central city". Founded in 1877, the group eventually purchased three downtown buildings in the 1880s. Within their walls, the WEIU offered lunchrooms to provide safe meeting spaces and inexpensive meals to women working in the city center, as well as an employment office, a clinic, and a pure milk station. The expanding

---

[13] See Sarah Deutsch, *Women and the City: Gender, Space, and Power in Boston, 1870-1940*, New York: Oxford UP, 2000, 18; Meyerowitz, *Women Adrift*, 46-50 [quotation, 50]; Ruth Bordin, *Woman and Temperance: The Quest for Power and Liberty, 1873-1900*, Philadelphia, PA: Temple UP, 1981; see also Daphne Spain, *How Women Saved the City*, Minneapolis: U of Minnesota P, 2001.

programs soon included vocational advising, a handicraft workshop, a consignment shop for women's work, kitchens selling nutritional food, school lunches, evening classes, milk distribution, and lecture series. Unlike the YWCA or the WCTU, the WEIU was a "class-bridging" organization that included on its board of officers working-class white and middle-class black women as well as professional white women. The WEIU sought to create, in Deutsch's words, "public space where middle-class and elite women could appear without being declassed and working women could appear in public without having their virtue questioned by being 'on the streets'". Moreover, because the group's activities included lobbying for laws protecting working women, laws that would change the city itself, it was hardly accidental that their buildings' physical location gave them "proximity to the corridors of power, [including] the state legislature and city hall". Eventually, as did settlement houses in a later era, the WEIU got the city of Boston to adopt several of their ventures. [14]

Still, as Deutsch cautions, "drawing a reciprocal relationship between women and urban space is not drawing an equation between women in public and women in power". Men still held the winning hand in the political game. But even male politicians, along with other urban residents on their way to work or shop, surely could not avoid noticing the visible evidence of women's public activism that the WEIU buildings or the WCTU Temple represented. Certainly, such edifices made the activism of some organizations manifest. Class, religious, and racial divisions still structured the access that different groups had to downtown locations. The WCTU got the land for its Temple courtesy of Marshall Field, the department store tycoon; the WEIU board had its ability to purchase downtown land smoothed by the well-connected men to whom the elite white women trustees were tied by blood or marriage. Compared to the Chicago YWCA, and compared to the need among urban black working women, the Boston Harriet Tubman House and the Chicago Phillis Wheatley House were small, under-funded, and located in out-of-the-way neighborhoods. Middle-class black women's organizations simply did not have a chance of purchasing the prime real estate that middle-class white women could obtain for their ventures. [15]

---

[14] Deutsch, *Women and the City*, 145-46.
[15] *Ibid.*, 23; Bordin, *Women and Temperance*, 142-48.

The monumental aspects of Chicago's YWCA on Michigan Avenue or the WCTU Temple on LaSalle Street, their visibility as symbols of Woman, made it hard for passers-by to ignore them. In a way, their very monumentality made it harder still to notice the exclusions they practiced. Chicago's YWCA, for example, voted in 1877 to deny black women entry into its boarding homes (though later, at the turn of the century, YWCAs took up the cause of interracial cooperation long before YMCAs did). Even white working-class women found themselves excluded from YWCA housing if they did not conform to the portrait of respectable and grateful clients their middle-class patrons had in mind. Although YWCA leaders, "envisioned their own role as that of mothers" to the young women who lived at the Y, and sought to "mask the class barrier between themselves and the younger working-class women they sought to protect", they were often chagrined to find that their clients did not see things as they did. Despite the benefit of low rents and access to middle-class perquisites such as parlors, libraries, pianos, gyms, and swimming pools, self-supporting women often resented the image of charity recipients that clung to their residence in Y facilities. They disliked feeling patronized and singled out, chafed at rules and regulations such as curfews, and resented being required to attend religious services. When they could afford it, clients lit out for furnished rooms, or shared flats or commercial boarding houses, where they could manage their own time and enjoy the freedom of the city when they chose.[16]

Monumentality of another sort characterized the historic houses that women's organizations labored to preserve, the history museums they created, the historical societies they fostered, the monuments they built, and the memorials they sponsored. Each in its own way, such edifices altered city and town spaces. The Mount Vernon Ladies' Association led the way for historic house preservation, raising money in 1859 to purchase George Washington's estate and save it from the businessmen who planned to turn it into a hotel. Soon, the ladies had made the site available for pilgrimage. As David Lowenthal has noted, such activity fundamentally changes even an existing structure; once marked, labeled, restored, moved to a new location, cleaned up, improved upon, and made into an historic spot, it loses its ordinariness and becomes notable – and noticeable. So, too, do the labors of the

---

[16] Meyerowitz, *Women Adrift*, 52-53.

groups doing the preservation. By 1919, there were a hundred historic house museums, almost all of them displaying houses in which famous and elite men had lived (or slept), almost all of them sponsored by women's organizations. The National Society of Colonial Dames, for instance, opened the Van Cortlandt House in the Bronx in 1896 and the Quincy Homestead (home of John and Abigail Adams) in Massachusetts in 1904.[17]

Women's groups were particularly active in sponsoring memorials to the Civil War dead. Decoration Day (later Memorial Day) began in 1865 as an African American project, as groups of women, men and children decorated the graves of Union soldiers buried in the Confederate states. Soon, Ladies' Memorial Associations began to champion the cause of memorializing the Confederate dead, either through creating special burial sites and raising funds to rebury sons of the Confederacy in them, through erecting the "ordinary soldier" monuments that appeared first in cemeteries but quickly came to dominate courthouse squares in small towns throughout the South, or through celebrating Confederate Memorial Day.[18] The women's auxiliaries of the Grand Army of the Republic took as part of their work the memorializing of the Union dead in the North, so that by 1900 the "ordinary soldier" statue in small-town Vermont was

---

[17] See Michael Wallace, "Visiting the Past: History Museums in the United States", in *Presenting the Past: Essays on History and the Public*, eds Susan Porter Benson, Steven Brier, and Roy Rosenzweig, Philadelphia, PA: Temple UP, 1986, 137-61; David Lowenthal, *The Past Is a Foreign Country*, New York: Cambridge UP, 1985, 263-88. For one example of organization women's roles in creating local historical societies, see Sandra Haarsager, *Organized Womanhood: Cultural Politics in the Pacific Northwest, 1840-1920*, Norman: U of Oklahoma P, 1997. See also W. Fitzhugh Brundage, "'Woman's Hand and Heart and Deathless Love': White Women and the Commemorative Impulse in the New South", in *Monuments to the Lost Cause: Women, Art, and the Landscapes of Southern Memory*, eds Cynthia Mills and Pamela H. Simpson, Knoxville: U of Tennessee P, 2003, 72.

[18] David Blight, *Race and Reunion: The Civil War in American Memory*, Cambridge, MA: Harvard UP, 2001, 279-84; Caroline E. Janney, "'To Honor Her Noble Sons': The Ladies Memorial Association of Petersburg, 1866-1912", in *Virginia's Civil War*, eds Peter Wallenstein and Bertram Wyatt-Brown, Charlottesville: U of Virginia P, 2005, 256-69; Gaines Foster, *Ghosts of the Confederacy: Defeat, the Lost Cause, and the Emergence of the New South*, New York: Oxford UP, 1987, 167-69; Kirk Savage, *Standing Soldiers, Kneeling Slaves: Race, War, and Monument in Nineteenth-century America*, Princeton, NJ: Princeton UP, 1997; Sims, *The Power of Femininity in the New South*, 142.

virtually interchangeable with the "ordinary soldier" monument in small-town Georgia. Indeed, enterprising marble and bronze companies sold the same model to both sides. And DAR members began devoting a good deal of energy to marking the grave-sites of Revolutionary War soldiers during the 1890s (and writing up their work in the DAR *Magazine of History*).[19]

Specific memorials to particular individuals or ideals sponsored by women's clubs and associations similarly altered public space. African American women organized in the 1870s to help build the Freedman's Memorial in Washington, DC. When it was dedicated in 1876, however, its design represented, to paraphrase Kirk Savage, a standing Lincoln and a kneeling former slave being helped to his feet. The women might have preferred a sculpture with a different message. Still, their work resembled that of other women's organizations, which, in erecting monuments to famous or ordinary men, reburying the Civil War dead and marking their graves, funding soldiers' homes, or claiming and preserving sites as "historic", reconfigured familiar surroundings and reworked the geography of everyday life.

These transforming labors generally came wrapped in the comfortable garment of feminine self-effacement. Few women's groups took women – either individually or collectively – as the object of their commemorative zeal. Despite the objections of women's civic groups, a "Memorial to North Carolina Women of the Confederacy" arose in Raleigh, paid for by the United Confederate Veterans; the women would have preferred that the money go towards something they considered more practical. On occasion, as in the case of a St Louis emancipation monument, women's groups proposed including individual heroines in a larger project, but few such ideas ever became concrete reality. More commonly, it was the bronze impression of an allegorical woman (such as "justice") or a representative type (such as the pioneer mother) that made it onto a public monument. As Mary Ryan has noted, such representations of womanhood "bore only a remote relationship" to actual "female people". Yet self-effacing

---

[19] Julie DesJardins, *Women and the Historical Enterprise in America: Gender, Race, and the Politics of Memory, 1880-1945*, Chapel Hill: U of North Carolina P, 2003, 66-69; Woden Sorrow Teachout, "Forging Memory: Hereditary Societies, Patriotism, and the American Past, 1876-1898", PhD diss., Harvard University, 2003, 139-74; Morgan, *Women and Patriotism in Jim Crow America*, 54-55.

rituals coexisted with the common practice of inscribing an organization's name somewhere on the edifices that women's groups sponsored, thereby ensuring that future generations would recognize the feminine labor behind the famous man, event, or place. Plaques noting that an item was "erected by" or "restored by" a DAR, UDC, or WCTU chapter graced many a statue or (in the case of the WCTU) marble water fountain in public parks or squares. A few groups were bolder, inscribing their officers' names as well, for posterity. In New York's Riverside Park, at 116th Street, an elaborate marble clean-water fountain completed in 1909 still bears the title of the Woman's Health Protective Association and the names of its officers.[20]

With the arrival of the United Daughters of the Confederacy in 1894, however, the combination of memorializing processes with feminine self-effacement took on a newly aggressive and insistent character. Genteel and determinedly anti-suffrage, the UDC membership nevertheless forcefully planted themselves in public squares of various types (both literal and metaphorical). Their startling success in getting their political and racial agendas into the public arena offers an important reminder that different women's organizations achieved different levels of public effectiveness. Founded in 1894, the UDC had 17,000 members by 1900; by 1917 it

---

[20] On the Memorial to North Carolina Women of the Confederacy, see Sims, *Power of Femininity*, 143-45. Cynthia Mills documents the existing memorials to Confederate women (in Arkansas, Florida, Maryland, Mississippi, North Carolina, South Carolina, and Tennessee), all of them funded by men's groups. See her article, "Gratitude and Gender Wars: Monuments to the Women of the Sixties", in *Monuments to the Lost Cause*, 183-200. Kirk Savage, in his book, *Standing Soldiers, Kneeling Slaves*, 111-12, discusses the Ladies Union Aid Society of St Louis' proposal to include Clara Barton, Dorothea Dix, and Mary Bickerdyke in an emancipation monument; it was never built. The quotation is from Mary Ryan, *Civic Wars: Democracy and Public Life in the American City during the Nineteenth Century*, Berkeley: U of California P, 1997, 67. The women of the North Carolina chapter of the DAR placed their name prominently on a 1908 plaque commemorating the Edenton Tea Party of 1774: see Sims, *Power of Femininity*, 140-42. Pioneer Women and pioneer mother statues date largely from the 1920s and 1930s, beginning in 1928, the DAR sponsored twelve "pioneer mother of the trail" sculptures following the "National Road" west from Maryland to California: see Morgan, *Women and Patriotism in Jim Crow America*, 133, and Lida Keck Wiggins, "Ohio's Madonna of the Trail", *Ohio History*, XLI, 1932, 161-66. For a description and photo of the New York Women's Health Protective Association fountain, go to http://nycgovparks.org/sub_your_park/historical_signs/hs_historical_sign.php?id=127 50.

may have had as many as 100,000 members.[21] Led by energetic and well-connected women such as Mildred Lewis Rutherford of Georgia, the UDC undertook projects on a variety of fronts. In order to rebury the Confederate dead languishing in Yankee burying grounds, for example, they lobbied Congress and state legislatures for enabling legislation – and for funds; the campaign resulted a massive 1903 exhumation of remains from Northern cemeteries and reburial in Arlington National Cemetery. They worked assiduously to try to make "War Between the States" the official name for the Civil War; they pressed for the assigning of only "Southern" textbooks – that is, textbooks with pro-Confederate interpretations – in Southern schools; and they saw to it that such textbooks got written and published.

So successful were they, that historian David Blight has suggested that, as "cultural guardians", the UDC "may have accomplished more than professional historians in laying down for decades … a [specific] conception of a victimized South", that is, a white South, during the Reconstruction era. They provided scholarships to the grandchildren of Confederate veterans and sponsored essay contests in schools, essays in which white children wrote paeans to the Ku Klux Klan. All of these efforts produced the Old South myth of the peaceful and contented population, enslaved and free, along with a New South myth that Reconstruction had been an unmitigated horror and a conviction that African Americans had declined racially since emancipation.[22] Indeed, insofar as Americans today continue to use terms such as "The South" and "Southerners" when they mean only white southerners, the successes of the UDC march on.

The UDC's work did not go unchallenged, however. The challenges, especially those mounted by the National Association of Colored Women, reveal significant contests among women's groups

---

[21] Blight, *Race and Reunion*, 278-79; Karen L. Cox, *Dixie's Daughters: The United Daughters of the Confederacy and the Preservation of Confederate Culture*, Gainesville: UP of Florida, 2003, 49-72; Janney, "'To Honor Her Noble Sons'", 263-64.

[22] Blight, *Race and Reunion*, 278; Sarah E. Gardner, *Blood and Irony: Southern White Women's Narratives of the Civil War, 1861-1937*, Chapel Hill: U of North Carolina P, 2004, 118-31, 162-69; W. Fitzhugh Brundage, *The Southern Past: A Clash of Race and Memory*, Cambridge, MA: Harvard UP, 2005, 12-54; Bessie Louise Pierce, *Public Opinion and the Teaching of History in the United States*, New York: Alfred A. Knopf, 1926, 154-64.

over what should be memorialized and who should have the power to shape public memory. These contests also highlight the competing claims that groups of organized women made for control of textbooks, historical interpretations, and historical memories. The UDC's effort to establish monuments to "the faithful slave" and especially to "Mammy" were emblematic of their view of history, and became the flashpoint for NACW counter-views. Beginning with an essay contest stirring white children to find "Stories of Faithful Slaves", the UDC helped build the first "faithful slave" monuments in Fort Mill, South Carolina in 1896. These activities had at stake key political issues, in particular whose interpretation of slavery, the Civil War, Reconstruction, and African American history would prevail. As part of that effort, the UDC began a two-decade campaign to erect memorials to a very specific figurative faithful slave – the "Southern Mammy" – in every state, along with a national Mammy memorial in Washington, DC. The US Senate even appropriated $200,000 for such a memorial in 1923, but the bill failed in the House. These activities brought the UDC into direct conflict with the National Association of Colored Women, which had already undertaken a heavy load of public labors, including protection for African American working women, promotion of kindergartens and free public schooling, and anti-lynching activism. In addition, the NACW promoted African American history and sought to preserve and memorialize the African American past. Among those efforts was the struggle to preserve Frederick Douglass' Washington, DC, home, Cedar Hill. The organization took custody of Cedar Hill soon after Douglass' death in 1895 and offered it as an alternative to house museums that celebrated slaveholders or erased their pasts as the owners of their own enslaved children.[23]

The proposed Mammy monuments horrified NACW members, who, along with the black press and the National Association for the

---

[23] See DesJardins, *Women and the Historical Enterprise*, 122-27; Blight, *Race and Reunion*, 284-91; Morgan, *Women and Patriotism*, 102-104; Cynthia Neverdon-Morton, *African American Women of the South and the Advancement of the Race, 1895-1925*, Knoxville: U of Tennessee P, 1989; Brundage, *The Southern Past*, 147-48. The best summary of NACW work remains Elizabeth Lindsay Davis, *Lifting as They Climb*, 1933, rpt. New York: G.K. Hall, 1996. See also Morgan, *Women and Patriotism*, 20-26, and 102-104, and Joan Marie Johnson, *Southern Ladies, New Women: Race, Region, and Clubwomen in South Carolina, 1890-1930*, Gainesville: UP of Florida, 2004, 44-57.

Advancement of Colored People (NAACP), mobilized every potential resource to oppose them. The NACW "rejected the messages implicit in the Mammy" idea; to its members, their purchase and restoration of Cedar Hill represented a positive alternative to the sort of racist imagery and demeaning depictions of black women embodied in the Mammy memorials. Hallie Q. Brown, who became president of the NACW in the early twentieth century, "called white women's bluff" by suggesting that if they were concerned about African Americans, white women would reject their complicity in the widespread lynching of black men and the poor conditions that working-class blacks faced on a daily basis. Charlotte Hawkins Brown, the North Carolina educator, proposed using the money set aside for the Washington "Mammy" memorial to fund the education of black children. Black clubwomen sent thousands of protests to Congress and to Vice-President Coolidge. At the same time, the NACW sponsored history programs comparable to those of the UDC, attempting to counteract its mythological version of the Old South. By transforming Frederick Douglass into a symbol of black manhood, they sought to resist the common caricature of their husbands, fathers, and sons as potential rapists. By naming their clubs and boarding homes after Harriet Tubman, Phillis Wheatley, and Ida B. Wells, they sought to raise awareness of black women who were definitely not mammies. By publishing texts and biographies, such as Hallie Brown's *Homespun Heroines and Other Women of Distinction*, they sought space for African American women's history on school and public library shelves.[24]

But the public monuments and memorials created or identified by different women's groups had different fates. Despite heroic efforts, the NACW's initiative to preserve Cedar Hill enjoyed little of the

---

[24] Hallie Brown, *Homespun Heroines and Other Women of Distinction*, Xenia, OH: Aldine Publishing, 1926; Joan Marie Johnson, "'Ye Gave Them a Stone': African American Women's Clubs, the Frederick Douglass Home, and the Black Mammy Monument", *Journal of Women's History*, XVII/1 (Spring 2005), 63-75; Johnson, *Southern Ladies*, 53-57; Micki McElya, "Commemorating the Color Line: The National Mammy Monument Controversy of the 1920s", in *Monuments to the Lost Cause*, 203-18; see also Angela David Nieves, "'We Gave Our Hearts and Lives to It': African-American Women Reformers, Industrial Education, and the Monuments of Nation-building in the Post-Reconstruction South, 1877-1938", PhD diss., Cornell University, 2001.

public approbation accorded to the Mount Vernon cause, except among the District of Columbia's African Americans. After quickly paying off the mortgage on the property, the organization struggled for years to keep the site up. Only in 1962, when the National Park Service took it over, did the Douglass home receive the sort of preservation that Mount Vernon and other historic homes had enjoyed for decades. And it hardly needs underlining that, in the era of Thomas Dixon's *The Clansman* and D.W. Griffith's *Birth of a Nation*, the NACW enjoyed only limited success in counteracting the powerful histories the UDC sponsored. The NACW's monuments, whether in the form of physical buildings, club names, or historical research, seldom enjoyed prominent, highly visible geographical locations; if they occupied center stage in the historical understandings of African Americans, they hovered on the periphery or faded into the fog of white Americans' historical memory. Nevertheless, through naming practices, literary club reading lists, and historical textbook promotion, the group kept alive among African Americans an alternative history – and memory – of the United States.[25]

Efforts to build and preserve monuments of various kinds or to capture downtown spaces for women's clubs and associations forged yet another form of visibility for women: political visibility. Whether one looks at African American women's desire to shape public understanding of the history of slavery, the YWCA's concern with the protection of the working girl, or the WCTU's physical temple advertising its broad-ranging agenda for temperance and social purity, one finds women's groups creating and pursuing political agendas. The examples are so numerous, indeed, that some historians and sociologists (such as Theda Skocpol) have argued that through their organizations, voteless women possessed almost as much political clout as they gained when they achieved full suffrage in 1920. Such an argument draws on some of the claims of the anti-suffragists – particularly their view that women could be "better citizens without

---

[25] See Davis, *Lifting as They Climb*, for a portrait of this world of activity. Phillis Wheatley clubs and associations were popular with many NACW chapters, but the women also named their endeavors after Sojourner Truth, Frances Ellen Watkins Harper, Harriet Tubman, and local heroes.

the ballot".[26] But such an argument ignores a phenomenon to which historians have recently begun to turn their attention: partial suffrage.

Although 1920 is often seen as marking the apex of the suffrage movement's success, historians have charted seismic shifts in the movement during the 1910s, especially the arrival in the suffrage coalition of large numbers of working-class women, as well as the emergence of a group of women calling themselves "Feminists". At least part of the reason for those changes in the suffrage coalition was that women had already entered and altered politics before 1910, with full or partial suffrage.[27]

Full suffrage during these years arrived in the Western territories and states by various mechanisms. In some instances, such as Wyoming and Utah, male legislators conferred suffrage by fiat for various reasons (Utah Mormons with plural wives hoped to maintain Mormon dominance over "gentiles"). More typically, women mobilized to achieve suffrage, using their clubs and organizations as grass-roots levers for change. California's 1910-1911 referendum campaign offers an excellent example. There, pro-suffrage women and their male supporters had to organize in order to convince male voters to approve the referendum. In the process, as Jessica Sewell has shown, they took over downtown streets in San Francisco and Los Angeles and redefined the spaces as "feminist political territory". Because both downtowns did not separate financial from shopping activity, with offices located above the major stores, women and men – workers and shoppers both – regularly mixed together on sidewalks. They passed by suffrage headquarters, strategically located in the same areas. At suffrage rallies, the banners read "Women are co-

---

[26] Theda Skocpol, *Protecting Soldiers and Mothers: The Political Origins of Social Policy in the United States*, Cambridge, MA: Harvard UP, 1992, 318-20, 464-65; Manuela Thurner, "'Better Citizens without the Ballot': American Antisuffrage Women and Their Rationale during the Progressive Era", *Journal of Women's History*, V/1 (Spring 1993), 33-60.

[27] Nancy F. Cott, *The Grounding of Modern Feminism*, New Haven, CT: Yale UP, 1988; Annelise Orleck, *Common Sense and a Little Fire: Women and Working-Class Politics in the United States, 1900-1965*, Chapel Hill: U of North Carolina P, 1995; Ellen Carol DuBois, *Harriot Stanton Blatch and the Winning of Woman Suffrage*, New Haven, CT: Yale UP, 1997; Ellen Carol DuBois, *Woman Suffrage and Women's Rights*, New York: New York UP, 1998, 176-209; see also Kristin L. Hoganson, *Fighting for American Manhood: How Gender Politics Provoked the Spanish-American and Philippine-American Wars*, New Haven, CT: Yale UP, 1998, 29-34.

workers; why not be co-voters?" Noontime speeches at major intersections could be sources of entertainment, and suffragist lunchrooms invited businesswomen and working-class girls to drink "Equality Tea" at bargain basement prices. The end result was not only a victory for the referendum but a validation of women's equal access to downtown public spaces.[28]

Short of the full-suffrage campaigns that were so successful in California and elsewhere in the West, women in some states gained partial suffrage. Illinois offers a case in point. There, after the 1870 formation of the Illinois Woman Suffrage Association, the state legislature passed a law permitting qualified women, married or single, to run for any school office created by law (that is, not by the Illinois State Constitution). By 1874 ten women were serving as County Superintendents of Schools (though they could not vote for themselves). Then, in 1891, Illinois women won limited suffrage. They could vote in any election held to elect school officials, using separate ballots and separate ballot boxes. (Those elections were usually held on the same day as general elections.) Soon, a decision by the Illinois Supreme Court permitted women to vote for and run for the office of University of Illinois Trustee. African American and white members of the Illinois Woman Suffrage Association (including Ida B. Wells and Jane Addams) campaigned for the election of Lucy Flower that year; she won. African American suffragists supported Flower because she measured up to their yardstick: she agreed to rely on the Fourteenth Amendment to oppose any restrictions on the admission of African American students to the University. By 1913 Illinois women were voting in presidential elections and all local elections not specifically named in the Illinois State Constitution,

---

[28] The best recent studies of how women won voting rights in the West are Holly J. McCammon and Karen E. Campbell, "How Women Won the Vote in the West: The Political Successes of State Suffrage Movements, 1869-1919", *Gender and Society*, XV/1 (February 2001), 55-82, and Rebecca J. Mead, *How the Vote Was Won: Woman Suffrage in the Western United States, 1868-1914*, New York: New York UP, 2004. See also Holly J. McCammon, Karen E. Campbell, Ellen M. Granberg and Christine Mowery, "How Movements Win: Gendered Opportunity Structures and U.S. Women Suffrage Movements, 1866 to 1919", *American Sociological Review*, LXVI/1 (February 2001), 49-70. For the Californian suffrage referendum campaign, see Jessica Ellen Sewell, "Gendering the Spaces of Modernity: Women and Public Space in San Francisco, 1890-1915", PhD diss., University of California at Berkeley, 2000.

though they continued to vote using separate ballots and separate ballot boxes. It was no accident, then, that the very states where women's associations were especially effective in lobbying for what Theda Skocpol has termed "maternalist" legislation, such as mothers' pensions and minimum wage laws for women workers, were states in which women were already voting.[29]

All of this political activity – along with the national and state campaigns for suffrage – brought women into public spaces in multiple ways. Women's organizations held annual conventions in public arenas such as hotels or theaters. In addition, women labored in mixed-sex organizations, especially unions, but also study clubs and professional associations. But as always, some had more access and more visibility than others, and spaces that were welcoming for some were hostile and dangerous to others.

To travel to meetings, rallies, and national conventions, women needed access to the railway, the streetcar, the subway, the public trolley, and the city sidewalk. Their presence shaped public arenas such as railroads, while also introducing new questions about which women would travel freely and how their exposure to the dangers of anonymous public space would be managed. As Amy Richter has suggested, the arrival of the railroad required Americans to rethink whatever boundaries they thought separated the spheres of men and women and to redraw, for yet another time, the line between public and private spaces. After all, on American-style trains, in which passengers occupied open seating (unlike the British-style compartment), a traveler "might sit for hours elbow-to-elbow with

---

[29] See Mark W. Sorenson, *Ahead of Their Time: A Brief History of Woman Suffrage in Illinois*, Springfield: Illinois State Archives, 2001; Steven M. Buechler, *The Transformation of the Woman Suffrage Movement: The Case of Illinois, 1850-1920*, New Brunswick, NJ: Rutgers UP, 1986; Lisa Gail Materson, "Respectable Partisans: African American Women in Electoral Politics, 1877 to 1896", PhD diss., University of California at Los Angeles, 2000, 14-60; Dubois, *Harriot Stanton Blatch*; Skocpol, *Protecting Soldiers*, 317. Partial suffrage states were concentrated in the Midwest and usually permitted women to vote in school elections and/or for local officials; by 1917, most Midwestern women also had presidential suffrage. In the former Confederate states, only Arkansas (1917) and Texas (1918) passed any form of partial woman suffrage; in both states, where the white primary had been instituted in order to disenfranchise African Americans, women (that is, white women) gained the right to vote in primary elections. See Anne Firor Scott and Andrew Mackay Scott, *One Half the People: The Fight for Woman Suffrage*, Urbana: U of Illinois P, 1982.

another passenger; she ate and slept among strangers". The newness of such arrangements challenged middle-class notions about the separateness of women's and men's worlds and brought significant alterations in the design and especially the comfort level of railroad cars. In Richter's view, the "public domesticity" that came to prevail on railroads, as well as in hotel lobbies, department stories, theaters, and public parks represented a "hybrid sphere – a social and cultural realm shared by women and men". In the process, an older view of public spaces as dangerous and masculine disappeared, to be replaced by a "vision of an orderly, comfortable, and safe realm" that was "no longer solely masculine".[30]

From the standpoint of women traveling to association meetings and conventions, the ladies' car was the most notable aspect of this "public domesticity". By separating women from men and providing creature comforts that turned the ladies' car into a replica of the middle-class parlor, railroad companies promised ladies safety, largely by separating them from rowdy male travelers, but also by offering upholstered seats and separate water closets. The ladies' car was generally considered the safest car on the train, too, because of its distance from the sooty and noisy engine. Gentlemen companions – as long as they were of the proper class and respectable demeanor – were permitted to use the ladies' car.

At the 1899 meeting of the National American Woman Suffrage Association, a proposal by an African American delegate and NACW member, Lottie Wilson Jackson, exposed the racially-based notion of safety that underlay the designation of a ladies' car. Lottie Jackson sought NAWSA endorsement for a simple proposition: that "colored women ought not to be compelled to ride in smoking cars, and that suitable accommodations should be provided for them". After debate, the resolution was defeated. The difficulties that African American women faced in getting safely and comfortably to national meetings were not a concern for the white delegates. They, after all, had access to the ladies' car. (Although Homer Plessy was the plaintiff in the famous 1896 case, it was women who brought the majority of lawsuits in state and federal courts challenging racial segregation on railroads – thirty-one cases out of forty-seven between 1855 and 1914.) Because

---

[30] Amy G. Richter, *Home on the Rails: Women, the Railroad, and the Rise of Public Domesticity*, Chapel Hill: U of North Carolina P, 2005, 6-8.

African American women could not routinely expect to claim the safety of the ladies' car, they faced considerably more danger when they traveled to meetings and conventions than did white women, including the danger of sexual assault in smoking cars and the danger of physical assault if their presence in the ladies' car was challenged. Ida B. Wells' 1885 suit against the Ohio and Southwestern Railroad resulted from an incident in which two white male passengers and the conductor physically dragged her into the smoking car.[31]

Perhaps the "public domestication" of the railroad – and comparable spaces – tamed public arenas and made them into more hybrid spaces. But of course spaces that were clearly domestic had their own hybrid character and their own dangers. Women who organized and ran national and city-wide voluntary associations generally required household help, especially if they were married and/or had children. Even without marriage and family, women needed servants to sustain and symbolize their middle-class status. While they were at meetings, someone – usually another woman – cleaned and cooked, sewed and did laundry. Homes need to be understood as containing both public and private spaces, and as places of waged work as well as of leisure or retirement from the world. Homes could be islands of safety to which middle-class women retired when they returned from their voluntary society labors. But for domestics, the middle-class home could present many dangers, the most evident of which was the danger of sexual seduction or rape.[32] As remains the case today, perceived danger was not the same as actual danger.

Through collective public activism, women claimed visibility for their organizations and for themselves in post-Civil War America. In doing so, they departed from the reticence that had characterized most voluntary association labors in the antebellum era. In the three ways

---

[31] Richter, *Home on the Rails*, 104; Barbara Y. Welke, "When All the Women Were White and All the Blacks Were Men: Gender, Race, Class, and the Road to Plessy, 1855-1914", *Law and History Review*, XIII/2 (Autumn 1995), 261-316; Patricia Schechter, *Ida B. Wells-Barnett and American Reform, 1880-1930*, Chapel Hill: U of North Carolina P, 2001, 43-44. Lottie Wilson Jackson was a delegate to the 1904 NACW biennial meeting; see Davis, *Lifting*, 1933, rpt. 1996, 43. On Wells, see also Mia Bay's essay in this collection.
[32] See Deutsch, *Women and the City*, 60-67.

that I have explored here – altering public spaces, building monuments, and exercising their rights to suffrage – women's groups sought to shape their members' access to public arenas and to reshape those arenas as well. When we examine the texts they produced or sponsored, including historic houses and museums, monuments and statues, voluntary society reports, political petitions, textbooks, holidays, and legal case depositions, we begin to see how very different post-bellum public life was from the antebellum version and how, in no small part, women's groups produced that difference. To be sure, their activism had many dimensions; it was fractured by racial and class divisions and deformed by contests over racial privilege. But like the African American suffragists and club members who brought suits against racial segregation on the railroads, by the end of the nineteenth century, most women took for granted their right to appear in public and to be safe, within certain limits, in doing so. And they could take it for granted because women's groups had taken concrete actions to remake the spaces and places generally termed "public".

DANGEROUS WORKING-CLASS WOMEN: MOTHER JONES, LUCY PARSONS, AND ELIZABETH GURLEY FLYNN

JANET ZANDY

Salutations and frames

They defy easy categorization. Flamboyant of speech, demur of dress, they emerged as public performers, testifying with their words and bodies to America's economic class war. For some, they were heroic leaders; for others, dangerous women. Frequently harassed, arrested, and jailed, Mother Jones, Lucy Parsons, and Elizabeth Gurley Flynn challenged the hypocrisy and class determinism of female gentility. Within the labor movement they were privately imperfect public saints who never relinquished their commitment to class struggle and liberation. From a historical distance, their lives enable us to see the myriad, often hidden ways by which class is framed.

To situate their lives within a context of class struggle, consider the difference between these two salutations: "Dear Reader", and "Fellow Workers and Friends". Each greeting raises salient questions about the position, literally and figuratively, of the author/speaker. Are we indoors or outdoors? Inside, reading a text or stood in a crowd hearing a speech? Are we sympathetic outsiders or comrades in the heat of a struggle? In the safety of our homes or on the street likely to be harassed or jailed? Fixed in one place or continually moving about? These questions stir us to imagine the physicality of performing and participating in labor activism, and also coax us to be self-conscious about how our own class positions frame our interpretive readings of the lives of working-class women organizers, agitators, and orators in the late nineteenth and early twentieth centuries.

With the more familiar "Dear Reader", we step back to 1861 and the publication of an extraordinary story, "Life in the Iron Mills", in *The Atlantic Monthly*. The author, Rebecca Harding Davis, asks her readers to imagine a cloudy day in a iron-works town and to look through the frame of a window of a decaying cottage to observe, through the industrial smoke and filthy rain, the pig iron mule trains and "the slow stream of human life creeping past".[1] Rebecca Harding Davis claims her readers' attention in a particular way:

> Stop a moment .... This is what I want you to do. I want you to hide your disgust, take no heed to your clean clothes, and come right down with me, here, into the thickest of fog and mud and foul effluvia. I want you to hear this story.[2]

From the perspective of middle-class respectability, Harding Davis portrays the lives and language of individual laborers, and calls for sympathetic awareness.[3]

The dangerous women considered in this essay did not dismiss sympathetic awareness. But their interests did not lie with the tender feelings of the middle class, sympathetic or not. Rather, they saw their life's work as developing the nascent and organic consciousness of workers (through newspapers, pamphlets, organizing, speeches, direct action and aid to the needy) as a way of achieving their larger goal – a radical change in the social order that exploits workers. Contemporary interpreters of their lives, turning from the familiar, text-based "Dear Reader" to the open, oratorical, "Fellow Workers and Friends", were asked to alter their class perspective and adjust their subjectivity. We shift our angle of vision from the human object, imagined, observed, and presented from the outsider's position (Davis' perspective), to a view that approximates the perspective of the subject of the gaze. We move from object to subject. We leave behind Rebecca Harding Davis' framed window, and, in some cases, domestic space entirely, and enter another world: the world of our second salutation and the focus of this essay.

Mother (Mary Harris) Jones, Lucy Parsons, and Elizabeth Gurley Flynn understood labor struggle as inseparable from domestic struggle – that is, securing a decent life for working-class women and their children. They themselves, however, rarely had secure domestic lives.

---

[1] Rebecca Harding Davis, *Life in the Iron Mills; or, the Korl Woman*, with a biographical interpretation by Tillie Olsen, New York: The Feminist Press, 1972, 12.
[2] *Ibid.*, 13.
[3] Davis' story raises complicated questions about middle-class representation of working-class lives beyond the scope of this essay. See Janet Zandy, *Hands: Physical Labor, Class, and Cultural Work*, New Brunswick, NJ: Rutgers UP, 2004, xiii, 1-5 and 180-91, for further analysis of the problems of cross-class representation.

To enter their world we must move outside the parlor, beyond the physical structure of houses and homes, and into the crowded spaces of the street and labor hall. We also must move outside the seeming stability of written literary texts and into the relative instability of speeches, oratory, and the remembered and reconstructed events of working-class memoir. The pace changes too. These women do not sit still: they peripatetically respond to another beat, the tempo of resistance or movement work.

They were social revolutionaries and radicals who sought to improve the immediate material conditions of working-class people and who advanced an ideal for a new society founded on principles of economic justice. Although they took ideological positions – socialist, anarchist, communist, feminist, trade unionist – they may be better understood as ideologically informed, yet pragmatic, shape shifters. At various times, they were each given the dubious distinction of being called "the most dangerous woman in America".[4] From the perspective of those on the other side of the class war, industrialists and their apparatuses of capitalist control in government, the judiciary, police, and the media, these women certainly were not considered – in any conventional sense – ladies.

The limited scope of this essay cannot encompass the fullness of their highly complicated lives. Instead, it presents selected incidents, writings, and speeches in order to shorten their historical distance from us, enabling us to perceive their public actions from a relational class perspective. In juxtaposing their lives, we can discern patterns to their nearly concomitant histories. First, they all engaged with a rhetoric of the body. Whether positioned on a platform or in a crowded meeting room, they would punctuate their rousing speeches with thrusting arms, hands, and fingers. Their own bodies were often in jeopardy, subject to exhaustion, abuse, beatings, and imprisonment. They were also acutely aware of how the laboring bodies of workers – men, women and children – could be evidence (exhibit A, so to speak) to advance their cause. The body itself became part of the performance, even pageantry, of labor struggle.

---

[4] See Elliott J. Gorn, *Mother Jones: The Most Dangerous Woman in America*, New York: Hill and Wang, 2001; Carolyn Ashbaugh, *Lucy Parsons: American Revolutionary*, Chicago: Charles H. Kerr, 1976, and Rosalyn Gurley Flynn Baxandall, *Words on Fire: The Life and Writing of Elizabeth Gurley Flynn*, New Brunswick, NJ: Rutgers UP, 1987.

Second, their rhetoric of domesticity, motherhood, and women's work tilted, reinvented, and upturned conventional notions of women's roles in domestic spaces and as mothers. They simultaneously embraced and challenged the ideal of house and home and viewed marriage in relation to the underpaid labor of men and as a perceived alternative to the drudgery of factory work. Marriage was no safe harbor for them personally; out of necessity as well as political mission, they cobbled together a means to support themselves and their families through movement work.

Third, they consciously invented a public, knowing self, using the interior experience of class oppression to forge an epistemology – a way of knowing and a way of being known – outside conventional institutions of learning and sometimes outside their affiliated male-dominated labor or political movements. Theirs is not the outsider's gaze, but the insider's savvy. This is a form of knowledge that emerges out of empathetic identification and shared lived experience. Part of it is an intimacy with suffering, struggle, physical harm, hardship, loss, sorrow, and death. They were no strangers to grief and with that came a sense of urgency that turned them into historical actors rather than passive victims. They were all striking individualists, yet linked inextricably to larger communal causes. More personally, as working-class women, they reveal and conceal their private selves.

Fourth, they practiced a secular spirituality. Although none was religious in any conventional sense, their ground of engagement in class struggle is inspired and, perhaps more importantly, sustained by something transcendent. Their lives were consecrated in a secular pursuit of something larger than themselves[5] – although they all certainly possessed robust individual egos. Their committed movement work may have shifted and changed with the given political and ideological circumstances, but they never succumbed to cynicism, capitulation, or co-option. Their work is aligned with a

---

[5] Their demonstrated secular spirituality should not be misconstrued as fanatical zealotry. To do so, especially from the protection and privilege of bourgeois stability, undervalues their ethos of class solidarity, sustained by a spine that was physical and spiritual. In this regard, their lives are similar to other prominent but often forgotten figures in class struggle – Agnes Smedley, Tina Modotti and Vito Marcantonio, to name only three. For another view of a consecrated life in relation to upward mobility, see Elizabeth Faue, *Writing the Wrongs: Eva Valesh and the Rise of Labor Journalism*, Ithaca, NY: Cornell UP, 2002, 4.

prophetic tradition of witnessing and agency. They combined, if you will, consciously or unconsciously, Isaiah and Marx.

Despite their unprivileged circumstances of birth and background, they harnessed their experiential knowledge to shape themselves into powerful, visible women. They transformed their individual interior consciousness and lived experiences into exterior agency and collective resistance.

Mother (Mary Harris) Jones (1837-1930)

> I asked a man in prison once how he happened to get there. He had stolen a pair of shoes. I told him that if he had stolen a railroad he could be a United States Senator. One hour of justice is worth an age of praying.[6]

Mother Jones defied the societal constraints of age and gender by using her wit, energy, anger, and oratorical power to challenge the powerful and, in her own words, "to educate the worker to a sense of the wrongs he has had to suffer … and to stir up the oppressed to a point of getting off their knees and demanding that which I believe to be rightfully theirs". She told a reporter in 1912, "I am simply a social revolutionist. I believe in collective ownership of the means of wealth."[7] It should be added that, although she was born in Ireland and educated in Canada, she was proud of her American citizenship, often drawing on American history and using revolutionary war pageantry to rouse America to live up to its democratic promises. In a 1902 speech she urged labor solidarity and renewed commitment to the "teachings of your forefathers who fought and bled and raised the old flag that we might always shout for liberty".[8]

The Autobiography of Mother Jones was published in 1925, when Mary Harris was eighty-eight and Mother Jones ninety-five (an age

---

[6] Mother Jones, "The Wail of the People", speech at Coney Island, NY, 28 July 1903, quoted in *Fellow Workers and Friends: I.W.W. Free-Speech Fights as Told by Participants*, ed. Philip S. Foner, Westport, CT: Greenwood Press 1981, 102.

[7] As quoted in *ibid.*, 24.

[8] As quoted in *ibid.*, 89. The forefathers she likely imagined were those in the mud and thick of battle rather than the slave-owning and class privileged founders. She was fond of evoking Patrick Henry's "Give me liberty or give me death".

discrepancy to be explained shortly).[9] Mother Jones (that is, Mary Harris) devotes the first and only paragraph to her childhood and gives her birth date as 1830. Her actual year of birth was 1837. This confusion about dates, while not so unusual for many immigrants of her generation, and rather typical of her proclivity for reworking the particularities of historical facts, also reveals something very significant about how she transformed herself from the private Mary Harris to the very public Mother Jones.[10] The transformation emerges, at least in part, out of traumatic losses that shook her private identity as wife and mother and caused her either to seek another public persona or succumb to grief.

The bare facts: she was born in Cork, Ireland. "My people", she writes, "were poor".[11] Around 1847 her father, Richard Harris emigrated to America with his oldest son, Richard. Mary's mother, Ellen Cotter somehow managed to hold together the remaining family of four children as they witnessed the dispossession, hunger and death caused by the potato famine. Richard sent for his family when Mary was around fourteen, and they settled first in Ontario, Canada where he found a job on a railway construction crew. Mary's early education was in Toronto. She attended a normal school with the intent of becoming a school teacher, learned dressmaking proficiently, moved to Michigan, next to Chicago, and then found a teaching job in Memphis, Tennessee, where in 1861 she met and married George Jones, an iron molder, and subsequently gave birth to four children. In 1867 her husband and all of her children died of a yellow fever epidemic, an epidemic that particularly struck the poor since they were unable to leave town. She buried her family, stayed in Memphis as a nurse to the diseased, and after the plague ended, returned to Chicago, where she supported herself as a thirty-year-old widowed

---

[9] Her *Autobiography* was originally published in Chicago by Charles H. Kerr in 1925. Philip S. Foner suggests that it may have been ghostwritten by Mary Field Parton based on Jones' oral and highly selective recollections (*Mother Jones Speaks: Collected Writings and Speeches*, ed. Philip S. Foner, New York: Monad, 1983, 21). Gorn agrees that the actual writer was not Mother Jones, who may not even have read the manuscript, noting that her oral language was sanitized into standard English and swearing was expunged (Gorn, *Mother Jones*, 280). Gorn observes that it is more adventure story than interior memoir: see his useful analysis (*ibid.*, 278-86).

[10] Dale Fetherling, *Mother Jones: The Miners' Angel*, Carbondale: Southern Illinois UP, 1974, 67.

[11] Mother Jones, *Autobiography of Mother Jones* (1925), rpt. Chicago: Arno, 1969, 11.

dressmaker. She soon lost her shop and home to the great Chicago fire of 1871. That is the summation of Mary Harris' life.

Her life as Mother Jones, a radical labor activist, begins around 1880. She gives her day of birth as 1 May 1830 (claiming retrospectively the international workers holiday as her date of birth). Her *Autobiography*, a construction of her public persona, can be read as a radical's *Pilgrim's Progress*. From her early awakening and membership in the Knights of Labor, to her identity as "the miner's angel", she anoints herself as "mother" to workers and their families struggling to survive. She devotes a chapter in her *Autobiography* to the "Haymarket Tragedy", describing the conditions in the city of Chicago – the impoverishment, strikes, and brutal police suppression. She not only describes the strikes and meetings on 1 May to launch the eight hour day movement and the rally on 4 May in Haymarket Square where anarchists spoke and a bomb was dropped, but notes the political climate of the city of Chicago – an acute assessment of media control and public opinion manipulation:

> The city went insane and the newspapers did everything to keep it like a madhouse. The workers' cry for justice was drowned in the shriek for revenge. Bombs were "found" every five minutes.[12]

She was fearless and a great storyteller. She used working-class rhetorical tools – sarcasm, humor, profanity, verbal assault – as well as lively music, performance, and street theater to cudgel, persuade, rouse, inspire, and love laboring people. Her public persona – the black tailored dress, bonnet, and bit of lace at the throat – was of the tireless grandmother and the insistent teacher, stern and loving. Wagging her finger at the crowd, she was the sympathetic, nagging, critical, all embracing, in-your-face "mother". Although she was involved in labor campaigns all over the country for child laborers, garment workers, streetcar conductors, steel workers, and brewery workers, her primary focus was the plight of miners, especially in the "medieval" state of West Virginia.

Beloved by the miners – men, women, and children, she was called the "miner's angel" – because she got down into the muck and dirt and lived with them. In a letter she describes one of her experiences:

---

[12] *Ibid.*, 21.

I have been up to My Ears in a Strike of the Miners here I have not had a moment to Spare 20 thousand men and women are here to be looked after I have not had a moment to Spare for the last Six weeks. I just got back after ten miles going and coming in a blizzard to a house away from civilization. I find the father down with Typhoid fever the Mother and Six children Shivering with cold no clothing not a thing to Eat.[13]

She shamed the male miners, attacking their acquiescence to their conditions, and badgering them to find their manhood through the union.[14] She organized miners' wives into "mop and broom" brigades who, with mops in one hand, babies in another arm, would intimidate scabs so they would not enter the mines.[15]

For many years she was a "walking delegate": a paid union organizer for the United Mine Workers traveling from region to region, state to state, strike to strike, raising material support and rousing the consciousness of working class people. In 1897 at Turtle Creek, Pennsylvania, just outside Pittsburgh, she orchestrated support for striking coal miners by getting local farmers to share their produce with striking families, developing alliances with local factory workers in support of the strike, visiting strikers' wives, involving them in battalions of pickets, and organizing children into parades with banners supporting the miners.[16] This multi-lateral effort is typical of the capacious nature of her organizing genius.

She became an underground reporter, writing about child labor conditions in her first published article, "Civilization in Southern Mills".[17] Working undercover, she wrote dramatically about the physical conditions mothers and children faced – "I have seen their helpless limbs torn off" – and contrasted the "blighted lives of the mill children with the coddled poodles of the masters".[18] Her description of labor in Southern mills links the degradation of the working body to the crushing of the human mind:

---

[13] Mother Jones, quoted in *Mother Jones Speaks*, 53.
[14] *Ibid.*, 36
[15] Gorn, *Mother Jones*, 79
[16] *Mother Jones Speaks*, 53.
[17] Mother Jones, "Civilization in Southern Mills", *International Socialist Review*, March 1901.
[18] Gorn, *Mother Jones*, 128.

Almost every one of my shop mates in the mills was a victim of some disease or other. All are worked to the limit of existence .... The factory operator loses all energy either of body or mind. The brain is so crushed as to be incapable of thinking, and one who mingles with these people soon discovers that their minds like their bodies are wrecked. Loss of sleep and loss of rest gives rise to abnormal appetites, indigestion, shrinkage of stature, bent backs, and aching hearts.[19]

She was dramatic, some might say histrionic – any place could be her stage. On 7 July 1903 she led a march against child labor. Putting the children textile mill workers at the front of the march, she led the walk from Philadelphia to President Theodore Roosevelt's summer home at Oyster Bay on Long Island. To increase publicity along the way, she used street theater, music, a pipe and drum band (evoking the American Revolution), and dressed several children as revolutionary war soldiers, linking the spirit of 1776 to the emancipation of child laborers.

In 1905 she and Lucy Parsons participated in the founding of the IWW (Industrial Workers of the World) in Chicago. In 1911 she lobbied for the release of imprisoned Mexican revolutionaries from US jails. Later, traveling to Mexico City, she understood the revolutionary fight to overturn the US-backed Diaz dictatorship as a hemispheric fight against rapacious capitalism. In an age without immediate visual communication, she traversed the country in order to describe evocatively the Colorado Ludlow Massacre of 20 April 1914 where twenty men, women and children were killed.

Although she had little enthusiasm for upper-class suffrage movements, observing that the ballot had not improved the lot of working-class men very much, I believe it is a mistake to judge her gender politics from the perspective of contemporary feminism. In a 1902 speech she said, "You will never solve the problem [of exploitation of labor] until you let in the women. No nation is greater than its women … women are fighters."[20] She had a working-class take on the role of women as mothers of the republic. As a symbolic Mother of the working class she turned the ideology of motherhood inside out to use it as a weapon in the class war. She revealed the

---

[19] Mother Jones, quoted in *Mother Jones Speaks*, 454-55.
[20] Mother Jones, quoted in *ibid.*, 92-93.

hypocrisy of bourgeois, sentimental definitions of motherhood in relation to working-class wives and mothers, who had to feed their families on the unlivable wages their men earned, and who often took in boarders or laundry or sewing (unrecognized jobs in the economy) so that their families could survive. Her badgering of the men in her audiences was a lever to destabilize the internal colonization of the poor and working class.

In his biography, *Mother Jones: The Most Dangerous Woman in America*, Elliot J. Gorn argues that Jones' *"Autobiography* must be treated less literally than metaphorically; its specific details are often incorrect, but the book is best thought of as akin to religious testimony, to bearing witness, to a pilgrim's story".[21] But hers was a particular kind of religious expression. She bore for fifty years a life of physical hardship, threats, no security, no home, and no close ties by turning her deep private grief into a secular spirituality. The struggle for the rights and dignity of laboring people was her religion. And that struggle was long and immense:

> I am not one of those who believe that individual freedom is going to drop down from the clouds …. The fight can be won, and will be won, but the struggle will be long and education, agitation, and class solidarity all must play a part in it. I have no patience with those idealists and visionaries who preach fine spun theories and cry down everybody but themselves. [22]

She was a pragmatist, willing to negotiate with political leaders to advance her cause, and she had a collective consciousness that grounded her as an individualist. She was wary of institutions, critical of labor bureaucrats, impatient with theories, and difficult to understand outside the context of her times. Without concern for her personal health, comfort, or well being, she traversed the industrial landscape of the United States, to speak for, teach, and improve the lives of the working class.

---

[21] Gorn, *Mother Jones*, 45.
[22] Mother Jones, quoted in *Mother Jones Speaks*, 249.

Lucy Parsons (1853?-1942)

> Anarchists know that a long period of education must precede any great fundamental change in society, hence they do not believe in vote begging, nor political campaigns, but rather in the development of self-thinking individuals.[23]

Lucy Parsons' long life is situated in the dialectic between her incisive critique of class oppression (and the judicial, governmental, and police apparatuses that serve the interest of the business class), and her revolutionary vision and hope for a new society of worker liberation (and, hence, the necessity for lectures, tours, pamphlets, and newspapers to advance radicals' educational imperatives). Lucy Parsons' individuality is inseparable from her radical, collective consciousness. However, her life story is less the trajectory of a singular, remarkable individual, typical of bourgeois biography, and more illustrative of an alternative *Bildung* in which the individual "I" is inseparable from the collective "we".

In a speech in London in 1888, for example, she locates her own experience within a larger cause:

> I have been treated with the greatest indignities in American prisons; but I do not complain .... I have thrown myself in the path of established order, and we who do so must expect to take the consequences .... Let none of us ... say "I suffered this; I have done this." The cause is above you and me.[24]

Although Parsons is acutely aware of race oppression, particularly the Klan violence she witnessed in Waco, Texas, she primarily argued that economic injustice is the foundational oppression. She saw her role as a movement leader – in one instance, quite literally at the head of the 1 May 1886 procession on Michigan Avenue, Chicago – and as educator, writer, rouser, fighter, even martyr to a larger vision of economic justice. Despite continual police brutality (particularly in Chicago), and denial of her First Amendment right of free speech, she sustained a sometimes violent, hot rhetoric of resistance and a public

---

[23] "The Principles of Anarchism", a lecture by Lucy Parsons, reproduced by the Lucy Parsons Project: http://www.lucyparsonsproject.org/writings/principles_of_anarchism.
[24] Ashbaugh, *Lucy Parsons*, 160.

persona that connected her (widowed, impoverished mother of two children) to a larger, nobler cause. Her life's work was situated within a continuum of complicated political permutations that included affiliation with the Knights of Labor, the International Working People's Association, the Industrial Workers of the World (IWW), the Anarchists, the Socialists, and, later, emerging Communist movements, and the International Labor Defense campaigns. She advocated an American version of syndicalism where workers would own and control the means of production. [25]

With Albert Parsons and her friend, Lizzie Swank Holmes, she wrote, edited, published, and sold numerous political newspapers and pamphlets, including *Alarm, The Liberator*, and, in 1891, *Freedom: A Revolutionary Anarchist-Communist Monthly*. Rejecting a view of the poor as helpless victims in order to appeal to the sympathetic sensibilities of the middle class, she wrote directly to the poor to rouse them into action. Her famous, perhaps notorious, essay, "To Tramps: The Unemployed, the Disinherited, and Miserable" was the cover article of the 4 October 1884 issue of the *Alarm*. "To Tramps" was a message of hope and of "revolution by deed" to those homeless and unemployed men who "tramped" the roads looking for work and who considered suicide as an alternative to dying of hunger. It was also a message of violence, dismissing the utility of written petitions, and advising tramps to "avail yourselves of those little methods of warfare which Science has placed in the hands of the poor man, and you will become a power in this or any other land. *Learn the use of explosives!*" Her militancy answered the violent rhetoric of Chicago's ruling class and its leading newspapers, typified by this (not quite tongue-in-cheek) quotation from the *Chicago Tribune*: "When a tramps asks you for bread, put strychnine or arsenic on it and he will not trouble you any more, and others will keep out of the neighborhood."[26] Although by the 1890s Parsons reassessed a political

---

[25] In her biography, Ashbaugh elaborates on Lucy Parsons' anarchist/syndicalist affiliations: "Lucy Parsons' vision of a future society was not of a society with no regulations whatsoever, but of a society of voluntary association in which the members of trade unions would voluntarily agree to regulations governing their behavior and which would be enforceable by members of the association. She chose to call this system 'no government,' but in reality, she advocated a syndicalist theory of society. She advocated workers' ownership and control over the means of production and distribution through their unions" (174).
[26] *Ibid.*, 182.

strategy of "propaganda by deed", advocating instead trade union activism, she never relinquished her belief that capitalism is founded on violence against the powerless – against children, the poor, and wage-earners. From the perspective of the Chicago police, she was the most dangerous woman in America. From Lucy Parsons' perspective she was acting and speaking out of an epistemology of experienced and observed economic violence. To understand her militant language we must attempt to see what she saw.

About her childhood and young adulthood very little is known. She was born in Texas, in or around 1853, of mixed black, Mexican, and Native American ancestry. Some biographical accounts suggest that she was a descendent of slaves. According to her biographer, Carolyn Ashbaugh, she used a variety of maiden names and claimed her Mexican ancestry through the name Gonzales perhaps to avoid the vicious racism she encountered. It is likely that she witnessed or was aware of the brutality of lynching and white vigilantism. She met Albert Parsons, a Confederate scout during the Civil War, in Waco where he edited a radical Republican paper, the *Spectator* and was shot at and threatened with lynching for attempting to register black voters. Given miscegenation laws at the time, it is difficult to say whether they were officially married. In 1873 she and Albert Parsons moved to Chicago where they lived in the poorest, most squalid working-class and immigrant neighborhoods. Albert Parsons found work as a printer, but soon after was fired and then blackballed for his radical labor organizing. Lucy Parsons supported the family, which would soon include two children, with her skills as a dressmaker. Her militant working-class consciousness was forged in the Chicago working-class movement of the 1870s and 1880s.[27]

In the history of prominent American women, if Lucy Parsons is remembered at all, it is less for her own writing and speeches and more as the grieving widow of Albert Parsons, one of the Haymarket radicals unjustly hanged for his radical beliefs (1886-87). What is less well known and acknowledged is how for fifty years she sustained a life – mostly impoverished – as a movement activist and social revolutionary opposed to wage slavery and ever hopeful of the class revolution. After the sentencing of the eight Haymarket defendants, she began a seven-week speaking tour declaring, "I am an Anarchist

---

[27] *Ibid.*, 182.

and revolutionist!".[28] In her public persona she turned the hot rhetoric of anarchism in the press to her advantage by using the public platform to advance arguments against child labor, starvation, and unemployment:

> You may have expected me to belch forth great flames of dynamite and stand before you with bombs in my hands. If you are disappointed, you have only the capitalist press to thank for it.[29]

Like Mother Jones and the Wobblies, she deliberately exposed religious hypocrisy. In a lecture entitled "The Religion of Humanity" she attacked pie-in-the-sky promises:

> We are tired of hearing about the golden streets of the hereafter. What we want is good paved and drained streets in this world.

She took a public position holding marriage and family as ideals, although her own family relationships were less than ideal.[30] Her daughter Lulu died in 1889. Her son Albert Jr. rebelled against his famous mother by enlisting in the army during the Spanish American War in 1898 and attending church services. Lucy Parsons had him committed to a hospital for the insane in 1899 where he spent the rest of his life, dying of tuberculosis in 1919.[31]

In 1905 she joined Mother Jones, Eugene V. Debs and others on the platform as Big Bill Haywood launched the Industrial Workers of the World. Like Mother Jones, Parsons linked child labor to the greater economic oppression of all workers. She was particularly sensitive to the plight of women workers under an oppressive capitalistic system, including prostitutes, addressing them as, "my sisters whom I can see in the night when I go out in Chicago". She raised women's issues at the IWW convention:

> We, the women of this country, have no ballot even if we wish to use it … but we have our labor …. Wherever wages are to be reduced the capitalist class uses women to reduce them.

---

[28] *Ibid.*, 109.
[29] *Ibid.*, 108.
[30] *Ibid.*, 201.
[31] *Ibid.*, 208-209.

She was remarkably prescient in her discourse, seeing the conditions that she daily witnessed in Chicago within a larger frame of world capital. In the same speech she said, "When we look around for cheap bargains … it simply means the robbery of our sisters, for we know that the things cannot be made for such prices and give the women who made them all fair wages".[32] She also presaged the sit-down strike: "My conception of the strike of the future is not to strike and go out and starve, but to strike and remain in and take possession of the necessary property of production."[33] In 1909 she edited and reprinted the famous speeches of the Haymarket martyrs while touring and lecturing to keep their memory and history alive and relevant. By 1912 she became more involved with the Syndicalist League of North America and continued her affiliation with the IWW. She criticized current anarchist theories in 1913, while lecturing to the unemployed, and moving from place to place on the West coast and into Canada as a "traveling propagandist".

She was arrested during a hunger demonstration and police brawl in Chicago in 1915. Street marching – the fight for public space – was a tool of struggle and a site for informing the public and developing solidarity among the working class: "What I wanted to do was to take some of the rags and poverty of the city and bring them on the street where everyone could see them."[34] By 1920, witnessing the destruction of the IWW and the violence of the Palmer Raids, she affiliated with the Communist Party and became involved with the International Labor Defense (ILD). She continued to speak at May Day rallies, lived an impoverished life with George Markstall, lost her eyesight, and died in a house fire in 1942. The anarchists and communists fought over who would conduct her funeral and Elizabeth Gurley Flynn delivered a moving tribute:

> She had her roots in the people, which gave her strength. She never lost faith in the power, courage, intelligence and ultimate triumph of the people.[35]

---

[32] *Ibid.*, 217.
[33] *Ibid.*, 218.
[34] *Ibid.*, 240.
[35] *Ibid.*, 265.

Her extensive library and papers survived the fire, but were apparently confiscated by the FBI with the connivance of the Chicago police. The FBI denied having them and they were never found.

Elizabeth Gurley Flynn (1890-1964)

> What is a labour victory? I maintain that it is a twofold thing. Workers must gain economic advantage, but they must also gain revolutionary spirit, in order to achieve a complete victory. For workers to gain a few cents more a day, a few minutes less a day, and go back to work with the same psychology, the same attitude toward society is to achieve a temporary gain and not a lasting victory. For workers to go back with a class-conscious spirit, with an organized and determined attitude toward society means that even if they have made no economic gain they have the possibility of gaining in the future.[36]

She was called the "Rebel Girl" by Joe Hill, the "East Side Joan of Arc" by Theodore Dreiser and "the saint in our house" by Western Wobblies.[37] Elizabeth Gurley Flynn was an orator extraordinaire, an agitator, a strike leader, a specialist in labor defense work (for Bill Haywood, Ettor and Giovannitti, Joe Hill, Tom Mooney, Warren K. Billings, and many others, including lesser known women activists), a Wobblie (joining in 1906), a frequently-arrested free-speech fighter, a founder of the American Civil Liberties Organization, a socialist, a communist, a political prisoner, an author, a newspaper columnist and reporter, a mother, a separated wife, lover, daughter, sister, and comrade. At the age of sixteen she launched her life as a public orator with a 1906 speech at the Harlem Socialist Club titled, "What Socialism Will Do for Women", a topic that she felt was safe from the interference of her self-important, disinclined-to-work father and which spoke to her sustained conviction that women could not become full and equal citizens under capitalism.[38]

---

[36] Elizabeth Gurley Flynn, Paterson Strike Speech, New York Civic Club Forum, 31 January 1914: http://www.spartacus.schoolnet.co.uk/USA/flynn.htm.
[37] Baxandall, *Words on Fire*, 1, 2, and 9
[38] See Elizabeth Gurley Flynn, *Rebel Girl: An Autobiography, My First Life (1906-1926)*, New York: International Publishers 1955, 57.

She planned a two-volume autobiography. The first, published with her preferred title, *The Rebel Girl: My First Life (1906-1926)*, was written when she was in her sixties and immersed in appeals against her conviction and those of others under the Smith Act. She served more than two years at the Federal Women's Reformatory at Alderson, West Virginia and wrote about her life as a political prisoner in *The Alderson Story*.[39] She had only begun an outline of the second volume, "My Second Life" (from 1927-1951), intending to describe her life as a communist, when she died in the Soviet Union at the age of seventy-four.

My focus is on her formative years. In her autobiography, she describes the episodes in her life in a clear, even calm, descriptive style notably different from the vitriolic voices of Mother Jones and Lucy Parsons. (She recognizes and honors both these early figures and recalls hearing Mother Jones speak and meeting Lucy Parsons at an IWW convention.) Unlike her radical foremothers, we learn more about her early life, her family, her reading, her absorption of the radical conversations of her household, her mother's sustaining work and her father's opinions and limited job prospects (he lost the sight of one eye as a child laborer in a Maine quarry pit), and her empirical knowledge of poverty. The details are revealing when seeking to understand both the formation of her intellectuality and political consciousness and her pronounced feminism. In many ways, Elizabeth Flynn had the life that her mother, Annie Gurley, was restrained from having because Annie had to support her younger siblings through her work as an expert tailor – paid work that she continued after her marriage to Thomas Flynn. Annie Gurley was an early advocate for women's rights, having heard Susan B. Anthony and Frances Willard in her youth, and she read widely. She appreciated women's public role away from the "endless monotony of women's household chores".[40]

So, one can imagine Annie Gurley's annoyance when the young Elizabeth married miner and IWW organizer Jack Jones on her first trip West. Jones and her father found jobs working on a railroad tunnel in Duluth but were soon fired for their labor agitation and they and

---

[39] Elizabeth Gurley Flynn, *The Alderson Story: My Life as a Political Prisoner*, New York: International Publishers, 1963, *passim*.
[40] Flynn, *Rebel Girl*, 30.

Elizabeth returned home to the South Bronx. Elizabeth Gurley Flynn writes:

> I can see my mother's pale face as this unemployed army appeared with suitcases full of dirty clothes .... My mother resented Jones's presence. She felt he should not have married me, so young a girl, so far away from home, without the knowledge of her parents .... She hated poverty and large families and was fearful that my life would become a replica of her own.[41]

Elizabeth Gurley Flynn was born in Concord, New Hampshire, and her family changed locations from New England to Cleveland, and back to New England as Tom Flynn found jobs as a civil engineer and poorly paid mapmaker. The family moved to New York City around the turn of the century, settling in the South Bronx where they lived in the same apartment for twenty-seven years. This was Elizabeth's home base, to which she would return from her innumerable organizing and "jawsmithing" trips.

Her education as a socialist and activist was also shaped by her acute sensitivity to poverty. This too provided her with an epistemology. Her description of her memory (even as a five-year-old) of the gray mills in Manchester foreshadows her important role in the Lawrence 1912 "Bread and Roses" strike. She recalled:

> The gray mills in Manchester stretched like prisons along the banks of the Merrimac River; 50 per cent of the workers were women and they earned one dollar a day. Many lived in the antiquated 'corporation boarding houses,' relics of the time when the mills were built .... A young woman mill worker, showing her hand with three fingers gone due to a mill accident, shocked me immeasurably.[42]

She was also a natural, gifted speaker, described by some as a prodigy. She learned to breathe deeply and use her diaphragm to throw her voice out. She writes of those early years:

> I began to speak on the street. I took to it like a duck to water .... Styles of speech have changed with the radio and public speaking systems, ... then we gesticulated, we paced the platform, we appealed

---

[41] *Ibid.*, 85.
[42] *Ibid.*, 36.

to the emotions .... Even when newly-arrived immigrants did not understand our words they shared our spirit.[43]

This was demonstrated during the IWW-led strike in Lawrence, Massachusetts in 1912 involving immigrant textile workers of twenty-five nationalities, speaking an estimated forty-five different languages. She said that half the time they did not know "whether the interpreters were telling them to stay out on strike or go back to work".[44] Bill Haywood advised the young Elizabeth (she was twenty-one years old at the time) "to speak English so these people could understand it". She recalled Haywood's rapport with the workers: "They roared with laughter and applause when he said:

> 'The AFL organizes like this!' – separating his fingers, as far apart as they would go, and naming them – 'Weavers, loom-fixers, dyers, spinners.' Then he would say: 'The IWW organizes like this!' – tightly clenching his big fist, shaking it at the bosses.[45]

The importance of the body as a tool of communication was not just the domain of men. Nor should we underestimate the vulnerability of the body, given the vicious police attacks that IWW speakers faced. Between 1906 and 1916 the IWW carried on twenty-six campaigns for the rights of free speech and assemblage. The West Coast IWW fights were aimed at organizing those migratory laborers being duped and cheated by employment agencies. Speakers faced police beatings, arrests and inhumane jail conditions. In December of that year, Elizabeth Gurley Flynn was limited in her public speeches because she was noticeably pregnant and some of the male leaders disapproved of the visibility of her pregnant body: "In those days", she writes:

---

[43] *Ibid.*, 62.

[44] Elizabeth Gurley Flynn, "Memories of the Industrial Workers of the World (IWW)", an address to students at Northern Illinois University DeKalb, Illinois, 8 November 1962: http://www.geocities.com/CapitolHill/5202/rebelgirkl.html.

[45] Flynn, *Rebel Girl*, 131-32. Flynn further comments on the relationship of language learning to organizing workers: "I learned from Bill Hayward in Lawrence, to use short words and short sentences, to repeat the same thought in different words if I saw that the audience did not understand. I learned never to reach for a three-syllable word if one or two [syllables] would do. This is not vulgarizing. Words are tools and not everybody has access to the whole tool chest. The foreign-born usually learned English from their children who finished school after the lower grades. Many workers began to learn English during these strike meetings" (*ibid.*, 131).

pregnant women usually concealed themselves from public view. It
doesn't look nice. Besides Gurley'll have that baby right on the
platform if she's not careful! one fussy old guy protested.[46]

Was Elizabeth Gurley Flynn the token woman in an all male
Wobblie crowd? Yes and no. She no doubt enjoyed the attention her
beauty, youth, and oratory brought her, but she also had a more
expansive imaginary for other women's roles in public spaces and in
struggle (more so than Parsons and Mother Jones). Although she was
literally bailed out by upper-class women many times, she was less
interested in cross-class coalitions than in organizing working-class
and poor women, speaking and writing on their behalf, and learning
from their militancy and struggle. She recognized the double work
lives these women faced: "The women worked in the mills for lower
pay and in addition had all the housework and care of the children."[47]
Like Mother Jones, she understood the importance of revealing to the
privileged public the living and working realities of children, but
unlike Jones, Gurley Flynn saw the children as more than victims or
props. She organized special labor schools for children, a resistance
education to counter the anti-strike attitudes and immigrant prejudice
in the public schools. She headed the famous Lawrence Children
Crusade that transported and placed children in homes of sympathetic
workers.[48] She sustained a lifelong commitment to the freedom of
women. Later in her life, 1945-1953, she chaired the Women's
Commission of the Communist Party, campaigned in support of black
women, and was Vice-President of the Congress of American women.

Two final descriptions of her public persona and speaking style by
those who witnessed them can help sum her up. The first is
anonymous but evocative:

> Elizabeth Gurley Flynn hypnotized the crowd before she had got far in
> her discourse. She has an odd manner of making what might be called
> short hand gestures, pot hooks, curves, dots and dashes written in the
> air. Soon they [the audience] were frowning when she frowned,

---

[46] *Ibid.*, 109. The Spokane struggle ended when the mayor realized that it was costing
the city too much money to limit the free speech of the IWW.
[47] Baxandall, *Words on Fire*, 16.
[48] The catalyst for the Children's Crusade came from the Italian striking families
themselves, who proposed that their starving children be sent to sympathetic families
as was done during strikes in Europe (*ibid.*, 18).

laughing when she laughed, growing terribly earnest when she grew moderately so.[49]

The second, by her friend, the journalist Mary Heaton Vorse, is similarly vivid:

> When Elizabeth Gurley Flynn spoke, the excitement of the crowd became a visible thing …. It was as though a spurt of flame had gone through the audience, something stirring and powerful, a feeling which has made the liberation of people possible, something beautiful and strong had swept through the people and welded them together, singing.[50]

This is a brief glimpse into the intersecting lives of three highly visible, outspoken, fearless, and determined women. Despite their differences, they hold certain traits and experiences in common: they all worked, supporting themselves and their families through their skills as seamstresses/tailors, or through their oratory, labor organizing, and publishing. They all were mothers – Mother Jones as a public mother after the death of her children, Lucy Parsons as a mother who lost one child and institutionalized another, and Elizabeth Gurley Flynn as a single mother relying on her mother and sisters to care for her son, who would eventually die a premature death. They all lived lives as organic intellectuals in a Gramscian sense, moving out of their sphere of birth but carrying with them a consciousness of class oppression and struggle. They were abused by police and courts, hounded for their political radicalism, and were very publicly visible women. And they all, I would argue, sustained their lives through a secular spirituality, a consciousness that grounded them, no matter the shifting ideological winds they encountered, in a determined pursuit of economic justice – especially for women.

How representative were they of the thoughts and politics of other women of their generation is a question worth further exploration. That they were historical actors there is no doubt. Their lives remind us that reform and change came out of struggle. Their lives attest to what has been gained, but also what was lost in the quelling of a socialist revolution in the United States. Elizabeth Gurley Flynn could

---

[49] From a newspaper clipping in the *Morning Public Ledger*, Kensington, NY, 28 August 1906, rpt. in Baxandall, *Words on Fire*, 75.
[50] Quoted in Baxandall, *Words on Fire*, 17.

have spoken for all them when in describing the Lawrence strike she said, "We talked of 'Solidarity,' a beautiful word in all the languages".[51]

---

[51] Flynn, *Rebel Girl*, 135.

VISIBLE WOMEN IN THE NEEDLE TRADES: REVISITING THE CLOTHING INDUSTRY IN THE LATE NINETEENTH AND EARLY TWENTIETH CENTURIES

MARGARET WALSH

The clothing industry and its workers have been sites of conflict for historians and activists alike. Debate has flourished in print and visual media in both the Progressive years of the late nineteenth and early twentieth centuries and in more recent times. Long hours, low wages, seasonal unemployment, child, female and immigrant labor, exploitative middlemen and employers, sexual harassment and lack of care for health and safety have been the main features of attention. Frequently these issues have been collapsed into discussions of the infamous site of the sweatshop, a site that has aroused outrage and moral repulsion despite recent efforts to suggest that sweating had positive attributes.[1] The recent sweatshop debate, like its predecessor in the early twentieth century, rendered visible what otherwise would have been invisible to the vast majority of the American population; so too did the great labor uprisings or the clothing strikes of the years 1910-1913.[2] But there is and was more to the ready-made clothing

---

[1] Nancy L. Green, *Ready-to-wear, Ready-to-work: A Century of Industry and Immigrants in Paris and New York*, Durham, NC: Duke UP, 1997, 137-60; Jefferson Cowie, "A Century of Sweat: Subcontracting, Flexibility, and Consumption", *International Labor and Working Class History*, LXI/61 (April 2002), 128-40; Nancy L. Green, "Fashion, Flexible Specialization and the Sweatshop: A Historical Problem", in *Sweatshop USA: The American Sweatshop: The Historical and Global Perspective*, eds Daniel E. Bender and Richard A. Greenwald, New York: Routledge, 2003, 37-55; Peter Liebhold and Harry R. Rubenstein, "Bringing Sweatshops in the Museum", in *Sweatshop USA: The American Sweatshop: The Historical and Global Perspective*, 57-73.

[2] Louis Levine, *The Women's Garment Workers: A History of the International Ladies Garment Workers' Union*, New York: B.W. Huebsch, 1924, 144-95; Joan M. Jensen, "The Great Uprisings: 1900-1920", in *A Needle, a Bobbin, a Strike: Women Needleworkers in America*, eds Joan M. Jensen and Sue Davidson, Philadelphia, PA:

industry than the sweatshop and industrial action. If the invisible women who sewed are to become visible alongside their activist sisters, a broader range of activities and socio-economic environments must be examined alongside the exposés and media coverage.

Indeed women's presence in the clothing industry needs to be perceived as layered. At the top of any pyramid of visibility were the union leaders such as Pauline Newman, Rose Schneiderman, Fannia Cohn, Clara Lemlich or Teresa Malkiel, who strove to improve working conditions. These notable women left much evidence of their actions and their stories have been told, more recently by women's and labor historians.[3] Less well known individually, but heralded collectively for the wrong reasons, were the workers of the Triangle Shirt Waist Factory who fell to their deaths in the disastrous fire of 1911.[4] Their counterparts laboring in other garment factories and clothing shops of the large cities were discussed both sympathetically and pejoratively by contemporary government inspectors, Progressive reformers, and newspaper reporters, and their images were at times recorded for posterity by documentary photographers whose work continues to be analyzed in academia. Such photographers as Lewis Hine and Jacob Riis also portrayed the outworkers toiling in their tenement homes for a pittance. These outworkers' lives were likewise documented in print through the distorted lenses of white middle-class reformers and commentators who reported their findings to governments and in the press. Certainly a variety of historians have refocused the lives of ordinary, frequently Jewish and Italian clothing workers more positively and have given them much more agency both within their communities and in their workplaces. Yet these anonymous lives need much more attention if their visibility is to be

---

Temple UP, 1984, 83-93; Ann Schofield, "The Uprising of the 20,000: The Making of a Labor Legend", in *A Needle, a Bobbin, a Strike: Women Needleworkers in America*, 167-82; Nancy Woloch, *Women and the American Experience*, third edn, New York: McGraw-Hill, 2000, 209-24.

[3] Alice Kessler-Harris, "Organizing the Unorganizable: Three Jewish Women and their Union", *Labor History*, XVII/1 (Winter 1976), 2-23; Mari Jo Buhl, *Women and American Socialism, 1870-1920*, Urbana: U of Illinois P, 1981, 176-213; Annelise Orleck, *Common Sense and a Little Fire: Women and Working-class Politics in the United States, 1900-1965*, Chapel Hill: U of North Carolina P, 1995.

[4] Richard Greenwald, *The Triangle Fire, the Protocols of Peace and Industrial Democracy in Progressive Era New York*, Philadelphia, PA: Temple UP, 2005, 25-56; Barbara M. Wertheimer, *We Were There: The Story of Working Women in America*, New York: Pantheon Books, 1977, 309-15.

other than the occasional glimpse, often through a veil in specialized history texts. This essay focuses on those females who populated the underside of the American clothing industry between the 1880s and the First World War.

Context

The layered nature of female visibility in clothing manufacture was of long standing, and needs to be placed in the larger context of women's place in the American labor force as a whole. Given the huge amount of academic attention paid to women's primacy in the home and the desirability of domesticity, it may be surprising to find how many women were visible, in print at least, or to use the more common term, were gainfully employed in the late nineteenth and early twentieth centuries. In 1870 1.8 million women comprised 14.7 percent of the total labor force in the United States. Forty years later in 1910 8.1 million female workers formed 21.2 percent of a rapidly increasing work force.[5] These figures are probably underestimates, as the census often failed to count married part-time workers, intermittent workers and those who worked at home.[6] Domestic service was the largest employer of women throughout the nineteenth century, comprising about half of the female labor force. It was followed by agriculture, with some 22 percent of gainfully employed women. However, with the spread of industrialization more women, about 19 percent of the total, worked in factories and smaller units of production.[7]

Within the manufacturing sector the clothing industry was the largest employer of women. Whether in small establishments, in factories or at home, women who sewed men's, women's, and children's clothing, hats and caps were a major economic, if not always an evident force. They possibly formed between 55 and 70 percent of all clothing workers in the late nineteenth and early

---

[5] *Statistical History of the United States: From Colonial Times to the Present*, 1976, intro. by Ben J. Wattenberg, New York: Basic Books 1976, 129.

[6] Claudia Goldin, *Understanding the Gender Gap: An Economic History of Women*, Oxford: Oxford UP, 1990, 219-27; Edith Abbott, W*omen in Industry: A Study in American Economic History* (1910), North Stratford, NH: Ayer Reprint, 1969, 232-33, 352-61.

[7] Janet M. Hooks, "Women's Occupations through Seven Decades", *Women's Bureau Bulletin*, no. 218, Washington, DC: US Department of Labor 1947, 52-62; Bettina Berch, *The Endless Day: The Political Economy of Women and Work*, New York: Harcourt, Brace Jovanovitch, 1982, 12-13.

twentieth centuries, though statistics are problematic, and vary geographically and within branches of the clothing industry.[8] Their presence in this particular industry was due to the nature of the work, which was deemed to be light and suitable to women. According to contemporary prescriptive literature and cultural mores women should not be gainfully employed, but should only fulfill the domestic duties of running a good household, and being a good wife and mother or a dutiful daughter or sister. Exceptions might be made for widows without financial support and women who helped to support a family; but ideally these exceptions would be temporary. In practice, many working-class women, particularly daughters, had to join the labor force in order to try and avoid poverty for themselves and their families. In many cities and particularly in large cities they became clothing workers.

This was not a new phenomenon in the late nineteenth century. Women had frequently been needleworkers, but in the eighteenth and early nineteenth centuries their work was very different from its later mechanized production. Then it was either located in the home where women hand-sewed clothing for their families, or in small and often elite dressmaking shops and tailoring establishments catering to the requirements of upper-class male and female clients. These two separate and distinct businesses operated a sexual division of labor. Men tailored clothing for male patrons while women seamstresses sewed for female customers. Like tailors, modistes and milliners were skilled artisans. Other women were employed in dressmaking establishments as apprentices, finishers, and helpers, and might through hard work gain some upwards mobility by becoming a fitter, trimmer, or forewoman. Women also entered or re-entered the men's clothing trade as unpaid help in the form of wives, or as paid help in the shape of hired workers who sewed the cheaper quality clothing. This pattern of fashionable clothing production remained for many years, even after the introduction and spread of the sewing machine in the 1850s facilitated the growth of ready-made clothing. It also sat

---

[8] Mabel Hurt Willet, *The Employment of Women in the Clothing Trade*, New York: Columbia UP, 1902, 53-55; US Congress, Senate, "Report on the Condition of Women and Child Wage Earners in the United States", in *History of Women in Industry in the United States*, IX, 61 Cong. 2 Sess. Report 645, 1910, 143-44; Daniel Bender, *Sweated Work, Weak Bodies: Anti-Sweatshop Campaigns and Languages of Labor*, New Brunswick, NJ: Rutgers UP, 2004, 108-109.

side by side with an "outside" system in which female wage-earners sewed a range of cheaper-end clothing for the southern and western trade and for the lower end of the urban market.[9]

After the Civil War women moved into the batch production and then the mass production of standardized, relatively cheap, but reasonable quality men's and women's clothing. Men's ready-made clothing developed first as a large scale industry in the 1860s and 1870s, following the improvement in techniques and machinery for cutting clothes to size that emerged as a result of demand for uniforms during the war. Originating in small clothing shops in the tenements of large cities, the entrepreneur or contractor hired some five or six female and male operatives and produced both whole garments and parts of men's garments, like sleeves, trousers, and cuffs. If successful, the entrepreneur increased the size of his shop. He also employed other female machine operators as outworkers. They took their work home and were paid by the piece rather than by the hour. Women's ready-made wear, as distinct from custom-made wear was initially batch-produced by women in the tailoring rooms of large department stores in the 1870s and 1880s. Here smaller lots of dresses were cut from dress patterns and sewn by machine, and were then given individual finishing touches, thereby providing the customer with a unique garment. Alteration workers offered a similar service for the growing number of ready-made items that were being sold in large department stores towards the turn of the twentieth century.[10]

By the late nineteenth century the clothing industry was a rapidly expanding and highly visible part of American economic and social

---

[9] Wendy Gamber, *The Female Economy: The Millinery and Dressmaking Trades, 1860-1930*, Urbana: U of Illinois P, 1997, 9-21; Christine Stansell, "The Origins of the Sweatshop: Women and Early Industrialization in New York City", in *Working Class America: Essays on Labor, Community and American Society*, eds Michael H. Frisch and Daniel J. Walkowitz, Urbana: U of Illinois P, 1983, 78-103; Ava Baron and Susan E. Clapp, "'If I didn't have my Sewing Machine...': Women and Sewing Machine Technology", in *A Needle, a Bobbin, a Strike: Women Needleworkers in America*, 20-59; Claudia B. Kidwell and Margaret C. Christman, *Suiting Everyone: The Democratization of Clothing in America*, Washington DC: Smithsonian Institution P, 1974, 19-64.

[10] Gamber, *Female Economy*, 190-228; Sarah A. Johnson, "The Industrial Development of Women's Clothing Manufacturing in American Department Stores, 1878-1900", in *The Consumption of Middle Class American Women's Clothing through Mail Order Catalogues, 1850 to 1900*, PhD diss., University of Brighton, 2003, 130-75; Kidwell and Christman, "Suiting Everyone", 75-164.

life. The statistics provided by the federal or state governments are at best estimates and are all subject to interpretative qualification. Yet even scattered figures suggest significant expansion and visible female workers. Men's ready-made clothing had already increased by 70 percent between 1870 and 1890, with its product value rising from $147,650,000 to $251,000,000. It continued to expand notably in the next twenty years. Women's clothing output rose fivefold between 1870 and 1890, from the relatively smaller baseline of $13,000,000, when the figures included the output from dress-making establishments as well as from factories, to $68,000,000. It then accelerated more quickly, reaching a product valued at $385,000,000 in 1910, a five and a half fold increase. By this time there were 153,743 female workers in women's clothing alone.[11]

The majority of these workers were located in the very large or metropolitan cities. New York was the leading centre of production. In 1900 the factory product of all clothing in that city was valued at some $209,000,000. By that time the women's clothing industry in particular had expanded dramatically and there were 830 shops in the Lower East Side making only women's suits and cloaks. Chicago came a poor second with an output valued at approximately $47,000,000, followed by Philadelphia at $28,000,000 and Baltimore at $20,000,000.[12] This concentration of clothing manufacture in large cities stemmed primarily from the availability of workers who increasingly were immigrants or their children born in the United States.

By 1900 less than one quarter of the female workers in the women's clothing trade in large cities, with a population over 50,000 were native-born white Americans. Initially these immigrants were German and Irish, but in the 1890s Russians and Italians dominated. Particularly noticeable, however, was the growing preponderance of Jewish clothing workers. In 1897 60 percent of Jewish (or, to contemporaries, "Hebrew") immigrants in New York worked in the needle trades both as small entrepreneurs and as machine operators.

---

[11] Victor S. Clark, *History of Manufactures in the United States* (1916-28), 3 vols, New York: Peter Smith, 1949, II, 446-47 and III, 222; Louis Levine, *The Women's Garment Workers: A History of the International Ladies Garment Workers' Union*, New York: B.W. Huebsch, 1924, 515.

[12] US Bureau of Census, 1902, *Statistical Atlas, Twelfth Census of the United States, 1900*, Washington, DC: US Government Printing Office, 1902, 87-88, and plate 199; Clark, *History of Manufacturers*, II, 446; Bender, *Sweated Work, Weak Bodies*, 33.

Emigrating mostly from Germany at first, such Jewish immigrants during the course of the nineteenth century increasingly came from Russia. Only when Jewish wives withdrew from the trade did the female workers in New York become more varied. By 1913 34 percent were Italian. But Jews were the largest group of immigrant operatives even in Chicago where garment workers were more ethnically diverse.[13]

Not all clothing workers in the years 1870-1910 were women. The industry was populated by both women and men, but the proportions of each sex varied depending on the use of machine technology, the flow of immigrants into specific cities and the availability of alternative occupations for men. Estimates derived from the censuses and government surveys suggest that in 1860 85 percent of the workers in ready-made women's wear were female. This proportion remained steady or increased slightly so that in 1880 it was 88 percent. It subsequently declined to 66 percent in 1890 and 63 percent in 1905 as the industry became more mechanized. Women comprised 56 percent of the clothing and sewing trades as a whole in 1900. More specifically in New York City, 58 percent of the operatives in the women's clothing industry were male in 1890. This declined to 54 percent of the operatives in 1910 and 50 percent in 1920. In Chicago in the early twentieth century women formed 52.6 percent of the clothing workers while in Baltimore at the same time they comprised 43.4 percent. In the male clothing industry in the early twentieth century women comprised a smaller proportion, about 36 percent of the shop.[14]

The context of the American clothing industry in the nineteenth century suggests that it is an important site for examining working women who were visible in contemporary public space if viewed in

---

[13] US Congress, Senate, "Clothing Manufacturing", in *Reports of the Immigration Commission: Immigrants in Industries*, XI, pt 6, 61 Cong. 2 Sess., Report 633, 1911, 253-661; Levine, *Women's Garment Workers*, 12-17; Bender, *Sweated Work, Weak Bodies*, 25-31; Elizabeth Ewen, *Immigrant Women in the Land of Dollars: Life and Culture on the Lower East Side, 1890-1925*, New York: Monthly Review Press, 1985, 25; Jo Ann Argersinger, *Making the Amalgamated: Gender, Ethnicity and Class in the Baltimore Clothing Industry, 1899-1939*, Baltimore, MD: Johns Hopkins UP, 1999, 13-14; Susan A. Glenn, *Daughters of the Shtetl: Life and Labor in the Immigrant Generation*, Ithaca, NY: Cornell UP, 1990, 92.
[14] US Congress, Senate, 1911, 405, 429; Green, *Ready-to-wear*, 167; Glenn, *Daughters of the Shtetl*, 109.

actuality rather than ideologically. Certainly many of these women
were ignored, pitied or treated as cultural deviants. But the subsequent
academic debates that have been engendered by the problematic
statistics of official bodies, the writings of investigative journalists or
muckrakers, the photographs of contemporary reformers, the reports
of social workers, and the output of historians, have created different
layers of visibility for these workers. As well as establishing their
presence, research has perceived clothing workers as one of the
clearest examples of working-class women's lives. Such visibility
should further challenge the concepts of female respectability that
revolve round white middle-class women and the artificial dichotomy
of public and private spheres that has dominated so much scholarship
in women's studies.

The spaces of female clothing workers
As Nancy Green so aptly pointed out "garments can be made just
about anywhere", and indeed they were in the United States in late
nineteenth century.[15] Despite the improvements in sewing and cutting
machinery, clothing was still made in homes and in small shops as
well as in large factories. Thanks to the division of labor that made it
possible for workers to specialize in putting together or finishing parts
of garments with their own sewing machine, a proportion of the
industry was located in their homes, frequently in tenement buildings.
Small contractors also continued to run their own workshop, again
often located in tenements. Here they could directly supervise their
handfuls of workers. These two decentralized production modes were
frequently referred to as the "outside" process, since they involved
collecting pre-cut garments and sewing parts of these garments. At the
same time larger manufacturers decided to bring their workforce into
their newer establishments where they could supervise the most cost-
effective use of their improved industrial sewing machines and cutting
machinery. In this inside process workers completed all stages of
production, from cutting to finishing garments. However, given the
seasonal fluctuations in clothing demand, all clothing entrepreneurs
wanted to avoid or at least to minimize fixed capital costs, a regular

---

[15] Green, "Fashion, Flexible Specialization", 43.

workforce, and regulations. They thus looked to a variety of production modes, some of which were more visible than others.[16]

The private space of the home becomes public
Most entrepreneurs used outside workers whose home was their site of gainful employment. Contractors and sub contractors, especially in metropolitan cities, encouraged workers to turn their homes into workplaces. Here untrained, unskilled, frequently immigrant women with family responsibilities could earn money on piecework if they worked for long hours. Evidence abounds concerning these women and children, who have been called the "toilers of the tenements".[17] The official reports of State Factory Investigating Commissions and Bureau of Statistics, the Federal Government *Report on the Condition of Women and Child Wage Earners*, the social investigations of such reformers as Edith Abbott, Mary Van Kleeck, Mary Kingsbury Simkovitch, and Sophonisba P. Breckinridge, or the more inflammatory articles in *The Survey* or the *New York World*, sometimes accompanied by the graphic photographs taken by photographers like Lewis Hine or Jacob Riis, all clearly pointed to overcrowded and unsanitary working conditions, which lacked fresh air, public utilities and amenities, and involved long working hours for pitifully low wages, the employment of children, and their exclusion from education. Whether this information was reported in clinically neutral words accompanied by statistics or written as muckraking exposés for the purpose of demonstrating that conditions needed to be improved, it clearly informed the reading public that there were clothing workers who labored in less than ideal circumstances.[18]

---

[16] Green, "Fashion, Flexible Specialization", 37-55; Green, *Ready-to-wear*, 144-55; Levine, *Women's Garment Workers*, 8-23; Baron and Clapp, "'If I didn't have'", 1984, 38-41; Argersinger, *Making the Amalgamated*, 9-13.

[17] Elizabeth S. Sergeant, "Toilers of the Tenements: Where the Beautiful Things of the Great Shops Are Made", *McClure's Magazine*, XXXV (July 1910), 231-41.

[18] US Congress, Senate, 1910, II, 215-318; New York State, *Preliminary Report of the Factory Investigating Commission*, Albany: Arcus Co., I, 1912, 83-89; New York State, *Second Report of the Factory Investigating Commission*, Albany, NY: J.B. Lyon Co., 1913, I, 90-123 and appendix 4, 669-705; Massachusetts Bureau of Statistics and Amy Hewes, *Industrial Homework in Massachusetts*, Boston, MA: Women's Educational and Industrial Union, 1915, 1-58; Mary Van Kleeck, *Artificial Flower Makers*, New York: Russell Sage Foundation, 1913, 90-117; Elizabeth C. Watson, "Home Work in the Tenements", *The Survey*, XXV/19 (1911), 772-81; Sergeant, "Toilers of the Tenements".

So what did these sources suggest? New York City was the centre of the clothing industry. Here, according to the 1902 *Annual Report* of the New York City Bureau of Labor Statistics, there were between 25,000 and 30,000 outworkers located primarily in the Lower East Side of the city. For married women, taking in sewing was a means of supplementing their husbands' irregular earnings and of contributing to family income while maintaining their domestic functions at home. Their labor and that of their children meant the difference between their families' survival and starvation and homelessness. Whether licensed or unlicensed, most of these Italian or Jewish women finished coats and trousers or made artificial flowers. Either they or their children, featured in photographs as well as described in writing, carried bundles of clothing and boxes of flowers from and to the contractors or middlemen who lived in the vicinity. They completed the work, often in the kitchen, either sewing or making flowers in between cooking and caring for children. Their daughters were quickly taught how to help, by pulling out basting threads, sewing on buttons or separating artificial flower petals. Soon older children could do the same work as their mothers, before and after school, if indeed they attended school. These were the toilers of the tenements.[19]

Social investigators, state government reports, and inspectors roundly condemned this labor and its location. "Homework" was carried out in the dark, dingy, overcrowded housing of tenement buildings where conditions were both dirty and unsafe. But equally, if not more appallingly in the eyes of these middle-class visitors and observers, was the merger of the world of work with the home. The kitchen was frequently the sewing room, and here both meals would be cooked and garments finished. For investigators the two worlds of paid work and the family should be kept separate and there should be a "proper" family life. Even more damning was the problem of sanitation and disease. Not only were the tenements filthy, but their occupants were often ill with a variety of infectious diseases. Contamination then became a major issue for reformers, concerned about the dangers posed to the community at large by germs on this home-produced clothing.

---

[19] Willet, *The Employment of Women in the Clothing Trade*, 94-133; US Congress, Senate, 1910, II, 215-54; Sergeant, "Toilers of the Tenements"; Watson, "Home Work"; Ewen, "Immigrant Women", 122-26.

They campaigned for legislation either to prohibit or to regulate the work. In the 1890s many states passed laws licensing and regulating tenement homework and restricting the age of tenement house workers. By 1901 inspectors in New York and Illinois were advocating the abolition of homework. But the regulations that were passed were of little effect. There was an insufficient government inspectorate to enforce the legislation, and furthermore middle-class investigators were loath to take away the income that often provided a family's living. Insisting that homes should be clean and regulated and that children went to school only meant that many immigrant families went hungry or were evicted because they could not pay the rent. Outworkers and reformers were caught in a vicious circle.[20]

The contractors' shop: publicly visible and condemned
Also caught in a vicious circle were those "inside workers" who were located in the neighborhood contractors' workshops. These petty entrepreneurs, who were also referred to as the "sweaters" in contemporary literature, operated "contract shops" where they usually carried out only some functions of making clothing. They located their workspaces in their apartments, in cheap and small warehouses, or converted lofts, and these shops were overcrowded, dirty, dark, unventilated, and unsafe, but they were cheap and convenient. In an industry that was seasonal and highly competitive, these small-scale operators bid against their counterparts for bundles of cut cloth from the wholesale manufacturers, who in turn were attempting to cut their own costs. Having collected the bundles from the manufacturers, they took these to their own shop or rooms, where they employed a handful of female and some male workers to complete parts of the suits, trousers, or vests of the men's ready-made clothing industry.

Between six and twenty workers might be employed, but many shops had five or fewer workers. Provided that the contractor had the space for a few tables, chairs, sewing machines, a stove, and irons, he could set his workers to completing specific tasks such as basting parts together, pressing these with heavy hot irons, and finishing the

---

[20] US Congress, Senate 1910, II, 215-54; New York State 1913, I, 90-123, appendix 4, 669-705; Josephine Goldmark, "Tenement Home Work and the Courts", *The Survey*, XXXV/21 (1916), 612-13; Bender, *Sweated Work, Weak Bodies*, 62-76.

parts, which were then returned to the manufacturer for a fixed price.[21] Conditions of labor were appalling. Inspectors frequently commented on this "system of making clothes under filthy and inhuman conditions" as a "process of grinding the faces of the poor".[22]

Though the clothing industry had regularly featured a contracting system, what was emerging in the late 1880s and 1890s was an industrial dualism, in which small and very small contact shops grew at an accelerated rate.[23] The increasing presence of these "sweatshops" was linked to the upsurge in East European Jewish immigration. At the time many observers reported this symbiosis with a marked degree of repugnance. Investigators considered that the dirt and danger together with immoral conditions in which women worked side by side with men were the result of a pattern of Jewish workplace degeneration and an un-American mode of working. Immigrants in the Lower East Side of New York City, whether female or male, were perceived as pale, gaunt haggard figures whose lives were blighted by long hours (ten to twelve hours a day and fourteen hours in the busy period), minimal pay and miserable conditions. They were a disgrace to the American nation, but the circumstances of female workers was particularly distressing because they were marginalized as transient workers and were relegated to less well paid jobs like basting or sewing on buttons.[24]

There is no doubt that women were among the sweaters of the clothing workshops and as such became visible in the public arena. Those middle-class reformers or would-be reformers who drew attention to the workshops, in written and visual records, portrayed women as victims of a debased system of manufacturing. If only these

---

[21] John R. Commons, "The Sweating System in the Clothing Trades", in *Trade Unionism and Labor Problems*, ed. John R. Commons, Boston: Ginn and Co., 1905, 316-29; Jesse E. Pope, *The Clothing Industry in New York*, New York: Columbia UP, 1905, 61-78; Levine, *Women's Garment Workers*, 18-23; Jacob Riis, *How the Other Half Lives: Studies among the Tenements of New York* (1901), New York: Dover Publications, 1971, 96-107; Glenn, *Daughters of the Shtetl*, 93-95; Argersinger, *Making the Amalgamated*, 10-11.

[22] Quoted in Levine, *Women's Garment Workers*, 22.

[23] Steven Fraser, "Combined and Uneven Development in the Men's Clothing Industry", *Business History Review*, LVII/4 (Winter 1983), 522-471.

[24] Willet, *The Employment of Women in the Clothing Trade*, 73-93; Commons, "The Sweating System in the Clothing Trades", 316-35; Bender, *Sweated Work, Weak Bodies*, 25-31, 42-60 and 105-31; Argersinger, *Making the Amalgamated*, 13-16; Glenn, *Daughters of the Shtetl*, 90-106.

newcomers really understood and were integrated into American culture, then they would either not be working or they would be working in cleaner and more regulated spaces. Yet most of these observers were also keenly aware that these immigrants had little choice. They had either come to "the land of dollars" to improve their living standards or to gain the freedom to practice their religion. Whether skilled needleworkers or not, on arriving in the country they were hired through family, social and religious connections. These young Jewish women, often speaking little or no English and in search of work, quickly learned that the clothing industry was the easiest and most accessible place to get a job. They and their second-generation peers often moved out of the workshops to the clothing factories, to be replaced by Italian girls. They subsequently moved into office work. But initially Russian-Jewish women were steered to a limited labor market in the workshops in order to help support their families. Their lives here were known and recognized, but it was beyond those investigating their low-waged and repellent conditions, as it was a century later at the end of the twentieth century, to raise enough support, official or otherwise to change their situation effectively.[25] Therefore there were two layers of visibility for the sweatshop worker: one that was portrayed in the media and government documents and one that was practically known to and accepted by most recent immigrants but which was ignored by the majority of society.

The factory girl and her place in the public arena
Young immigrant women, particularly Russian Jewish women in the 1890s and 1900s, sought work in the larger clothing factories as well as the small workshops. Run increasingly by entrepreneurs from their own ethnic groups, they were again pressured by cultural ties and lack of English to work in the clothing industry. Here they had the possibility of finding an improved working environment, but, as the industrial action that took place between 1905 and 1915 suggests, they did not do so. In this decade a hundred-thousand women in clothing

---

[25] Kathie Friedman-Kasaba, *Memories of Migration: Gender, Ethnicity and Work in the Lives of Jewish and Italian Women in New York, 1870-1914*, Albany: State U of New York P, 1996, 158-72; Glenn, *Daughters of the Shtetl*, 90-131; Ewen, *Immigrant Women*, 111-27, 242-62; Miriam Cohen, *Workshop to Office: Two Generations of Italian Women in New York City, 1900-1950*, Ithaca, NY: Cornell UP, 1992, 37-86, 147-77.

factories in New York City, Rochester, Chicago, Philadelphia, and Cleveland went on strike to obtain higher wages, improved working conditions and an end to subcontracting. What has been called "the great uprisings" thrust women into the public view, raising sympathy from some and outright hostility from others.[26] Their actions certainly led to a movement of women into trade unions, but without significant improvements in industrial relations.

What was the nature of the large clothing factory that stimulated radical action by many of its female workers? By the 1880s and 1890s some of the larger manufacturers, who had often merged together several smaller shops and wholesale dealers in men's ready-made clothing, moved into sizeable establishments in lofts or warehouses in the metropolitan cities. Here, using a minute division of labor at all stages of production, ranging from laying out and cutting cloth to finishing garments and adopting new technology, they aimed to accomplish considerably more cost-effective production of garments. The advent of newer, heavier, and more expensive sewing machines, sometimes powered by electricity, greatly enhanced the speed of production at the same time as contributing to the division of labor, with unskilled immigrant workers doing the less difficult tasks and the more experienced women sewing the more difficult seams. As in the sweatshops and the homes, women only stitched one part of a garment, in what became known as the task system.

Inside subcontracting within the factory created further distinctions between the learners and the more experienced workers. The introduction of cutting knives and then cutting machines, together with clothing patterns and the use of heavy pressing machines, not only encouraged separation of tasks, but facilitated separate occupations that were confined to males, particularly in the men's clothing industry. Indeed men, imbued by the ideal of the family wage as much as by the notion that women could not operate heavier machines, frequently held the higher-paid jobs in cutting and pressing. They also moved into machine operating in the higher-priced products such as the women's cloaks and suits, limiting women to auxiliary tasks like finishing and basting. So not only were there limited

---

[26] Jensen, "The Great Uprisings: 1900-1920", 83-93.

opportunities for female needleworkers, but there was gender segregation in many clothing factories.[27]

If women's work in these establishments was personally restrictive and gender segregated, were other conditions better than in the workshop or the home? The larger units of operation were at times lighter and cleaner, had more modern machinery, and could have electric power. In the better factories female machine operators considered that they had made progress in their working environment. But at times there were few discernible differences between the conditions of the factory and the shop. Machines were crowded together and floors were covered with debris. Safety hazards were common, with stairs and halls being dark and dangerous, toilets being dirty and broken, and exits and fire escapes obstructed. The machine rooms were subject to variations in weather, being extremely hot in the summer and cold in the winter. Even more problematic were the low wages, fines, and wage deductions, which, in addition to seasonal fluctuations when layoffs were common, created financial hardships and domestic instability. The work discipline imposed by supervisors and bosses and the sexual jokes and sexual harassment experienced by workers were frequent causes of complaint and made the job more irritating and miserable for factory girls. All these conditions pointed to a lack of care about and interest in unskilled workers who were easily replaceable, and it is no wonder that many female clothing workers were dissatisfied, took to organizing and went on strike.[28]

It was not uncommon for workers to take industrial action in the clothing industry in the late nineteenth century, but it was less usual for women to be involved in such action other than to set rates at the start of the season or occasionally through their membership of the Knights of Labor. Many male unionists were reluctant to involve their

---

[27] Pope, *Clothing Industry*, 61-78; Elizabeth B. Butler, *Women and the Trades: Pittsburgh 1907-1908*, New York: New York Charities Commission Committee, 1909, 101-26; Levine, *Women's Garment Workers*, 146-48; Glenn, *Daughters of the Shtetl*, 110-22; Bender, *Sweated Work, Weak Bodies*, 31-35; Jensen, "The Great Uprisings: 1900-1920", 85-86; Fraser, "Men's Clothing Industry", 527-28; Ewen, *Immigrant Women*, 245-50; Cohen, *Workshop to Office*, 66-68; Orleck, *Common Sense*, 31-50; Argersinger, *Making the Amalgamated*, 10.

[28] Ewen, *Immigrant Women*, 242-62; Glenn, *Daughters of the Shtetl*, 132-66; Louise C. Oldencrantz, *Italian Women in Industry: A Study of Conditions in New York City*, New York: Russell Sage Foundation, 1919, 65-75, 82-107; Bender, *Sweated Work, Weak Bodies*, 112-207.

female co-workers in their activities because they deemed them to be unskilled, transient workers who would retire from the labor force once married.[29] Only their growing numbers in the industry led to their recognition and grudging acceptance in the 1890s and 1900s. So when young militant shirtwaist workers walked off the job and took to the streets in 1909-1910 in the "uprising of the 20,000", they forced male leaders to reassess the role of women in the labor movement. Equally importantly, they drew the attention of the public to their industrial situation. When beaten and arrested on the picket line and joined by middle-class female allies in the shape of the Women's Trade Union League, they became newsworthy and generated considerable sympathy.

Such activism focused national attention on the plight of the female clothing workers. It also provided encouragement for other clothing workers in major cities to strike and to become involved in union campaigns. However, the end results were mixed. Some concessions in terms of hours, pay, and working conditions were gained, but many issues remained unresolved or soon returned to the *status quo ante*. Within two years, however, the fire at the Triangle Shirtwaist Factory in 1911, in which 146 working girls died and many more were injured, would once again remind Americans, albeit temporarily, of the problems of working women in the garment industry.[30]

Women in the late nineteenth century and early twentieth century clothing industry were always present, but their visibility was layered. Known intimately within their ethnic communities, they were respected there for their toil that helped sustain their families. Recognized by their employers and by their male co-workers as necessary parts of an industrial system, they were still regarded as dispensable because they were consigned to unskilled work and were

---

[29] Pope, *Clothing Industry*, 211-55; Levine, *Women's Garment Workers*, 32-43; Foner, *Women and the American Labor Movement*, 74-75, 86-87.

[30] Jensen "Great Uprisings: 1900-1920", 83-93; Joan M. Jensen, "The Great Uprising in Rochester", in *A Needle, a Bobbin, a Strike: Women Needleworkers in America*, 94-113; Schofield, "Uprising of the 20,000", 167-82; N. Sue Weiler, "The Uprising in Chicago: The Men's Garment Workers Strike, 1910-1911", in *A Needle, a Bobbin, a Strike: Women Needleworkers in America*, 114-39; Woloch, *Women and the American Experience*, 209-24; Glenn, *Daughters of the Shtetl*, 167-242; Orleck, *Common Sense*, 53-113; Ewen, *Immigrant Women*, 254-62; Foner, *Women and the American Labor Movement*, 133-83; Levine, *Women's Garment Workers*, 64-195; Argersinger, *Making the Amalgamated*, 83-102.

deemed to be transient. Publicized, as outworkers, "sweated labor", and strikers, they were both pitied and condemned as being unfeminine and un-American. History has at times given them an honorable place, either as part of the industrial working class or as at the forefront of industrial feminism. More recently, rather than being perceived as victims, they have been awarded much more agency both within the labor force and their communities. That they should always be remembered in the public domain as visible is incontestable.

WOMEN'S EMPLOYMENT IN THE PUBLIC AND PRIVATE SPHERES, 1880-1920

S.J. KLEINBERG

> Whatever opinions may be held as to the proper sphere of woman, the fact is that, to a considerable extent, woman's place to-day is no longer in the home. In addition to her social contributions to the preservation and welfare of mankind, the contributions of her sex to economic production in its commercial aspects are of such substantial proportions that not only is it impossible to ignore them as a factor in industrial process, but they are worthy of serious study as an important element in this progress.[1]

Barbara Welter's influential article, "The Cult of True Womanhood", articulated a disjuncture in women's roles between the public and private spheres of life, in which women's lives were presumed to be private while men's lives were public.[2] This essay rejects the way this model sets the purportedly public and private spheres in opposition to each other for several reasons. Firstly, the construct could only apply to those families wealthy enough to sustain a wife outside the labor force who did not generate some income, whether by taking in boarders, selling butter and eggs, or doing some remunerated labor.[3] Secondly, the terms "public" and "private" have little salience in a society in which the state – itself a form of " public" – increasingly

---

[1] Joseph A. Hill, *Women in Gainful Occupations, 1870-1920* (1929), New York: Joseph Reprint Corporation, 1972, xv.

[2] Barbara Welter, "The Cult of True Womanhood", *American Quarterly*, XVIII/2 (Summer 1966), 151-74.

[3] Joan Jensen, *Loosening the Bonds: Mid-Atlantic Farm Women, 1750-1850*, New Haven, CT: Yale UP, 1986, 79-144; Suzanne Lebsock, *The Free Women of Petersburg: Status and Culture in a Southern Town, 1784-1860*, New York: W.W. Norton, 1985.

regulated family matters that were previously private, including children's education and employment as well as women's work outside the home.[4] A third reason for rejecting a sharp differentiation between these supposedly separate spheres is that many families' homes were not private in any meaningful sense. African American women, for example, lived in a world which denied them privacy, most obviously under slavery, but also, still, in a postbellum world in which these women's employment after marriage largely took place in white people's homes or farms.[5] Moreover, the sentimental fiction Welter cites depicts the private world of the household as a sanctuary and haven, but that in no way characterized the pre-Civil War slave quarters or postbellum sharecropped farms or urban tenements where everyone could hear their neighbors' business.[6]

Welter drew upon antebellum ladies' magazines as her primary source. She described the true woman's place as being "by her own fireside – as daughter, sister, but most of all as wife and mother". Her article reflected the world of affluent white women with at least enough education and leisure time to read the newly published women's magazines of this era. The portrait she drew did not depict women as wage laborers, slaves, immigrants, or subsistence farmers. Instead, it presented a picture of American womanhood that essentialized affluent, small town and urban white women as "true women", while ignoring the lived realities of most women's experiences: women of all ages, races, and ethnic groups worked inside and outside the household.[7]

Along with Nancy F. Cott's *Bonds of Womanhood* and Carroll Smith-Rosenberg's "Female world of love and ritual", Welter's widely quoted article established the notion of separate spheres, with

---

[4] S.J. Kleinberg, "Children's and Mothers' Employment in Three Eastern Cities", *Social Science History*, XXIX/1 (Spring 2005), 45-76; Eileen Boris, *Home to Work: Motherhood and the Politics of Industrial Homework in the United States*, Cambridge: Cambridge UP, 1994.

[5] Pete Daniel, *Breaking the Land: The Transformation of Cotton, Tobacco, and Rice Cultures Since 1880*, Urbana: U of Illinois P, 1985, 49, 77, 198-200, 277-78; Tera W. Hunter, *To 'Joy My Freedom: Southern Black Women's Lives and Labors after the Civil War*, Cambridge, MA: Harvard UP, 1997, Ch. 3.

[6] S.J. Kleinberg, "Technology and Women's Work: The Lives of Working-Class Women, Pittsburgh, 1870-1900", *Labor History*, XVII (Winter 1976), 58-72.

[7] Mary Kelley, in her article, "Beyond the Boundaries", *Journal of the Early Republic*, XXI/1 (Spring 2001), 73-78, provides an excellent critique of the "Cult of True Womanhood".

women supposedly located in the home and men outside it.[8] The popularization of these constructs in historical discourse has turned both the Cult of True Womanhood and the doctrine of separate spheres into paradigms that, in the words of Nancy Hewitt, "established concepts and categories that now shape the analysis of all groups of American women".[9] While it is the case that economic and political changes occurring in the late eighteenth and early nineteenth centuries moved production and politics away from the household and into the marketplace, it is also true that different groups of women related in divergent fashions to the economy, household, and politics.[10] Race, marital status, age, class, ethnicity, and region, amongst other factors, were and are crucial determinants of women's activities, whether voluntary, domestic, or remunerated, a point to which I will return in the second part of this essay.

In trying to move this discourse on from the initial polarities of inside/outside the home and private/public, Alison Easton, R.J. Ellis, Janet Floyd, and Lindsey Traub urged historians and literary critics to think about the "complex scene of multiple publics and counter-publics with which women of varied groups and classes could engage, either in activity outside the home, in public activities within domestic settings or in the workplace".[11] This can be accomplished by focusing on specific spaces, on how women's appearances in particular zones were negotiated and represented within a wide range of historical, cultural, and material cultural texts as well as within literary texts. It also requires us to think about how women and the society in which they lived negotiated the complex meanings of the terms public and private. For, as Alice Kessler-Harris observes, women's employment in the "nonfamily workplace (itself public) therefore had something of

---

[8] Nancy F. Cott, *The Bonds of Womanhood: "Women's Sphere" in New England, 1780-1835*, New Haven, CT: Yale UP, 1977; Caroll Smith-Rosenberg, "The Female World of Love and Ritual: Relations between Women in Nineteenth-century America", *Signs: A Journal of Women in Culture and Society*, I/1 (Autumn 1975), 1-29.

[9] Nancy Hewitt, "Beyond the Search for Sisterhood: American Women's History in the 1990s", in *Unequal Sisters: A Multicultural Reader in U.S. Women's History*, eds Vicki L. Ruiz and Ellen Carol DuBois, New York: Routledge, 1990, 2.

[10] See Barbara Easton, "Industrialization and Femininity: A Case Study of Nineteenth-century New England", *Social Problems*, XXIII/4 (April 1976), 389-401.

[11] Alison Easton, R.J. Ellis, Janet Floyd and Lindsey Traub made this appeal in their call for papers for the "Visible Women" colloquium held at King's College University of London in June 2005.

a disruptive quality, simultaneously providing a potential vehicle for female political power and the focus of resistance among men who clung jealously to the male turf".[12] Women and men took their complex understandings of public and private into the workplace as did their employers.

Concepts of public and private
This essay questions the extent to which a model of womanhood that even implicitly contrasts public and private can apply to women from different racial, age, regional, and ethnic groups. American women had diverse employment configurations, based largely upon demographic and socioeconomic demarcations. Women's increased labor force participation did not necessarily represent a move from private to public in the Gilded Age and Progressive Era, in part because the concept of domesticity followed women into the workplace, but also because so many women earned their daily bread in the purportedly private space of the home itself. The public/private paradigm of women's employment essentializes young women's labor force participation, principally in the Northeast and Midwest, at the same time that it ignores older women, those in the South and, to a lesser extent, the West, who moved fluidly between these spaces as part of their daily lives, whether participating in remunerated labor or not.

By examining the conceptual trajectory taken by the historians of women in the last forty years and the ways in which employment altered in the nineteenth and early twentieth centuries, I hope to show that the conceptualization of women's work in terms of a rigid, mutually exclusive public-private divide obscures and hides much of women's work itself, to the detriment of many women workers inside and outside the home. I will then explore how women's employment patterns changed and developed in the Gilded Age and Progressive Era (1880-1920), a crucial time period for understanding society's attitudes towards women's employment and the uses of the home as a site of economic endeavor.[13]

---

[12] Alice Kessler-Harris, *Gender and Labor History*, Urbana: U of Illinois P, 2007, 159.

[13] See, for example, Alice Kessler-Harris, *In Pursuit of Equity: Women, Men, and the Quest for Economic Citizenship in 20th-century America*, New York: Oxford UP, 2001; and Boris, *Home to Work*.

The general history of women's participation in the formal economy has been an area of scholarly concern for some forty years. Writing in 1969, Gerda Lerner described the changes that took place as an industrial culture, based on an egalitarian ideology (for whites), replaced the hierarchical agricultural world of pre-Revolutionary North America. Lerner notes that the "Puritan world view" expected women of all marital statuses to labor on the farm, and in the home and the shop. Industrialization had many effects: it separated the home from most aspects of remunerated labor, and in the process redefined home as an emotional site rather than a workshop. By separating women's labor into that done in the home (by married women and their helpers, whether daughters or paid servants) and that performed in dedicated industrial spaces – factories, workshops, and the like – usually by single women, industrialization demanded both a new definition of work and a division of women's experiences according to marital status, age, and class.[14] Women's opportunities contracted with the professionalization of medicine, the expanding scale of manufacturing, and the formalization of the economy in the early national era. Yet, as Lerner observes, "the slogan 'woman's place is in the home' took on a certain aggressiveness and shrillness precisely at the time when increasing numbers of poorer women *left* their homes to become factory workers".[15] These women were outside the concern of the "publishers and mass media writers", who increasingly posited middle-class women's world as domestic and apart from economic activity. Such framing might have suited their readers, but was largely outside the experience of poorer women.

The dichotomy of public versus private spheres, while never wholly accurate even for affluent white women, fails entirely when historians consider the situation of Native American women engaged in agriculture and gathering or enslaved African American women,

---

[14] Jeanne Boydston, in *Home and Work: Housework, Wages, and the Ideology of Labor in the Early Republic*, Oxford: Oxford UP, 1990, discusses changing definitions of work in the nineteenth century. See also Boris, *Home to Work*, on the controversy that arose over industrial home work at the end of the nineteenth and beginning of the twentieth century, precisely because middle-class reformers did not want the home to be used as a workplace.

[15] Gerda Lerner, "The Lady and the Mill Girl", *Mid-Continent American Studies Journal*, X/1 (Spring 1969), 13.

whether they worked in domestic jobs or in the fields.[16] Indeed, Lerner herself was one of the first women's historians to include African American women in the historical record in her documentary history, *Black Women in White America.* However, most other historians ignored women's lives under slavery until the 1980s, when the silence was broken by Paula Giddings' *When and Where I Enter,* Jacqueline Jones' *Labor of Love, Labor of Sorrow,* Deborah Gray White's *Ar'n't I a Woman?,* and various edited collections concerned with women's lives during slavery.[17]

Other authors have subsequently complicated the story sketched by Lerner, adding depth and richness to our understanding of American women's work through a consideration of racialized gender and class. They have investigated slavery, industrial disputes, Native American women's distinctive economic contributions, immigrant women, women in the South and the West, and women working in a broad variety of occupations, including domestic service, agricultural production for market, nursing, teaching, and medicine.[18]

---

[16] See Ramona Ford, "Native American Women: Changing Statuses, Changing Interpretations", in *Writing the Range: Race, Class, and Culture in the Women's West,* eds Susan Armitage and Elizabeth Jameson, Norman: U of Oklahoma P, 1997, 42-68. For an inclusive historiography of antebellum women's work, see Inge Dornan and S.J. Kleinberg, "From Dawn to Dusk: Women's Work in the Antebellum Era", in *The Practice of U.S. Women's History: Narratives, Intersections, and Dialogues,* eds S.J. Kleinberg, Eileen Boris, and Vicki L. Ruiz, New Brunswick: Rutgers UP, 2007, 83-105. Edward Pessen, in *Riches, Class, and Power before the Civil War,* Lexington, MA: D.C. Heath, 1973, maps the growth of wealth in the antebellum period as derived from commerce. There is no mention of women in this account of riches, classes, and power, except as the wives of wealthy men.

[17] Gerda Lerner, *Black Women in White America: A Documentary History,* New York: Pantheon, 1972; Paula Giddings, *When and Where I Enter: The Impact of Black Women on Race and Sex in America,* New York: William Morrow, 1984; Jacqueline L. Jones, *Labor of Love, Labor of Sorrow: Black Women, Work, and the Family from Slavery to the Present,* New York: Basic Books, 1985; Deborah Gray White, *Ar'n't I a Woman? Female Slaves in the Plantation South,* New York: Norton, 1984; *The Afro-American Woman: Struggles and Images,* eds Sharon Harley and Rosalyn Terborg-Penn, Port Washington, NY: Kennikat Press, 1978; and *All the Women Are White, All the Men Are Black, but Some of Us Are Brave: Black Women's Studies,* eds Gloria T. Hull, Patricia Bell Scott, and Barbara Smith, Old Westbury, NY: Feminist Press, 1981.

[18] Alice Kessler-Harris, *Out to Work: A History of Wage-earning Women in the United States,* New York: Oxford UP, 1982; Kessler-Harris, *Gender and Labor History;* Thomas Dublin, *Women at Work: The Transformation of Work and Community in Lowell, Massachusetts, 1826-1860,* New York: Columbia UP, 1979;

An increasing number of studies have enhanced our understanding of women's employment by considering it from more than one perspective. Wendy Gordon's investigation of single women's independent migration to textile towns in England, Scotland, and the United States is an example of such work and points to an important aspect of women's economic history, namely its implicitly or explicitly comparative structure.[19] Such a framework helps overcome the binary public-versus-private divide by demonstrating both the extent to which women moved between home and workplace and that for many women the home was their workplace. This point obviously holds for domestic servants, but it also characterizes a large number of female mill workers for whom the American textile manufacturers provided company housing, where their tenure in their dwellings depended upon their work status. Many urban and some rural women also combined household tasks with wage-earning either by taking in boarders or through the domestic production of goods, stigmatized by reformers as sweated labor, and by the early twentieth century the subject of regulatory campaigns.[20]

Jensen, *Loosening the Bonds*; Faye E. Dudden, *Serving Women: Household Service in Nineteenth-century America*, Middletown, CT: Wesleyan UP, 1983; Daniel E. Sutherland, *Americans and Their Servants: Domestic Service in the United States from 1800 to 1920*, Baton Rouge: Louisiana State UP, 1981; Lebsock, *The Free Women of Petersburg*; Marli Wiener, *Mistresses and Slaves: Plantation Women in South Carolina, 1830-1880*, Urbana: U of Illinois P, 1998; White, *Ar'n't I a Woman?*; Jennifer L. Morgan, *Laboring Women: Reproduction and Gender in New World Slavery*, Philadelphia, PA: U of Pennsylvania P, 2004; Mary Roth Walsh, *Doctors Wanted: No Women Need Apply*, New Haven, CT: Yale UP, 1977; Theda Perdue, *Cherokee Women: Gender and Culture Change*, 1700-1835, Lincoln: U of Nebraska P, 1998; Ramon Gutiérrez, *When Jesus Came, the Corn Mothers Went Away: Marriage, Sexuality and Power in New Mexico, 1500-1846*, Stanford, CA: Stanford UP, 1991; Susan Reverby, *Ordered to Care: The Dilemma of American Nursing, 1850-1945*, Cambridge: Cambridge UP, 1987; *Hidden Histories of Women in the New South*, eds Betty Brandon, Virginia Bernhard, Elizabeth Fox-Genovese, Theda Perdue and Elizabeth Turner, Columbia: U of Missouri P, 1994; Gail MacLeitch, "'Your Women Are of No Small Consequence': Native American Women, Gender, and Early American History", in *The Practice of U.S. Women's History: Narratives, Intersections, and Dialogues*, 30-49.

[19] Wendy M. Gordon, *Mill Girls and Strangers: Single Women's Independent Migration in England, Scotland, and the United States, 1850 -1881*, Albany: State U of New York P, 2002.

[20] David Katzman, *Seven Days a Week: Women and Domestic Service in Industrializing America*, New York: Oxford UP, 1978; Dublin, *Women at Work*; Boris, *Home to Work*; S.J. Kleinberg, "Seeking the Meaning of Life: The Pittsburgh

In the postbellum era, white women workers moved away from agricultural and domestic work first to industrial employments and later towards white-collar jobs.[21] In recent years, historians have acknowledged that the focus on northern industrial employment hid many women's ways of life, whether in southern textile mills and tobacco factories, western rural communities, or on farms throughout the United States.[22] Women of color continued to work largely in agriculture and in service jobs and were thus hidden from the wider public gaze during their working lives. The private nature or remoteness of their work site meant that little effort was made to regulate their employment or working conditions, despite the penchant Progressive reformers showed for restricting female economic endeavors for their supposed "own good".

Supreme Court decisions, such as *Muller v. Oregon*, accepted that women's relation to the economy and the state was fundamentally different from men's and could be regulated in ways that would be an unacceptable breach of men's right to earn a living as they saw fit. By ruling that state legislation could abrogate women's rights to contract their labor freely, the Court reflected Progressive reformers' sentiment that society (or a particular stratum of it) had a need and a right to regulate women's work outside the home in order to protect their ability to care for their homes and families. Such rulings only applied to women working in industrial establishments, and rarely, if ever, covered female domestic servants or agricultural laborers, who remained largely outside the white reformers' purview in the Progressive Era.[23] Urged on by Progressive reformers who wished to protect women from exploitation in the market place, state legislatures purported to protect motherhood by banning women from working over ten hours per day in industrial and similar establishments, but at

---

Survey and the Family", in *The Pittsburgh Survey Revisited*, eds Maurine Greenwald and Margo Anderson, Pittsburgh, PA: U of Pittsburgh P, 1996, 88-105.

[21] Ileen A. DeVault, *Sons and Daughters of Labor: Class and Clerical Work in Turn-of-the-century Pittsburgh*, Ithaca, NY: Cornell UP, 1990.

[22] See, for example, *The Practice of U.S. Women's History*; Susan Armitage and Elizabeth Jameson, *The Women's West*, Norman: U of Oklahoma P, 1987; *Writing the Range: Race, Class, and Culture in the Women's West*, eds Armitage and Jameson; Vicki L. Ruiz, *From Out of the Shadows: Mexican Women in Twentieth-century America*, New York: Oxford UP, 1998.

[23] See Louis Brandeis and Josephine Goldmark, *Women in Industry* (1908), New York: Arno Press, 1969; and Nancy Woloch, *Muller vs. Oregon: A Brief History with Documents*, Boston, MA: Bedford Books of St Martin's Press, 1996.

the same time simply ignored the widespread overwork amongst household and farm workers, who were seemingly invisible or working in a supposedly healthy environment. Many states passed statutes similar to Oregon's in the first two decades of the twentieth century. In doing so they defined the occupations and time of day or night in which women could or could not work. These were occupations such as the retail trade and light manufacturing in which men, and single and married women all worked in potential economic competition with each other.[24] The laws applied to women, regardless of marital status or their desire to have children, but not to men. They prevented women from competing on an equal basis with men for employment and effectively restricted women's economic opportunities, gendering their citizenship and relation to the state.

By regulating women's working conditions and occupations, protective legislation treated women as children who needed safeguarding and undermined the principle of equality before the law. This legislation was based upon a viewpoint that women should be in the home rather than in the labor market and that work outside the home was dangerous and undesirable. These laws were based upon the assumption that there should be a sharp dichotomy between public and private space and that women should be viewed as potential or actual mothers to be kept within the purported privacy of the home. They treated motherhood as women's primary and preferably only function, and tried to keep remunerated labor out of the home by opposing tenement house and other home-based industries that would enable women to both care for their home and families and use their homes to produce an income.[25]

The regions varied in their proclivity to pass gendered protective legislation, with most of the laws regulating women's relationship to the labor force being in the North and the West. Given the structure of the southern economy it is not surprising that few states south of the Mason-Dixon Line enacted such laws.[26] Their economies depended upon cheap labor, whether in the textile and tobacco industries, in the

---

[24] Kessler-Harris, *In Pursuit of Equity*, 30-33.

[25] Boris, in *Home to Work*, makes this point eloquently. For contrasts with British employment legislation, see Vivien Hart, *Bound by our Constitution: Women, Workers, and the Minimum Wage*, Princeton, NJ: Princeton UP, 1994.

[26] Chapter 3 of S.J. Kleinberg's *Widows and Orphans First: The Family Economy and Social Welfare Policy, 1880-1939*, Urbana: U of Illinois P, 2006, discusses regional variations in protective legislation.

fields, or in the home.[27] Southern states made few concessions to either the family wage ideology (the belief that men should be paid a sufficient wage to support their family without help from women or child wage earners) or its close cousin, protective legislation, which restricted the hours women could work and their occupations in the belief that ensure women's primary focus should be domesticity and the production of healthy babies.[28] It did not, in the perception of either white southern factory or land owners, serve the public weal if either poor white farmers, factory workers or African American field workers and domestic servants were protected from the harsh conditions and low wages pertaining in their industries.[29]

Nor did the southern elite regard private world of the family as the appropriate site of either poor black or white women's labor.[30] Alice Walker presents an example of labor coercion in *The Color Purple* when Sofia refused to be the mayor's wife maid, and is beaten and thrown into prison for her challenge to southern mores.[31] Her desire to keep her labor for her family defied a society that expropriated African American women's labor, as did African American servants and laundresses' collective protests in some southern cities against low wages in the 1870s and 1880s. Their efforts to resist the dominant culture had limited success largely because the white elite which ran the political system used the power of the state to squash their protests. Nevertheless domestics and washerwomen went on strike, a public activity, in order to press their employers for higher wages. Tera Hunter's account of private domestic workers' protests against low wages by parading through the streets of Galveston and Atlanta illustrates how African American women appropriated public spaces

---

[27] Hall, *Like a Family*, Ch. 2.

[28] Annie G. Porritt, *Laws Affecting Women and Children in the Suffrage and Non-suffrage States*, New York: National Woman Suffrage Publishing Company, 1917; see also Ch. 5 of Kleinberg, *Widows and Orphans*, 2006.

[29] Shirley Wilson Logan, "'What Are We Worth': Anna Julia Cooper Defines Black Women's Work at the Dawn of the Twentieth Century", in *Sister Circle: Black Women and Work*, ed. Sharon Harley, New Brunswick, NJ: Rutgers UP, 2002, 146-63.

[30] Jacqueline Dowd Hall *et al.*, *Like a Family: The Making of a Southern Cotton Mill World*, Charlotte: U of North Carolina P, 1987; Delores E. Janiewski, *Sisterhood Denied: Race, Gender, and Class in a New South Community*, Philadelphia, PA: Temple UP, 1985; Hunter, *To 'Joy My Freedom*, 58-62, 134.

[31] Alice Walker, *The Color Purple*, New York: Harcourt, Brace, Jovanovich, 1982, 75-79.

because individually they met little success in negotiating higher wages. Hunter concludes that domestic workers' strikes in the 1870s and 1880s demonstrated "an astute political consciousness by making women's work carried out in private households a public issue – exploding the myth of the separation between private (family and household) and public (business and economic) spheres".[32] Arrests, fines, and proposed city taxes indicated that the white political elite would not tolerate black women's attempts to make their private grievances public.

Southern states did not enact protective legislation for industrial, agricultural, or domestic labor because they did not wish to protect poor white or African American women's place in the home. Subsequently the purportedly private location of many women's economic activities, among other factors, resulted in their exclusion from major employment and welfare legislation during the New Deal. Many New Deal programs effectively relegated women to the economic sidelines by giving them relief rather than employment.[33] Important and innovative legislation such as the Social Security Act, which provided retirement pensions for workers in certain occupations, mostly in the industrial sector of the economy, ignored women's occupations, especially those undertaken by women of color. Neither domestic service nor agricultural labor, the two primary occupations of African American women, was covered by the act.[34] The NAACP protested against this exclusion to little avail. Southern senators and congressmen objected to the inclusion of these occupations. They were horrified at the prospect of their wives and other white women having to collect Social Security payments from their black household workers, claiming that this intruded the Federal government into their private domestic spaces. They also opposed the

---

[32] Hunter, *To 'Joy My Freedom*, 94.

[33] Alice Kessler-Harris, "Designing Women and Old Fools: The Construction of the Social Security Amendments of 1939", in *U.S. History as Women's History: New Feminist Essays*, eds Linda K. Kerber, Alice Kessler-Harris, and Kathryn Kish Sklar, Chapel Hill: U of North Carolina P, 1995, 87-106; Robyn Muncy, *Creating a Female Dominion in American Reform, 1890-1935*, New York: Oxford UP, 1991, Ch. 5.

[34] United States Congress, *Economic Security Act: Hearings Before the Committee on Ways and Means, House of Representatives*, 74th Congress, First Session on H.R. 4120, *A Bill to Alleviate the Hazards of Old Age, Unemployment, Illness, and Dependency, to Establish a Social Insurance Board in the Department of Labor, to Raise Revenue, and for Other Purposes*, Washington, DC: Government Printing Office, 1935, 590, 600, 796.

collection of Social Security taxes from agricultural workers as impractical.[35] Thus regional racialized and gendered economic differences resulted in the development of distinctive approaches to the location and legal framework of women's employment. The supposedly private site of the home became a reason to discriminate against a large group of workers and demonstrates the politicization of the private, thus making it simultaneously reserved for the family and subject to public regulation – or neglect.

The growth of women's employment
Such politicization of women's work can be seen in the statement made by Joseph A. Hill (1929), writing for the Census Bureau about *Women in Gainful Occupations: 1870 to 1920*, who observed that "the interest in women's occupations lies not so much in the number occupied or in the amount of work that they are doing as in the change that is taking place in the character of their occupations and the extent to which their work takes them away from the home which was once the sole field of occupational activity for most women".[36] Moreover, Hill situates the Census Bureau's analysis of women's occupations in terms of the movement of women from the presumably private home to the public world of employment, whilst acknowledging both that the actual amount of work performed by women at home depended on their interests, thoroughness, and presence of servants. Given such variability, women's economic contributions could not be monetized, at least not by measures then accepted by the Census Bureau. Hill also cautions that much of women's unremunerated work outside the home had a public nature, since they formed the majority of church and unpaid welfare workers. In other words, some women's work was in the public gaze, even though it was not work for wages. Even confining the notion of work to the narrowest definition of paid labor and despite efforts to regulate certain areas of female employment during the Progressive Era in the North and West, the proportion of economically active women over the age of sixteen rose from 15

---

[35] Gareth Davies and Martha Derthick, "Race and Social Welfare Policy: The Social Security Act of 1935", *Political Science Quarterly*, CXII/2 (Summer 1997), 217-35.
[36] Joseph A. Hill, *Women in Gainful Occupations: 1870-1920*, Washington, DC: US Bureau of the Census, Government Printing Office, 1929, 4.

percent in 1870 to 24 percent in 1910 and 1920.[37] Yet while more women entered the labor market, demographic characteristics still influenced whether women worked and at what jobs, and many women continued to work in what were essentially private spaces, either in the home or in remote rural areas, where their labor was hidden from view. This particularly pertained to middle-aged women (over-represented in the ranks of domestic servants) and those from racial minorities, whose employment was constrained by the family economy or prejudice and a disproportionate number of whom toiled for wages in purportedly private spaces, leading to the conclusion that one woman's private or domestic space could be another's public one.

Quite clearly, economic activity had a gendered dimension, although other factors also shaped whether and where a person worked. Class, race, ethnicity, and locality broadly determined what type of work a man would do, but not whether he would work at all or whether his employment took place in the private or public sphere. Age, however, had a marked role in men's continued presence in gainful employment; by the turn of the century employment tapered off after the age of sixty-five for many men. According to US Census, "men take up some occupation almost as a matter of course, and usually follow it the greater part of their lives". For women in 1900, however, the "adoption of an occupation, although by no means unusual, is far from being customary, and in the well-to-do classes of society is exceptional". Nine out of every ten men over the age of sixteen had jobs, compared with two out of ten women.[38]

Many historians in the last four decades have explored the extent to which class, race, and ethnicity influenced women's employment, with some acknowledgement that marital status played a significant role in determining whether a woman worked for pay in the Gilded Age and Progressive Era. For white women marital status was the best predictor of gainful employment in these years. Labor force participation rates were much higher for African American women of

---

[37] *Ibid.*, 4, 30. It is important to be wary, when using printed tables, concerning two potentially confusing factors. Many tables refer only to "nonagricultural pursuits", thereby eliminating many African American women from the data. Secondly, some of the tables look at women as a proportion of the total workforce (male and female), while others analyze women's employment as a proportion of all women.

[38] United States Department of Commerce and Labor, Bureau of the Census, *Statistics of Women at Work: Based on Unpublished Information Derived from the Schedules of the Twelfth Census, 1900*, Washington, DC: Government Printing Office, 1907, 9.

all ages, but even their employment levels decreased after marriage.[39]
Moreover, the trajectory of white and black women's employment
was not the same: African American women's employment levels
decreased in the twentieth century, while those of white women
increased.

Yet while historians have recognized the importance of some
demographic variables in explaining women's labor force
participation, they have overlooked the importance of age as a factor
in women's employment, perhaps because age and marital status co-
vary to a great extent. Since women tend to get married at a certain
age (usually before the age of twenty-four in this era) their marital
status explains much, but not all, of their level of economic activity, at
least for white women. The vast majority of Euro-American women in
postbellum America married by the age of twenty-three or so and
dropped out of the labor force (if they had entered it at all) either when
they married or with the birth of their first child. This generalization
characterized urban women in the late nineteenth and early twentieth
centuries, but does not hold for rural women, especially those in the
South. Nor does it encompass what we know to be true, namely that
many women dipped in and out of the labor force in response to their
families' economic needs and ages of their children, but were not
recorded by the Census as being gainfully employed.[40]

Rural black women married at a younger age than their urban,
white, or northern counterparts, establishing homes as tenant farmers
or sharecroppers when they were as young as twenty. Their presence
in the farm labor force accounted for much of the productivity of
southern agriculture before and after the Civil War, as they both

---

[39] There are many excellent histories of women's labor force participation in this
period. Kessler-Harris' *In Pursuit of Equity* provides a recent formulation of the
issues. Also see Christine E. Bose, *Women in 1900: Gateway to the Political
Economy of the 20th Century*, Philadelphia, PA: Temple UP, 2001; Ruiz, *Out of the
Shadows*; Theresa L. Amott and Julie A. Matthaei, *Race, Gender, and Work: A
Multicultural Economic History of Women in the United States*, Boston, MA: South
End Press, 1991.

[40] Hill, *Women in Gainful Occupations*. While it is difficult to quantify the number of
women who worked outside the home but were not counted as such by the Census,
my own family's experience suggests it was a widespread practice. The 1920 US
Census lists my grandfather as having a food store, but my grandmother as having no
occupation. Yet she worked with him in the store even when the children were quite
young, solving the childcare dilemma by simply locking my father and his brother and
sister into their tenement house apartment while she was at work.

produced and reproduced at an early age. Their postbellum private decision to marry was based upon the availability of land to be rented or sharecropped, rather than the need to save up to start married life.[41] However, early marriage also reflected the prevailing socio-economic and political attitudes in which whites made it difficult or impossible for blacks to own land. Thus private decisions, women's labor force participation, and public, even if never legislated, policies intertwined in the rural South.[42]

One of the most significant changes in women's employment during the Gilded Age and Progressive Era and to an even greater extent later in the twentieth century was the aging of the gainfully employed female population. This occurred for two separate but interrelated reasons. The proportion of very young working women (those with ages between ten and fifteen) fell by nearly 50 percent between 1890 and 1920, as states (especially in the North and the West) banned their presence in the labor force, using the public power of the state to override parents' private decision to bolster the family economy through their children's waged labor.[43] Girls were, in effect, removed from the public world of work and put into the arguably more sheltered environment of schools.[44] This had subsequent implications for the types of jobs undertaken by women as their education levels increased. It also had ramifications for the family economy as mothers began to replace their daughters as ancillary breadwinners.[45]

---

[41] Stewart E. Tolnay, *The Bottom Rung: African American Family Life on Southern Farms*, Urbana: U of Illinois P, 1999, 49-72, discusses the timing of marriage in different groups within society.

[42] Gilbert Fite, *Cotton Fields No More: Southern Agriculture, 1865-1980*, Lexington: U of Kentucky P, 1984 and Daniel, *Breaking the Land*, explore the agricultural systems of the South that excluded African Americans from a significant degree of land ownership.

[43] William A. Link, *The Paradox of Southern Progressivism, 1880-1930*, Chapel Hill: U of North Carolina P, 1999, writes about the way in which southern states exempted child agricultural labor even when they legislated against children's employment in this era.

[44] Barbara Miller Solomon, *In the Company of Educated Women: A History of Women and Higher Education in America*, New Haven, CT: Yale UP, 1985, 45-47, 115-18; John L. Rury, *Education and Women's Work: Female Schooling and the Division of Labor in Urban America, 1870-1930*, Albany: State U of New York P, 1991.

[45] Kleinberg, "Children's and Mothers' Employment".

Table 1
Proportion of Women Employed in each Age Group: 1890-1920

Ages	1890	1900	1920
	's	's	's
10-15	10.0	10.2	5.6
16-24	29.0	31.6	37.6
25-44	15.6	18.1	22.4
45-64	12.6	11.4	17.1
65+	8.3	9.1	8.8

Source: US Department of Commerce, Bureau of the Census 1960, 71

Young women in their late teens and early twenties underwent a great increase in economic activity, with nearly two-fifths of this group holding jobs by 1920. It is this group of women whose employment has been described as moving "From Home to Office" (to borrow the title of Elyce Rotella's study of female employment in this era), although the characterization of the shifting locus of employment applies principally to white women.[46] However, as shown in Table 1, older women's employment also increased, with that of twenty-five to forty-four year olds rising by about one-quarter and that of middle-aged women (ages forty-five to sixty-four) also climbing. The employment levels of elderly women remained essentially static throughout this period, as it did for much of the twentieth century. By 1920, the proportion of women between the ages of twenty-five to sixty-four who had jobs rose from 28.2 percent in 1890 to 39.5 percent. This presaged one of the major shifts in the female labor force, namely its domination by middle-aged women. Yet, as explored above, this increase in employment came despite, not because of, public policy, which in the guise of protective legislation attempted to regulate women's employment along maternalist lines.

Even within these generalizations about women's level of economic activity by age, there were significant racial/nativity differences in the age profiles of women workers according to race/ethnicity. While the labor-force participation rates of younger

---

[46] Elyce Rotella, *From Home to Office: U.S. Women at Work, 1870-1930*, Ann Arbor: U of Michigan P, 1981; also see Joanne J. Meyerowitz, *Women Adrift: Independent Wage Earners in Chicago, 1880-1930*, Chicago: U of Chicago P, 1988; Hunter, *To 'Joy My Freedom*; Evelyn Nakano Glenn, *Unequal Freedom: How Race and Gender Shaped American Citizenship and Labor*, Cambridge, MA: Harvard UP, 2004.

native-born white women (ages sixteen to twenty-four) with either native- or foreign-born parents rose between 1900 and 1920, that of foreign-born women in this age group fell slightly, perhaps because more of them stayed on in school. Thus, two things seem to have occurred simultaneously for this age group: more of them entered the labor force and more of them stayed on in school to complete a high school education.[47] These apparently contradictory trends are explained by a third factor: the census recorded far fewer young women as simply being "at home", that is, neither in school nor in the labor force.[48]

An increasing number of young women and their families viewed education as the way to obtain desirable jobs opening up in the white-collar sector of the labor force after the turn of the twentieth century. They benefited from public investment in education as they worked their way up the class hierarchy.[49] In this way they attempted to move their employment from domestic service and factory labor into the supposedly more respectable ranks of the white collar workers.[50] Their education completed, these women demonstrated their success by wearing white blouses or dark dresses to work, depending upon whether they worked in offices or department stores. According to Susan Porter Benson's research, department store saleswomen refused to wear uniforms, as some of their employers would have preferred, because they took them to signify a "badge of service", and thus to be abhorrent.[51] They wished to work in a public place and also to retain their autonomy through their own choice of dress. They rejected anything that smacked of domestic service with its uniforms or the dowdy clothes fit only to be worn on an assembly line.[52]

Not all women were able to use their education to escape less socially desirable employment. The patterns of African American

---

[47] DeVault, *Sons and Daughters of Labor*, 27-38, 42-44.

[48] Kleinberg, "Children's and Mothers' Employment".

[49] Michael W. Apple, in his *Ideology and Curriculum*, New York: Routledge, 1990, examines the way in which American society used education as a tool of assimilation and transmission of social values.

[50] DeVault, in *Sons and Daughters of Labor*, 45-47 examines education from a gendered class perspective in Pittsburgh. She finds that skilled workers' children made up a significant portion of the Commercial Department of Pittsburgh's high schools, although unskilled workers' children were less well represented.

[51] Susan Porter Benson, *Counter Cultures: Saleswomen, Managers, and Customers in American Department Stores, 1890 -1920*, Urbana: U of Illinois P, 1988, 236.

[52] Hunter, *To 'Joy My Freedom*, 182.

women's employment are complex. Persistent discrimination kept many from achieving access to the upper ranks of the female employment hierarchy. While they had the highest rates of economic activity in all age groups, some began to withdraw from employment while others persisted in the labor force. The decrease in work rates was most marked among younger women and in sharp contrast to the employment patterns of native-born white women. Between 1900 and 1920 the proportion of economically active sixteen to twenty year-old black women decreased from 50 to 38 percent. To some extent, the lower rates reflect the impact of the Great Migration, the massive exodus of African Americans from the southern United States. Northern states provided educational opportunities that were rare for blacks in the South, and young black women stayed in school longer as a result. At the same time educational opportunities also began to expand in the South, so that more stayed on at school there, especially in urban areas.[53]

Table 2
Employment by Age and Racial/ Nativity Group: 1900-1920

Age	NBW-NP		NBW-FP		FBW		AfAm	
	1900	1920	1900	1920	1900	1920	1900	1920
	's	's	's	's	's	's	's	's
16-20	20.8	25.0	40.0	45.2	56.8	52.0	49.6	38.0
21-24	21.3	32.5	37.8	48.8	41.5	37.7	45.6	45.0
25-44	12.9	18.4	19.5	24.6	16.6	18.6	41.7	45.2
45-64	10.5	12.4	11.9	15.6	9.7	11.8	38.8	41.8
Total	14.6	19.7	25.4	29.0	19.1	18.8	43.2	43.1

Sources: United States Department of Commerce and Labor, Bureau of the Census 1907, 12; and United States Census Office 1935, vol. 5, 275
NBW-NP: Native-born whites with native-born white parents
NBW-FP: Native-born whites with foreign-born white parents
FBW: Foreign-born Whites
AfAm: African Americans

While there was little change in black women's employment levels among twenty-one to twenty-four year olds, the increase in

---

[53] Anderson, in *Education of Blacks in the South*, Chs 5 and 6, discusses changing educational patterns in the South. See also Heather Andrea Williams, *Self-taught: African American Education in Slavery and Freedom*, Chapel Hill: U of North Carolina P, 2005.

employment levels of women ages twenty-five to forty-four suggest that these women, many of whom had children, were even more engrossed in economic activity than their mothers had been. This increased level of employment occurred among all racial and nativity groups, as did that of women ages forty-five to sixty-four. For white women, whether native- or foreign-born, the rates of economic activity moved up from about 10 to about 12-16 percent, while for black women it rose from 39 to 42 percent. While these shifts were not that large, they nonetheless indicated the beginnings of a long-term trend, namely the increasing monetization of older women's endeavors.

The changing age/employment patterns can be attributed to a number of long-term trends in the USA's economy and society. As family sizes shrank, women had fewer domestic responsibilities and a shorter period of intensive childcare. Various aspects of domestic technology, including indoor plumbing, electricity, gas, and the appliances that accompanied them, made their home lives easier to manage. This points to an interaction between the home and the workplace and suggests the extent to which they influenced each other. As women at home desired labor saving devices they provided a market for objects made by other women (and men) in factories and sold in shops. In other words, private domestic demand provided public employment for other workers, many of them women, outside the home.[54] Yet another factor undergirded the rising level of employment among older women workers. These women increasingly used their labor not just to buy new forms of technology, but also to enable their children to stay in school longer. At the same time that child labor levels fell across the United States those of older women rose. In three cities I have examined intensively elsewhere, namely Pittsburgh, Fall River, and Baltimore, the employment levels of married women increased significantly between 1880 and 1920.[55] By

---

[54] James R. McGovern, "The American Woman's Pre-World War I Freedom in Manners and Morals", *Journal of American History*, LV/2 (September 1968), 321. On the working-class use of domestic technology, see Kleinberg, "Technology and Women's Work"; Matthews, *Just a Housewife*; Ruth Schwartz Cowan, *More Work for Mother: The Ironies of Household Technology from the Open Hearth to the Microwave*, New York: Basic Books, 1983.

[55] Kleinberg, *Widows and Orphans*. The increase was from 3 to 6 percent in Pittsburgh, from 16 to 25 percent in Fall River and from 5 to 14 percent in Baltimore between 1880 and 1920.

the early twentieth century older women also had higher levels of
education than their foremothers and therefore were better placed to
take jobs opening up in the white collar sector of the economy. In
effect they educated themselves not just for a job after leaving school,
but also for later in life.

However, older and younger women worked in different sectors of
the economy, with older workers having a much lower presence in the
public (that is, visible employments that attracted more attention –
such as factories, shops, and offices) than younger ones. For women
as a whole (remembering that the category of employed women was
numerically dominated by younger workers throughout this period),
the proportion in white-collar jobs more than doubled, at the expense
of manual, agricultural, and, especially, service sector jobs. By 1920
nearly two-fifths of all women workers had moved into clerical, sales,
teaching, and other white-collar jobs. By then, they were as likely to
work in manual occupations such as factory labor as they were to be
in service industries, with farming becoming less prevalent as
mechanization and hard times began to affect the agricultural sector of
the economy.[56]

Table 3
Sectoral Analysis of Women's Employment

Employment	1900		1910		1920	
	All	Middle Age	All	Middle Age	All	Middle Age
	's	's	's	's	's	's
White Collar	17.8	10.4	26.1	15.7	38.8	24.2
Manual	27.7	18.3	25.7	18.7	23.8	21.8
Service	35.5	43.8	32.4	42.8	23.9	39.3
Agriculture	18.9	27.6	15.7	23.7	13.5	14.7

**Calculated from: US Department of Commerce, Bureau of the Census
1960, 74; Ruggles et al., 2004.** Middle-Age defined as ages 40 to 64

While middle-aged women participated in the sectoral shifts in a
way that resembled that of the labor force in general, they remained
especially enmeshed in domestic service, mostly but not entirely

---

[56] Paula S. Fink, *Agrarian Women: Wives and Mothers in Rural Nebraska, 1880-
1940*, Chapel Hill: U of North Carolina P, 1992 describes women's agricultural work
through prosperity and depression.

working in other people's homes. Older women workers preferred where possible to live in their own homes with their families and do cooking, washing, or cleaning on a daily basis.[57] Among all employed women the percentage of service workers fell from 36 to 24 percent. However, the picture was quite different for middle-aged women: in 1900, 44 percent were service workers; in 1920, 39 percent were servants, a much smaller decrease than that experienced by their younger counterparts. Between 1910 and 1920 alone the proportion of women undertaking household work for others dropped by 20 percent. The largest decreases were in the categories of servants, dressmakers and seamstresses not in factories, and laundresses (not in laundries), precisely those occupations preferred by older women and especially by African American women. The census attributed the decrease in the proportion of women who worked as servants to several factors, including the simplification of housework, the use of restaurants, and the proliferation of mechanical improvements in housekeeping equipment. These changes left women without other skills facing a declining market for their services.[58] Even though the proportion of women working in white collar jobs as professionals, clerical, and shop assistants also doubled, middle-aged women remained much less likely than their daughters to hold these jobs, while prejudice restricted the ability of women of color to leave domestic service.

As Table 4 makes clear, the expansion of the white collar sector of the economy benefited mid-life white women, but the proportion of middle-aged African American women with such jobs was, even by 1920, only one-tenth that of white women. While the percentage of white women in agriculture almost halved between 1880 and 1920, that of middle-aged black women remained quite high (38 percent in 1880 and 35 percent in 1920). Similarly, the proportion of mid-life white women in service sector jobs declined from 42 to 35 percent during the Progressive Era, while that of black women decreased only slightly, from 60 to 57 percent. At the same time that white women ages forty to sixty-four edged out of manufacturing and industrial pursuits (from 28 to 26 percent), African American women made some progress in this sector, moving up from 1.5 to 5.2 percent. In summary, middle-aged white women shifted away from the agricultural and service jobs that employed nearly three-fifths of them

---

[57] Hunter, *To 'Joy My Freedom*, 50-57.
[58] Katzman, *Seven Days*, 61, 286; Hill, *Women in Gainful Occupations*, 34-39.

in 1880, but just over two-fifths in 1920. By contrast, 98 percent of black women worked in these two occupational categories in 1880 as did 92 percent in 1920. In other words, middle-aged African American women remained overwhelmingly in the more private sectors of the economy while white women in this age group enjoyed a greater diversity of employment.

Table 4
Sectoral Analysis of Black and White Middle-Aged Women's Employment: Women ages 40-64

	Agricultural		White Collar		Service		Manual	
	1880	1920	1880	1920	1880	1920	1880	1920
	's	's	's	's	's	's	's	's
White	16.7	9.4	13.1	29.7	41.9	34.9	28.2	26.1
Black	37.8	35.4	0.5	2.8	60.3	56.6	1.5	5.2

Source: as for Table 3

These data indicate a changing and indeed, a multi-tiered economy in which younger and older women and black and white women had distinctive niches. Younger and white women increasingly moved into the more visible sectors, while older and black women remained concentrated in service and agricultural occupations. This matters because the legislation that increasingly regulated women's employment essentially ignored the purportedly more private occupations in the domestic and agricultural sectors of the economy. Thus "public" and "private" come to have different meanings from those delineated in the ideologies of the separation of spheres and the Cult of True Womanhood. In the early twentieth century "private" can be construed as neglected and overlooked, as was the case with the 1935 Social Security Act, which deliberately omitted domestic servants and agricultural workers from its retirement and unemployment coverage. It also made no provision for middle-aged women who had spent their lives looking after their families and were stranded by their husband's death or divorce in a no-woman's land of few employment choices and little money.[59] In this context, "private" meant neglected and "public" meant some, albeit gendered,

---

[59] The broader issues in this field are examined through one woman's experience in Patricia Huckle, *Tish Sommers: Activist, and the Founding of the Older Women's League*, Knoxville: U of Tennessee P, 1991.

recognition of women's participation in the economy. Therefore the terms have a certain utility in their recognition of prescriptive roles, but overemphasis on an extreme polarization between them obscures the diversity and range of women's experiences in the Gilded Age and Progressive Era.

"If Iola Were a Man": Gender, Jim Crow and Public Protest in the Work of Ida B. Wells

Mia Bay

"If Iola were a man, she would be a humming independent in politics", reported a leading black journalist, T. Thomas Fortune, after first meeting "Iola" (the pen name of Ida B. Wells), "she has plenty of nerve, and is sharp as a steel trap".[1] Written in 1888, this assessment of the first famous African American female journalist highlights the gendered terrain that Wells had to traverse as she assumed prominence in African American cultural leadership. Born in 1862 to slave parents, Wells was a woman often taking on traditionally male roles: firstly as the breadwinner of her household at age sixteen, after her parents died in a yellow fever epidemic that swept the Mississippi Valley in 1878, and then as the first black female owner and editor of a newspaper, seeing herself as an heir to Frederick Douglass.

Yet, despite performing these roles, Wells' life, thought, and activism were shaped by her gender. Wells is most famous today for her denunciations of lynching. But her career as an activist began before that, as did her development of a trenchant analysis of the sexual politics of white supremacy, so evident in her anti-lynching campaign. Both grew out of Wells' experiences as a black woman in a public sphere within which she was forced to question conventional understandings of gender and sexual relations, by virtue of the fact that the Southern white ideology of chivalry rarely applied to black women. Growing up in late nineteenth-century Mississippi and Tennessee, Wells came of age at time when segregation not only eroded the social and civil equality of all blacks, it also challenged them in gendered terms. Disenfranchisement was an assault on the racial manhood of black men, while many Jim Crow practices made a mockery of any claims by African American females to womanhood.

---

[1] Article by T. Thomas Fortune, *The New York Age*, 11 August 1888, 1.

In short, white supremacy confronted black men and women differently, launching Wells into a public career that would not have been the same "if Iola were a man".

As Patricia Schechter notes, Wells' critique of lynching centrally engaged with these gender-and-race intercalations. Her campaign against lynching "made black women visible in the dynamics of southern lynching and sexualized racism", and in so doing transformed lynching into a women's issue.[2] In particular, Wells mobilized middle-class African American women, who became lynching's earliest public critics. The impact of the anti-lynching work of Wells and other African American women has been well chronicled. Their efforts helped feminize American reform by defining opposition to lynching as "women's work" and through their campaigns generating widespread public disapproval for lynching both in the North and abroad, paving the way for biracial movements against lynching and Jim Crow in the twentieth century.[3]

Less clear, however, is why it was lynching that provoked such unprecedented public activity among African American women. Although Wells' crusade helped transform the understanding of lynching into a powerful symbol of the racial terror that was Jim Crow, lynching was only one of many forms of racial violence that Southern whites inflicted on African Americans in the late nineteenth-century South. Southern black communities were terrorized by white capping, race riots, oppressive and exploitative labor relations and a severely discriminatory justice system that placed many blacks in a penal servitude that was "worse than slavery" and as lethal as lynching.[4] Lynching was usually a crime against men, and worse still, it was ideologically linked to the "indelicate" subject of rape – a topic

---

[2] Patricia Schechter, "Unsettled Business: Ida B. Wells Against Lynching, or How Anti-lynching Got Its Gender", in *Under the Sentence of Death: Lynching in the South*, ed. W. Fitzhugh Brundage, Chapel Hill: U of North Carolina P, 1997, 296.

[3] *Idem.*, 292. For Wells' impact on public opinion, see also Hazel Carby, "'On the Threshold of Woman's Era': Lynching, Empire, and Sexuality in Black Feminist Theory", in *"Race", Writing, and Difference*, ed. Henry Louis Gates, Jr., Chicago: U of Chicago P, 1995, 301-16; and Ch. 2 of Gail Bederman's *Manliness and Civilization: A Cultural History of Gender and Race in the United States, 1880-1917*, Chicago: U of Chicago P, 1995.

[4] Leon Litwack, *Trouble in Mind*, New York: Vintage, 1999, 422-44; David M. Oshinsky, *Worse than Slavery: Parchman Farm and the Ordeal of Jim Crow Justice*, New York: Free Press, 1997, 209-13.

which respectable black women were reluctant to discuss. Indeed, although black women were often the victims of rape and other forms of sexual violence, they generally avoided any public discussion of these issues in favor of what Darlene Clark Hine has called "a culture of dissemblance". Designed to shield "the truth of their inner life and selves from their oppressors", this culture discouraged black women from mobilizing against the endemic sexual and racial violence they suffered, for fear of perpetuating "derogatory images and negative stereotypes of black women's sexuality".[5] Under pressure to create positive images of themselves as women, black females were also reluctant to discuss the daily sexual and racial denigration they faced under Jim Crow – at least directly.

Ironically, the constraints that nineteenth-century black women faced when it came to discussing Jim Crow's many assaults on their gender may help explain the powerful appeal anti-lynching held for Wells and her contemporaries, especially since, when African American women were raped or otherwise assaulted, "nobody is lynched and no notice is taken".[6] Indeed, both Wells' anti-lynching work and the appeal her campaign held for other black women are best understood by reference to the contested character of black womanhood in the South and black women's awareness of the limitations of Southern chivalry. Wells' career as a journalist and activist took shape around such contestation.

As Wells would find out early in her career, both black women and black men were traditionally seen as lascivious and morally loose in white racial thought. These negative representations of African American sexuality first took shape during the slavery era, when they functioned as both a justification for and a reflection of the slaves' lack of power to contract legitimate liaisons or exercise complete control over their sexuality.[7] But white attacks on black sexuality took on renewed vitality in the years following Reconstruction, when they

---

[5] Darlene Clark Hine, "Rape and the Inner Lives of Black Women in the Middle West: Preliminary Thoughts on the Culture of Dissemblance", *Signs*, XIV/4 (Summer 1989), 917.

[6] Ida B. Wells, "Southern Horrors" (1892), rpt. in *Southern Horrors and Other Writings: The Anti-lynching Campaign of Ida B. Wells, 1892-1900*, ed. Jacqueline Jones Royster, Boston: Bedford Books, 1997, 58.

[7] Gray White, *Ar'n't I a Woman: Female Slaves in the Plantation South*, New York: W.W. Norton, 1985, 28-34, 38-40; Patricia Morton, *Disfigured Images: The Historical Assault on Afro-American Women*, New York: Praeger, 1991, 46-47.

were often mobilized in the service of white attempts to reclaim power in the South.[8] As part of their concerted effort to drive African Americans out of politics, the white Democrats who retook the South after Reconstruction branded black men as rapists who lusted after white women.[9] Likewise, the Democratic Party's white supremacy campaigns denigrated black women as well: when the Redeemers built political campaigns around protecting the virtue of white women, they underscored the implication that black women did not require similar protection. As a consequence, even in the post-emancipation era it was difficult for black women to speak out or make themselves heard on the issue of race – something that had long been the case but which now became, effectively, as acute as it ever had been under slavery.

By contrast to African American men, who published voluminously on race and racism, even educated black women remained largely silent on the issue of racism's characterizations of racial differences until almost the turn of the century. At that time, Wells' anti-lynching campaign helped inspire black women across the country to speak out against not only lynching, but also the ways in which racism and Jim Crow denigrated black women. In doing so, they spoke with a consciousness that their voices had not been heard before. "Too long have we been silent against unjust and unholy charges", African American journalist Josephine Ruffin told the First National Conference of Colored Women in 1895, adding, "we can not expect to have them removed until we disprove them ... *ourselves*".[10]

Black women like Ruffin and Wells still find too small a place within the historiography of race and racial thought. For whether they focus on black or white thought, classic studies of eighteenth- and nineteenth-century American racial thought, such as George Frederickson's *The Black Image in the White Mind*, Winthrop Jordan's *White over Black*, and Wilson Jeremiah Moses' *The Golden Age of Black Nationalism*, draw on discussions of race and racial

---

[8] Beverley Guy-Sheftall, *Daughters of Sorrow: Attitudes Toward Black Women, 1880-1920*, New York: Carlson, 1990, 43-57.

[9] Glenda Elizabeth Gilmore, *Gender and Jim Crow: Women and the Politics of White Supremacy in North Carolina, 1896-1920*, Chapel Hill: U of North Carolina P, 1996, 82-89.

[10] Josephine Ruffin, "Address of Josephine Ruffin, President of the Conference", *The Women's Era*, 2 (August 1895), 14.

difference written almost exclusively by men.[11] This neglect matches what generally happened throughout the nineteenth century: anti-slavery societies, suffrage organizations, and temperance clubs organized by white women frequently excluded black members; and the rights and reforms that white feminists sought on behalf of their gender were often envisioned as pertaining to Anglo-Saxon women only.[12]

Meanwhile, racism confronted African American women all the more destructively as a consequence of this exclusion. In an era when black people were often held to be inferior to white people in much the same way as women were to men, black women faced the additional jeopardy of finding that their race excluded them from full title to their gender. These difficulties make it vital to recover black women's perspectives on nineteenth-century racism. The dilemmas that public discourses on race posed for black women can shed light on how gender shaped both the construction of racist ideology and black women's responses to it. Indeed, the activism of Ida B. Wells and other turn-of-the-century black women was borne of such dilemmas, and illuminates the ways in which black women's challenges to lynching and Jim Crow built on a careful rethinking of the relationship between race, gender and political power in the post-emancipation public sphere.

"Mute and voiceless": African American women confront nineteenth-century racial thought
Wells was, of course, far from the first black woman to ponder this relationship. The nineteenth-century reticence of African American women on racial subjects did not stem from indifference. Throughout the nineteenth century black women were prominent in community

---

[11] George Frederickson, *The Black Image in the White Mind: The Debate on Afro-American Character and Destiny, 1817-1914*, Hanover, CT: Wesleyan UP, 1987; Winthrop Jordan, *White Over Black: American Attitudes toward the Negro, 1550-1812*, Chapel Hill: U of North Carolina P, 1968; William Jeremiah Moses, *The Golden Age of Black Nationalism, 1850-1925*, Hamden, CT: Archon Books, 1978.
[12] For a brief history of discrimination in the nineteenth-century women's movement, see Rosalyn Terborg-Penn, "Discrimination Against Afro-American Women in the Women's Movement, 1830-1920", in *The Black Woman Cross-culturally*, ed. Filomina Chioma Steady, Cambridge, MA: Schenkeman Co., 1981, 310-15. On the racial ideology of the woman's movement, see Louise Michele Newman, "Laying Claim to Difference: Ideologies of Race and Gender in the U.S. Women's Movement, 1870-1920", Ph.D. diss., Brown U, 1992.

activism for racial uplift, were a mainstay in black mutual aid societies – sometimes outnumbering the men – and also organized female literary and benevolent organizations. Scant records exist of these groups, but it is clear that these organizations were formed with an acute awareness of white allegations of black inferiority. They were repeatedly dedicated to the highly race-conscious goals of racial "uplift" and "elevation".

But prior to Wells' anti-lynching campaign, black women engaged with American racial thought only fleetingly, and often indirectly. Throughout the nineteenth century, only a relatively small number of black women could read and write, and a smaller number committed any of their thoughts to paper. But the scarcity of public discussion on race by nineteenth-century black women cannot be entirely explained by the limits imposed on black women because of their restricted access to education. Among the black women who participated in their community's organizations were educated black women qualified to speak for themselves. They included some of the most privileged, well-off, and well-educated African Americans of the era, such as Charlotte Forten, who descended from a prosperous Philadelphia family that had never been enslaved, but also female members of black activist families such as the Douglasses and the Redmonds and individuals such as Maria Stewart, a self-educated working woman. Far from inarticulate, these women wrote poems, letters, essays, speeches, fiction, and autobiographies.

Moreover, these educated black women were acquainted with their male contemporaries' ideas about race. During the antebellum era, the scholarly Charlotte Forten attended lectures on race issues, and even recorded her own ethnological opinions about the origins of the American Indians in her diary.[13] Likewise, in a talk in 1875, author and activist Frances Harper presented a confident review of ethnology, before going on to dismiss the subject altogether. "Ethnologists may differ about the origin of the human race", she told a Pennsylvania audience, "Huxley may search for protoplasms, and Darwin the missing links, but there is one thing of which we may rest assured – that we all come from a living God and that He is the common

---

[13] Charlotte Forten Grimke, *The Journals of Charlotte Forten Grimke*, ed. Brenda Stevenson, New York: Oxford UP, 1988, 108.

Father".[14] But African American women's references to race and ethnology were invariably brief. The nineteenth-century literature of black revisionist work on ethnology – which provides one of richest single source available on the era's black racial thought – does not contain a single work written by a woman.[15]

In part, this female silence was a consequence of the masculine cast of nineteenth-century discourse on race. To a large extent, the political and ethnological questions that dominated nineteenth-century racial discourse were off-limits to women of both races by virtue of their specialized subject matter. White writers typically celebrated the masculine virtues of their own race, identifying courage, manliness, intellect, and independence as Anglo-Saxon virtues lacking in the lesser races, while black male writers often invoked a history of white savagery to recast the Anglo-Saxon as a hyperaggressive, hyper-masculine being who took his celebrated virtues of courage and manliness too far: "See them in the gloomy forests of Germany, sacrificing their grim and gory idols", wrote William Wells Brown in 1876, deriding the white race's savage past, "drinking the warm blood of their prisoners, quaffing libations from human skulls; infesting the shores of the Baltic for plunder and robbery; bringing home the reeking scalps of enemies as an offering to their king".[16]

Indeed, black women received limited attention in the racist invective of the pre-emancipation era – which may be another reason why black women did not engage the subject of race more frequently. Throughout this era, white thinkers denounced the Negro's status among the races of man largely by reference to masculine measures of difference. Samuel Morton's studies of skull size, for example, supported arguments that the black race lacked the mental capacity for self-government, which targeted men more than women, since women as a group were not given credit for such abilities. Likewise, black men were also the primary target of the highly traditional, patrilineal accounts culled from the scriptures that, in a polygenetic challenge to Scripture questioning whether the race descended from Adam, were

---

[14] Frances Ellen Watkins Harper, "The Great Problem to be Solved" (1875), rpt. in *A Brighter Coming Day*, ed. Frances Smith Foster, New York: The Feminist Press, 1990, 220.
[15] Mia Bay, *The White Image in the Black Mind: African American Ideas about White People, 1830-1925*, New York: Oxford UP, 2000, 6, 192.
[16] William Wells Brown, *The Rising Son; or, The Antecedents and Achievements of the Colored Race*, Boston: A.G. Crown, 1876, 85-86.

twisted into denunciations of African Americans as sons of Ham. Only in the post-emancipation era did black women move directly into American racial theory's line of fire. This shift reflected diverse developments, such as the rising social and educational status of women of both races, the growing sexual demonization of African Americans under Jim Crow, and new racial agency accorded to women in evolutionary thought.

By the 1890s, these developments combined to create a concerted ideological assault on the gendered characteristics of both black men and women that would ultimately break black women's long silence on the subject of race. In the post-emancipation South, African American men and women alike entered the public sphere as a free people for the first time, as a result of a long struggle that forced defeated white Southerners to scramble to create new ways to maintain the white supremacy that had been guaranteed to them when blacks were enslaved. With freedom, it was not longer enough for Southern apologists to question the manhood of a race of people they believed to be naturally suited to slavery. Rather, black struggles for freedom and autonomy in the post-emancipation South pushed whites to malign the gendered characteristics of black women as well as black men. From Reconstruction onward, the race as a whole suffered from discriminatory laws and labor practices, and widespread mob violence. And, especially in the 1880s and 1890s, whites moved to suppress black men's political participation with gender-specific challenges to their voting rights – a male prerogative – as well as vicious attacks on black male sexuality that branded black men a dangerous threat to white women.

Meanwhile, the status of black women in the post-emancipation public sphere was subject to similarly gender-specific challenges against their claims to womanhood, which deemed them wholly outside the protection of the chivalry that white Southerners mobilized to protect white women. Assumed to be lascivious by nature, even after slavery ended black women still received no protection against sexual assault in Southern courts – which remained almost exclusively under white control even during Reconstruction. Moreover, Southern whites also went out of their way to demonstrate that they considered black women unworthy of the courtesy and respect their society accorded to white women – as Wells would find out. Whites assumed that all Negroes lagged behind the Caucasian race in development, making black women unworthy of the courtesies accorded white ladies, who were held to possess the kind of highly developed moral character that African American women lacked. As members of a race "still controlled by animal impulses", black women merited no protection. On the contrary, by the turn of the century, many white commentators had begun to suggest that black degeneracy was caused by black women. Races rose or fell on the strength of their women, the Social Darwinist thought of that day maintained, and white commentators often took a dim view of black women in particular. Typically regarding them as too animalistic to lead their race on an evolutionary path toward the civilized gender ideals embodied in white women, white commentators even accused African American women of being the root cause of the inferiority of their race. "It is her hand that rocks the cradle in which the little pickaninny sleeps", wrote Eleanor Tayleur in a turn-of-the-century article on the "Social and Moral Decadence" of the Negro woman. Labeling the Negro woman as "the Frankenstein product of civilization", she went on to characterize black women as "a great dark, hopeless mass ... leading ... lawless and purposeless lives in the cane and cotton field, or herded together in the cities".[17]

By the 1890s, black women could no longer remain in silence in the face of this newly hyperbolic racist invective, which singled them out as the primary carriers of racial inferiority. African American men did not always challenge white assaults on the morality and femininity of black women; and even when they did, black men could not be expected "to fully and adequately reproduce the exact voice of the black woman" – as African American educator Anna Julia Cooper noted in *A Voice from the South* in 1892. Black women could not longer remain "mute and voiceless" in the face of attacks on their group, Cooper wrote, lending her own voice to this cause.[18] Throughout the 1890s and onward, Cooper, Wells, and other black women would begin to speak out on behalf of their race and gender, abandoning the domestic ideology of true womanhood in favor of racial self-defense.

---

[17] Eleanor Tayleur, "The Negro Woman: 1. Social and Moral Decadence", *The Outlook*, LXXIV (10 January 1904), 266-71.
[18] Anna Julia Cooper, *A Voice from the South*, Xenia, OH: The Aldine Printing House, 1892, 1, 31.

Leading this charge was Ida B. Wells, whose analysis of lynching opened up a new discussion of the ways in which Southern black women were often exploited and victimized by white men. Wells launched her crusade against lynching in 1892, thereafter becoming the target of a variety of white critics who were all too willing to defame her morality as a black women. Denounced as a "slanderous and nasty-minded mulattress" in the *New York Times*, Wells was also accused of speaking out against lynching in the hopes of an "income" rather than an "outcome",[19] and was described as a "black harlot", whose public appearances were designed to secure a white husband.[20] Although troubled by such commentaries, Wells refused to be silenced by attacks on her womanly reputation. A product of her difficult upbringing, Wells' courage in the face of slander inspired other black women to attack not just lynching, but the racial denigration of black women as well, and to examine the connections between the two – the links between gender and Jim Crow. Far from self evident, the interplay between gender and white supremacy went largely unexamined by most Americans in the 1890s. But as a brief review of Wells' early career can demonstrate, during this period race and gender shaped African American women's lives in ways that gave them a unique perspective on the racial thought of their era, and ultimately propelled them to take their battle for womanhood into the public sphere.

"Like a lady": black women in the Jim Crow public sphere
Wells' road to becoming a political journalist is a case in point, since it was the result of her clash with the utterly confounding race and gender politics of her region. It began with nothing more complicated than a trip to work. In the years immediately following the deaths of her parents, Wells supported herself and her siblings by working as a teacher. Only minimally educated herself, Wells' lack of teaching credentials initially limited her employment opportunities to teaching positions in Mississippi's rural black schools which had few grades and required little in the way of teaching qualifications. But these also paid poorly, so Wells relocated her family to Memphis in 1883 in the hope of passing the city's schoolteachers' examination, to allow her to

---

[19] "British Anti-Lynchers", *New York Times*, 2 August 1894.
[20] Quoted in Linda O. McMurray, *To Keep the Waters Troubled: The Life of Ida B. Wells*, New York: Oxford UP, 1998, 177.

teach in better schools at a better salary. A job in Memphis would also, Wells hoped, spare her the long weekly journey to the farming communities in which she taught. Still teaching in rural schools as she prepared for the Memphis exam, Wells was no doubt tired of commuting on what was then a new, modern convenience in passenger travel: the railroad.

In the 1880s, Jim Crow segregation was still taking shape in the South and railroad cars were not yet segregated by race, but taking a seat on a train was a complex proposition for middle-class black women. Trains typically consisted of a locomotive followed by two passenger cars: a "smoker" or second-class car, and a "ladies' car" or first-class car. Removed from the soot and noise of the engine, not to mention the tobacco smoke filling the "smoker", the "ladies' car" was supposed to be reserved for ladies and the gentlemen who accompanied them.[21] More comfortable than the smokers, which had hard wooden seats and few other amenities, the ladies cars had upholstered seats and their own water closets. In addition to such amenities, they also offered respectable women of the late nineteenth century shelter from over familiar male passengers – since they were set aside for women and couples. In the South in 1880s, however, as Ida found out on one of her trips home from school, such cars were increasingly segregated by race rather by gender, and reserved for middle-class whites. Having bought a first-class ticket, Wells boarded the train and seated herself in the "the ladies' coach of the train as usual" only for the conductor to refuse her ticket, telling her he could not take it in the ladies' car.

Initially, their exchange was polite. Wells would later testify: "He said that he would treat me like a lady … but that I must go to the other car". She replied, "If he wished to treat me like a lady, he would leave me alone", and remained where she was. The conductor finished collecting tickets from the other passengers and then returned, moving Wells' bags and umbrella to the forward car in an attempt to dislodge her. She told him "that the forward car was a smoker, and as I was in

---

[21] On the ladies' cars and black women's legal claims to them, see Barbara Welke, "When All Women Were White and All Blacks Were Men: Gender, Class, and the Road to Plessey: 1855-1914", *Law and History Review*, XIII/2 (Autumn 1995), 261-317, and Barbara Welke, *Recasting American Liberty: Gender, Race and Railroad Revolution, 1865-1920*, Cambridge: Cambridge UP, 2001, Ch. 9. On female travelers on American railroads, see Amy G. Richter, *Home on the Rails: Women, Railroads and the Rise of Public Domesticity*, Chapel Hill: U of North Carolina P, 2005.

the ladies' car I intended to stay".[22] Losing all patience with Wells, the conductor then grabbed her arm and tried to drag her out of her seat. Determined not to move, Wells managed to retain her seat by hanging on to her chair and sinking her teeth into his hand.

At twenty-one years old, Wells had grown up to be a petite woman, less than five-feet tall, but she put up an impressive fight. She now "braced her feet against the seat in front and was holding on to the back, and as he had already been badly bitten he didn't try it again himself". Instead, he sought assistance from the baggage clerk and another man, and they dragged Wells out of the first-class car. As the three men carried her out, they were congratulated by "the white ladies and gentlemen in the car", some of whom even "stood in their seats so that they could get a good view and continued applauding the conductor for his brave stand".[23]

Wells' altercation dramatized the day-to-day indignities that African American women could expect to find in the public sphere, especially traveling by rail. It also dramatized the dilemma they faced in responding to such indignities. Writing in 1892, Anna Julia Cooper reflected that black women who sought to defend their claims to womanhood were caught in a double bind. Extended few courtesies by white train officials even when allowed to travel, black women often received no assistance in getting on or off the train, or carrying luggage. At stations with no raised platform, for example, "gentlemanly and efficient railroad conductors" would help their white female passengers off the train and then "deliberately fold their arms and turn away when the black woman's turn came to alight – bearing her satchel and bearing besides another unnamable burden inside her heaving bosom and compressed lips".[24] Yet black women always had to accept that any protest would only make them look even less ladylike to scornful white audiences, who never saw middle-class white women having to fight to be treated courteously. "The feeling of slighted womanhood is unlike any other emotion of the soul", Cooper reflected mournfully. "Its first impulse of wrathful protest and self-

---

[22] Ida B. Wells, *Crusade for Justice: The Autobiography of Ida B. Wells*, ed. A. Duster, Chicago: U of Chicago P, 1970, 18.
[23] *Ibid.*, 19.
[24] Cooper, *Voice from the South*, 90.

vindication is checked and shamed by the consciousness that self assertion would lead to further attack".[25]

Wells ended up on the platform with "the sleeves of my linen duster torn out", but otherwise unharmed, and still fighting.[26] She got off at the next station rather than accept a seat in the smoker, returned to Memphis by wagon and filed a suit in the Tennessee State Court. Charging the railroad with both assault and discrimination, she complained that the conductor had laid "violent hands on her" and that the railroad had refused to provide her with the first-class seat she had purchased.[27] Moreover, even before her first suit was settled, Wells found herself compelled to launch another one, after again being refused entry to the ladies' car during another trip to Woodstock in May 1884. And she also wrote about her suits, publishing her first articles about them in a local Baptist newspaper, *The Living Way*.[28]

Wells ultimately lost both her suits, but not before receiving an education in Southern law as it applied to her race and her gender that would teach her to question the meaning of Southern chivalry and lay the foundation for her anti-lynching campaign. In filing her suits, Wells joined a long line of African American men and women who fought for a place on common carriers in nineteenth-century America. Blacks frequently encountered segregation or even outright exclusion on steamboats, railroads, and streetcars, especially after emancipation, when four million ex-slaves were suddenly free to travel for the first time. Forged through a series of African American challenges to segregation and exclusion, nineteenth-century American law typically required common carriers to serve blacks, but such carriers were not necessarily required to provide equal accommodations. In other words, common law gave "passengers a right to passage", but "not a right to choose a seat".[29]

Indeed, when it came to dividing up passengers, common carriers were allowed to adopt any "reasonable regulation" they chose. However, if segregation by race was one such regulation, segregation by gender was an older, more widely established division, as can be

---

[25] *Ibid.*, 91.

[26] Wells, *Crusade for Justice*, 19.

[27] Wells, quoted in McMurray, *Keep the Waters Troubled*, 89.

[28] No copies of *The Living Way* survive, but the early articles on Wells' lawsuit that it carried received mention in the New York *Globe*, starting in May 1885. See McMurray, *Keep the Waters Troubled*, 90.

[29] Welke, "When All Women Were White", 324.

seen in the convention of the ladies' car. Indeed, the necessity of dividing passengers by sex was so well established that, as segregation cases began to multiply during Reconstruction, this tradition of separate accommodations for women became the "socially irrefutable analogy for separating passengers by race". The resulting tortured analogies, however, collapsed when confronted with middle-class black women such as Wells. Black women could claim access to the ladies' car by virtue of a "common law tradition privileging separate superior facilities for women". And it was a tradition that they took advantage of, filing the majority of challenges to racial discrimination on common carriers in the nineteenth century. However, by the 1880s, such suits were further complicated by the fact that black women's challenges to railroad segregation had helped push the Southern states toward Jim Crow laws legalizing the separation of railroad passengers by race. Tennessee, for example, passed a law in 1881, requiring railroads to provide "separate but equal" accommodations for black railroad passengers, aimed to block African American challenges to racial discrimination on the railroads by providing a more systematic sanction for racial discrimination.[30]

An early victim of this new Jim Crow law, Wells received an education in the shifting status of black women under Southern law. She did win both cases in the lower courts, where she saw her right to ride in the ladies' car affirmed as a matter of class and gender, rather than race. James O. Pierce, an ex-Union soldier from Minnesota, whom Wells had the good fortune to draw as Judge in one of her cases, characterized Wells as "a person of lady-like appearance and deportment, a school teacher, and one who might be expected to object to traveling in the company of rough or boisterous men, smokers or drunkards". As such, he concluded, she was entitled to ride in the ladies' car, and he awarded her $500 dollars in damages.[31] But that was the last affirmation of her qualifications as a lady that Wells would receive in her court battles.

---

[30] Joseph Cartwright, *The Triumph of Jim Crow: Tennessee Race Relations in the 1880s*, Memphis: U of Tennessee P, 1976, 106; Kenneth W. Mack, "Law, Society, Identity and the Making of the Jim Crow South: Travel and Segregation on Tennessee Railroads, 1875-1905", *Law and Social Inquiry*, XXIV/4 (Fall 1999), 377-409.

[31] *Ida Wells vs. The Chesapeake, Ohio and Southwestern Railroad*, Declaration, 23 January 1884.

When news of the verdict came out, Memphis' white newspaper scoffed "DARKY DAMSEL GETS DAMAGES", and expressed outrage over "What it Cost to Put a Colored Teacher in a Smoking Car".[32] Bolstered, doubtless, by such sentiments, the railroad appealed both cases, and launched a smear campaign against Wells. The details of what one black newspaper described as "a shameful attempt to tarnish the character of the fair prosecutrix" have been lost, but the trial transcripts of the case suggest that the railroad succeeded in persuading the court that Wells was no lady after all.[33] Throughout the case, Hollis Cummins, the Railroad's lawyer, argued that all the seats on railroads trains were equal, while at the same time portraying Wells as an overly aggressive colored woman who insisted on seating herself where she was not wanted.

The Tennessee State Supreme Court's ruling on the case involved similar reasoning. Issued in 1887, it reversed the lower court's decision, declaring that "the two cars were alike in every respect". Transforming the common law of the ladies car into Jim Crow law, the court noted that the rear car was set aside for "white ladies and their gentleman attendants", so implying that women of color should expect to sit elsewhere. Wells was the problem, the court stated. She complained that there was smoking in the forward car – which the court did not admit was commonly known as the "smoker" – while "another [white] passenger says no one there was smoking". Her purpose, the Court concluded, "was to harass with a view to this suit", and "her persistence was not in good faith to obtain a comfortable seat for a short ride".[34]

The Supreme Court ruling also reversed Wells' award for damages, making the young teacher, who supported several people on $85 a month, responsible for $200 in court costs. But the bitterest pill for Wells was the import of the decision for African American rights more generally. "I feel so disappointed", Wells wrote in an 1887 diary entry on the ruling, "because I had hoped such great things from the suit for my people generally":

---

[32] Wells, *Crusade for Justice*, 19.

[33] *The Cleveland Gazette*, 11 December 1886, quoted in McMurray, *Keep the Waters Troubled*, 29.

[34] Robert T. Shannon, *Report of Cases Argued and Determined in the Supreme Court of Tennessee*, Louisville, TN: Fetter Law Book Co., 1902, LXXXV, 616.

I have firmly believed all along that the law and the world ... would, when we appealed to it, give us justice. I feel shorn of that belief and utterly discouraged, and just now if it were possible would gather my race in my arms and fly far away with them. O God is there no redress, no peace, no justice in this land for us. [35]

Wells' anguish was more justified than she then knew. By the end of the 1890s it became clear that her case had been one of many State-level steps on the road to Plessey v. Ferguson, the famous 1896 Supreme Court Case ruling that blacks could be relegated to separate but equal accommodation. Moreover, for Wells, a child of the Civil War era, the case helped signal the death of Reconstruction. As she later observed in her autobiography, her case marked the tragedy that the Civil Rights Act of 1875, written by abolitionist Charles Sumner to provide federal protection for citizens' rights under the Constitution and national law, had been subsequently declared unconstitutional by the US Supreme Court in 1883. Had it stood, the Civil Rights Act would have allowed Wells to pursue her case at Federal Court level. That it was struck down, Wells noted acerbically, signaled that "the South did not want or intend to give justice to the Negro after robbing him of all sources from which to secure it". "The supreme court of the nation", she concluded, "told us to go to state courts for the redress of grievances; when I did so I was given a brand of justice Charles Sumner knew the Negroes would get when he fathered the Civil Rights Bill during Reconstruction".[36] But in Wells' anguish and the insights it brought, a writer and an activist was born – one who from this experience turned to journalism.

Calling herself "Iola", a name with a rural twang to underscore her origins, she wrote "in a plain common sense way on the things which concerned our people".[37] Although often published in the "Women's Column" of newspapers, Wells wrote about racial discrimination and politics as well as more lady-like subjects, and her work reflected her awareness of the import of these issues for men and women alike – one of the lessons of her railroad cases. "Iola" was a tremendous success. By her late twenties, Wells' byline had appeared in black newspapers across the country, making her the leading female writer

---

[35] Ida B. Wells, *The Memphis Diary of Ida B. Wells*, ed. Miriam DeCosta-Willis, Boston: Beacon Press, 141.
[36] Wells, *Crusade for Justice*, 20.
[37] *Ibid.*, 24.

among black journalists; she became known as "Iola, the Princess of the Press". She also entered the business end of the news, buying part ownership of the Memphis *Free Speech and Headlight*, a black paper, in 1889. However, Wells' new business would not last long. In 1892, it was destroyed in the aftermath of a brutal triple lynching that rocked black Memphis and forever changed her life. Like Wells' conflict in the ladies' car, the incident seemed to begin over nothing and spiraled outward to expose the gendered vulnerabilities of black men and women in the Jim Crow South.

"The battle for womanhood is the battle for race": from anti-lynching to the National Association of Colored Women

The trouble that would galvanize Wells' anti-lynching campaign began one March night, when a group of black and white boys quarreled over the outcome of a game of marbles in a black neighborhood known as the Curve. Later that evening, their parents joined in, after the father of one of the white boys whipped a victorious black player. Outraged, several black men confronted the white father at his home, which was next door to the People's Grocery Store, an African American-owned joint-stock grocery store, where Memphis blacks often congregated after work. The dispute subsequently moved into the store, where armed white men clashed with armed black men who had assembled to guard the place. Three white men were wounded before the store's protectors and patrons fled. Over the next several days a white mob terrorized the inhabitants of the Curve, looting the People's Grocery Store, and dragging more than thirty black men off to jail in a show of racial domination that ended with the lynching of three black men. Taken from jail and lynched four days after the initial conflict were Thomas Moss (a good friend of Wells), Calvin McDowell, and Will Stewart. All three were proprietors of the People's Grocery Store but largely blameless in the disputes. None had fired shots – indeed, Moss was not even present during the shootout. Rather, his offence, and those of his partners, Wells later concluded, seems to have been the success of the store, which competed directly with a white-owned store across the street.

Wells would always maintain that prior to this event she had given little thought to lynching. Like "many another person who had read of lynching in the South", she said she had believed that, "although lynching was irregular and contrary to law and order" the motives behind it were defensible – "unreasoning anger over the terrible crime of rape led to lynching ... perhaps the brute deserved death anyhow and the mob was justified", and that only events in Memphis opened her eyes "to what lynching really was".[38] A powerful story of personal revelation, Wells' account of learning "what lynching really was" helped generate outrage over these Memphis events by dramatizing the circumstances behind the murder of three up-and-coming young businessmen who had been among Wells' friends and neighbors. However, evidence that Wells had taken note of earlier lynchings can be found in Wells' one surviving diary, which dates back to her Memphis years. Written between 1886 and 1889, this diary mentions several lynchings, including the 1886 murder of a black woman that shook Wells to the core. Usually stoic in her diary, Wells discussed this 1886 lynching with an anguish and frustration echoing the feelings she expressed on losing her railroad suits. Lynching clearly haunted Wells long before 1892, as did an awareness that white violence often had nothing to do with rape. Indeed, Wells seems to have been left feeling powerless and vulnerable in the aftermath of the 1886 lynching, which suggested that black women could be murdered with impunity in her home state.

"Wrote a dynamitic article to the G[ate] C[ity] P[ress] almost advising murder", she wrote in her diary on 4 September 1886, describing an editorial she wrote protesting against the public murder of the black woman in Tennessee that year. Accused of poisoning a white woman, the victim had been "taken from the county jail and stripped naked and hung up in the court house yard and her body riddled with bullets and exposed to view!" Still disturbed by the murder and its gruesome aftermath even after her editorial went to press, Wells lamented in her diary "Oh my God! Can such be and no justice for it?" But at the same time, she also worried about the perils of expressing her outrage publicly. No copies of her article exist today, but whatever response the article advised, she was also thinking, "it may be unwise to express myself so strongly".[39]

Wells expressed no such hesitation in 1892, however, perhaps because she knew everyone involved, perhaps because the events made her realize that she must "tell the whole truth".[40] Busy selling

---

[38] *Ibid.*, 64.
[39] Wells, *Memphis Diary*, 102.
[40] Wells, *Crusade for Justice*, 69.

subscriptions to *Free Speech* in Natchez when the lynching occurred, Wells witnessed none of the events. But she returned to find her friend "Tommie" Moss dead and blacks fleeing Memphis. The lynching marked Wells' first personal experience of such violence, the first of its kind in Memphis. Rocked by racial violence during the Civil War era, Memphis had come to offer a measure of security and political power to blacks during Reconstruction, and managed to enjoy relatively peaceful race relations as African American political power in Tennessee was eroded. Though lynching was at an all-time high in the South as the nineteenth century entered its last decade, vigilante violence had not occurred in Memphis prior to 1892, so its black community saw the murders of three of its leading men as a violation of their trust in the city.

Wells' personal involvement made her sense of violation all the more powerful. Moss, McDowell and Stewart were aspiring young black men, living by the rules that African Americans were supposed to obey in order to advance themselves and their race. Moss was a particularly poignant case in point. "A favorite with everybody", Moss worked by day as a mail carrier (the *Free Speech* was on his route) and by night in the black business he had co-founded and co-owned. An eminently respectable man who taught Sunday school, he died with religious literature from his last class in his pocket. But, despite this exemplary life, "he was murdered with no more consideration than if he had been in a dog" for defending his property.[41]

Wells' feelings were even more outraged by the way the three men were discussed in the white press. Although none had been accused of any serious crime, following their deaths, they were defamed as criminals. *The Memphis Scimitar*, for example, defended their lynching by reference to a noble battle for racial purity, in which no crime was actually specified, but some sort of sexual transgression was implied. "Whenever it comes to the conflict between the races", its editors declared, "the *Scimitar* is for the grand old Anglo-Saxon every time, no matter what the original cause". Meanwhile, the Memphis *Appeal-Avalanche* lost sight of the facts altogether in its rush to defend Memphis' reputation. When "an unprotected woman is assaulted", it declared, "chivalrous men in the neighborhood will forget that there are such things as courts".[42]

---

[41] *Ibid.*, 55.
[42] Quoted in McMurray, *Keep the Waters Troubled*, 138.

Among other things, the Memphis lynching revealed to Wells that whites defamed lynch victims as rapists even when no rape had been alleged. Outraged as she had been about earlier lynchings, Wells had never investigated lynch mobs' grounds for their actions, or these actions' circumstances. Now she began to suspect that many lynchings were little more than "an excuse to get rid of Negroes who were acquiring wealth and property and thus keep the race terrorized and 'the nigger down'".[43] Wells' suspicions built upon her own railcar encounter with defamation and sexual slander. Having been unjustly accused of being both a whore and troublemaker herself, Wells knew from experience that character defamation often served to police social boundaries and support racial hierarchies.

Her suspicions were confirmed when she began her researches into lynching. She found the Memphis events were not unusual: two-thirds of the victims of lynch mobs were never even accused of rape. She also found that accusations of rape often relied on the flimsiest of evidence. Wells' discoveries about lynching enraged her, inspiring her to run a series of anti-lynching editorials in *Free Speech*. Some focused on local events: she castigated white Memphis, and especially its law enforcement officials, who claimed to be unable to identify the lynchers of Moss, Stewart, and McDowell. African Americans, she concluded, had little choice but to "leave a town which will neither protect our lives and property, nor give us a fair trial in court, but takes us out and murders us in cold blood when accused by white persons".[44] But Wells also publicly challenged the veracity of the rape allegations so frequently used to justify lynchings, and put her life at risk in the process.

In the 21 May *Free Speech* editorial, she wrote:

> Nobody in this section of the country believes the threadbare old lie that Negroes rape white women. If Southern men are not careful, they will over reach themselves and public sentiment will have a reaction; a conclusion will be reached which will then be very damaging to the moral reputation of their women.[45]

---

[43] Wells, *Crusade for Justice*, 64.

[44] *Ibid.*, 52.

[45] Wells, "Southern Horrors", 49-72.

Wells was out of town when her editorial came out, which turned out to be fortunate. With its publication, a white mob descended on the offices of *Free Speech*, shutting it down permanently. Although Wells was not immediately identified as the author of the unsigned editorial, its author was threatened with death and dismemberment. The editors of one white Memphis paper, who assumed the author was male, threatened to tie "the wretch who has uttered these calumnies to a stake at intersection of Main and Madison Sts., brand him with a hot iron, and perform on him a surgical operation with a pair of shears".[46] Wells' gender would do nothing to protect her. After her authorship was revealed, local whites let Wells know that if she returned "they would bleed my face and hang me in front of the court house".[47]

The violence that drove Wells out of Memphis underscored both the racially exclusive character of Southern chivalry and the dangers such chivalry held for black women. Although civilized men were not supposed to assault women, Wells' gender offered her no protection from these ugly threats. Her race put her entirely outside such protection. Barred from returning to Memphis, Wells did not, however, abandon her public campaign against lynching.

Instead, she traveled to New York, where African American club-women embraced "the lonely homesick girl … in exile for speaking out against lynching". They launched Wells on a public speaking career that would take her across the Northern states and eventually to Britain. Her lectures on lynching described the events that led to her exile, and defended the name of "the many Southern girls traduced by lying tongues".[48] As she stood before her audiences, Wells testified as a female victim of Jim Crow. Her eyes often filling with tears as she told her story, Wells was living evidence of the fact that black women had no protection from Jim Crow. Intermixing the personal and the political, she emphasized lynchings hurt not just black men, but black women and children as well. Among its victims was the "baby daughter of Tom Moss", who, although "too young to express how she misses her father, toddles to the wardrobe, seizes the legs of his letter-carrier uniform, hugs and kisses them with evident delight and stretches her little hands to be taken up into arms that will never more

---

[46] Wells, *Crusade for Justice,* 66.
[47] Ida B. Wells' words can be found in the Kansas City *American Citizen*, 1 July 1892.
[48] Patricia Ann Schechter, *Ida B. Wells-Barnett and American Reform, 1880-1930*, Chapel Hill: U of North Carolina P, 2001, 18.

clasp his daughter's form". Another victim was the baby's mother, whose tears fell "thick and fast" as she thought of the "sad fate" of the father of her children.[49] But Wells' discussion of lynching went well beyond such heart-wrenching vignettes by offering a gendered analysis of Jim Crow stressing that the racial terrorism white Southerners directed against African Americans was by no means limited to assaults against men.

Wells repeatedly emphasized that the way white Southern men treated black women proved that they were "not so desirous of punishing rapists as they pretend. The utterances of leading white men show that with them it is not the crime but the *class*." The region's white leaders were "apologist[s] for the lynchers of the rapists of white women only":

> Governor Tillman of South Carolina … declared he would lead a mob to lynch the Negro who raped a white woman. So say the pulpits, officials and newspapers of the South. But when the victim is a colored woman it is different.[50]

In her lectures and pamphlets, Wells bitterly contrasted white men's sexual assaults against black women, which usually went unpunished, with love affairs between white women and black men, which, if discovered, often resulted in a lynching. "White men lynch the offending Afro-American, not because he is a despoiler of virtue", she contended, "but because he succumbs to the smiles of white women".[51] A powerful indictment of lynching as a crime against black men, Wells' critique of lynching also spoke on behalf of black women by exposing the racial and sexual double-standards that allowed white men to victimize black women with impunity. An attack on "the white man's civilization and the white man's government", Wells' work gave voice to grievances previously concealed by the quiet culture of dissemblance adopted by middle-class black women.

Wells' anti-lynching campaign offered black women a new mode of racial self-defense, within which African Americans could address the vilification of black women as a race problem, rather than a shameful personal one. By exposing the sexualized racism at the heart

---

[49] Quoted in McMurray, *Keep the Waters Troubled*, 179.
[50] Wells, "Southern Horrors", 58.
[51] *Ibid.*, 54.

of Jim Crow, her campaign against lynching made the defense of black females a matter not only of racial uplift but also of public protest. Indeed, the influence of Wells' campaign on the public discourse of African American women can be seen in the foundation of the National Association of Colored Women (NACW) – the first national black women's organization. The organization originated in 1895, when Josephine Ruffin organized the First National Conference of Colored Women, a gathering of black women's club members, who would reconvene to form a permanent affiliation as the NACW the following year. Both Ruffin's meeting and the new organization saw clubwomen across the country rallying to defend themselves against the moral and sexual defamation they were subjected to by a Southern newspaper editor.

Aroused by Wells' anti-lynching campaign, a Missouri editor named James W. Jacks had outspokenly attacked black women: The race was "devoid of morality", and its women were "prostitutes … natural liars and thieves".[52] English women need not protest against lynching, Jacks maintained in a public letter to British reformer Florence Balgarme, a supporter of Wells' campaign. Jacks' attempt to discredit Wells by an extended attack on the morality of black women suggests that Wells' gendered analysis of Jim Crow hit home among white Southerners. But his letter also exposed a militant mood that Wells' work had helped generate among black women, who no longer dodged any public reference to sexualized racism as they mobilized against Jacks. "There was a time when our mothers and sisters could not protect themselves from such beasts", one of the participants in the meeting that founded the NACW commented, "but a new era has begun and we propose to defend ourselves".[53] Likewise, the Conference's organizer, Josephine Ruffin, noted that black women could no longer be reduced to "mortified silence" by charges of a "delicate and humiliating" nature.[54] Their public protests built on Wells' gendered analysis of racism, as can be seen in the maxim emblazoned on their letterhead: "*the battle for womanhood is the battle for race*".[55]

---

[52] Originally published in *The American Eagle*, Jacks' letter was republished in the Kansas City *American*, 12 July 1895.
[53] P.G., quoted in Richard T. Greener's typed manuscript report of the convention founding the NACW, located in the Boston Public Library's Rare Book Room.
[54] Ruffin, "Address of Josephine Ruffin, President of the Conference", 14.
[55] Quoted in Elizabeth L. Davis, *Lifting as They Climb*, Chicago: Race Relations Press, 1933, 17.

Wells had made lynching into a subject that allowed black women to speak to the violations and humiliations that they suffered in the public sphere, without even addressing them in detail. Wells' campaign against lynching, as critic Alison Piepmeier notes, discussed the female victims of racial violence without "the graphic detail that characterized her reports on black male victims", instead using "the language of true womanhood and sentimental literature" to discuss black women, and making them "sentimental victims on a par with white women".[56] In attacking the rape myths with which white Southerners justified lynching, Wells was afforded an opportunity to expose the racist sexual stereotypes that made interracial sex into rape only when it involved black men and white women. And more broadly, she was able to speak to the intolerable contradictions between gender, race, and sexuality at play in the daily lives of black women under Jim Crow. Wells' critique of lynching was grounded in these contradictions. It underscored that navigating public space was difficult and dangerous for black women as well as men – and encouraged other black women to confront the dangers they faced.

---

[56] Alison Piepmeier, *Out in Public: Configurations of Women's Bodies in Nineteenth-century America*, Chapel Hill: U of North Carolina P, 2004, 181.

"Outdoor relief": Sarah Orne Jewett, Annie Adams Fields, and the Visit in Gilded Age America

Alison Easton

In the 1880s in Massachusetts and Maine two women who shared a household were each at work on a book. Annie Adams Fields, cultural hostess, poet and founder/director of the Associated Charities of Boston, was setting down her prescription for a reformed version of charitable assistance. This successful manual, *How to Help the Poor*, was published in 1883. Meanwhile, Fields' companion, Sarah Orne Jewett, was writing her third novel, *A Country Doctor* (published in 1884). This narrative about a young woman growing up in rural Maine and eventually starting to train as a doctor would consolidate the focus of Jewett's fiction, in particular the life of postbellum communities of rural, seaport and factory-town Maine.[1]

On the face of it, these two works have nothing in common. Fields writes of a system of helping the poorest of the urban poor, the city's desperate and near-destitute, who were almost never the subject of Jewett's fictions despite her part-time residence in Boston over nearly three decades. True, Jewett's novel does begin with a widowed, homeless, suicidal young woman, returning to die in her mother's

[1] Like many of Jewett's readers, I am deeply indebted to Terry Heller, whose authoritative website, The Sarah Orne Jewett Text Project (http://www.public.coe.edu/~theller/soj/sj-index.htm), has made freely available all known Jewett writings, including many periodical items never reprinted, plus much of Fields' work. Without it this essay would not have happened. The Sarah Orne Jewett Text Project is used here for all citations of Jewett's and Fields' texts, and in most cases page numbers will not be cited. The Project's website does not provide paginations for the texts it holds on-line, so I have adopted the expedient of providing chapter references for such texts. Thanks also to Tess Cosslett and Charlene Avalone, my fellow editors, and to the British Academy, which funded my paper on this topic for the Society for the Study of American Women Writers international conference, Philadelphia, 2006.

farmhouse. The tale, however, then charts the fostering of her child in this rural community, her growth to young adulthood, and her subsequent encounter with her father's upper-class family. The novel thus moves within and across a set of overlapping socio-economic worlds: agricultural neighborhoods apparently little touched by industrialization, except when farmers' children leave to work in factories and shops; the gentry's houses in the country and seaport with their wealth, power, and high culture; and the life of the professional classes serving all levels of society and having wider connections to a metropolitan, indeed international world of knowledge. It is through the narrative device of visiting – all kinds of visiting, neighborly, medical, friendly, familial and helping – that Jewett explores complex cross-class interactions such as these. She deployed this trope, her commonest narrative device, in at least thirty-seven of her tales and novels.

Judith A. Roman has observed that Fields' charitable work was the one unshared thing in her life with Jewett, her companion from 1881 until Jewett's death in 1909.[2] I want, however, to demonstrate how reading the subject of visiting across the work of both these women allows us to see the connections between social and charitable visiting, to understand what visiting involved for diverse groups of women as an act of moving into and within spaces that were deemed public despite their home-based setting, and to consider what re-envisaging of the "public" might be going on for these authors. This was a major period of transition, when America was consolidating into an advanced capitalist industrial economy, engendering permanent class divisions and, among many other things, changing possibilities, good and bad, for women of different classes and ethnicities. In particular, for my present purposes, these wider developments altered both attitudes to social rituals of association, already well established mid-century, and the patterns of charitable visiting that had existed earlier in the century. Fields (born 1834) and Jewett (born 1849) lived through this transition, demonstrating how earlier expectations and values were brought to bear on a radically changing America and were themselves changed.

However, in exploring shifting boundaries between public and private in various kinds of visiting in the Gilded Age, I do not intend

---

[2] Judith A. Roman, *Annie Adams Fields: The Spirit of Charles Street*, Bloomington: Indiana UP, 1990, 108.

to suggest that before this era all women had been sequestered in the home entirely without involvement in anything other than the domestic. Clearly we cannot align nineteenth-century women with the home, the domestic and the private in some starkly dichotomous opposition to a public world of men and work: what was evolving in the course of the century was more multi-layered and contradictory. Part of my argument will be that understandings of the public/private distinction became inextricably bound up with the social and economic worlds created by advanced industrial capitalism. I draw particularly on the work of Linda Kerber for the following analysis.[3]

As Kerber argues, a distinction between public and private goes back at least to Ancient Greece, which aligned the private with child-bearing and the public with a world of action based on choice. But new republican politics, capitalist commercial relations and industrial technologies were central in reformulating these distinctions in America in the course of the nineteenth century. It was the social world created by this new economic order that would eventually dislodge pre-nineteenth-century forms of domesticity from their almost exclusive role in defining most free white women's lives. For our present purposes, this affected the act of visiting and its representations.

Capitalism put the traditional patriarchal version of "separate spheres" under great strain, though it took the entire century to break the notion down. New social relations needed to be defined or the old order patched up and reconstructed, since "the patriarchal variant of separate spheres was not congruent with capitalist social relations".[4] The notion of an exclusive female private sphere persisted only in those middle-class households where women were either not part of the labor market or were invisibly earning within the home. Since capitalism's ethos of universal, free competition ostensibly required "unattached individuals freely negotiating with each other in an

---

[3] Linda K. Kerber, "Separate Spheres, Female Worlds, Woman's Place: The Rhetoric of Women's History", *Journal of American History*, LXXV/1 (June 1988), 9-39. See also Carole Pateman, *The Disorder of Women: Democracy, Feminism and Political Theory*, Cambridge: Polity, 1989, 142-61; Cathy N. Davidson, "No More Separate Spheres!", *American Literature*, LXX/3 (September 1998), 443-63; and Monika M. Elbert, *Separate Spheres No More: Gender Convergence in American Literature, 1830-1930*, Tuscaloosa: U of Alabama P, 2000.
[4] Kerber, "Separate Spheres, Female Worlds, Woman's Place: The Rhetoric of Women's History", 21 and 22.

expansive market", women were pushed as wage-earners into what had previously been defined as the public.[5] But women had even less power than working men to negotiate and often found themselves doing work replicating housework. Therefore, the idea of separate spheres persisted, structuring the industrial labor market along gender lines.

As a result, longstanding distinctions between men's and women's lives increasingly could not be aligned with the private/public distinction. This produced a complex relationship between a persistent but shifting notion of separate spheres and the actual lived conditions of work and home in this industrial capitalist society where, for instance, workplace and home might indeed be one and the same, or where one might earn one's living in the home of another woman. Not surprisingly, the meanings of the two terms, "public" and "private", were publicly contested in this period; as Mary Ryan observes, public and private were "cultural constructions imposed on a complex world".[6]

Bringing these understandings to bear upon the home, the scene of all kinds of visiting, we should note that the desire for privacy, as S.J. Kleinberg demonstrates, was a function of two key aspects of the nineteenth century: first, immigration, making for an "increasingly heterogeneous population" (so a less easy sense of community identity beyond one's door), and second, appalling urban conditions created by industrial capitalism (a "civilized life", the bourgeois notion of the home as sacred space, therefore required seclusion from direct contact with the barbarities of the new economic order).[7] Class conditions came to be expressed in differentials between, rather than within, households, and as Kleinberg discusses, meanings ascribed by different classes to their houses diverge ever more widely. Rather than indicating stability and prosperity, homes of the poor were places where money was earned and neighbors intruded, and their multi-functioned rooms did not allow the segregation of public and private activities.

---

[5] *Ibid.*, 21.

[6] Mary P. Ryan, *Women in Public: Between Banners and Ballots, 1825-1880*, Baltimore, MD: Johns Hopkins UP, 1990, 6.

[7] S.J. Kleinberg, "Gendered Space: Housing, Privacy and Domesticity in the Nineteenth-century United States", in *Domestic Space: Reading the Nineteenth-century Interior*, eds Inga Bryden and Janet Floyd, Manchester: Manchester UP, 1999, 142.

Bourgeois ideology might fantasize home as haven, but middle-class women throughout the nineteenth century had as much resisted the separation of home and work as they celebrated the distinction, seeking to establish a continuum between the two worlds and seeing their own efforts as part of the world in which men worked.[8] Home and work worlds were seen as different, but not as separate. Some middle-class women understood that the same economic forces created both the bourgeois home on the one hand and the sweatshops, factories, agribusinesses and slum dwellings on the other, and that in all of these places women worked. Some embarked on activities beyond the home designed to alleviate suffering, embracing values incongruent with capitalism. While women's philanthropy was deemed private activity in the antebellum period, philanthropy takes on a public character in the postbellum period:[9] if middle-class visitors to poverty-stricken homes were less concerned with working-class privacy (despite the fact that the working class did try to keep their doors shut to them), it was because charitable visitors deemed these home conditions a matter of public concern.[10] In an age where government regulation came reluctantly, piecemeal and insufficiently, the "public" came to mean both the general community where civic opinion is formed, and the area of the world under the power of the state – a power which was resisted by the business world of "private capital".[11] Privacy came to mean both a privileged status of withdrawal from the world whereby the supply of personal

---

[8] Stephanie Coontz, *The Social Origins of Private Life*, London: Verso, 1980, Chs 6 and 7.

[9] See also Anne Boylan's essay in this present volume.

[10] See Martin Hewitt, "District Visiting and the Constitution of Domestic Space in the Mid-nineteenth Century", in *Domestic Space: Reading the Nineteenth-century Interior*, 121-41.

[11] See Baym's use of Habermas in *American Women Writers and the Work of History, 1790-1860*, New Brunswick, NJ: Rutgers UP, 1995, 5-6. See also Nancy Cott, "'Giving Character to Our Whole Civil Polity': Marriage and the Public Order in the Late Nineteenth Century", in *U.S. History as Women's History: New Feminist Essays*, eds Linda K. Kerber, Alice Kessler-Harris, and Kathryn Kish Sklar, Chapel Hill; London: U of North Carolina P, 1995, 107-21. Linda Mahood, in *Policing Gender, Class and Family: Britain, 1850-1940*, London: U College London P, 1995, explores in the British context an increasing intervention in family life by outside agencies, and a shift to a public patriarchy and to classification, surveillance and discipline.

information could be limited, and the freedom from interference by external agencies.[12]

Nina Baym argues that, in earlier historical periods before most men vacated the home during daylight hours, "it was obvious that public and private spheres were metaphorical rather than actual places, that public and private were different ways of behaving in the same space".[13] I want to suggest that visiting, in the various late nineteenth-century forms that Fields organized and Jewett imagined, continued to be a form of public behavior in the home space. This modified the nature of the space in which visiting took place, and, more importantly, changed the idea of the public.

Historically, we know that both social visiting and charitable visiting were considered public events.[14] It was an act of association primarily for women, and the home was an acceptable or necessary space within which women might congregate or intervene. This home, depending on class status, might or might not contain reception rooms, for example a parlor, as an intermediate space.[15] Charity visitors, on the other hand, would commonly enter rooms where cooking, bathing, sitting and sleeping all took place, so that the home became the site for what historians are now terming the "social", an intermediate space between public and private which outside agencies of dominant institutions create by intervening in, classifying and disciplining the lives of the indigent.[16] Social visiting among the middle and upper classes also contained elements of regulation (this time, within a caste).

Visits of whatever kind were distinctive events, and as such revealing and sometimes enabling. People left their own homes to enter the customarily intimate space of another home, carrying with them elements of exterior life – the journey made, clothes worn and a social script designed to predetermine interactions (whether social etiquette, or the highly structured investigative visit to the poor). Normal routines were suspended, meals if served felt special, and people were brought into conjunction in ways that were not quotidian.

---

[12] Cott, "'Giving Character to Our Whole Civil Polity'", 110-14; see also Hewitt, "District Visiting", 133-34.

[13] Baym, *American Women Writers*, 11.

[14] C. Dallett Hemphill, *Bowing to Necessities: A History of Manners in America, 1620-1860*, New York: Oxford UP, 1999, 193.

[15] *Ibid.*, 182.

[16] Mahood, *Policing Gender*, 63, 151-54.

Although social visiting was supposed primarily to be an act between equals, these sites commonly became an interface between people who might not be equal.[17] Indeed, experiencing differences between participants may have been as significant as finding similarities, and this raised disturbing questions in a purportedly democratic society believing in equal association. So, visiting troubled settled distinctions and indicated boundaries, but also allowed passage between social groups, opened possibilities and made connections. This stepping out was mostly positive, protected, communal, licensed and well-meaning, but was also challenging in its non-quotidian nature, and raised questions about knowledge, power, empathy, conciliation, social change and social cohesion.

Fields' *How to Help the Poor* concerns new forms of what was called "outdoor relief". This was a technical term denominating support for the poor that did not involve residential care such as poorhouses and reformatories, but it is a resonant phrase for this volume's present concerns about public space. It is notable that Fields starts her manual with two scenes involving homes forced open to outsiders: she describes, first, a well-to-do woman in her own house fielding a series of requests from beggars coming to her door asking for money or for support to get money, and second, a man from the same class hearing screams and feeling obliged to enter the working-class tenement to investigate and offer help. Fields' book addresses concerned middle-class persons amid a public crisis: as Fields observes, a million dollars had been given in poverty relief in one year alone in Boston. Her analysis is underpinned by more than a decade of her philanthropic initiatives in the face of economic depression (1873-1877) and, in the 1880s, the repercussions of massive industrial unrest and acute class conflict. The new industrial order of the Gilded Age, as Eric Arnesen argues, raised critical questions about the "morality of capitalist industrialization, the compatibility of political democracy with economic concentration, and the very fate of the Republic".[18] Symptomatically, *How to Help the Poor* sold 22,000 copies in the first two years because it offered a response to this crisis.

---

[17] Hemphill, *Bowing to Necessities*, 151-54.
[18] Eric Arnesen, "American Workers and the Labor Movement in the Late Nineteenth Century", in *The Gilded Age: Essays on the Origins of Modern America*, ed. Charles W. Calhoun, Wilmington, DEL: Scholarly Resources, 1996, 44.

Inspired by European and British models proffering longer-term alternatives to simply giving money, Fields had spearheaded the setting up of a system of investigation that reported back to a central board.[19] This board pooled knowledge, offered practical help (jobs, childcare, cafés, housekeeping advice, and legal enforcement of responsibilities), and then monitored progress. This system was distinct from state relief – besides, the state did not regard itself as having a central role in ameliorating extreme poverty until the appalling 1890s depression.[20] Though Fields notes a Christian imperative informing her agenda, her scheme was not traditional Christian almsgiving – and most Gilded Age clergy denied or ignored the social evils of poverty in their sermons to the comfortably situated until the 1890s.[21] Instead, hers was consciously a modernizing system that prefigured the professionalization of social work.

The fundamental distinction between the truly helpless who deserve financial welfare and those deemed able, if given practical assistance, to work and live in reasonable comfort was a well established philanthropic principle in this period,[22] but, by framing poor relief as a visit, Fields moderates its basic conservativism. The motto of her first philanthropic association, the Cooperative Society of Visitors (1875), was "not alms but a friend".[23] Clearly this was not visiting between friends in a personal sense, not least given the huge power differential between moneyed visitor and impoverished host. Nonetheless, something complex is happening in Fields' account, as elements of the social visit are combined with regulatory charity functions. It is the poor under some duress who invite the well-to-do into their homes. No money is handed over, and the visit involves a sort of conversation, but one whose contents are put on record. So, to ask for outdoor relief meant to enter the public realm – as Fields notes, a charity visitor "investigates". This involves the recording of intimate

---

[19] Nathan Irvin Huggins, *Protestants against Poverty: Boston's Charities, 1870-1900*, Westport, CT: Greenwood Publishing, 1971, 163-177; Roman, *Annie Adam Fields*, 1990, especially Ch. 6.

[20] Michael B. Katz, *In the Shadow of the Poorhouse: A Social History of Welfare in America*, 10th Anniversary edition, New York: Basic Books, 1996, 147-50.

[21] Paul A. Carter, *The Spiritual Crisis of the Gilded Age*, DeKalb: North Illinois UP, 1971, 144-47.

[22] Katz, *In the Shadow of the Poorhouse*, 17-19, 91-99.

[23] Rita K. Gollin, *Annie Adams Fields: Woman of Letters*, Amherst: U of Massachusetts P, 2002, 167.

knowledge (that is, material indubitably of the private realm) whose confidentiality she stresses but whose contents would be shared among helping bodies. No wonder only the absolutely desperate, historians tell us, asked for this kind of help.[24] And for all her emphasis on being a friend and on "communication" and "sympathy" (her words), Fields does not mystify what is happening:

> Visiting the poor does not mean entering the room of a person hitherto unknown to make a call. It means that we are invited to visit a miserable abode for the purpose first of discovering the cause of that misery ....We are at great disadvantage: we go without authority, and often without knowledge; we are met sometimes with distrust and possible dislike.[25]

It is clear that this meant visitors stepping out of their own safety zone, even if in many ways they took their own values with them. Fields does recognize the difficulties and contradictions.

This kind of visit, then, seems to be both private and public: it does not obliterate this classic distinction but in acknowledging and connecting private realities and public responsibilities, it changes the meanings of both. Home remains the central space, refigured here as a space of potential reform and care, where a family will eventually acquire the housekeeping skills and working opportunities so as to live comfortably and privately. Furthermore, although the visitors have no authority and offer their services individually, they report to an institution, which may invoke the law (for example, in relation to housing regulations, provision for dependents or drunkenness). Poverty is addressed case by individual case, but Fields is well aware of the charity work's important wider significance – hence publishing a book. While denying there is a political agenda and making no critique of capitalism, this work raised enormous public questions; she

---

[24] Sarah Deutsch, *Women and the City: Gender, Space, and Power in Boston, 1870-1940*, New York: Oxford UP, 2000, 46-50; see also *Lady Bountiful Revisited: Women, Philanthropy, and Power*, ed. Kathleen D. McCarthy, New Brunswick, NJ: Rutgers UP, 1990, 3, 7, 11; Katz, *In the Shadow of the Poorhouse*, 3.

[25] Annie Adams Fields, *How to Help the Poor*, Boston: Houghton Mifflin, 1883, Ch. 3. See also Hewitt, "District Visiting", on the issue of working-class responses to charitable visiting.

herself invokes the sentiment that to do nothing is to affect "the common weal".[26]

Annie Fields had known Charles Dickens personally, and her move from literature to charity work was inspired by him. It seems likely that, in turn, Jewett would have been affected by Fields' work or shared her concerns. In addition, the hospitality that Jewett and Fields offered in their Boston house to the socially concerned cultural elite, continuing Fields' previous life as a cultural hostess, might well have fed into Jewett's notions of an ethically meaningful sociability. Jewett was not an elite nostalgic conservative, but a member of a liberal elite. While being no social radical, she was knowledgeable and thoughtful, a witness intervening quietly in central issues of her time.[27] Her tales respond in multiple, subtle ways to this period of massive social change, and given her deep interest in class relations, visiting thematically offered great possibilities of encounter and exchange. Similarly to Fields' visits, her fiction works on an individual basis, demanding successive acts of attention – the act of listening by characters and readers – as knowledge accumulates over time and study is required.[28] Her tales, where they explore charitable action, envisage no need of money; instead, as in *How to Help the Poor*, there is an efficacy in listening, talking, co-operation and (a key word for Jewett) friendship.

---

[26] Fields, *How to Help the Poor*, Ch. 2.

[27] Jewett's politics have become a matter of intense debate: see, for example, *New Essays on "The Country of the Pointed Firs"*, ed. June Howard, Cambridge: Cambridge UP, 1994; Nancy Glazener, *Reading for Realism: The History of a U.S Literary Institution, 1850-1910*, Durham, NC: Duke UP, 1997; Marjorie Pryse, "Sex, Class, and 'Category Crisis': Reading Jewett's Transitivity", *American Literature*, LXX/3 (September 1998), 517-49, Josephine Donovan, "Jewett on Race, Class, Ethnicity, and Imperialism: A Reply to Her Critics", *Colby Quarterly*, XXXVIII/4 (December 2002), 403-16. The study I am presently engaged on, "Relating Class: Jewett and Gilded Age America", will develop arguments made here and previously. See Alison Easton, "Introduction: History and Utopia", in Sarah Orne Jewett, *The Country of the Pointed Firs and Other Stories*, ed. Alison Easton, Harmondsworth: Penguin, 1999, vii-xxii.

[28] As Susan K. Harris observes, in *The Cultural Work of the Late Nineteenth-century Hostess: Annie Adams Fields and Mary Gladstone Drew*, New York: Palgrave Macmillan, 2002, the society hostess' skills of being a listener were carried over into helping contexts, 123.

"In Shadow", a wonderful chapter in Jewett's first novel, *Deephaven* (1877), constitutes a primal scene. The novel has proceeded up to this point by a succession of mostly happy scenes suggesting small-town networks of mutual support and respect, where the two young gentlewomen protagonists, intimate friends holidaying at a family home, visit or receive visits from a wide social range of neighbors – much preferring the fishing and farming families, whose questioning they come to understand is not "impertinence", to the "chill" of polite exchanges with their social equals or the absurdities of the decayed gentry. But two complex visits to a nearly destitute farm profoundly disturb this class-crossing friendliness. The protagonists happen upon the farm's desperate poverty during their day excursion, and then, hoping to render assistance, they return weeks later only to find the farmer and his wife dead and their family about to be scattered. The surrounding landscape, whatever its clear romantic attractions, is shown as enmeshed in economic and class meanings – mortgages, purchases, ineluctable historical changes in agriculture, commerce and industry. This farmer's poverty is not presented as a universal condition (the poor you always have with you), but caused by the particular industrial, economic and technological conditions of this advanced capitalist nation (for example, competition from Western agribusiness). Although the chapter keeps threatening to collapse into a sequence of ironic reversals, it does try hard for an inclusive vision – the interchanges between the characters, where each class attempts to imagine others' lives, create a dialogue, both literally (since in these remote places this is what visitors do), but also psychologically as each engages with the other's otherness. Understanding, however, goes in one direction, with the farmer teaching the young women (who have not earned a cent of what they have) the comparative meaning of money, and reasserting the value of his work and of himself as if to cancel out the charity involved in their over-generous payment for services.

Charity becomes a complicated transaction, with the women torn between their sense of being intruders and the sense that they have failed to help. The tale invokes two sets of transcendent values: first, on the national Fourth of July holiday, the farmer living off his own land – the epitome of early republicanism – is found struggling even for mere subsistence; second, a profound belief in the Christian afterlife does not, however, cancel out the poverty of the living world, represented at the chapter's very end by the deserted farmhouse, a home padlocked, fireless and forsaken. The attempt at social inclusiveness is baffled, leaving ineradicable class difference, inequality, and distance: "I wonder how we can help being conscious, in the midst of our comforts and pleasures, of the lives which are being starved to death in more ways than one."[29]

A Country Doctor (1884), Jewett's third and favorite novel, written at the same period as *How to Help the Poor*, addresses the bewildering impotence that those *Deephaven* protagonists had felt. This novel has commonly been read as a parable of Jewett's journey to her life's work as published writer. It concerns a young woman, Nan Prince, stepping out into public space, where she will find socially useful, self-fulfilling work, finally rejecting a gentlewoman's life of socializing and holidays. *How to Help the Poor* had likened the charity visitor to a doctor visiting – as a doctor, Nan Prince's visiting will be both legitimate (doctors step between public and private) and alarming (women entering a male profession).

Symptomatically it is through the public/private motif of the visit that the plot winds its way through all the difficulties which both Nan's mixed class inheritance (descendant of urban professionals and of farmers and shop assistants) and her choice of "so uncommon a purpose" pose for individuals, class and gender groups, neighborhoods and hence, the nation.[30] The accounts of these visits would seem randomly episodic if one did not understand the profound questions about community, social division and responsibility being explored through this motif. In wry, affectionate detail, early chapters delineate long-established patterns of entertaining or assistance among rural farming neighbors. There is too Nan's adoptive parent, the rural doctor, whose professional visits throw a web of connection over the

---

[29] Sarah Orne Jewett, *Deephaven*, Ch. 11. This understanding is repeated in another early tale, "Miss Sidney's Flowers" (1874/1879), in which a rich Boston woman, unvisited by her social equals except dutiful relations and insulated in her grand house that now abuts a major thoroughfare, awakens to a new kind of charity when she steps outside, and opens her eyes and her heart to a nearby street peddler, threatened by the almshouse. Though offering inadequate solutions, the tale shows her "trying, in a frightened, blind kind of way, to be good and useful". The only other stories of middle-class urban charity efforts are "Nancy's Doll" (1876) and "Paper Roses" (1879). Another early tale, "A Lost Lover" (1878), concerns a vagrant, a figure seen entirely negatively in this period, here partly recuperated, but "the distance between them seemed immense" (Katz, *In the Shadow of the Poorhouse*, 95).

[30] Sarah Orne Jewett, *A Country Doctor*, 1884, Ch. 12.

community, half private, half public (since everyone sees him on his rounds), and who also entertains privately fellow professionals from metropolitan and international worlds. Nan's choice of profession is played out between her two homes: the rural community of her doctor guardian and her mother, and secondly her estranged upper-class family to whom she proposes a reconciliatory social visit. This aunt and her maid expect to embarrass Nan, given her humble upbringing, but finally end up feeling that "the visit must not come to an end" and that Nan must embrace an upper-class female destiny. At a climactic disciplinary tea-party, the social arbiter of this class opines that a woman's act of keeping a house is "the best service to the public", but Nan refuses their demand to abandon her medical ambitions and submit to the pleasant but meaningless entertainments of a gentlewoman's "more retired place".[31]

Not unlike Fields' recognition that helping people of a different social class cannot be simply friendship, *A Country Doctor* demonstrates the growing sense at this period that these two kinds of visiting (social and professional) have become two very different ways of behaving because of enormous social divisions created by the Gilded Age economy. Once, humorously, Nan during a pleasure trip and to the dismay of her conventional suitor, briskly resets a farmer's dislocated collarbone, but later cagily describes this visit to her upper-class friends as "a pleasant call at the farmhouse".[32] Only Nan's unique cross-class upbringing puts her at ease in all situations, and by choosing to be a doctor she resolves for herself the issue of how to step out positively into multi-classed public spaces.

Throughout her career Jewett returns repeatedly to the topos of the visit. By finding patterns across the range of her writings on visiting and by focusing on a handful of tales in more detail, I want to ask what understandings does her work create out of this special public/private space? Home, the traditional setting for women, remains important here, but the focus is on women stepping out into the public by opening their home to a visitor or by traveling to enter another's home space, and this act is seen to have meanings for community and nation. Jewett's concern for homes and with homelessness reflects historical aspects of a society in radical

---

[31] *Ibid.*, Ch. 18.
[32] *Ibid.*, Ch. 17.

transition, a democratic society showing huge tensions: the aftermath of the Civil War (a surprising number of tales mention it); Northeastern rural depopulation and manufacturing changes; the growth of cities; industrial employment patterns; aspirations towards gentility by country dwellers; changes in how communities deal with the destitute; and an uncharitable world (see, for example, her Christmas and Thanksgiving tales, reaching out beyond the family at a time when these public holidays, traditionally associated with alms giving, were increasingly being privatized).[33]

In Fields' *How to Help the Poor*, because of immense economic and social inequalities, being public in a notionally private space provoked disturbance that was controlled by strong regulatory measures of charity work. In some Jewett fictions, however, visiting becomes a space which softens the sharpness of social divisions, or at least disables their power to separate and threaten. Rather than a dichotomized world, there appears instead to be a continuum, with the distinction between private and public shifting about in the course of a visit. This is partly because differences of wealth and class are played out in dialogues within smaller, definable communities (for example, rural townships) rather than in the far more bifurcated city. Jewett takes the same ideal, but one-sided, vision of friendship at the heart of *How to Help the Poor* and imagines how it might operate in her fictional communities. Although Jewett's impulse is utopian, the tales deal with the constraints, limitations and indissoluble differences of historical actuality.[34]

Jewett understood how historical conditions affected her suffering characters, even when causes lay geographically distant. These tales show the fundamental inequities of the era's economy, linking this with the failure of postbellum communities to aid their indigent members and with their view of the poorhouse as a just dessert. In this context the word, "neighbor", becomes a key moral term for Jewett. In the "Growtown Bugle" (1888), the protagonist invests in a far-away western boom town while her New England small town neighbors "starved within the sound of her voice"; in "The Gray Mills of Farley" (1898) the manager of a shut down factory, whose shareholders have benefited from too high a dividend, is visited by desperate employees,

---

[33] Stephen Nissenbaum, *The Battle for Christmas*, New York: Alfred A. Knopf, 1996, 8-10, 62-63, 82-84.
[34] Easton, Introduction, xix-xx.

whom he characterizes as his "neighbors" and whom he struggles to help with loans, odd jobs and seed potatoes in a deliberately-attempted act of "right living" in a "selfish" age;[35] in "The Night Before Thanksgiving" (1895/1899) a rapacious neighbor, who threatens the sick and old with the poorhouse, accuses one woman of having been "too generous to worthless people [an orphan] and coming to be a charge on others".[36]

But other tales chart the eventual triumph of sympathy and care in a plot where it is a visit that effects the transformation in the characters' fortunes, often to the mutual benefit of both visitor and visited. Help usually does not require money, so is more like a gift – that is, an individual but public act in response to a situation requiring community knowledge and action. It brings assistance to the needy while simultaneously asserting a fundamental equality between giver and receiver.[37] This is neither commercial exchange (as in a capitalist economy), nor Western/Christian charity (where the recipient has no chance of reciprocating), nor the emerging forms of professional philanthropy. As Marcel Mauss defines it, a gift involves the obligation to give, to accept and to reciprocate; it is a principle of community and of justice, and it must create solidarity and friendly feelings between people, or it is not a gift.[38] Collectivities, not individuals, impose these obligations. As Mary Douglas observes, Mauss' gift economy contrasts with the capitalist market economy that had neglected to address adverse changes in social relations caused by alterations in modes of production.[39] Those changes constituted both the underlying context and impulse for Jewett's tales.

So, in some of Jewett's tales social and charitable visits are elided; characters, while still recognizing crushing endemic financial disparities, meet as equals, are able to talk openly, and both receive

---

[35] Sarah Orne Jewett, "The Gray Mills of Farley", 1898.

[36] Sarah Orne Jewett, "The Night Before Thanksgiving", 1895/1899. The distribution of potatoes, seemingly a little sentimental to present-day readers, has historical precedents (see Katz, *In the Shadow of the Poorhouse*, 47). A number of Jewett's stories briefly note the specific economic roots of this hostility towards helping: "A Visit Next Door" (1884), "Mrs. Parkins' Christmas Eve" (1890-91), "Aunt Cynthy Dallett" (1899), "A Business Man" (1886), and "Miss Manning's Minister" (1883).

[37] See also, for example, Jewett's stories, "Jack's Merry Christmas" (1881), "An Empty Purse" (1895), "A Visit Next Door" (1884), and "Miss Esther's Guest" (1893).

[38] Marcel Mauss, *The Gift: The Form and Reason for Exchange in Archaic Societies*, trans. W.D. Halls, London: Routledge, 1990.

[39] Mary Douglas, Foreword to Mauss, *The Gift*, x.

and bestow gifts. "The Town Poor" is Jewett's finest exploration of this.[40] Mrs Trimble, a prosperous widow and active business woman, comes to pay a social call on former neighbors. These elderly sisters were left virtually destitute by their well-to-do, inappropriately philanthropic father, and are now othered by the township's inhabitants and officials as the "town poor" and auctioned off to the lowest bidders who can house them (an impoverished family themselves). Historically, this system of pre-workhouse care was generally recognized as abusive,[41] and Jewett's tale should be read in the context of national debates about poverty, inequality, the adequacy of various forms of public assistance and the question of responsibility, as well as in relation to the efforts of private volunteers like Fields. Out in remote winter-bound farmland, where "no-one came visiting", Mrs Trimble and her companion find "the golden spirit of hospitality" in these pitiful women who have almost nothing to give their visitors (their private possessions sold off), rearrange the meager furniture so as to accommodate their guests and serve tea. In a room that is an intimate space but not a home, the town poor are hidden from public awareness until their guests leave with the determination to reverse their own and everybody else's past actions, and to restore their hosts to their former home.

I have argued that the "In Shadow" chapter in *Deephaven* represented Jewett's starting place for exploring charitable visiting. Four years previously, her very early "The Best China Saucer" initiated an exploration of the social visit with a similar sense of a virtually unbridgeable divide between classes. Nineteenth-century social visiting usually functioned to define and maintain a class, and in this profoundly unequal democracy this would happen only between social equals.[42] However, in this quietly subversive children's story, the wonderfully unruly, deprived lower-class little neighbor invites herself to tea with the bored upper-class girl with her dolls' tea party, good food and fine china. The "guest" only gets as far as the garden, since her "hostess" has been expressly forbidden to allow into inside the house this neighbor child, who "teaches you bad words and bad manners". But her mother's other pronouncements on the absolute

---

[40] Sarah Orne Jewett, "The Town Poor", 1890.

[41] *Maine: The Pine Tree State from Prehistory to the Present*, eds Richard W. Judd, Edwin A. Churchill, and Joel W. Eastman, Orono: U of Maine P, 1995, 230.

[42] Hemphill, *Bowing to Necessities*, 151-54.

politeness required towards disliked guests and kindness due to the disadvantaged give the small hostess license to entertain. The result, both funny and disturbing, is theft, smashed china, guilty feelings and a glimpse of another harder world and, as in the *Deephaven* scene, there is a walking funeral, this time imagined as a comic dream burying the broken saucer.[43]

Perhaps in reaction to this, Jewett's subsequent stories of social visits seem to take as their premise (or promise) some advice from her novel for adolescents, *Betty Leicester*: "wherever you may put two persons, one is always hostess and the other always guest, either from circumstances alone or from their different natures, and they must be careful about their duties to each other."[44] (Jewett loved this novel, and her favorite chapter has the upper-class heroine preparing tea for her hostess' servants whom she is visiting in their own home – an odd, if well-intentioned, scene.) How those of a different class – for example, servants – fit into this model of social relations is something pursued in her tales of social visits. I shall briefly discuss three of them. These, contrary to nineteenth-century social codes, involve bringing together persons of differing status and power. They move in unexpected ways in relation to public/private behaviors, lay open needs and desires that are the consequence of social inequalities, and end up thinking freshly about gentility and sociability.

A rigidly maintained, conventional public is treated by Jewett as a matter of high comedy. In "The Guests of Mrs. Timms" (1894/95), formal visiting, which should facilitate social connection, instead prevents it. Two friends take up the invitation of an old acquaintance in another town to visit her anytime soon, only to find themselves completely unwelcome and received with minimal politeness. The wonderfully absurd journey and visit are played out in the traditional spaces of stage coach (jockeying for one's preferred seat), streets, gates and front doors, and a parlor kept so darkened that the guests stumble and can barely see one another. The rooms the visitors do not get asked into are the bedroom, where bonnets would be taken off (the signal for real hospitality), and the back sitting room into which the

---

[43] See Sarah Way Sherman's excellent analysis, "Party Out of Bounds: Gender and Cass in Jewett's 'The Best China Saucer'", in *Jewett and Her Contemporaries: Reshaping the Canon*, eds Karen L. Kilcup and Thomas S. Edwards, Gainesville: UP of Florida, 1999, 223-48.

[44] Sarah Orne Jewett, *Betty Leicester*, 1890, Ch. 1.

purring cat has been quickly booted. When previously out at their church convention, the three women had been apparently equal – "'as if she was a sister'" – but their home spaces are nervously guarded against over familiar visitors by latches, bolts and locks. Because they all rank each other by subtle gradations of status, they exist in a state of constant tension between the attractions of being noticed by a "superior" and the twitchy difficulties of knowing the degree of intimacy they may assume or wish. Formalities simply serve to conceal these private desires, embarrassments and dislikes. Rigid demarcations of public and private are thus articulated with ridiculous preoccupations with status. Only outside these constraints of bourgeois etiquette do we glimpse women who run down the garden path to welcome unexpected friends, let them fully enter their homes, and behave by Christian values they ostensibly espouse and quote.

In contrast, at the centre of Jewett's greatest novel, *The Country of the Pointed Firs* (1896), lies a utopian vision of sociability, embodied in the elderly Mrs Blackett on Green Island whom the novel's urban upper-class narrator is invited to visit. Mrs Blackett is neither wealthy nor powerful, but an ordinary countrywoman whose family subsists on farming and fishing on an isolated island. The narrator, however, is inspired to redefine social visiting:

> Her hospitality was something exquisite, she had the gift which so many women lack, of being able to make themselves and their houses belong entirely to a guest's pleasure .... Sympathy is of the mind as well as the heart, and Mrs. Blackett's world and mine were one from the moment we met .... I wondered why she had been set to shine on this lonely island on the northern coast. It must have been to keep the balance true, and make up to all her scattered and depending neighbors for other things which they may have lacked.[45]

The distinctions between private and public and between the prosperous and poor no longer operate in this celebration of a hospitality that temporarily dissolves social difference. This is marked out by the spaces in which the visit takes place. Mrs Blackett comes out to greet her visitors by the shore, and then, though the main path to the house leads to the kitchen, the visitor is taken instead through the front door ("kind of formal", they admit) so that she can be honored

---

[45] Sarah Orne Jewett, *The Country of the Pointed Firs*, 1896, Ch. 10.

by being received in the "best room", a parlor whose presence on this remote place is appreciated for what it offers her community.[46] They then move, "as if by common instinct", to the old kitchen, a place of conversation and entertainment where even the householders themselves use the best china each Sunday evening. The two other places that the narrator is admitted to are both deeply private: Mrs Blackett's bedroom, a "place of peace", where she is encouraged to sit in Mrs Blackett's chair and is told she will be remembered for this; and secondly Mrs Blackett's daughter's "sainted" place, a point in the island where her favorite healing herb grows and where she recalls for the narrator the complexities of her relations with both her dead husband and with an earlier lover lost through social snobbery.[47]

The Country of the Pointed Firs is structured by a series of visits – tourist, medical, neighborly, pastoral – and unsurprisingly thematizes friendship and neighborliness. In an America of mass immigration and internal migration, to be told, "I shan't make a stranger of you" is a resonant gesture.[48] In the painfully shy man, William Blackett, we see someone to be initiated in these essential "affairs of social life" (Chapter 9), that offset the geographical, economic and social separation and loneliness of the scattered township they live in[49]; and in Mrs Fosdick, another of the novel's visitors, we see the person who, we are told, can introduce "a new impulse and refreshing of social currents", and knows how to visit, "as if to visit were the highest of vocations" (this is another visit that gravitates, after initial formalities, to the kitchen).[50]

By contrast, "In the lives of each of us . . . there is a place remote and islanded", and this is embodied in Joanna, a self-isolated hermit alone on a tiny island, dressed for best in the afternoons in her "livin-room".[51] She has no parlor, but clearly something ceremonious and social survives. She rejects the formality, interference, and inquisitive intrusion of all the other neighbors, but can recognize the love offered by the truly caring visitor. Even the aspirations to gentility, satirized in "The Guests of Mrs. Timms" and identified by the historian Richard

---

[46] *Ibid.*, Ch. 8.
[47] *Ibid.*, Chs 11 and 10.
[48] *Ibid.*, Ch. 8.
[49] *Ibid.*, Ch. 9.
[50] *Ibid.*, Ch. 12.
[51] *Ibid.*, Ch. 15.

L. Bushman as spreading throughout America in the nineteenth century at various social levels, are both honored and transcended.[52] The old seaman, Elijah Tilley, has been entertaining the narrator in the kitchen, so he is bound by neither bourgeois conventions nor, surprisingly, by gender conventions. But he also shows her his parlor, a "sadder and more empty" conventional public space furnished with carpet, vases and fine china, where nonetheless she respectfully imagines the aspirations, cost, and devoted care involved in its modest creation.[53]

In his study of nineteenth-century American gentility, Richard Bushman notes that refinement was associated with the city and with an "exalted society of superior beings", and that the difficulty of combining gentility with comfort was also an issue.[54] He argues that, as capitalism encouraged consumption and hence access to genteel culture increased, the sense of class distinctions became confused in American society. It seems to me that Jewett is intervening in this cultural phenomenon. She was not confused about class: she understood the limits to mobility and access, and recognized the nation's profound social inequalities. Hers is not a nostalgic ruralism, but a would-be utopian critique of this new industrial capitalist social order. Among her fiction are tales where, through the device of the visit, rural working people encounter the lives of the socially advantaged. These explore rituals of gentility and sociability, redefine comfort, sincerity and refinement, and open up the conventionally private to the public. In so doing the visit takes on wider meanings for community and nation.

"Martha's Lady" (1897/9) centers on a new, gauche servant from a "stony hill farm", who learns the fine mannered ways of a traditional upper-class house in a New England small town through the intervention of her mistress' visitor from Boston, a delightful, kind, young cousin, Miss Helena.[55] The servant, Martha, indeed, learns not so much her mistress' stuffy formalities, but the beautiful, generous,

---

[52] Richard L. Bushman, *The Refinement of America: Persons, Houses, Cities*, New York: Alfred A. Knopf, 1992.

[53] See *ibid.*, 251-52, 264-67. See also Katherine C. Grier, *Culture and Comfort: Parlor Making and Middle-class Identity, 1850-1930*, rev. edn, Washington, DC: Smithsonian Institution Press, 1988, and Jack Larkin, *The Reshaping of Everyday Life, 1790-1840*, New York: Harper Row, 1988, 122-26.

[54] Bushman, *The Refinement of America*, xix.

[55] Sarah Orne Jewett, "Martha's Lady" (1897/9).

affectionate hospitality of her charming younger guest. Forty years later, this guest, after marriage, life abroad, and widowhood, returns to visit again, and, without being told, realizes that Martha has remembered her with silent, enduring love and has followed her teachings with profound devotion all these long years apart.[56]

Early in the tale Martha's mistress states that a maidservant is essential when one has guests, but this is later revised in descriptions of how Martha, adopting the refinement of the gentry of a previous age, gradually determines that the household will be run daily in unusually beautiful, stately ways, so that, though remaining always in service, she becomes a little like the house's hostess. The tale offers an image of a more satisfying life than that of either poverty-strained hill farms or middle-class withdrawal and stasis. In finding her love object in a higher-class woman, figured as a friend, the protagonist discovers imagined access to something beyond basic daily housekeeping. This love is utterly private (readers alone see her twice in her bedroom quietly contemplating her souvenirs of Helena), and is given public expression only in the way she runs the house as Helena had shown her. Her devotion bestows dignity, not servility. This would be a disturbingly sentimental conclusion on Jewett's part but for the visibility that this tale (and others by Jewett) gives to Martha's work as a servant, and the clear recognition that class differences are never actually transcended.[57]

The tale explores perfect hospitality, politeness, and self-forgetfulness, and disengages from the fashionable opposition

---

[56] "The Queen's Twin" (1899), another important contemporary tale by Jewett, though very different in tone (it is a comedy), shares important themes with "Martha's Lady": the hostess of lower social status than her guests, a higher class love object, glimpses of refinement, the idea of hospitality, and a sense of the tale having meanings beyond impoverished rural Maine.

[57] Intense debate about servants by magazines and academics reached its height in the Gilded Age where being a lady was predicated on having domestic servants. See Daniel E. Sutherland, *Americans and Their Servants: Domestic Service in the United States from 1800 to 1920*, Baton Rouge: Louisiana State UP, 1981. Jewett makes an interestingly confusing comment: "Nobody must say that Martha is dull, it is only I (letter 64, 1911) – objecting to privileged readers' possible boredom with the lives of servants, reminding readers that this servant's characterization is limited by her creator's powers to imagine and express her, and possibly hinting at some projection onto or identification with Martha on Jewett's part. Note also the language of Jewett's will (see *The Sarah Orne Jewett Text Project*), where she left $1000 to one servant "in remembrance of his faithful friendship and service to my family and me".

between comfort and gentility that historically was a dilemma of social aspiration. The importance of being welcomed is emphasized: "The beautiful old house stood wide-open to the long-expected guest." Visitors are treated with a ceremoniousness that honors but does not distance (this is not the bourgeois paradigm of Mrs Timms and her guests), and the visitors play their part understanding their hostess (Helena puts into words what her aunt's maid has felt and believed). Moreover, this "fine art of housekeeping" is given broader significance, reaching beyond both the domestic realm and minor New England townships – this narrative, spanning forty years, explicitly comments on aspects of the social, political, and moral evolution of the nation through the nineteenth century. The tale starts with images of opening to a wider world: the initial image of "chairs placed near together" in the front yard invokes past hospitality when the family's grandfather quoted Dr Johnson to his daughters: "'be brisk, be splendid, and be public.'" The tale proceeds to contrast this with a mid-nineteenth-century narrowing of sympathies, an over-emphasis on discretion and status, and a "provincialism and prejudice" that denied beauty and hardened "open mind and affectionate heart".

Charlene Avallone traces a female-authored model of reformed social relations earlier in nineteenth-century America based on sociable conversations, independent of money market and political parties.[58] This conversational culture – tea-talk rather than the protocols of formal visiting – sought to extend the practices of private society into public institutions, offering an alternative model to andocentric culture. Constituted by a utopian discourse of "nurturance, mutual exchange, pleasure, and shared resources", this social functioned as a synecdoche of national social formation as well as a metonym of female power.[59]

In order to imagine this kind of sociability, Jewett's tales blur the distinction between public and private – a distinction that only the reasonably well-to-do could maintain and which Jewett refuses. However, although the deeply moved Miss Helena asks to be kissed goodnight by Martha at her story's end, Jewett's depiction of such a

---

[58] Charlene Avallone, "Catharine Sedgwick and the Circles of New York", *Legacy*, XXIII/2 (2006), 115-31.

[59] Charlene Avallone notes, in e-mail correspondence with the author, 8 August 2006, that most of the nineteenth-century writers envisaging this kind of social interaction were more interested than Jewett in maintaining social hierarchies.

friendship underlines the permanence of class difference (something that, despite Annie Fields' best efforts, her charity work and her manual had confirmed). This visiting is, then, recognized by Jewett as a model of how social relations should, but do not, exist in Gilded Age America, and can therefore only be glimpsed as an alternative to the realities of a grossly unequal nation where socially maintained distinctions between public and private merely served to perpetuate divisions.

PART II

STEPPING OUT: BODIES, SPACES AND THE CULTURAL REPRESENTATION OF VISIBILITY

NEGOTIATING VISIBILITY:
LOUISA MAY ALCOTT'S NARRATIVE EXPERIMENTS

LINDSEY TRAUB

> "Oh, oh, Jo! You ain't going to wear that awful hat? It's too absurd! You shall *not* make a guy of yourself," remonstrated Meg.
> "I just will though! It's capital; so shady, light and big. It will make fun; and I don't mind being a guy, if I'm comfortable."[1]

> A woman ... is almost continually accompanied by her own image of herself .... From earliest childhood she has been taught and persuaded to survey herself continually .... She has to survey everything she is and everything she does because how she appears to others, and ultimately how she appears to men, is of crucial importance for what is normally thought of as the success of her life. Her own sense of being in herself is supplanted by a sense of being appreciated as herself by another.[2]

Louisa May Alcott's fiction shows how she understood that the visibility of women is not just an issue of public versus private, nor of external observation only, but involves, for the individual woman, simultaneous processes of self-surveillance and self-construction. In her writing for both adults and children she adopted strategies that explore the implications of these processes, while at the same time becoming one of America's best selling authors throughout a hundred and fifty years of social and cultural change. From her own subject position – white and middle-class – Alcott illustrated how, in the

---

[1] Louisa May Alcott, *Little Women,* (1868), ed. Elaine Showalter, New York: Penguin Books, 1989, 123.
[2] John Berger, *Ways of Seeing,* Harmondsworth: Penguin, 1972, 46.

evolution of women's cultural presence, a personal innovation or discovery, however small, can effect the penetration of a cultural site, an intervention in the cultural status quo. For the conscious and self-directed woman – as Jo March becomes in *Little Women* – such interventions might be exhilarating (as well as frightening), an opportunity for self-expression or the performance of change. For a self that is constructed of internalized prescriptions, such as her sister Meg's, exposure to the authority of cultural assumptions and possible censure must have been experienced as painful risk. However, if the risk were taken and survived, as they were by Polly in *An Old-fashioned Girl* and Christie in *Work*, then that *status quo* might, however gradually, be modified. In this essay, by focusing upon four consecutive but very different novels by Louisa May Alcott, *Moods* (1864), *Little Women* (1868), *An Old-fashioned Girl* (1870) and *Work: A Story of Experience* (1873), I hope to suggest something of the development of Alcott's understanding of the significance of visibility and its relation to agency and cultural change, from the end of the Civil War into the Gilded Age.

Louisa Alcott was herself peculiarly well placed to perceive and to interpret aspects of the development of American women's cultural presence in this period, since her own experience involved crisscrossing class and cultural boundaries. She was born in 1832 and brought up mainly in Concord, the daughter of Bronson and Abigail ("Abba") May Alcott. Her father was a key member of the Transcendentalist circle, a close friend and protégé of Ralph Waldo Emerson. In the Alcott household however (and they were not alone in this), the radical exhortations of Transcendentalism to self-reliance, self-culture and self-analysis were subtly adulterated by a simultaneous insistence on feminine self-control and self-effacement. Thus the mixed message Louisa received from earliest childhood was an imbrication of radicalism and conservatism.

The Alcotts also experienced extreme poverty, in spite of their prosperous family and social connections. Abba May Alcott had sacrificed social standing and domestic comfort to Bronson's indigent intellectualism. She and her daughters, Anna and Louisa, were forced by necessity to work for money, with their hands and their heads, inside and outside their home. So, while Louisa's fiction presents employment as a known and precarious reality, it is also suffused with reference to occluded social status and an acquaintance with leisure and high culture, in spite of an absence of income. She dreamed of and relished success, enjoyed her creativity and her celebrity as an increasingly high profile author, and actively supported women's causes, but protested to the last that she wanted above all to be a good daughter.

From her first sensation thrillers onwards, Alcott's work shows recognition that, through internalization and continuous modification of the effect of their visibility, women can sometimes exert a degree of control over it. In these early thrillers, published anonymously in non-literary magazines like *Frank Leslie's Illustrated Newspaper* and *The Flag of Our Union*, the gleeful irony surrounding the parade of actresses and adventuresses who court and survive self-exposure suggests an imagination free from the restraints of feminine literary propriety. Alcott's assurance and ingenuity in handling the material and mechanics of the genre are the more extraordinary, given that it was her first resort to writing fiction that would be successful. That she would continue to write and publish those stories while working on the more prescribed pieces for *The Atlantic Monthly*, the experimental *Hospital Sketches* (1863) and *Success* (begun in the early 1860s but only published, in 1873, as *Work: A Story of Experience*), the tentative *Moods* and the ultimately triumphant *Little Women* demonstrates the complex relationship between her knowledge, her imagination and her literary performance.

The effect of beauty, primarily on men and used consciously to secure the heroine's ends, is the most obvious – and spirited – deployment of women's visible social power in many of her early stories. There are several variations on the manipulations of Pauline in the early "Pauline's Passion and Punishment" (1863):

> "Manuel, am I beautiful tonight?"
> "How can you be otherwise to me?"
> "That is not enough. I must look my fairest to others, brilliant and blithe, a happy-hearted bride whose honeymoon is not yet over."[3]

But from as early as "A Whisper in the Dark", Alcott suggests that a woman's relationship with her appearance is a complicated

---

[3] Louisa May Alcott, "Pauline's Passion and Punishment" (1863), rpt. in *Louisa May Alcott Unmasked: Collected Thrillers*, ed. Madeline Stern, Athens: U of Georgia P, 1995, 9.

ontological process, with subtle ramifications in the formation and expression of the individual female self. The very young heroine is shown viewing herself as a pleasing object, to which she responds with candor rather than conventional modesty:

> I surveyed myself in the long mirror as I had never done before, and saw there a little figure, slender, yet stately ... ornamented with lace and carnation ribbons which enhanced the fairness of neck and arms, while blond hair, wavy and golden, was gathered into an antique knot of curls behind, with a carnation fillet, and below a blooming dark-eyed face, just then radiant with girlish vanity and eagerness and hope.
> "I'm glad I'm pretty!" [4]

Using the first person, Alcott dramatizes the moment at which the young woman first learns to objectify herself, by analyzing her reflection in a mirror "as I had never done before". What she sees, however, she records impersonally: "*the* fairness of neck and arms ... *a* blooming dark-eyed face" – the absence of the personal pronoun "my" severs image from self. The objectivity of the self-survey establishes her prettiness as a welcome fact, which, derived from a mirror reflection, enables her to visualize what others will see when they look at her. The very expression, "appearance", and the question, "How do I look?" refer to being seen by another, not to appearing or looking in any active sense. The reflection of herself in the "look" of others is essential to Sybil's control of a situation, or loss of it. When she is kidnapped and held against her will, deprived of both human company and a mirror, the absence of an image of her own face is the most disorienting experience of all. In the same year, "A Pair of Eyes" is remarkable, even among Alcott's many other experiments with "looking", since within its narrative the dominant gender relation in the process of "looking" is reversed when the male first person narrator finds himself in the power of a woman's relentless and manipulative gaze.[5]

Conscious control of their visibility gives Alcott's thriller heroines rich opportunities within her inventive and transgressive plotting.

---

[4] Louisa May Alcott, "A Whisper in the Dark" (1863), rpt. in *Louisa May Alcott Unmasked: Collected Thrillers*, 4.
[5] Louisa May Alcott, "A Pair of Eyes" (1863), rpt. in *Louisa May Alcott Unmasked: Collected Thrillers*, 59-81.

However, the kind of exploration of female sexual and social power afforded by the conventions of melodrama and gothic fable was only feasible under the literary conditions peculiar to these genres. The material was established as exotic and the conventions distanced the content from any suggestion of reader emulation or moral sanction. But realism, the ascendant form in nineteenth-century fiction, and middle-class domestic realism in particular could not readily accommodate the sort of fantasies and revelations that Alcott offered in her sensation writing. Increasingly, successful literary fiction offered a picture of real contemporary life and Louisa Alcott worked at such fiction even while she mastered and then abandoned its denigrated alternative.

Alcott's domestic realism illustrates the subtlety and complexity of women's relation to and experience of their visibility, as part of her exploration and literary validation of female subjectivity. Nancy Armstrong has argued that in this period of social flux and mobility – the long nineteenth century – the household emerges as a locus of power and interest in fiction, where social status is loosely implied as middle-class, rejecting earlier aristocratic models and set in absolute definition against working-class deprivation. Within this domestic theatre the domestic woman performs, her body, according to Armstrong, used neither in aristocratic display, nor for working-class labor, whilst her inner life and moral development assume prime importance.[6] The admission of a necessity for hard domestic work into the lives of both the Alcotts and *Little Women*'s March family, who most resemble the Alcotts, was manipulated in such a way that the possible implication that the families become déclassé was trumped by the implication that, rather, their conduct under such duress underlined their status as gentlewomen. Physical labor is an unexpected burden, to be borne for the opportunity it provided for a display of moral courage.

Alcott, then, draws upon her own cultural education to depict the promotion, within a domestic context, of a significant and scrutinized inner life with emotional and physical self-effacement effecting, simultaneously, the relocation and control of a woman's potential. Almost needless to say, a prescriptive effacement of the female body only signals an increased cultural interest in and concern about its

---

[6] Nancy Armstrong, *Desire and Domestic Fiction: A Political History of the Novel*, Oxford: Oxford UP, 1987, 76.

significance and its activities. With the interesting exception of *Moods*, much of Alcott's fiction illustrates how the inner lives of her characters are engaged in monitoring their own spiritual progress in conjunction with their visible behavior, as a combined expression of not only their moral health but also the concomitant quality of their social standing.

Louisa Alcott's first full-length novel, *Moods*, challenges self-effacement while exposing the risks involved in attempting self-realization. She worked on it intermittently from 1860 to the autumn of 1864, when it was eventually published. Her journal suggests it was a mixed experience of frustration and satisfaction, in marked contrast to the facility and amusement with which she concurrently produced and published her lucrative thrillers. It is arguable that, while the stylized and playful conventions of gothic fiction were liberating for a lively critical imagination, those of domestic fiction were confined by the same propriety that circumscribed the life it drew upon. The awkward but revealing novel Alcott finally produced is about sexual confusion and unhappy marriage, though, perhaps tellingly, she was later to deny that this was her intention. She dramatizes the complex tensions surrounding the social presence of a naïve young woman, her coming to consciousness and descent into a moral and sexual impasse. The problems of visibility that Alcott cloaked in theatricality in her melodramas are painfully exposed and explored in *Moods*.

In her telling of the girlhood, courtship and marriage of Sylvia Yule, Alcott presents the tragic consequences of a young woman's unconsciousness of her visibility. The men who fall in love with her in effect trespass, as it were, into intimacy with her across a field of vision unguarded by self-visualization. An early scene is one of the most significant in this respect. Seventeen-year-old Sylvia, rebelling against pursuits like dress fittings, piano lessons, and morning calls, prefers her own company, the run of a good library, and working in the garden of her comfortable, semi-rural family home. She is busy with this last activity when Geoffrey Moor, an older family friend, calls on the family unannounced. Looking out of the window he sees "a slender boy, in a foreign-looking blouse of grey linen; a white collar lay over a ribbon at the throat, stout halfboots covered a trim pair of feet, and a broad-brimmed hat flapped low on the forehead". When the "boy" pulls off the hat to fan "his" face, Moor is startled to see it is Sylvia:

> Holding the curtain between the window and himself, Moor peeped through the semi-transparent screen, enjoying the little episode immensely. Sylvia fanned and rested a few minutes, then went up and down among the flowers, often pausing to break a dead leaf, to brush away some harmful insect, or lift some struggling plant into the light; moving among them as if akin to them and cognizant of their sweet wants. If she had seemed strong-armed and sturdy as a boy before, now she was tender fingered as a woman, and went humming here and there like any happy-hearted bee.
>
> "Curious child!" thought Moor, watching the sunshine glitter on her uncovered head, and listening to the air she left half sung. "I've a great desire to step out and see how she will receive me. Not like any other girl, I fancy."

This extraordinary scene, where a young woman is watched unawares, is of course redolent of Eve and Persephone. The references are unmistakable: innocent, alone, at one with nature – and fatally endangered by the watcher. It also recalls Susanna and Bathsheba, betrayed by voyeurs. But this is contemporary nineteenth-century America, and the victim, while intensely feminine, is presented as androgynous and to be apostrophized as "Curious child!"

What is Alcott doing? She offers Sylvia as an admirably charming sight, with her "trim" feet and tender fingers, a "happy-hearted bee". At the same time privacy, androgyny and immaturity not only do not protect her but seem to combine to make her irresistible to Moor. The invitation to the reader to admire Sylvia's charm proposes that it is healthy, while the direction of the references signals something more sinister. Indeed the text continues: "But before he could execute his design, the roll of a carriage was heard in the avenue, and pausing an instant, *with head erect like a startled doe*, Sylvia turned and vanished, dropping flowers as she ran".[7] Sylvia's unconsciousness and her doe-like flight identify her as prey.

This double message is more than merely the sign of an unresolved ambivalence on Alcott's part. It also demonstrates what the book goes on to explore: that a woman who is not conscious or in control of her own visibility is vulnerable. In the early chapters of the novel Alcott stresses Sylvia's "innocent unconsciousness", while displaying her as

---

[7] Louisa May Alcott, *Moods* (1864), ed. with an introduction by Sarah Elbert, New Brunswick, NJ: Rutgers UP, 1991, 21 (emphasis added).

others see her (in the case of this extract, Geoffrey Moor): "Figure, posture, and employment were so childlike in their innocent unconsciousness, that the contrast was all the more strongly marked between them and the sweet thoughtfulness that made her face singularly attractive with the charm of dawning womanhood."[8] Relationships develop, subsequently, on a river camping trip, on which Sylvia is allowed to accompany her brother Mark, Geoffrey Moor, and a friend of Moor's, a powerful, lone wolf figure, Adam Warwick. The adult men watch her constantly, and Alcott describes in detail what they see. Although she is barely conscious of their attention, Sylvia warms to them both in her declared search for a man to be "a friend", in preference to the unreliability of "love" – "because men go where they like, see things with their own eyes".[9]

Both men fall in love with her, and though Moor articulates his feelings on their return home, she finds it is Warwick with whom she shares a silent but powerful attraction. At the same time she develops an interest in her appearance, asking her more worldly sister if she is pretty and being told in reply:

> "Now I think everyone finds you very attractive because you try to please. ..."
>
> Sylvia had never asked that question before ... she went away to make a lampless toilet in the dusk, which proved how slight a hold the feminine passion for making one's self pretty had yet taken upon her.[10]

Sylvia is not shown to objectify her visibility, once aware of it, nor to exercise control over how she is seen by the man to whom she is drawn. Indeed, Warwick disappears from the scene, to disentangle himself from a repented engagement to a Cuban beauty ("Pauline's Passion" rewritten, as it were). Sylvia marries Moor by default, persuading herself that quieter emotions will suit her best. Renewed but belated contact with Warwick produces an anguish that brings on depression within her passionless marriage. Talking in her sleep, she alerts her husband to her trouble and confesses her true love. Finally, though gentle and civilized, Moor's courtship and marriage to Sylvia

---

[8] *Ibid.*, 23.
[9] *Ibid.*, 25.
[10] *Ibid.*, 75.

are acknowledged as predatory, even by himself. He understands that he took advantage of her immaturity: "'I should have known it, and left you to the safe and simple joys of girlhood. Forgive me that I have kept you a prisoner so long; take off the fetter I put on, and go, Sylvia.'"[11] Since that is not really an option for a mid-century wife, Moor leaves instead, traveling to Europe, joined by Warwick, who is drowned saving Moor's life in a shipwreck. Moor returns home to find Sylvia terminally ill. She dies in his arms as the novel ends.

Summarizing the plot of the novel in this way emphasizes its implausible mechanics, but their function is to break the intense moral impasse created by the fictional themes. This is a serious problem for Alcott because the dilemma and suffering she evokes for both Sylvia and Moor are intense. Sylvia has attempted "being in herself", to use John Berger's phrase, and found it to be dangerous. She is not, in Nancy Armstrong's sense, "a domestic woman" because she finds it impossible to comply with the prescription that Armstrong identifies for that figure, which Alcott went on to make central to the lives of the March sisters in *Little Women*: "The domestic woman executes her role in the household by regulating her own desire."[12]

In *Moods*, Alcott did not reconcile the demands of her provocative subject and the treatment of it available to her as a novice realist attempting to present difficult, intimate experience. The taboo nature of the material was such as to render narrative candor and transparency unworkable, creating distortions in the plot. Richard Brodhead has argued in his discussion of Alcott's relations with *The Atlantic Monthly* and its effect on her subsequent career that soon after writing *Moods*, she gave up trying to satisfy the literary conditions of *The Atlantic Monthly* and moved from an exploratory to a more didactic mode.[13] Four years later, in *Little Women*, Alcott had developed a narrative method that gave her continuous control over reader-reception of her topical, sensitive, though less shocking material. Susan K. Harris, in writing about *Work*, aptly describes the

---

[11] *Ibid.*, 70.

[12] Armstrong, *Desire and Domestic Fiction*, 81.

[13] Richard H. Brodhead, *Cultures of Letters: Scenes of Reading and Writing in Nineteenth-century America*, Chicago: U of Chicago P, 1993, 79-89.

technique: "the narrator … continually monitors her narratee's interpretations."[14]

With the history of the March family, Alcott returned to the fiercely contested cultural site of transition from girlhood to womanhood, with its own familiar, diverse discourse. The contribution of her work to this discourse, that was so deeply concerned with the evolution of women's visibility and cultural presence, was so influential that the books have remained continuously in print for the best part of a hundred and fifty years. The domestic realism of *Little Women* certainly teaches self-regulation but its advocacy of the examined inner life is always humane. Though its family resemblance to an advice or conduct book has been well noted,[15] the writing has an engaging naturalness, based on Alcott's own reminiscence of girlhood.

The March girls begin their saga at home, in genteel poverty like the Alcotts', enjoying what Geoffrey Moor in *Moods* called "the safe and simple joys of girlhood". Home is a place for preparation and reflection from which, in the case of Meg and Jo, to set out to work in other people's homes. It is also a space for rehearsal of the skills needed before being what the sophisticated Belle Moffat calls "out". Though it is no part of their parents' plan for the girls to be out in society, the expression is significant in identifying a key element in the transition from child to woman – becoming visible. To be out is no longer to be sheltered by the seclusion of home, or the protection of family gatherings. But it signifies more than a private/public dichotomy.

To be out is to be placed in full view, looked at, sized up, responsible for one's own behavior and available for marriage. The March girls might scorn to be associated with such an expression, but at "Vanity Fair", in the Moffats' house, Meg discovers painfully different ways in which she can be seen and her appearance can be interpreted by others. The overt lesson is about personal vanity and narcissism, but the story also serves as one of Alcott's many warnings

---

[14] Susan K. Harris, *Nineteenth-century American Women's Novels: Interpretive Strategies*, Cambridge: Cambridge UP, 1990, 175.

[15] See, for example, Sarah Klein, "Bringing up Jo: *Little Women*, Female Rhetorical Activity and the Nineteenth-century American Conduct Book Tradition", in *Domestic Goddesses*, ed. Kim Wells: http://www.womenwriters.net/domesticgoddess/klein alcott.htm.

about the significance of visible performance. Meg, the innocent sixteen-year-old in her shabby white dress, is unconscious of her ability to please and satisfy a certain kind of morally authoritative onlooker. She thus penetrates the cultural site of the Moffats' two parties quite differently: as innocent Meg and subsequently as precocious Meg, a little figure in blue silk with tight boots, elaborate curls and earrings, dressed by her nouveau riche hostess. Overhearing disappointment and disapprobation, and on being rebuffed by Laurie, her friend and neighbor, she is introduced to the inescapable relationship between visibility and cultural authority.

The delicious risk involved in submitting herself to the Moffats' taste and judgment necessarily involves offence to others whose approbation she values even more, and with whom she realizes she identifies herself more closely. By letting Belle Moffat manipulate the quality of Meg's visibility according to her own cultural assumptions and expose her, momentarily, as if out, Meg learns why the experiment felt so exciting and dangerous, but made her so unhappy. It is not that Meg is not familiar with the idea of what is or is not proper – she is her sisters' monitor of simple propriety – but her experience demonstrates that propriety is a complexly nuanced and mutable process, not a monolithic moral entity.

It is this mutability of propriety and with it the possibility for cultural change that Alcott explores most effectively through the behavior of Jo, who is always "scandalizing Meg with her queer performances".[16] Alcott's repeated application of pressure on etiquette, the notions of the proper or essential femininity surrounding Jo, moves interestingly towards modernity. In *An Old-fashioned Girl*, Alcott was to take this technique further, applying it to the shape of the whole book. In *Little Women* it is Jo's "scrapes" and attitudes that pose questions which successive generations of readers responded to.

Jo whistles because it is boyish, is deeply disappointed not to be a boy and, if putting up her hair is the significant sign of being a young lady, then she declares she will "wear it in two tails till I'm twenty".[17] She can be visibly male in her own home-made dramas "to her heart's content" before an audience of girls in her home, where such performances are enjoyed and "no gentlemen were admitted".[18]

---

[16] Alcott, *Little Women*, 47.
[17] *Ibid.*, 3.
[18] *Ibid.*, 16.

Whatever else this androgyny implies, her boyishness is continuously used as a means of discriminating between false delicacy and healthy moral instincts, and frequently the tests are the outcome of some dilemma over a question of visibility. Early in the novel, for instance, Jo and Meg are invited to a private party where there will be dancing. Jo has spoiled her gloves with spilled lemonade but Meg cannot countenance her not dancing or dancing without gloves – "'gloves are more important than anything'".[19] Jo's response goes deeper: "'Then I'll go without. I don't care what people say.'" As they go to the party the sisters smile affectionately together over the importance to their mother of a clean handkerchief: "'It is one of her aristocratic tastes, and quite proper, for a real lady is always known by neat boots, gloves and handkerchief'", replied Meg, who had a good many little "aristocratic tastes" of her own.

These decidedly bourgeois "aristocratic tastes" are soon to be chastened in the course of Meg's development into the model domestic woman. Jo is more concerned with her need to keep the large burn in her dress (caused by her habit of standing with her back to the fire, like a gentleman) out of sight of the other guests. She is generally anxious about not doing the wrong thing and Meg promises to guide her with a code of raised eyebrows and nods (not winks, as Jo suggests).[20] In the event Jo has a hugely important evening making friends with Laurie, out of sight, hidden in a curtained recess, he from shyness, she to escape from the frustration of constraint placed on her because her visibility becomes so compromised by social errors. It is the antithesis of the traditional, romantic ballroom encounter, with roles reversed: "Laurie's bashfulness soon wore off, for Jo's gentlemanly demeanor amused and set him at his ease."[21]

The scene is also the antithetical pair to Meg's experience at the Moffats' ball that is still to come. Jo's "queer performances" have made it impossible for her to conform with the relatively simple social demands of the Gardiners' party – she has messed up her gloves and burned her dress and wants to talk to the young men on equal terms. Her visibility is an embarrassment to her sister, who tries to control her using the agreed visual signals. Meg's solution is to become invisible and in so doing she is able to establish one of the most

---

[19] *Ibid.*, 24.
[20] *Ibid.*, 26.
[21] *Ibid.*, 29.

significant relationships in the book, and on her own terms. In the course of the book she will learn how to control her visibility on terms she can accept, without significant loss of individual expression or innovation. Indeed, she first kisses the man who will become her husband in the street.[22] Meg, however, the conscientious conformer, finds herself out of her depth at the Moffats', when she fulfils a longing to conform to a cultural model that turns out to be unacceptable to those she most respects. She discovers that a dissonance between visibility and self-perception is not necessarily "queer" – her estimate of Jo – but can equally result from an inappropriate performance of femininity.

Laurie's devotion to Jo validates her unconventional behavior. The romantic male lead, with his almost feminine beauty and sensitivity, small feet, and shyness, is assigned to love the tomboy, whose small misdemeanors and eccentricities are repeatedly linked to dilemmas over how she will be seen. The sunhat he sends her horrifies Meg and she remonstrates: "'You shall not make a guy of yourself'", to which Jo replies: "'I just will though! It's capital; so shady, light, and big. It will make fun; and I don't mind being a guy, if I'm comfortable.'" The hat then "deserved a vote of thanks, for it was of general utility", a verdict making everyone laugh and relax, and easing a potentially awkward social moment.[23] Jo's integrity is thus established as robust and self-reliant, allied to a social sense that is more altruistic than self-regarding – the opposite of narcissistic, through this direct flouting of the rules of visible femininity.

However, this independence comes at a cost. In a corresponding scene much later in the book, Jo is subjected to the torture of morning calls with her youngest sister, Amy, and shows that she has learned to modify her behavior, though not always to order, in spite of a resigned conformity in appearance. Amy is a far more sophisticated being than the earlier teenage Meg and knows how to direct Jo's toilette to make her agreeable, because "'I want people to like you'",[24] thus recalling the social aesthetic of Sylvia's sister in *Moods*. After minute analysis of Jo's finished effect, Amy asks for her "best deportment". Jo promises to comply, having "played the part of a prim young lady on the stage". She is prim to immobility at the first house, relaxed to

---

[22] *Ibid.*, 480.
[23] *Ibid.*, 123.
[24] *Ibid.*, 288.

indiscretion at the second (but much liked and enjoyed by her audience), and left to her own devices at the third, where she ends up playing with the children in the garden.

The chapter develops a serious point, however, as Jo tries to persuade Amy not to fulfill the planned call on their Aunt March. Amy reminds her of the pleasure a formal call from her nieces "in style" will give the old lady – and family benefactor – and goes on: "'Women should learn to be agreeable, particularly poor ones; for they have no other way of repaying the kindnesses they receive.'"[25] They then disagree about the nature of influence and its relation to conscience in social relations. Amy is convinced that without wealth or position they have no influence over, for example, young men of whom they disapprove, so have no right to show their disapproval:

> "We should only be considered odd and Puritanical."
>
> "So we are to countenance things and people which we detest, merely because we are not belles or millionaires, are we? That's a nice sort of morality."
>
> "I can't argue about it, I only know it's the way of the world; and people who set themselves against it, only get laughed at for their pains. I don't like reformers, and hope you will never try to be one."
>
> "I do like them, and I shall be one if I can; for in spite of the laughing the world would never get on without them. We can't agree about that, for you belong to the old set, and I to the new; you will get on the best, but I shall have the liveliest time of it. I should rather enjoy the brickbats and hooting I think." [26]

This is an unprecedented social and political avowal by Jo, and Alcott's strong sense of the social reception of open non-conformity necessitates, if not a retraction, an unenviable consequence. Unfortunately, Jo is now tired and has lost self-control. The conversation in her Aunt's parlor goads her into angry candor: "'I don't like favors; they oppress and make me feel like a slave; I'd rather do everything for myself, and be perfectly independent.'" Thereby, as Alcott comments, "Jo deprived herself of several years of pleasure, and received a timely lesson in the art of holding her tongue".[27]

---

[25] *Ibid.*, 295.
[26] *Ibid.*, 296.
[27] *Ibid.*, 297.

Amy, the conservative who likes to please, is taken to Europe, and Jo is punished by being left behind – though she does not thereby lose the reader's sympathy and respect. Most importantly, Alcott has firmly connected Jo's non-conformity with reform and the future, in direct contrast to Amy's assumptions about female compliance and expectation of dependence. So, at the conclusion of the novel, even as Jo shares ecstatically in the mutual revelation of love with Friedrich Bhaer, Alcott establishes a crucial compromise with domesticity. Wiping away her lover's tears of joy and relieving him of some of his parcels (they have encountered each other out shopping in the rain), Jo neatly combines familiar characteristics and adages of the feminine, past and future, by declaring:

> "I may be strong-minded, but no-one can say I'm out of my sphere now, – for woman's special mission is supposed to be drying tears and bearing burdens. I'm to carry my share, Friedrich, and help to earn the home. Make up your mind to that."[28]

In *Little Women* Alcott was able simultaneously to challenge and reassure her readership within a seamless narrative. Over the following two years, in producing *An Old-fashioned Girl* she developed this combination rather differently, by appearing to write one kind of book which turned into quite another. With her insistence that her little heroine's quiet country upbringing and reactions are old-fashioned, in contrast to the brash behavior of her urban nouveau riche friends, Alcott apparently recruits a conservative readership. Throughout the novel Alcott draws attention to the moral significance of visibility, as the Shaws and their friends flaunt their wealth in the elaborate costumes of their young women and children, while these pursue meaningless or inappropriate relationships and brittle courtships. But while they embody a highly visible and unhealthy aspect of contemporary social life at the beginning of the Gilded Age, it is Polly, the modestly dressed, "old-fashioned girl" who comes to represent Alcott's vision of the future. For, in the second half of the book (originally published as a sequel), Polly insists on earning her own living as a free-lance music teacher, renting a room in lodgings, and going about the streets to her pupils' homes, sometimes snubbed

---

[28] *Ibid.*, 480.

by the rich friends of her friends and sometimes acknowledged with warmth.

Having firmly established Polly's moral superiority, Alcott goes on to give her freedom to ally herself with women of the future. The first of these is Miss Mills, Polly's landlady, an elderly Boston reformer and friend to the poor. To her Polly confides her discomfiture at trying to discuss serious, social subjects with the rich and thoughtless girls in Fanny Shaw's sewing circle:

> "They call me old-fashioned now, and I'd rather be thought that, though it isn't pleasant, than be set down as a rampant women's rights reformer," said Polly ....
> "I'm not a 'rampant women's rights reformer,'" [said] Miss Mills. ... "but I think that women can do a great deal for each other if they will only stop fearing what 'people will think' and take a hearty interest in whatever is going to fit their sisters and themselves to deserve and enjoy the rights God gave them .... I don't ask you to go and make speeches, only a few have the gift for that, but I do want every girl and woman to feel this duty." [29]

That Polly calls her "women's rights reformer" "rampant" suggests the extreme and unwelcome visibility of this figure in Polly's perception. Miss Mills reclaims the reformer by first dissociating herself from Polly's clichéd version and then identifying herself with another, subtler one. She recognizes that Polly's distaste centers on "mak[ing] speeches", but instead of deprecating this iconic activity of the women's movement as undesirable for Polly, Miss Mills valorizes it by claiming that it requires special talent – indeed a "gift" – that Polly does not possess.

Polly's other new friends are self-supporting female artists, through whom Alcott energetically promotes the idea of an independent way of life for women. In the shared studio, "Art, morals, politics, society, books, religion, housekeeping, dress, and economy" are discussed "with feminine enthusiasm and frankness", whilst Polly "suck[ed] on her orange in public with a composure that would have scandalized the good ladies of Cranford". Fanny Shaw, Polly's rich, materialistic guest, is deeply impressed when Polly introduces her to these young women, thinking to herself: "'Men must respect such

---

[29] Louisa May Alcott, *An Old-fashioned Girl* (1870), New York: Puffin Books, 1991, 194.

girls as these .... Yes, and love them, too, for in spite of their independence they are womanly.'"[30] In practice, the friends are making visible their own version of womanliness and embodying their ideal, both in their own lives and through the work of one of them, Rebecca the sculptress. She is a professionally creative woman, working on the statue of a female figure, the outcome of a discussion between the friends about "the coming woman". Polly shows it proudly to Fanny: "'There she is, as you say, bigger, lovelier and more imposing than any we see nowadays, and at the same time, she is a true woman.'"[31]

Alcott underscores the parallel processes of embodiment at work in this scene by moving away from the statue to the living young women who are looking at and interpreting it: "For a minute the five young women sat silent, looking up at the beautiful figure before them ... each unconscious that she was helping, by her individual effort and experience, to bring the day when their noblest idea of womanhood should be embodied in flesh and blood, not clay."[32] The friends disagree about what the statue should hold in her hand "as the most appropriate symbol". The sculptress rejects a scepter ("'the kingdom given them isn't worth ruling'"), a man's hand ("'my woman is to stand alone and help herself'"), and a child ("'she is to be something more than a nurse'"), and finally agrees that the ballot box should be laid at her feet, along with a needle, pen, palette and broom to represent the range of her talents. The familiar and culturally circumscribed phrase, "true woman", is appropriated by Alcott and contextually transposed to show its openness to reinterpretation.

Such an obvious symbolic figure and such explicit responses would have been unthinkable in *Little Women*, least of all one rejecting so blatantly the familiar icons of the female in the name of the "true woman". Though Alcott had drawn her readers' attention to the significance of individual visibility and even suggested its potential relation to cultural change, *Little Women*'s narrative ultimately presents the home circle as the most rewarding arena for her heroines to enact their lives. *An Old-fashioned Girl* by contrast, a novel that initially presented itself as a reactionary moral tale, ends by radically undermining that traditional recommendation, as Alcott

---

[30] *Ibid.*, 244-45.
[31] *Ibid.*, 240.
[32] *Ibid.*, 246.

addressed her audience with the agency of one who knows she is listened to:

> There is a good deal more of this sort of silent suffering than the world suspects, for the "women who dare" are few, the women who "stand and wait" are many. For women often sew the tragedy or comedy of life into their work as they sit, apparently safe and serene at home, yet thinking deeply, living whole heart histories and praying fervent prayers while they embroider pretty trifles or do the weekly mending.[33]

This painful and unwilling invisibility – indeed home itself – was exactly what the next Alcott heroine, Christie Devon in *Work: A Story of Experience* (serialized 1872, published 1873), rejected at the very opening of her novel, in her determination to join the working world. However, *Work* is not a record of working-class experience and Christie is not a working-class girl. The book is an exhortation to women not to fear independence but be prepared to find fulfillment and active self-reliance through paid work, which may be humdrum and arduous, but is not morally inferior to the financial dependence of marriage. Though an orphan and not rich, Christie is tenacious of her status as a gentlewoman. Her rebellious decision to leave home on the farm is underpinned by the middle-class luxury of financial choice. Raised in security, Christie rejects dependence on her grudging uncle or on a loveless marriage. Never having been in want, Christie sees self-supporting work, away from home, as the way to spiritual fulfillment and psychological health: "I'm willing to work, but I want work that I can put my heart into, and feel that it does me good, no matter how hard it is. I only ask for a chance to be a useful and happy woman".[34]

However, though decidedly one of the "few" who "dare", Christie finds there is no easy way through or out of the world in which the many are living from sheer necessity. She endures insult, privation, and despair to the point of contemplating suicide, but not outright squalor. Though she does not experience "the fatigue and publicity of a shop",[35] this Alcott heroine involves herself with the extreme

---

[33] *Ibid.*, 332.
[34] Louisa May Alcott, *Work: A Story of Experience* (1873), ed. with an Introduction by Joy S. Kasson, New York: Penguin Books, 1994, 11.
[35] *Ibid.*, 23.

visibility of acting on the public stage and with the tragic invisibility of a seamstress and a fallen woman. Love, marriage, widowhood, and motherhood, though fully treated, are only incidents in her life. Interestingly, though Christie's responses and actions are expressed in detail, there is little attention drawn, on the part of the narrator and Christie herself, to how she appears to others. It is as if her self-liberating act has released her from the impotence of being interpreted by others through her appearance. Perhaps in the phrase of Polly's friend, Miss Mills and like Jo March, she has stopped "fearing what 'people will think'", and so left behind concern over visual clues and nuances central to Meg's class anxiety. She knows who she is, under a series of disguises and, especially as an actress, she maintains her integrity from within.

Christie's work fleshes out Alcott's enlarged conception of "the true woman" as she illustrated it in *An Old-fashioned Girl*. Even her spell in the theatre is described in terms of just another job, among ordinary hard-working people; it is the danger of insincerity and narcissism, not cruder forms of immorality, that makes her give it up. There is no suggestion of challenge to male activities and the book is not about equal opportunities or the frustration of major talents. Its didactic emphasis is on the building of inner strength, dignity and self-confidence, through work already available to women. *Work* is a fiction with the positive agenda of supporting the emergence of a young woman from conventional seclusion and dependence into various forms of visible activity in nineteenth-century urban culture. But occasionally it also offers unselfconscious insight into and expression of the fears and sensibilities of women like Alcott who found themselves, through taking up paid work, on the class borderlines of expanding, democratic America:

> There are many Christies, willing to work, yet *unable to bear the contact with coarser natures* which makes labor seem degrading, or to endure the hard struggle for the bare necessities of life when life has lost all that makes it beautiful. People wonder when such as she say they can find little to do; but to those who know nothing of the pangs of pride, the sacrifices of feeling, the martyrdoms of youth, love, hope, and ambition that go on under the faded cloaks of these poor gentlewomen, who tell them to go into factories, or scrub in kitchens,

for there is work enough for all, the most convincing answer would be, "Try it." [36]

Work is not an angry book like, say, Fanny Fern's *Ruth Hall,* and it has quite different interests. But its class and cultural values are sometimes sharply articulated, with a revealingly essentialist quality underpinning its sense of class difference and with a more personal slant brought to the politics of race. The abolitionist Alcott (alias Christie Devon) is honored to work as a maid-of-all-work with a black cook, Hepsey, once a runaway slave. Christie is deeply moved by Hepsey's experiences and her dream of saving money to free her family. However, Alcott/Christie draws the line at working with Irish women, who, she claims, would scorn to work with black women. She assures her prospective employer: "'I have no objection to color, ma'am.' An expression of relief dawned upon Mrs. Stuart's countenance, for the black cook had been an insurmountable obstacle to all the Irish ladies who had applied."[37]

Nonetheless, the novel's conclusion, where friends assemble at Christie's plant nursery, unites those characters who have demonstrated self-reliance across the lines of class, color and age (no Irish included), in a utopian image of female co-operation and harmony. Christie's home is a place of work: not only domestic work but a thriving business that she runs with her husband and continues after his death. Her experiences on the borders of class and color have also been shown to give her a unique role to play in mediating between philanthropic gentlewomen and working-class women in urgent need of representation. However, this is a female world and there is no confrontation with male resistance – even the powerful male enablers have fallen into the background by the end. So, while offering lively descriptions of Christie's succession of working contexts and unsparing accounts of her suicidal despair and bereavement, Alcott is ultimately less concerned with accurate realism than with investing the experience of working with a high moral value, legitimizing and dignifying the growing presence of women in the labor force in postbellum American society. As Susan Harris concludes, "The truly radical emphasis of the novel lies in its advocacy of women's freedom to explore the world and to determine

---

[36] *Ibid.,* 117 (emphasis added).
[37] Alcott, *Work,* 19.

the shape of their own lives", though I also agree with her that, to temper this, "Rather than fighting for open job markets, in *Work* Alcott is trying to redefine women's possibilities and to lay the foundation for a society based on cooperation rather than competition, nurturance rather than manipulation".[38]

Louisa Alcott did not greatly extend these ideas in her subsequent fiction, though she continued actively to support women's causes until she died in 1888. But these four novels, the central work of her mid-career and probably her strongest, trace a remarkable trajectory in the presentation of the female subject and her relation to visibility. In just under a decade, from the Civil War to the recognizable beginning of the Gilded Age, the novels move from the anguished discovery that for a woman to be visible is to be vulnerable, to the representation – albeit idealized – of a self-reliant confidence, a woman "being in herself", who can negotiate openly and successfully, as Christie does, with domesticity and employment and with class and race and gender, without being misinterpreted.

---

[38] Harris, *Nineteenth-century American Women's Novels*, 175.

"PEOPLE WILL THINK YOU HAVE STRUCK AN ATTITUDE": FASHIONABLE SPACE IN EMMA DUNHAM KELLEY-HAWKINS'NOVELS

R.J. ELLIS

Halfway through her second novel, *Four Girls at Cottage City* (1895), Emma Dunham Kelley introduces a startling difference between what this novel has to say about the propriety of attending dances and dramas and the attitude advocated less than four years earlier by some of the characters in her first novel, *Megda* (1891). Whereas in *Megda* the balance had come down heavily against young adults' participation in or attendance at drama productions and dances, the four young female protagonists in *Four Girls at Cottage City* (Jessie, Allie, Vera, and Garnet) reach the conclusion that dramas are not necessarily dangerous to their moral health. Their debate is a pressing one, because the four girls are vacationing alone in Cottage City, a resort on the island of Martha's Vineyard, where entertainments and dance venues are thick upon the ground, yet are also good Christians, seeking to work out how they should behave in a resort finding its origins in an antebellum alcohol-free Methodist Camp Meeting Ground.[1] The young women are perhaps aware of Cottage City's sober origins (for example, they identify a Church they might attend at the first opportunity), yet they are also enticed by the resort's attractions and decisive when finding dancing and theater going permissible. This article sets out to explore why such a sharp change in attitude towards dancing and dramas occurs in Kelley's fiction between 1892 and 1895, and what trying to answer this question reveals about the process of stepping out in the late nineteenth century for young women.

A starting point for such an enquiry is to note the way in which the later novel, *Four Girls at Cottage City* deliberately invites comparison

---

[1] Dona Brown, *Inventing New England: Regional Tourism in the Nineteenth-century*, Washington, DC: Smithsonian Institute Press, 1995, 75-104.

between itself and *Megda*.[2] The passage in which *Cottage City*'s four protagonists countenance participation in promenading, band concerts, dance, and drama as legitimate social activities for Christians is closely followed by a surprising cross-reference between Kelley's two novels:

> "I have just discovered that this cottage [where the girls are vacationing] is the same described in 'Megda,' where she and 'Del' and 'Laurie' came that summer, and this is the very room they occupied." …
>
> "I've read that book," said Vera.
>
> "Which character did you like best?" asked Allie….
>
> "… *I* liked 'May' best," said Jessie, emphatically. "She was the bravest.…"
>
> … "Why, wait until you read the sequel to the book," said Vera, "perhaps 'May' will be married in that."
>
> "Is there a sequel to 'Megda,'" asked Allie.
>
> "Not yet, but there is going to be." [3]

On one level this is merely a species of advertisement, placed in *Four Girls at Cottage City* by Kelley, in order to announce an intended sequel to *Megda* that, so far as is known, was neither published nor even written. However, the conversation also operates self-reflexively. Though such reflexivity was common enough in fiction by the late nineteenth century, in this instance it seems to me to be particularly complex – a complexity sign-posted by the way it is so heavily underscored in the text: the four girls' discussion of *Megda* goes on for nearly a page and is quite out of line with the rest of the book.

Four Girls at Cottage City works broadly within the general expectations of the sentimental's "classic realist" mode and its

---

[2] See Emma Dunham Kelley, *Megda*, Boston: James H. Earle, 1891, and Emma Dunham Kelley-Hawkins, *Four Girls at Cottage City*, Boston: James H. Earle, 1898 (all subsequent references are to these editions, unless otherwise stated: *Four Girls at Cottage City* was published under the name Kelley-Hawkins and will be cited as such). Holly Jackson, in her article, "Mistaken Identity: What if a Novelist Celebrated as a Pioneer of African-American Women's Literature Turned Out Not to Be Black At All?", *The Boston Globe*, 20 February 2005 (http://www.boston.com/news/globe/ideas/articles/2005/02/20/mistaken_identity/), discovered that this 1898 edition is a reprint of a novel first published in 1895 (Providence, RI: Continental Printing Co.). Thanks are due to Alison Easton for her perspicacious suggestions.

[3] Kelley-Hawkins, *Four Girls at Cottage City*, 113-14.

maintenance of "illusionism", in Catherine Belsey and Colin MacCabe's words.[4] Kelley's insertion of a self-reflexive cross-reference between her two novels somewhat disrupts this general maintenance of realist illusion, instead drawing attention to the status of *Four Girls at Cottage City* as fiction. In part this move is prompted by a need for self-publicity on Kelley's behalf. Little is known about this author, though recently Holly Jackson claims to have uncovered evidence of Kelley's modest family background on Rhode Island.[5] Quite possibly, therefore, an important motive underlying Kelley's writing was to earn money – hence such self-publicity. Yet the author is also openly signaling that a fiction is being read and that its readers need to be aware of this. I think this is part of a dialogue that Kelley's omniscient narrator sets up with the reader as part of the book's didactic procedure – its offering of moral instruction. Kelley constantly inserts authorial asides that are particularly open, direct and sustained:

> But right here let me warn my readers against practicing this habit – discussing the qualities, good, bad and indifferent, of your friends and acquaintances .... Better let your tongue keep silent forever, than run the risk of hurting anyone in the eyes of others ... it is very seldom, if ever, that we meet with anyone who has not *one* good quality. Make the most of that .... We have all heard, of course, that "Money is the root of all evil." I would like to change the word "Money" to that of "Gossip" .... Methinks I hear a loud "Amen!" from the many persecuted ones.[6]

Indeed, Kelley's prominent authorial presence even invites the reader into complicity, marked by the repeated use of the first person plural: "That same evening finds our girls in their room"; "That afternoon, a trifle earlier than usual, our young people walked to Mrs. Hood's."[7]

Kelley's asides plainly offer moral instruction, in line with the Sunday School sentimental genre; in particular her novel draws upon Pansy's *Four Girls at Chautauqua* (1876), an intertext to which it is

---

[4] See Catherine Belsey, *Critical Practice*, London: Methuen, 1980, 69-70; Colin MacCabe, "Realism and the Cinema: Notes on Some Brechtian Theses", *Screen*, XVII/3 (Autumn 1976), 7-27.
[5] Jackson, "Mistaken Identity".
[6] Kelley-Hawkins, *Four Girls at Cottage City*, 223.
[7] *Ibid.*, 323, 358.

heavily indebted (as I will show).[8] But Kelley's asides, far more than Pansy's, also critically engage the reader, who must decide how far to accept the first person plural's invitation to adopt the proffered authorial position. The reader thereby becomes involved in an inspection of the text and its incidents, in parallel with the omniscient narrator's commentary. In the process, the reader must come to inspect the girls' inspection both of each other (especially) and of themselves. What results is a complex circulation of surveillance and (self-)questioning.

In large part this (self-)inspection is internal – to do with conscience and issues of morality and ethics – allying Kelley's novels to the Sunday School novel genre that came to prominence in the late nineteenth century, following in the wake of, say, Pansy's many writings and Martha Finley's "*Elsie*" series, which began in 1868 with the publication of *Elsie Dinsmore*.[9] But also, for Kelley's female characters, her girls, it has much to do with inspection of self and others in terms of presentableness: their (self-)presentation. An important motif in both novels by Kelley is a recurrent stress on how the girls monitor their own and each other's external appearance.

Since Kelley's two novels are usually described, with some justice, as sentimental Sunday School fictions, such a stress on taking care of appearance strikes a somewhat odd note, for it raises the issue of vanity. Why is an insistence on appearance so prominent in Kelley's texts? What is it doing? Beyond, that is, mobilizing the stock device of invoking Ecclesiastes' jeremiad, "vanity of vanities, all is vanity" – a mobilization which anyway hardly seems to apply, since there is an over-riding sense in both novels that the young females' self-

---

[8] Indeed, I have already passed over one possible debt that Kelley owes to "Pansy". *Four Girls at Chautauqua*, like *Four Girls at Cottage City*, alludes to its own sequel, but in a much more conventional way, since *Chautauqua Girls At Home*, the planned sequel, was to be published, in 1877. See "Pansy" [Isabella Macdonald Alden], *Four Girls at Chautauqua*, New York: Lothrop Publishing, 1876, p. 452; "Pansy" [Isabella Macdonald Alden], *The Chautauqua Girls at Home*, New York: Lothrop Publishing, 1877. On these issues, see, for example, Jane Tompkins, *Sensational Designs: The Cultural Work of American Fiction, 1790-1860*, New York: Oxford UP, 1985, 122-46; Trygve R. Tholfsen, "Moral Education in the Victorian Sunday School", *History of Education Quarterly*, XX/4 (Winter 1980), 77-99; and, more generally, Anne M. Boylan, *Sunday School: The Formation of an American Institution 1790-1880*, New Haven, CT: Yale UP, 1988.

[9] See Martha Finley, *Elsie Dinsmore*, New York: Dodds, Mead, 1868, and subsequent volumes in the "*Elsie Books*" sequence.

inspection is not ironically criticized as vanity but rather seen as a sign of careful discrimination and a desire to maintain tasteful restraint. Again, a contrast with *Four Girls at Chautauqua* is established; the way Kelley's novels focus upon detailed attention to external appearance fits poorly even with Pansy's example of the Sunday School sentimental genre, which by and large remains more exclusively focused upon the female protagonist's internal moral progress and the dilemmas this progress poses – so that, for example, discussions of some of the characters' concern with 'dress' in *Chautauqua* are framed by a commentary pointing out the vanity of such a preoccupation. By contrast, whilst coping with Christian moral dilemmas remains an important theme in Kelley's novels, this is far from the girls' only concern, and *Four Girls at Cottage City* deliberately highlights this distinction by blatantly announcing its intertextual ambitions in its very title. Kelley wants us to dwell on the differences between her novels and the Sunday School genre.

The texts' close attention to the girls' varying degrees of whiteness provides a useful starting-point when considering this divergence from generic expectation, since whiteness is a marker of not just ethnicity but also class and refinement. So detailed can Kelley's attention to skin shade become that *Megda*'s extraordinary insistence on detailing color and color-gradations has already been well attended to, for example by Molly Hite.[10] One way of understanding why this attention exists is to note the inclusion, as a frontispiece to *Megda*, of a photographic portrait of Kelley and an ambiguity this portrait creates. Its reproduction in the Schomburg Library edition is unhelpful, since it makes Kelley appear darker than she does in the original edition of *Megda* published in 1891 (see Figures 8.1 and 8.2). Even so, Claudia Tate noted the ethnic ambiguity of Kelley in this frontispiece photograph and proposed that Kelley's race might have been read differently by white and black audiences.[11] Kelley's ambiguous appearance – her off-white skin-tone and her smart, respectable dress – raises the issues of whether she was white, what

---

[10] Molly Hite, Introduction, in Emma Dunham Kelley, *Megda*, Schomburg Library Edition, New York: Oxford UP, 1988, xxvii-xxxvii.

[11] See Claudia Tate, *Domestic Allegories of Political Desire: The Black Heroine's Text at the Turn of the Century*, New York: Oxford UP, 1996; Claudia Tate, *Psychoanalysis and Black Novels: Desire and the Protocols of Race*, New York: Oxford UP, 1998.

her class position is and, inescapably, what her ethnic identity might be.

Figure 8.1 Frontispiece to the first edition of *Megda* (1893)
Figure 8.2 Frontispiece to the Oxford Schomburg Library Edition of *Megda* (1988)
Figure 8.3 "The New Negro Woman", in "Rough Sketches: A Study of the Features of the New Negro Woman" (1904), by John Henry Adams

I do not, however, want the issue of race to become the main focus of this essay, though I must note the only clear mention of America's African American population in either novel is a reference to the uppermost balcony in theaters – referred to in *Four Girls at Cottage City* as "nigger heaven" – which the young people identify as the place in which they will need to sit if they attend the theater during their vacation. This has been taken by Deborah McDowell to be an indication of the girls' racial identity,[12] but the four girls themselves also point out that they are not at all wealthy and the plain implication is they must sit in "nigger heaven" (although doubtless in a segregated part of this area) for the pressing reason that they can only afford the cheapest, third-tier seats (whereas, of course, African Americans could not enjoy any choice).

Taking issue with McDowell, Holly Jackson claims to have uncovered conclusive evidence that Kelley was white.[13] By doing so

---

[12] Deborah M. McDowell, Introduction, in Emma Dunham Kelley-Hawkins, *Four Girls at Cottage City*, ed. Deborah E. McDowell, Schomburg Library Edition, New York: Oxford UP, 1988, xxvii-xxxviii.

[13] Jackson, "Mistaken Identity". In this respect, it is worth noting that Pansy's *Chautauqua* describes the face of one of its protagonists darkening with emotion, for may have provided inspiration to Kelley, when the latter insists on the 'darkness' of

she compounds earlier debates about Kelley's alignment with the issue of race. For example, Carla L. Peterson argues that Kelley sought to offer a vision of what it would be like to live in a modern world in which racial difference no longer existed.[14] Similarly Claudia Tate suggested in 1998 that *Megda* was, in a sense, raceless.[15] Peterson's and Tate's suggestions point to how Kelley's two novels will continue to need to be approached in a context where their author's ethnic identity remains uncertain, since, no matter what her genealogy seemingly indicates about her identity, her photographic appearance certainly suggests some inter-ethnic derivations. Tate's proposal that *Megda* was raceless perhaps points to the way in which Kelley, given her own ambiguous appearance, was possibly uneasy or unsure about her racial identity, even though she and all her family had always classified themselves as white in a small New England community that would not have been tolerant of passing.[16] This may be why, apart from the books' manifestations of a constant concern with skin tone, there is no explicit racial dimension to either *Megda* or *Four Girls at Cottage City*.

Yet, counter to Toni Morrison's insistence that white remains characteristically "unvoiced" in white writing, Kelley's two novels, and especially *Megda*, repeatedly voice the whiteness of some of the protagonists and the relative darkness of others.[17] This could legitimate Jackson's contention that Kelley's novels explore white anxieties about racial distinction and the ambiguities that weaken the color line and make it permeable. However, I would rather argue that, by eliding racial discussions from her text so entirely, Kelley shifts attention away from the color line. Instead, her fiction on the one hand focuses upon Sunday School sentimental issues to do with Christian morality and ethics and, on the other, upon an exploration of the ways in which late nineteenth-century redefinitions of leisure and its pursuits generate both change within Christian moral boundaries and

---

some of her characters. Kelley, like Pansy, may simply be referring to the emotional intensity of the characters when describing their complexion as 'dark'. See Pansy, *Chautauqua*, p. 54; Kelley, *Megda*, p. 77.

[14] Carla L. Peterson, *Doers of the Word: African-American Women Speakers and Writers in the North, 1830-1880*, New York: Oxford UP, 1995.

[15] Tate, *Psychoanalysis and Black Novels*, 22-23.

[16] See Jackson, "Mistaken Identity".

[17] Toni Morrison, *Playing in the Dark: Whiteness and the Literary Imagination*, Cambridge, MA: Harvard UP, 1992, 48-53.

an increasing permeability between different socio-economic and
ethnic (if not racial) groups through their leisure activities.

At this time, also, the conflict between the customary assumption
of a foundational relation between outward appearance and ethnic,
racial and socio-economic identity and the escalation in opportunities
to alter appearance during the often gender-and-class-bridging pursuit
of leisure was becoming ever more pronounced. For example, one
source of anxiety about the reliability of the boundary between the
appearance of blacks and whites – for both blacks and whites – was
the rapid rise in the availability and use of commercial skin whitening
cosmetics, raising the intensity of the debate about whiteness,
appearance and self-inspection.[18] Such issues were a source of anxiety
on both sides of the color-line. For example, in a skeptical moment,
Anna Julia Cooper maintained that all the black man sought in a black
woman was "the three R's, a little music and a good deal of dancing, a
first rate dress-maker and a bottle of magnolia balm".[19] Magnolia
balm was a key ingredient in the proliferating number of commercial
cosmetics used to whiten the skin – cosmetics based, typically, on
traditional homemade domestic recipes circulating orally in folk
culture but, by the 1890s well-developed, in adaptations by
entrepreneurs, as mass-produced skin-lighteners.[20] Possibly the
iterated (self-)inspection of skin-color in Kelley's novels is a sign of a
concern over such exploitation of racial ambiguity. However, I want
to argue that Cooper's mention of "magnolia balm" was – more
importantly – also part of a larger set of socio-economic
developments.

Peiss makes the point that a whole beauty industry was emerging at
the turn of the century: for whites, this was clearly signaled by the rise
of a cosmetics industry generally, and this was tracked by African
American developments, as Annie Turnbo Malone and Sarah
Breedlove (aka Madam C.J. Walker) developed cosmetic treatments,
such as, respectively, Poro and Wonderful Hair Growth. Peiss
describes this as the emergence of a "beauty culture".[21] The aim of

---

[18] Kathy Peiss, *Hope in a Jar: The Making of America's Beauty Culture*, New York:
Metropolitan Books, 1988, 30-45.

[19] Anna Julia Cooper, *A Voice from the South*, Xenia, OH: The Aldine Printing House,
1892, 75.

[20] Peiss, *Hope in a Jar*, 10-11.

[21] Peiss, *Hope in a Jar*, 4.

such cosmetics was to alter appearance – in itself establishing the contingency of this method of assessing, indeed measuring, any individual.

Consequently, there was a deal of controversy surrounding such treatments when used to conceal any kind of ethnic identity, for this raised issues concerning the confrontation between Blacks' ethnic pride and the existence of hierarchies that valorized white skin.[22] Furthermore such treatments implicated issues of class, for the use of cosmetics raised the possibility of women passing themselves off as of a different, higher class – their skin seemingly unexposed to the rigors of the workplace and pampered to preserve its softness. Consequently, the insistence in Kelley's novels on fashion as a means of showing both decorum and stylishness imbricates her characters in contemporary 1890s debates concerning appearance, both in terms of her girls' skin color and class and in terms of their self-scrutiny. In Kelley's novels this is clearly related to the processes by which her girls step out. Thus, in Chapter 9 of *Four Girls at Cottage City*, as Vera and Jessie anticipate going out on the town "when the gentlemen come to call for us", Vera urges Jessie "to 'roughe' [*sic*] yourself", though self-consciously covering herself by adding, "as 'Sairey' says", in a reference to the alcoholic nurse and layer-out of the dead in Charles Dickens' *Martin Chuzzlewit*, who had become infamous for both her malapropisms and her slatternly lack of gentility.[23] Indeed, the girls are constantly working at their toilet in this book in a way that puts as much distance as possible between themselves and "Sairey", in preparation for their ventures out into the Cottage City

---

[22] See William B. Gatewood, *Aristocrats of Color: The Black Elite, 1880-1920*, Bloomington: Indiana UP, 1990, 151-70 *et seq.*

[23] Kelley-Hawkins, *Four Girls at Cottage City*, 128; Charles Dickens, *Martin Chuzzlewit* (1844), rpt. London: Wordsworth Editions, 1994, 678. When Dickens' Sarah (Sairey) Gamp says, "rouge yourselves", she is addressing her male companions and means to say "rouse yourselves". Her malapropism is intended to raise the comic image of her mistakenly instructing the men around her at the time to apply rouge. When Vera urges Jessie to "roughe" herself, she may merely, jokingly, by way of a literary pun, be telling Jessie to rouse herself. Yet, unavoidably, the idea that Jessie should rouge as well as rouse herself before meeting their male companions is suggested, not least because the play between "rouge" and "rouse" has, as it were, a mediating term: "arouse". The vein of quiet eroticism running through Kelley's work needs to be noted here as well; her steady illumination of her females' graces may in part be queer.

resort, even as they give themselves the appearance of emotional arousal.[24] The sense is they need to get their toilet just right.

In this respect, it is noteworthy that both of Kelley's novels are an unusually awkward fit when located within the sentimental novel genre, because almost all of the events in both are set outside the home.[25] The young female protagonists constantly move in public arenas – the school, the Church, the street, and the holiday resort and its entertainment venues – that is to say, fully in the public's gaze as well as each other's. In this sense, Kelley's novels track what Peiss characterizes as a process of "going public" in the late nineteenth century.[26]

To treat with this central feature of Kelley's novels, it is important to break from relating this "going public" to re-articulations of a distinct public-private binary (valuable though these articulations have been), and instead to turn to a more complex engagement with consumption, and in particular the cultural emergence of leisure. As work for women became less domestic and more shaped by the workplace and work hours from the antebellum period onwards,[27] so leisure space became ever more commonplace (and common space) and more defined as such: the dance hall, vaudeville, theater and other entertainments, and the incorporation of these in amusement and holiday resorts. For youths, and young women in particular, these ever-proliferating leisure areas were spaces they could move into by going out. As Peiss puts it, "It was in leisure that women played with identity, trying on new images and roles, appropriating the cultural forms around them".[28] Though the leisure resort played a significant (if minor) role in *Megda*, it is in *Four Girls at Cottage City* that it

---

[24] Kelley-Hawkins, *Four Girls at Cottage City*, 170.

[25] The only substantial exception is to be found in four pages at the very start of *Four Girls at Cottage City*, when the sisters Garnet and Jessie Dare are at home; but even in this case the two are impatiently awaiting the arrival of their two friends so that they can set off on their vacation (Kelley-Hawkins, *Four Girls at Cottage City*, 9-12) This also establishes one further debt to *Four Girls at Chautauqua*, which is also, unconventionally, set outside the home for the most part, albeit in a Methodist camp meeting ground, not Kelley's leisure resort.

[26] Peiss, *Hope in a Jar*, 7.

[27] Sara Evans, *Born for Liberty: A History of Women in America*, New York: Free Press, 1989, 98-100, 115-17, 120-22, 130-36; Christine Stansell, *City of Women: Sex and Class in New York City, 1789-1860*, New York: Knopf, 1986, 120-28, 156-63.

[28] Kathy Peiss, *Cheap Amusements: Working Women and Leisure in Turn-of-the-century New York*, New York: Temple UP, 1986, 62.

becomes the defining space for the narrative. Though in Cottage City the four girls conspicuously take on a particular form of Christian charity (charity visiting), they also regularly meet and interact with two males in leisure pursuits – and a sexual subtext is clearly intimated. So the "pretty pink" of Vera's cheek, that might have stemmed from running up stairs (as is suggested) or else from the application of "roughe", in fact stems from pleasurable embarrassment (and arousal) over a discreet but public compliment paid to her by one of the two young men in *Four Girls at Cottage City*. The issue in Cottage City's leisure spaces becomes that of bringing into balance pleasure, propriety, reputation, and their relationship to class status.

Vera's embarrassment is a measure of the care that is needed in this arena. A problem in this respect was how the rise of cosmetics and attention to fashion in the closing dozen or so years of the nineteenth century meant that appearance was no sure a sign of class or, indeed, even ethnicity, unless relatively minute observation was undertaken (how much rouge to use, for example, and what sort of rouge). Symptomatically, the Gibson Girl, when she appeared in this same period, arranged things so that she did not always clearly convey her class in her appearance.[29] The predominance of leisure space in the summer resort itself, still residually regarded as suspect (a space of idleness), in itself reinforced the idea that propriety of behavior needed to become a compensatory means of defining class and brought the issue of frivolity to the fore.[30]

Self-inspection thus becomes highly instrumental surveillance, monitoring the interfaces between the dictates of fashion, the constraints of respectability, and the play between the two. This was a critical issue for many women (particularly African American women). As Paula Klassen puts it, "clothing was a necessary and evocative medium".[31] In other words, clothes made a fashion statement. Klassen mainly discusses this fashion statement in terms of the search for respectability, and this is certainly fair enough, since Klassen's focus falls upon African American women. Respectability

---

[29] Martha H. Patterson, *Beyond the Gibson Girls: Reimagining the American New Woman*, Urbana: U of Illinois P, 2005, 40-45.

[30] Cindy S. Aron, *Working at Play: A History of Vacations in the United States*, New York: Oxford UP, 1999, 5-6.

[31] Paula E. Klassen, "The Robes of Womanhood: Dress and Authenticity among African-American Methodist Women in the Nineteenth-century", *Religion and American Culture*, XIV/1 (Winter 2004), 39.

was, for African American women, and religious African American women in particular, of especially central importance, not least because of an unavoidable defensive reaction to white negative stereotyping of black women, impugning their propriety and their sexual propriety in particular.[32] But we are also treating here with what I like to think of as "material Christianity", a material culture within which socio-economic class and aspirations to being "classy" become condensed in a Christian moral discourse of propriety of dress, appearance and behavior.

Yet fashion, as well as being a sign of proper piety, is also a class statement invoking degrees of refinement, intended "to delineate social hierarchies and to define communities" that were steadily becoming much more difficult to define.[33] Or as Dodson expresses it, "Aspirations toward social respectability, and the creation of distinctive cultural ethos, were internal aspects of community survival".[34] The point I want to emphasize is that not only can a careful, nuanced sense of fashion contribute to both these objectives, but also it can become the terrain for the negotiation of tensions between the two: conformity and distinctiveness. Both sit together to constitute a dynamic social organization for young women to move not only betwixt and between, liminally, but also against – resisting such borderings – since "personal liberty" was one objective of the conduct of the "new woman" (conduct broadly understood to include assertive female responses across different socio-economic groups to the nexus of socio-cultural developments I have been outlining).[35]

It seems to me, in this respect, that Kelley's fiction is exploring this dynamic, tension-filled but expressive arena. "The public presentation of an elegant self and group", in Dodson's phrase,[36] is not an untroubled or unified field, but involves tensions between self and group and a concern for outward appearance that is not shaped solely by considerations of piety and chastity but also by significations

---

[32] See Jualynne E. Dodson, *Engendering Church: Women, Power, and the AME Church*, New York: Rowman and Littlefield, 2002, 42-64; see also Evelyn Higginbotham, *Righteous Discontent: The Women's Movement in the Black Baptist Church, 1880-1920*, Cambridge, MA: Harvard UP, 1993, 185-229.

[33] Klassen, "Robes of Womanhood", 42.

[34] Dodson, *Engendering Church*, 42.

[35] Winifred Harper Cooley, *The New Womanhood*, New York: Broadway Publishing Co., 1904, 31.

[36] Dodson, *Engendering Church*, 43.

mobilizing nuances of self-expression, choice, and class that can run the risk of sharp criticism (with over-attention to appearance regarded as a trespass into vanity). Klassen, for example, notes how the Reverend A.W. Talbert in 1881 is already describing the way in which, if the reader

> … visit some fashionable chapel on the Sabbath … he will find a great display of finery …. And after services are over you will hear some stylish sister say to another, "Oh, didn't Sister A have on a sweet dress" …. Now just ask her of the minister's text and she will say, "I can't remember it." [37]

In this way we can see exactly what Klassen means when she writes that dress had "an important symbolic role".[38] Klassen is writing of particular issues related to sexual and racial stereotyping: modesty, decency and the use of clothing by women "to establish themselves as legitimate public figures".[39] Klassen's emphasis therefore falls on the need to avoid garish show in search for respectable dress.

Yet Klassen's specific points also have wider resonance for my argument, to do with issues of legitimation and class and ethnic discrimination. These broader issues switch attention to the complexity of fashion's finely nuanced, multi-layered social meanings and their inescapability in the totality of consumer culture (since, under the commodity code, all dress and every dress signifies as a fashion statement). My point is that fashion statements at this time work, more than ever before, in several ways. They have become not just a question of propriety or of countering sexist and racist allegations of immodesty or over-sexuality in public, but also a means of self-expression and self-definition within a carefully inflected and closely surveyed consumerist fashion corpus. A complex doubling is involved here: Klassen is right to speak of clothing as a "badge of honor and source of protection". Clothing (and other appearance) codes are a statement about respectability and status increasingly dependant on fine distinctions, and if these external restraints are balanced by the way that appearance is also a self-expressive means of demonstrating discernment (taste) within a group, to do with

---

[37] Klassen, "Robes of Womanhood", 61.

[38] *Ibid.*, 42.

[39] *Ibid.*, 34.

stylishness, it must also be noted that this last is yet dependent upon further in-group surveillance and self-surveillance.[40] Fashion subsists in such carefully checked self-expressive eddies of identification.

That Kelley leaves the socio-economic status of her four girls unclear is, therefore, informative. All we glean is that they must be very careful with their money. The girls might fairly be said to be liminally positioned in class terms and therefore necessarily extra anxious about the minutiae of appearance and conduct. As such they stand as indicators of how, in an ever more class-mobile society, the increasing fluidity and falling costs of fashionability were confusing ready distinctions of class status, which as a consequence needed to be re-established by other behavioral means. Or, as the conservatively-inclined Garnet puts it to the more risqué Jess in *Four Girls at Cottage City*, "Don't stand in the middle of the street, Jess, people will think you have struck an attitude".[41]

In Garnet's admonition we can see how alert the vacationing girls are to the risks inherent in stepping out: the possibility of losing respectability. Indeed, one could debate here just what "striking an attitude" implies – its complex connotations. At the least it firstly suggests that Jess runs the risk of appearing as if she wishes to put herself on show, displaying herself in a way not wholly respectable – a loss of class. More disturbingly, the unwitting performance might secondly cast doubt upon her chasteness. (Here recall that the third tier "heaven" of the theater, where the girls propose to sit, was also the haunt of prostitutes seeking custom below, in the stalls.) I need hardly add that these risks Jess runs are inextricably intercalate, thirdly, with the way in which the girls' ethnic identities are also left ambiguous. What is generated by these three conjunctions is a fraught tension between the need for young people to bring ever more interpretive effort to casual leisure encounters and the increase in uncertainty over the grounds for any such interpretations.

My claim then is that Garnet's caution to Jess alerts the reader to the complex risks of going out to participate in the late nineteenth-

---

[40] Hazel Carby is certainly right to speak of how, for African America women, this reaching for respectability was also, in an important way, subversive – a means of fighting racist stereotypes by dressing like ladies. See Hazel Carby, *Reconstructing Womanhood: The Emergence of the Afro-American Woman Novelist*, New York: Oxford UP, 1987, 32.

[41] Kelley-Hawkins, *Four Girls at Cottage City*, 29.

century proliferation of leisure entertainments and activities, such as the theater or (in this case) the promenade. In all this we are of course dealing with the rise of consumerism. Whilst the negative aspects of this rise are manifold, a new modern culture, as Peiss points out, is also emerging – of fluid exchange in a social field invested by discriminations conjoined with careful, deliberate choices.[42] This provides a new means of definition: such terms as "the New Woman", "the New Negro", and "the New Negro Woman", mobilize a whole range of emancipatory aspirations and personal statements within a group about style, as a way of projecting (sex) appeal and of adjusting and altering appearance.[43]

Consequently, Church-going clothes in *Four Girls at Cottage City* are carefully selected:

> When the girls were ready they looked each other over critically .... A fairer sight could scarcely be asked for than they in their summer dresses. Vera was dressed all in soft black, that made her white skin and golden hair look perfectly lovely. Allie wore a pretty, cool-looking dress of white and nile-green. Garnet and Jessie wore cream, which was most becoming to their rich complexions. [44]

"Nile-green": the precise shade is specified, in a fashion-based fine distinction with overtones of commercialized exoticism, created by modern industrial dyes, and in itself therefore a signification of modernity. Such nuances provide a means of making a personal statement, one that may carry connotations of commodification – here within a discourse of the Egyptian other – but one that may also provide a means of self-definition. Indeed, one woman in the Church congregation is identified by one of the girls, Jessie, by means of describing the fashion that she sported: "'… did she [the woman whom the girls want to identify] have on a lovely lace dress and a hat just one bed of pansies?'"[45] This does indeed identify the woman for the other three girls, though simultaneously it identifies Jessie as rather over-concerned with fashion (the link to the Reverend Talbert's

---

[42] Peiss, *Cheap Amusements*, 3-4, 6-8.

[43] See, generally, Patterson, *Beyond the Gibson Girls*; Joan Jacobs Bromberg, *The Body Project: An International History of American Girls*, New York: Random House, 1997.

[44] Kelley-Hawkins, *Four Girls at Cottage City*, 52.

[45] *Ibid.*, 55.

strictures is inescapable). The reference to 'pansies' I take here to be an allusion also to "Pansy" and the way that Pansy's discussions of her girls' appearance in *Chautauqua* (sometimes in no little detail), carry a censoriousness readiness to detect traces of vanity. By contrast, in Kelley's text, even the conservative Garnet, like Jessie, happily wears "cream", with its transformative effect on skin-tone. All this is a ratcheting-up of the implications of the admiring glances that Megda has bestowed on her friends in their Sunday best in Kelley's previous novel. Fashionableness is clearly something to be celebrated.[46]

For Kelley, therefore, the negotiation between the need for respectability in dress and the allure of fashion's adjustments to appearance provide a means for the establishment of a web of relations – a web woven between intimate social relations involving advice, opinion, critique, display, and honesty versus flattery, and broader issues to do with increasing social mobility and class. Fashion as a means of showing both decorum and stylishness becomes increasingly the point at issue, as it invests clothing, cosmetics and patterns of behavior. And making this point brings me back to my opening identification of a sharp difference between the two books concerning the propriety of dances and theatricals.

In *Megda*, condemnation of Megda's love of both theatricals and dancing is forthrightly advanced by the young clergyman, Mr. Stanley – one of *Megda*'s central characters. *Four Girls at Cottage City*, by contrast, shows much greater tolerance for leisure pursuits, as in its warm portrait of promenaders moving between concerts, walking to and fro, "laughing and talking".[47] Indeed, *Four Girls at Cottage City* specifically features the girls debating the rectitude of theater going and reaching the conclusion that it would do "not the least bit of harm … unless the play is immoral". Then, even more specifically, a few pages later, one of the girls, Garnet, quotes at some length a fictitious article by the Reverend Madison Peters in "*Munyon's Monthly Magazine*", entitled "The Common Sense View of the Theatre". The

---

[46] Kelley, *Megda*, 110. Garnet's and Jessie's use of cream before going out is symptomatic of the desire to appear fashionable (fashionably pale), in my argument, but it also must resurrect the debate that Holly Jackson has stirred up by proposing that Kelley was white, given the common contemporary use of magnolia balm in creams intended to whiten rich African American complexions.

[47] Kelley-Hawkins, *Four Girls at Cottage City*, 40.

Rev. Peters' article reaches the conclusion that "the theatre is here to stay",[48] and, in a paraphrase by one of the girls, urges "Let every man be persuaded in his own mind".[49] A debate unfolds about this conclusion, during which Vera "thoughtfully" makes the following point:

> "I know some good people – Episcopalians and Universalists – who go to the theatre every week of their lives … and … they go to balls and dances until 2 o'clock in the morning. Sundays they go to Church all day and *enjoy* going too, and their lives are all good and just, as they should be." [50]

Similarly Jess launches into a spirited defense of dancing:

> "To tell the truth, girls," she [Vera] said, "I would hate to give up dancing."
> "Who said anything about being obliged to?" asked Jessie …. "…Just as though anyone couldn't be just as good when they danced as when they didn't. It doesn't hurt anyone to shake their foot a bit …" and Jessie sprang out of her chair and waltzed lightly around the room.
> Vera leaned against the table and watched her. How lightly and gracefully the slender, girlish form glided over the floor ….
> "I would dance to-night if I knew I was going to die tomorrow. It's no sin, and I would go to Heaven just as quick." [51]

This defiance begs the question as to why such a change of position had occurred between Kelley's two novels, especially given the deliberate self-reflexive mention of *Megda* in the pages of *Four Girls at Cottage City* – inviting the reader to read both books and hence encounter this sharp contradiction.

An obvious first point to make in considering this change is to note the dates of composition of the two novels. *Megda*, published in 1891, came out four years before *Four Girls at Cottage City*. This is a matter of only a few years, but at the time the leisure and fashion industries were moving up a gear in their rates of change. This was true of both

---

[48] *Ibid.*, 81, 99, 102.
[49] *Ibid.*, 106.
[50] *Ibid.*, 105.
[51] *Ibid.*, 274. Compare this exchange to one in Pansy's *Esther Reid* (1870), London: Thomas Nelson and Sons, 1901, pp. 213-216.

the white and the African American fashion industries. For example, starting in 1890, the *Colored American Magazine* carried a fashion column, written by "Madame Rumford", whilst Julia Ringwood Costen founded the *Afro-American Journal of Fashion* in 1891, to follow the example of recently-established white women's and fashion magazines, such as *The Ladies' Home Journal*, edited by Louisa Knapp, which first appeared in 1883, published by the Curtis Publishing Company as a supplement to the *Tribune and Farmer*; *Woman's World*, founded in 1884; and the *Ladies' Home Companion* (1886), which began its life in Cleveland in 1874 as *The Home*.[52] This period also saw the expansion of opportunities for dancing of various kinds, in commercial halls, in organized dances sponsored by a range of organizations, and in a rapid increase in the number of summer resorts. Peiss traces the shift from the 1860s and 1870s into the 1900s. This was a period of cultural transition for dance, during which such an indulgence became more acceptable, even if still "remain[ing] morally suspect to some".[53] These changes in attitude to dance, and to drama, were part of a broader cultural shift, in which, also, as Peiss notes, "Putting on finery, promenading the streets, and … [attending] resorts" became elements of "an important cultural style" at the turn of the century.[54]

Picking out these cultural reconfigurations, which made the allure of fashion and the appeal of leisure pursuits all the more irresistible, helps me pull into focus how Kelley in *Four Girls at Cottage City* deliberately establishes a dialectic between her two novels' modes of engagement with the expansion of leisure and amusements that was all part of a paradigm shift in the construction of self-identity. Leisure spaces such as resorts and dancehalls were places in which, performatively, the participant could explore self, identity and the space between desire and respectability. That *Four Girls at Cottage City* is almost entirely set in a summer resort is therefore highly significant, for the girls can consider things differently, in an environment in which, Cindy Aron argues, women, who usually outnumbered men, could "exercise autonomy and influence" in a way

---

[52] Peiss, *Hope in a Jar*, 212.
[53] Peiss, *Cheap Amusements*, 90. "Pansy" reminds us that the debate had been a long one, for in 1876 she had briefly observed that dancing and Christianity need not always be mutually exclusive. See "Pansy", *Four Girls at Chautauqua*, pp. 373-74.
[54] Peiss, *Cheap Amusements*, 57.

rarely possible otherwise.[55] The shift in attitude between *Megda* and *Four Girls at Cottage City* is a negotiation of these differences, but it is not one with any clear-cut resolution. My claim is that it cannot be, and that Cottage City has been carefully chosen as the resort where *Four Girls at Cottage City* and part of *Megda* is set, since it was a space where these issues were particularly contested.

"Cottage City" was in fact an umbrella term, used to describe three adjoining developments. The first was Wesleyan Grove, the 1835 Methodist Meeting Camp Ground that by the 1860s had witnessed the building of a substantial number of permanent cottages. Adjoining it, Oak Bluffs had been established in 1867, a development undertaken by speculators seeking to cash in on the growing vacation business in the area; Vineyard Highlands, the third, was a response in 1870 by the Methodists, who feared commercialization might overwhelm them if they did not expand.[56] During the next two decades, the distinctions between the three eroded. Indeed, by 1907 Oak Bluffs had become the new general name for the area, and it was to become (instructively, in terms of permeability between groups) an area visited by many African Americans.[57] Yet also, in the 1890s, a Methodist influence still persisted. Thus, though in 1885 a reporter commented on Cottage City's bicycle and tricycle races, its ball games, boat races, and swimming matches (that may well have revealed female forms in wet costumes), and though alcohol was commonly consumed in Cottage City by 1890, some awareness still remained of the resort's temperance origins and its early avoidance of frivolous pursuits, particularly if these involved promiscuous mixed-sex entertainments – as these were sometimes censoriously denominated.[58]

Kelley's girls, vacationing in Cottage City, must negotiate these shifting messages, in a way that Pansy's four girls do not in their Methodist Sunday School camp ground founded in 1874, only two year's before *Four Girls at Chautauqua*'s publication and barely a decade before Kelley's two novels appeared. Things are changing fast: as Jess dances (in private, significantly) near the end of *Four Girls at Cottage City*, the enjoyment she experiences is tempered by the way that, even at the same time as she declares that she will "dance, dance,

[55] Aron, *Working at Play*, 9.
[56] See Brown, *Inventing New England*, 75-104.
[57] Hite, Introduction, xxx; Jackson, "Mistaken Identity".
[58] Aron, *Working at Play*, 72, 77, 73.

dance", she goes on to add, "until the Heavens fall" and, Kelley notes, "her cheeks were crimson".[59] Again, physical exertion, the use of "roug[h]e", arousal, or embarrassment (or a coalescence of all four) may be the cause of this facial coloration – though perhaps we are intended to understand that, this time, embarrassment predominates.

The interplay between consumption, self-expression and respectability is complex here. The girls are going through processes of learning about the signification systems of leisure, and shades of fashion, and about their relative but also proscribed control over how they can figure in these – how they present themselves in theater audiences, concert attendance, participation in theatrics, promenading and, above all, dance. As Kathy Peiss puts it, dance was a terrain for learning about and practicing the "cultural management of sexuality, intimacy and respectability".[60] Indeed, these combined fields together constitute a large arena of subtle significations and discriminations. Dress was one further important terrain. As Peiss explains, "Dress was a particularly potent way to display and play with notions of respectability, allure, independence, and status and to assert a distinctive identity".[61]

Even in the far more reserved *Megda*, this comes across clearly:

> "Ethel Lawton looked fine this morning, Girlie .... She had on a large hat with ever so many plumes. She was as white as a snowdrop, and her hair shone like gold .... She looks very delicate; her skin is almost transparent."
>
> "Oh, yes, she is strong enough," answered Meg hastily. "... But her new suit is green, Hal – an emerald green velvet, and it is perfectly lovely. I was in the house when it was brought home from the dressmaker's; no doubt it looks black to you as it shades on the dark. Her hat is imported." ...
>
> [Meg] looked in Laurie's seat – so did Hal – and both thought her looking prettier than ever in her new suit of navy blue cashmere trimmed with chinchilla. All the girls had on their new suits and looked very pretty.
>
> Meg never questioned whether it was right or wrong to think of such things in church. She never turned in her seat to stare at anyone ... but she could not keep her thoughts from dwelling, first upon one

---

[59] Kelley-Hawkins, *Four Girls at Cottage City*, 274
[60] Peiss, *Cheap Amusements*, 89-90.
[61] *Ibid.*, 63.

thing, then upon another, instead of keeping them strictly upon the sermon.

This morning Meg did not venture to look at Mr. Stanley until Hal touched her foot softly with his. Looking at him to see what he might want and seeing his eyes fastened earnestly upon the pulpit, Meg turned her head quickly and looked, too .... What was her embarrassment to meet Mr. Stanley's dark-blue eyes gazing earnestly at her. There was nothing in that certainly; the look was a grave, unobtrusive one; but Meg flushed hotly beneath it and dropped her eyes, at the same time feeling deeply angry with herself for doing so. As for Hal, mischievous fellow, he was obliged to turn his head and look out of the window. [62]

What this passage offers is a complex conjunction: an exploration of appearance and a lesson about the politics of its surveillance. This comes across in how the erotic connotations residing in the unstated but obvious attraction of Megda for the intense young clergyman are placed alongside the also unstated but just as obvious language of fashion, to do with respectability, taste, style, and display. The two are wittily intermingled. (I want to note, if only *en passant*, what a fine sense of comedy Kelley possesses, as she dissects her eponymous protagonist's oscillations between self-evasion and self-knowledge.)

Megda is, as it were, here walking the tightropes of a proliferating consumer culture, as her stepping-out occurs. She does indeed need to keep her wits about her. This is a constant underlying theme in Kelley's fiction, beneath the staples of the Sunday School genre that treat with the need for proper piety in church (Megda is implicitly criticized for her impiety). That it remains an underlying theme becomes quite apparent as Kelley's novels unfold and even as, progressively, issues of spiritual progress come to dominate their plots. Noting this progression towards moral conservatism reminds us of the way that the endings of the two novels end up in what Nina Baym describes as a "land of happy endings",[63] a conservative terrain perhaps best set to one side in analyzing the sentimental genre's impact, since such endings actually function as "a cover – or cover-up – for a more radical vision of female potentialities embedded in the

---

[62] Kelley, *Megda*, 108-111.
[63] Nina Baym, *Woman's Fiction, A Guide to Novels by and about Women in America, 1820-70*, 2nd edn, Urbana: U of Illinois P, 1993, 11.

text".[64] In reading Kelley's novels, if we avoid merely surrendering to being swept up by their happy, moralizing endings, we encounter a complex exploration of the individual's interaction with the subtly-inflected, (self)expressive languages of consumer culture that saturate the two novels' artful explorations of leisure pursuits, entertainments and fashion.

These codes expound the modes of negotiation that need to be learned by the new woman – and the extent to which these impact across boundaries of ethnicity and class is well-illustrated by placing the portrait of the New Negro Woman which appeared in *Voice of the Negro* in 1904 alongside *Megda*'s frontispiece daguerreotype of Kelley (see page 182). The two are startlingly similar, and their juxtaposition makes plain how the New Woman and the New Negro Woman are not just about asserting and developing female autonomy, "personal liberty" and/or race pride, and female and/or black culture but also about dealing with, or, rather, fashioning and learning the dialects of the ramifying effects of modern capital, its consumer orientations, and its effects on classification. Megda and *Cottage City*'s four girls are learning of the complications that this entails, in terms of negotiating the emerging signifying fields of the commodity code. Both *Megda* and *Four Girls at Cottage City* trace the way that these complications are becoming ever more embedded in consumer culture's cross-class proliferation in the 1890s. But, where in 1892 Megda admires her friends' dress sense and worries about the propriety of undertaking private theatricals, *Cottage City*'s girls in 1895 go on to negotiate more complex issues to do with cosmetics, vacation conduct, dancing, public theater attendance and even street promenading.

For this reason, it may not be best to follow past critics by focusing so much upon the importance of Kelley's color, white, black or other. This is why Scott McLemee's suggestion that Kelley, if revealed as "white", should as a writer be "re-forgotten" seems entirely mistaken.[65] Even if we were sure that Kelley were white, her novels still centrally call for an acute self-awareness and a recognition of both the tension-filled potency of community constraint and the counter-importance of self-expression when actively managing

---

[64] Susan K. Harris, *Nineteenth-Century American Women's Novels: Interpretive Strategies*, Cambridge: Cambridge UP, 1990, 12-13.
[65] Scott McLemee, "In Black and White", *Inside Higher Education*, 1 March 2005, 7.

modern consumption. This active, decorous management of style is surely part of what Alison Piepmeier calls the "multiple, transitional, strategic, playful, contested … modalities of embodiment" that position women as neither fully victims nor fully active agents.[66] What Kelley makes apparent is just how constant women's active, performative management of such modalities of embodiment needed to be as the turn of the century approached, whilst the sharp contrast between the negative and positive verdicts upon dances and theatricals advanced by *Megda* and *Cottage City* respectively underline how volatile the expanding cultural field of leisure was becoming as public morals shifted.

---

[66] Alison, Piepmeier, *Out in Public: Configurations of Women's Bodies in Nineteenth-century America*, Chapel Hill: U of North Carolina P, 2004, 2.

"MAGNIFICENT EQUIPMENT": BODY, SOUND AND SPACE IN THE REPRESENTATION OF THE FEMALE SINGER

JANET FLOYD

The figure of the female singer was the object of intense interest during the late nineteenth and early twentieth centuries in the United States. This period, as Elizabeth Johns points out, saw a "national obsession with singing".[1] But, while singers of both sexes were celebrated and discussed, praised and pampered, it was the female singer who attracted the greatest cultural attention. Given contemporary sensitivities about women in public life, some of the debates surrounding this figure were predictable. The singer raised questions about the spaces, private or public, in which a woman might appropriately display powers understood as inherent or God-given. The successful singer was uncomfortably positioned, having, on the one hand, a duty to use a gift perceived to be peculiarly consonant with the feminine and, on the other, experiencing exposure to the extraordinary publicity surrounding popular female singers. But these debates stretched beyond and outside contemporary preoccupations about women's place. The figure of the female singer, so central to the highly popular performances of the opera, oratorio and lieder of the era, the sound that she made, and its expansive power gave her a further cultural resonance. In this essay, I want to consider how three fictions – Rebecca Harding Davis' "The Wife's Story" (1864), Mary Hallock Foote's "The Fate of a Voice" (1886) and Willa Cather's *The Song of the Lark* (1915) – address themselves to the figure of the female singer, and the questions of agency and power that this female figure raised.[2]

---

[1] Elizabeth Johns, *Thomas Eakins: The Heroism of Modern Life*, Princeton, NJ: Princeton UP, 1983, 131.
[2] Rebecca Harding Davis, "The Wife's Story" (1864), rpt. in *Life in the Iron Mills and Other Stories,* ed. Tillie Olsen, New York: The Feminist Press, 1972, 177-222; Mary Hallock Foote, "The Fate of a Voice" (1886), rpt. in *The Last Assembly Ball and the*

The question of visibility is germane to my discussion. I want to discuss the interesting and unusual way in which the singer's publicly visible body is visualized and described before going on to consider the disposition of the singer's body in space. But I will also explore the significance of audibility, the sound made by these female singers and their power to fill space with sound. This too is critical to the significance of this figure.

One of the most striking aspects of the way in which the female singer was represented was the explicitness with which her body was described. Richard Leppart has proposed the general argument that "whatever else music is 'about,' it is *inevitably* about the body". If the "product" of music "lacks all concreteness and disappears without trace", the "visual experience of its production is crucial to musicians and audience alike for locating and communicating the place of music and musical sound within society and culture".[3] We think of Gilded Age Americans as preoccupied with what Miriam Bailin describes as the "rigid inhibition of physical and emotional exposure", but bodily power and its public display was the *sine qua non* of operatic and concert performance.[4] Thus, one of the most pressing questions raised by the female singer during this period had to do with the relationship between the singer herself – this female with a mind, a soul, a career – and the powerful sound made by her body. Was the spirit of the woman projected into her singing or was she marginal to the sound that her body was able to make? As Thomas L. Riis suggests, there was a well-developed discussion of the singer as a kind of vessel, a "performing object, a music box so to speak ... a singing body".[5] But the possibility that the voice produced by physical activity existed

---

Fate of a Voice, Boston and New York: Houghton, Mifflin, 1889, 215-75; Willa Cather, *The Song of the Lark* (1915), Oxford: Oxford UP, 2000.

[3] Richard Leppart, *The Sight of Sound: Music, Representation and the History of the Body*, Berkeley: U of California P, 1993, xv, xxi.

[4] Miriam Bailin, *The Sickroom in Victorian Fiction: The Art of Being Ill*, Cambridge: Cambridge UP, 1994, 22.

[5] Thomas L. Riis, "Concert Singers, Prima Donnas and Entertainers: The Changing Status of Black Women Vocalists in Nineteenth-century America", in *Music and Culture in America, 1861-1918*, ed. Michael Saffle, New York: Garland, 1998, 69. For an interesting discussion of the spirituality attributed to the singer, see Elizabeth Johns, *Thomas Eakins: The Heroism of Modern Life*, Princeton, NJ: Princeton UP, 1983, 130-32.

apart from the woman allowed an almost forensic attention to her body.

Here, for example, is Walt Whitman considering the physical work of the singer and describing almost warring elements between the singer and the voice:

> [The voice] forms, or rather gathers the tone in the back of the mouth, and makes none of the fearful work with the mouth itself that gives such a distorted appearance to English singers. In the good Italian singer, the mouth, lips, cheek, etc. are at ease, perhaps illumined with a gentle smile even during astonishing vocal performances .... The back of the mouth, the throat, great interior energy and muscular alertness are necessary, all under the espionage of a severe taste, permitting no severe attempts, but pleasing and natural simple effects.[6]

The singer is engaged in modeling a self-effacing femininity and controlling the impact of her voice on her body. She maintains the "gentle smile" of the Victorian ideal throughout – and in spite of – the intensity of her physical activity. The resounding "energy", the swelling sound that she makes, must be reined in by her "severe taste", and that relationship of restraint is conveyed through the word "espionage", the activity of a spy, someone who watches without participation. The effect of the passage, nevertheless, is to fasten our attention on the (in this case well managed) physical workings of the body itself.

As the presence of singing and singers extended during the later part of the nineteenth century, artists and writers were as likely to celebrate singers' "magnificent equipment" as to think of these women as vessels. In some part, the interest in the "equipment" of the female singer recalls the developing fashion during the period for the Junoesque female figure.[7] One thinks of the expansively healthy figures painted by Edward Simmons for the New York Courts in 1894 or indeed the bodies of Sarah Orne Jewett's Mrs Todd in *The Country*

---

[6] Walt Whitman quoted in Robert D. Faner, *Walt Whitman and Opera*, Philadelphia: U of Pennsylvania P, 1951, 57-58.

[7] The term "magnificent equipment" is drawn from Willa Cather's description of a singer in "Three American Singers", *McClure's Magazine*, 42 (December 1913), 34: "her physical equipment is magnificent."

of the Pointed Firs and Charlotte Perkins Gilman's Herlanders.[8] But in the case of the singer we are not only asked to envision a particularly magnificent body, but also to think about different elements of the body at work. We might expect to read of the glamorous physical appearance of the singer, but it is surely interesting to find ourselves asked, in the late nineteenth-century text, to focus on her throat and bosom. Foote's Madeline Hendrie, for example, in "The Fate of a Voice", appears in the predictable décolleté, but it is not the expensive fabric to which our attention is drawn, but to her "soft throat swelling" as she sings and "the heart that beat under the laces that covered [her] white bosom".[9]

It is not uncommon, as perhaps these quotations suggest, for representations of the female singer during this period to lend this evident physicality a sexual dimension. For example, John Singer Sargent, painting the lieder singer Mrs George Batten in 1897, places her bosom, framed by a long thick necklace, at the centre of the portrait, painting her low-cut dress in broad strokes of white and gold.

Sargent's Mrs Batten is not only magnificently equipped; she is shown in a quasi-sexual state of transport. Above her solid neck, the subject's face is tilted back, her eyes are almost closed, her vivid red lips are parted, showing white teeth. The artist is apparently at pains to represent the singer taken over by

Figure 9.1 John Singer Sargent, *Mrs George Batten Singing* (1895). Courtesy of Glasgow City Council (Museums)

[8] Sarah Orne Jewett, *The Country of the Pointed Firs* (1896), rpt. in *The Sarah Orne Jewett Text Project*, ed. Terry Heller (http://www.public.coe.edu/~theller/soj/sj-index.htm); Charlotte Perkins Gilman, *Herland*, (1915), rpt. New York: Pantheon Books, 1979.
[9] Foote, "The Fate of a Voice", 261.

the sound produced from her body, but we are presented here with an image of a respectable woman completely engaged in her physical life.

The meaning of the female singer's appearance was nuanced by the music that she performed, though this too often had an explicitly physical dimension. Oratorios offered women disembodied roles of spiritualized, if not angelic, commentary. But the great Italian operas of the era often showed female transgression punished by lingering disease and death.[10] In contrast, the German repertoire that dominated American classical music making during this period also included operas by Beethoven and Wagner that gave a majestic grasp of events to physically active, even physically passionate women characters.

Clearly, the way in which gender was understood in these music events is at least as complex as it is significant. Barbara Freedman, discussing the female singer, cites Hélène Cixous' comment that "men and women are caught up in an ideological theatre where the multiplication of representations, images, reflections, myths, identifications renders all conceptualizations null and void".[11] Such a comment should remind us that we generalize about the ways in which the classical repertoire of late nineteenth-century America positioned female singers in physical terms at our peril, but it may also alert us to the multiplicity of femininities available to the singer, many of which directly addressed women's physical life as well as providing roles so demanding as to bring her physical strength and the strength of her voice to the audience's immediate attention.

Of course, choice of repertoire might or might not lie in the hands of the singers and this raises another important issue with respect to the female singer's power: her imagined relationship, sexual or otherwise, with a largely hidden cast of powerful male characters with lives of a worldlier cast than her own. Few representations of female singers during this period fail to make reference to the conductors,

---

[10] This kind of argument is made in Lesley C. Dunn and Nancy A. Jones, *Embodied Voices: Representing Female Vocality in Western Culture*, Cambridge: Cambridge UP, 1994, and Catherine Clément, *Opera, or the Undoing of Women*, trans. Betsy Wing, Minneapolis: U of Minnesota P, 1988.

[11] Barbara Freedman, "Frame-up: Feminism, Psychoanalysis, Theatre", in *Performing Feminisms: Feminist Critical Theory and Theatre*, ed. Sue-Ellen Case, Baltimore, MD: Johns Hopkins P, 1990, 72. Freedman's quotation comes from Hélène Cixous, "Sorties", in *New French Feminisms*, eds Elaine Marks and Isabelle de Courtivron, Amherst: U of Massachusetts P, 1996, 96.

producers, agents, and managers, who directed, defined, managed, and marketed them. In an important depiction of the world of the great operatic singer, George Eliot's poetic drama, *Armgart*, the vital and ambitious heroine is buffeted by the various and uncompromising perspectives of her manager, her teacher and her lover. We see the overbearing attempts of those around her to steer her future – and her voice – to their own ends.[12]

Figure 9.2 Thomas Eakins, *The Concert Singer* (1890-92). Courtesy of the Philadelphia Museum of Art

The power of men over the singer is at issue across the range of representations of female singers, whether or not they are concerned, as Eliot plainly is, with questions of a woman's artistic independence. Thomas Eakins' "Concert Singer", for example, painted in 1892, gives his subject, Weda Cook, the face of an unsophisticated young woman and a dress of radiant pink. This girlish creature must surely be the mere vessel for the delivery of Mendelssohn's *Elijah*, as the presence of the authoritative hand and wrist of the conductor at the left hand corner of the painting suggests. Eakins even writes the words we are to imagine his figure singing on the frame of the painting. Yet even here the absence from the painting of the head and body of the man supposedly directing the singer draws attention to the power and importance of the voice and the person of the singer.

A difficult question of agency, then, lies at the heart of the representation of the female singer, from her relationship to her voice to the politics of her relationships with those involved in her career. But even when she seems most at the service of what is thought of as her gift, most dominated by her bodily powers, directed or

---

[12] George Eliot, *Armgart*, in *Jubal and Other Poems*, Edinburgh and London: Blackwood, 1870, 67-136.

compromised artistically by the more or less invisible men who are presumed to manage her performance, still, in one key respect, she faces a trial of her strength that she must win without assistance: the subjugation of the audience. This was the period in which massive constructions were erected to house the enormous audiences for opera. The New York Metropolitan Opera, for example, was built with 3615 seats.

Scholars have made much of the strictures imposed on the behavior, and specifically the bodies, of audiences for orchestral and operatic performance as a result. We might think of the work of the female singer, serving her gift, as reinforcing that required passivity. Representations of the female singer during this period, however, frequently make much of the opera house and concert hall audience as predominantly arenas of sensuality. The singer faces the promiscuous and instinctual crowd, the savage beast to be tamed, the mass preoccupied with mere fashion and display until – or unless – it is dominated by her predominantly physical feat of performance. In fictions of the period that describe other kinds of staged appearances, performers are clearly implicated in and diminished by their audiences' unpredictable, irrational and sensual response. Verena Tarrant and Carrie Meeber in James' *The Bostonians* (1896) and Dreiser's *Sister Carrie* (1900) are examples that come immediately to mind. But where these performers stimulate, even inflame, their audiences, the great singer is dignified as well as empowered by her instrument and the audience is rightly subjugated by it.

The emphasis on the singer's "equipment" and the positioning of this figure in a triangle of complex and challenging relationships with management and audience add up to a particular mode of female visibility in the late nineteenth and early twentieth centuries. But if what we have here is a highly, even extravagantly, visible woman, when we turn to the fictions about female singers, we are faced with texts that set the figure of the singer in an altogether broader cultural arena. The body of the singer remains crucially important, as does the power of the sound that she makes. The significance of these attributes, however, is traced in spaces far beyond the concert hall and the opera house.

Rebecca Harding Davis' "The Wife's Story" is dominated by the dream-memory of the narrator, Hester, who writes an opera and arranges to sing the leading role. Hester is convinced of her own talent, but finally she casts her art aside in favor of the private life. Davis shows no interest in plotting the figure of a female singer achieving access to the public sphere: she glosses over the process of finding a producer, for example. What is clearly much more important is Hester's covert preparation for her début and the nightmare of self-exposure and humiliation that she dreams. Davis' apparent preoccupation is with the singer's body, the power of the sound she can or cannot make and the reasons for this. Indeed Hester's nightmare is cast almost exclusively in terms of the inadequacies of the would-be singer's body: there is no attempt, for instance, to describe the opera itself or the female character that Hester has invented. We see Hester look at herself in her dressing room and see herself through the responses of others, before she appears onstage and at the moment at which her body is exposed. She is fleshless. Her "bare neck" and shoulders are "bony" and "coated with chalk". She has a wart on her lip. Her face and throat are "clammy" with fever.[13] When, onstage at last, Hester opens her mouth to sing, no noise comes out of her throat and the whole enterprise collapses. Sharon M. Harris has argued that Hester's problem is that she is without talent and "incapable of original thinking".[14] I would suggest that we are not asked to make a judgment about Hester's artistic talent but rather to consider the implications of the inability of her fleshless and unhealthy body to sing – or her nightmare that this is so.

The problem does not lie primarily with the opera house. From the start of the story, we see Hester attempting to control her body – she sends her baby away to a wet nurse, for example, and she physically separates herself from her husband and his family. Alternative bodily destinies are played out in the parallel drawn between Hester and her husband's neglectful and feckless first wife. Hester's predecessor is characterized as "diseased" and with "skin white, hanging loose from the flesh".[15] We begin to see the same repellent flesh quality in Hester, looking at herself in the mirror as she prepares to go onstage. Her predecessor is called a "foul vampire". As Hester creeps out of the theatre, she seems literally to have become a vampire herself: she

---

[13] Davis, "The Wife's Story", 210-12.
[14] Sharon M. Harris, *Rebecca Harding Davis and American Realism*, Philadelphia: U of Pennsylvania P, 1991, 110.
[15] Davis, "The Wife's Story", 202-203.

thinks she sees her husband dead on the ground "with a single drop of blood on the neck".[16]

Hester is not the only figure hampered by physical malfunction. "The Wife's Story" makes constant reference to ill health in terms of blood, breathing and disease. Hester has a "fever in the blood" as she works on her opera, but her husband Daniel, it seems, is in need of new blood. His marriage to Hester provokes him to remark, "This is putting new blood into my veins", while their estrangement prompts the comment that "we were too old" for "the fever of the blood called love".[17] There are constant references to breathing: Hester cannot, in the end, make sound come out of her throat, while Daniel's nostrils have a "blueness" about them.[18] References to "choking", surely the antithesis to singing, are rife in the narrative: Hester chokes in response to her little stepson's comments; Daniel twice chokes on his words; there are references to the choking sound of water. Thus, while physical breakdown is the result of Hester's endeavor, both she and Daniel have been in poor health: Hester has what she refers to as "the same old half-sickness" while Daniel has "a secret disease".[19] Nor is there an affirmative figure in a state of natural health. Jacky, Daniel's ward, is a sincere and "natural" creature and yet her face is "red" and her "small teeth determined as a steel trap" Interestingly, she, like Hester, cannot sing: her voice is "rough … like a cuckoo's".[20] Reference to an ailing or unattractive natural state even permeates the surrounding landscape. The cliffs at Newport are as "ghastly" in their bareness as Hester's shoulders, as "ashen" as Daniel's skin.[21]

Hester's longing to sing and inability to do so form the heart of a narrative of debilitation so wide-ranging as to suggest a general malaise in the culture. It may be that she is insufficiently wifely or over-ambitious and that her family is unhappy as a result. It may even be that she is less talented than she believes. Much more important, though, is the loss of physical power and the strangulation of physical expression that can be explored in a representation of a woman unable to sing.

---

[16] *Ibid.*, 214.
[17] *Ibid.*, 186, 194.
[18] *Ibid.*, 205.
[19] *Ibid.*, 210, 205.
[20] *Ibid.*, 180, 210, 202, 184.
[21] *Ibid.*, 206.

In a comparable way, Willa Cather's *Künstlerroman, The Song of the Lark*, examines what makes it possible for Thea Kronberg to sing. The novel makes much of how Thea's voice, identity, and success issue from her physical life. As Hester is bony and chalky, so Thea's body is described as animal, vital, and full of potential (and indeed scarcely gendered). She is described by her teacher Harsanyi as

> Like a horse, like a tree! …. She came to me like a fine young savage, a book with nothing written in it …. She is not quick, but she is solid, real.[22]

Thea has, in Cather's terms, the essential American body: coming from Northern European forbears, she is said to be "the sort that used to run wild in Germany" – full of strength and "the hardier feeling of action and daring", "tall and shining". Yes, Thea has "a big personality …. Brains, of course. Imagination, of course."[23] But it is the body that she has been born with, with its unconscious inheritance and memory, which provides the bedrock of her success. Her voice is powered and directed by her ethnic and regional inheritance, so, once accessed, the exercise of body and voice is instinctual.

If the singer's body and her physical health and vitality are central to her realization both as a visible woman and as a signifier of cultural health, so too is the space in which her power can most dynamically be exercised. It is interesting to find Foote, Cather and, more obliquely, Davis, drawing the West into their narratives of the singer's healthful power. Certainly, it is not surprising, during this period, to find the healthful body and its powerful exercise linked to a region that was associated with physical and social regeneration. Foote and Cather made their careers as writers of the Far West, and one expects them to return to such ground. The references to the West in "The Wife's Story" are less central to the plot, and yet they are interleaved within the narrative in a way that makes it difficult to avoid asking why they are there. The West is represented in terms of physical strength, in Daniel's muscle, in the "big square-built frames" of the men folk, and their "grave downright-looking faces". It signifies nature and purity: Teddy, Daniel's young son, is "as rough as a boar",

---

[22] Cather, *Song of the Lark*, 176.
[23] *Ibid.*, 271, 401, 379.

Jacky too is "rough" but hers is a "pure roughness" – "everything about the girl had been clean since she was born".

Westernness is also understood in terms of a cast of thought: Daniel's family has a "tough appreciation of fact beyond theory", and a way of "coming at the marrow and meaning of a scene or person … with a sheer subtilized common sense".[24] In staging a recovery, Hester and Daniel remake a style of Western life – a homestead, self-sufficiency, distance from the city, isolation – and recover their health. Hester's ambitions are erased in the process, but then the inhibited, choked society of rural New England and urban New York have made it impossible for her or her husband to realize their powers.

In a different but comparable way, Cather insists that, while Thea is stifled by Colorado's provincialism, nonetheless it is precisely the Westernness on which she can draw that enables her to reach the heights that she achieves. Similarly, "The Fate of a Voice", having finally situated Madeline in a "vague and rapidly lessening region known as the frontier", leaves her to sing in a massive and diversely populated space: "in the camps of engineers, within sound of unknown waters, on mountain trails, or crossing the windy cattle-ranges, or in the little churches of the valley towns."[25]

"The Fate of a Voice" and *Song of the Lark* both include important episodes that show the singer breaking free of expectations for their sex in the West. In both texts, the singer and her lover climb up into the kind of majestic, deserted canyon landscape so familiar to their contemporaries from painting and photography. In both, the ascent's erotic charge is suggested in references to panting and glowing faces; and in both cases the singer is portrayed rejecting the everyday satisfactions of married love in the face of the landscape they can see before them; we see both perching precariously but in profound and powerful solitude on the high rocks. The claim that Madeline and Thea can make to this exalted landscape is crucial to both scenes. We see Madeline changing the architecture of what is already a churning geological landscape, as she dislodges a rock, "the uppermost segment of a loosened column".[26] Thea, meanwhile, looks at the landscape and sees in it an extreme of independence that reflects her own temperament and aspirations:

---

[24] Davis, "The Wife's Story", 182, 184, 185, 187.
[25] Foote, "The Fate of a Voice", 274-75.
[26] *Ibid.*, 348.

Each tree grows alone, murmurs alone, thinks alone. They do not intrude upon each other. The Navahos are not much in the habit of giving or of asking for help. Their language is not a communicative one .... Over their forests there is the same inexorable reserve. Each tree has its exalted power to bear.[27]

In these Western landscape scenes, then, we return to the singer as a figure of a woman of indisputable power. Our sense of the scale of this feminine figure's powers and potential is magnificently evident in these huge spaces. She moves beyond the constraints of convention into a broader setting. But, for all the emphasis on the singer's magnificent equipment, visibility is only half the point. It is the sound that the singer makes that gives her power, whether she is visible on the stage or invisible in the Far western landscape.

Both Carolyn Abbate and Elizabeth Wood, exploring the cultural meaning of the powerful soprano voice, have suggested that its volume obliterates all constraints of gender, place and space. Abbate talks about how the operatic singer "drowns out everything in range"; she describes this voice's quality, triumphant and terrifying, as almost of roaring. Wood, in a similar reference to the irresistible power of the voice, writes of the soprano's "thrilling readiness to go beyond natural limits", "to overflow sonic boundaries".[28] We see precisely this breaking-free from constraint in the image of natural explosion that Cather uses to describe Thea singing the sextet from *Lucia di Lammermoor* with the men of the Mexican community in Moonstone Colorado: her "soprano voice, like a mountain jet, [shoots] up into the light". Foote has Madeline speaking of her desire to "sing to multitudes" and to enforce an "intoxicating silence" that it takes "hundreds" to make.[29]

The positioning of powerful female singers at the border between natural and unnatural, actual and supernatural, has a long tradition and is shaped by notions of singing women as irresistibly beautiful and

---

[27] Cather, *Song of the Lark*, 251.
[28] Carolyn Abbate, "Opera; or the Envoicing of Women", in *Musicology and Difference: Gender and Sexuality in Music Scholarship*, ed. Ruth A. Solie, Berkeley: U of California P, 254-55; Elizabeth Wood, "Sapphonics", in *Queering the Pitch: The New Gay and Lesbian Musicology*, eds Philip Brett, Elizabeth Wood, and Gary C. Thomas, London: Routledge, 33.
[29] Cather, *Song of the Lark*, 202; Foote, "The Fate of a Voice", 227.

tuneful but also as monstrous and malign. The significance of the sirens of myth often lies in their power to lure men to destruction; while the power to sing ("of arms and the man") is given to the male subject in classical writing, the power of the siren occupies a very different register of meaning. It is both erotic and indifferent to human pain and desire. Both Foote and Cather have their singers perform and practice the Heine poem, "Die Lorelei", set to music by both Liszt and Schubert. The Lorelei, a siren figure from German legend whose singing up on a rock lures sailors to their death, was a popular subject in the late nineteenth century.

Neither Madeline nor Thea are heartless *femme fatales*, though. Nor do they draw their menfolk men to destruction. Though in both fictions we see them positioned, albeit rather precariously, on the top of rocks with their lovers looking up from below, in both cases they are registering the desire for a separation from the usual destiny of a woman and for the exercise of a multi-dimensional power. Cather and Foote draw on the trope of the siren to mark a gap between the realm that the singer's "fateful voice" (as Foote puts it) allows her to occupy and the more earthbound context of the men around her. It is the sound that she makes, the voice, huge, invisible, and difficult to locate, that sets her apart and places her upon another plane of action. Certainly, Madeline's lover, Hugh Aldis, experiences Madeline's singing of "Die Lorelei" as a "delicious pain" and hears her voice as "pure" and "pitiless" "[celebrating] its own triumph and another's allurement and despair".[30] But then this is a character that does not wish to look upwards, as it were, for inspiration. He would prefer only to hear "the music of those silences" between Madeline and himself. In *The Song of the Lark*, the character of Dr Archie (who has acted as Thea's sponsor) is able to reach an understanding that Thea has been exalted by her magnificent voice and has the power to bring an intensity of experience to thousands of others. While his own successes in Colorado have brought him distinction and the kind of profile that makes meeting with the now-successful Thea achievable, nonetheless Dr Archie comes to recognize that it is "not appropriate to feel affection for her".[31]

Therefore Thea and Madeline are sirens in the sense that they have a special power and occupy a particular realm: Steven Connor

---

[30] Foote, "The Fate of a Voice", 261-62
[31] Cather, *The Song of the Lark*, 349.

describes the way in which "the voice ... inhabits and occupies space ... it ... actively procures space for itself". This is what Madeline's voice does. We habitually think of women as struggling to be heard during this period. In the figure of the singer, we have a voice that creates its own space and which cannot be resisted. As Connor says, "We cannot shut off hearing as we can seeing. We cannot ... 'listen away' as we can look away."[32] So while, for example, Aldis' attempt to penetrate rock and uncover wealth in the West seems dwarfed by the massive surrounding landscape, Madeline's intervention in the West at the end of the story is a "free exercise". Her triumph in the New York Academy has been a mere foretaste of the power exercised by the sound of the voice "singing in the Wilderness". This sound presages the dawn of a new American culture: "the day of art and beauty which is coming to a new country and a new people."[33] And now it is not delivered to a paying audience but expands out, in the form of sound, from the heartlands of America.

In *The Song of the Lark*, the link is even more firmly made between singing and the victorious domination of space. Thea is constantly imaged as increasing her powers: performing Wagner, she is "so far from shrinking she expanded"; she exists "in more space than she occupied by measurement".[34] Jacques Attali has written about the way that music can "Make people Forget, Make them Believe, Silence them. In all these cases, music is a tool of power."[35] Like Madeline's voice, Thea's has this power. Singing Wagner, she becomes a warlike creature, rising "into the hardier feeling of action and doing".[36]

This is the symbolic landscape of myth. But in one of the most interesting scenes in Cather's novel, Thea's voice expands to enclose the Mexicans who are seated rather worshipfully around her. In singing "for a really musical people", Thea draws the Mexicans to "[turn] themselves and all that they had over to her". In a more military image, Cather describes Thea feeling "as if all these warm-

---

[32] Steven Connor, *Dumbstruck: A Cultural History of Ventriloquism*, Oxford: Oxford UP, 2000, 12, 16-17.

[33] Foote, "The Fate of a Voice", 275.

[34] Cather, *Song of the Lark*, 314.

[35] Jacques Attali, *Noise: The Political Economy of Music*, trans. Brian Massumi, Minneapolis: U of Minnesota P, 1985, 21.

[36] Cather, *Song of the Lark*, 401.

blooded people débouched into her".[37] The word "débouche" is an interesting one, evoking as it does the movement (characteristically by soldiers) from a confined space into open country. Thea's music draws the Mexicans from their confinement (in spatial and economic terms) into the space created by the sound she makes. But while they have the sense of release from constraint, they have moved into Thea's powerful orbit: "open, eager, unprotected" they have "débouched *into her*" (my italics).

What is the significance of these powerful voices if not as a fantasy of a benign power over people and space: an imperialism of sound? In describing "sound imperialism" in the Victorian soundscape, John M. Picker refers to the experience of struggling to be heard, an experience we associate with women during this period.[38] In Davis, Foote, and Cather, however, it is not the female singer but the concert and opera audiences that must be silenced. Foote's and Cather's audiences learn – or are mesmerized into – submission and then give themselves up to applause. As Christopher Small puts it, the audience really has "nothing to contribute to [the] course [of the performance of music]".[39] The sound of the soprano's voice, storming through space, far from being transgressive, seems to express an ideal of subjugation that dissolves conflict in an uplifting experience of trance.

Linda and Michael Hutcheon have drawn our attention to the way in which the opera houses of the era celebrated imperial power.[40] Small too has written of the scale and decorative ebullience of such buildings, the importance given to such spaces and the wealth and power mobilized to create them. Foote and Cather both respond to the magnificence of the opera house and concert hall and both affirm contemporary assumptions about the civilizing work of such spaces.

It is possible to conclude, then, that the figure of the singer may evoke victorious and even aggressive domination of space and people. The sound that she makes is, as Abbate and Wood aver, "limitless"; it defies "boundaries". And yet, the question of sound and audibility is a complex one that brings me back to my earlier argument about the

---

[37] *Ibid.*, 200.
[38] John M. Picker, *Victorian Soundscapes*, Oxford: Oxford UP, 2003, 4-6.
[39] Christopher Small, *Musicking: The Meanings of Performing and Listening*, Hanover, CT: UP of New England, 1998, 27.
[40] Linda and Michael Hutcheon, *Opera: Desire, Disease and Death*, Lincoln: U of Nebraska P, 1996, 4.

singer's agency. As I have suggested, the source of the sound that the singer makes is difficult to grasp. It may be God-given or instinctual or the work of thought, or indeed none of these things. The agency of the singer herself is uncertain. Is this victorious figure simply the creation of others for profit? Is there a struggle for power that the triumph of the singer masks? There is a triumphalism in these figures, certainly, but the terms of their victory are difficult to assess, as Thea narrows her life down to the performance of opera and Madeline becomes invisible. These are public figures but the sphere in which they move is difficult to summarize. Meanwhile, Davis' Hester fails to sing in the theatre and rediscovers health by refusing a life of performance.

The female singer was a strikingly visible figure in the late nineteenth and early twentieth centuries. She was understood to possess extraordinary physical and bodily powers. She made an extraordinarily loud noise. She dominated the huge and status-laden spaces of the concert hall and the opera house. Indeed I have argued that the singer offered a body – a woman's body – that could appropriately be visualized, described, and analyzed. This opportunity to dwell upon the body of a woman that the singer offered and the writing that it produced offers us another route for approaching the implications of women's greater visibility in the late nineteenth century: the appearance of a woman, even her display of her self and her body, were not always and necessarily problematic, while the failure to perform in public or to be heard could be a way of envisioning a life of profound lack of fulfillment. Further, looking at fictions across the period between the Civil War and World War I, we can find examples of writers using this figure to explore the body in its cultural as well as its physical dimensions. The cultural power of the healthy woman's body is significant to all three of the writers discussed here.

At the same time, this is a figure that defies limits, regardless of her femininity, the state of her intimate life, even her personality. Much has been claimed about the difficulty that women across classes experience in being heard, and these claims have been rehearsed again and again in arguments about public and private, centers and margins, power and exclusion. What is perhaps most interesting about the singer, in the end, is the way in which she moves outside these kinds of claims and determinisms. In her performance lies an engagement with the limits of visibility, the complex qualities of space and the strange and unpredictable sound of the voice.

THE PAINFUL PRODUCTION OF VERENA TARRANT: JOHN LOCKE AND *THE BOSTONIANS*

PETER RAWLINGS

Spectacle

"Much in the nineteenth century", remarks Asa Briggs, "had the sense of a 'great spectacle,' particularly for the curious and entranced eye".[1] At the centre of Henry James' *The Bostonians* is a struggle, conducted largely in ocular terms, over how Verena Tarrant as "the cynosure of every eye" will be produced.[2] In general, it is counter-intuitive to regard "becoming visible" in the later nineteenth century as anything

---

[1] Asa Briggs, *Victorian Things*, Harmondsworth: Penguin, 1988, 104.

[2] James, *The Bostonians*, Harmondsworth: Penguin, 1978, 234. My on-going research indicates that there is a much higher frequency of words relating to the eye and vision in James' fiction than in other novels and short stories of the period. In *The Bostonians* the word ratio is approximately 1:676. This seems fairly constant in James: *The Portrait of a Lady*: 1:697; *Washington Square*: 1:684; *The Wings of a Dove*: 1:729; *The Golden Bowl*: 1:890. In William Dean Howells' *The Rise of Silas Lapham* (published in 1885, the year before *The Bostonians*), the ratio is 1:1220; similarly in Thomas Hardy's *The Mayor of Casterbridge* (1886) it is 1:1212. Predictably, given that Dickens "understood more clearly" than many other Victorian writers "all the metaphors of the eye" (Briggs, *Victorian Things*, 119) and given the visual preoccupations of the novel, the ratio in *The Pickwick Papers* (1836-37) is 1:607. (In James' short story "Glasses" [1896] the most optical of his works, the frequency rises to 1:411.) If Mrs Wix in James' *What Maisie Knew* is afflicted by an "obliquity of vision" (a squint) as she attempts to apply her "straighteners" to the moral confusion around her (Chicago: Herbert S. Stone and Co., 1897, 31), "the whole moral vision of Boston" is in Miss Birdseye's "displaced spectacles" (James, *The Bostonians*, 31). Mrs Wix's "goggles", as she sees them, "reminded" Maisie "of the polished shell or corslet of a horrid beetle" and in *The Bostonians*, "Mr Grace's … big head" is rendered even more repulsive by his "eye-glasses". If glasses disfigure in James, they also draw attention to the problem of seeing straight or far in the world of experience. Such preoccupations were at the forefront of John Locke's meditations in *An Essay Concerning Human Understanding* (1690) on the contingent nature of truth and knowledge. The proliferation of glasses in *The Bostonians* signifies just how difficult it was to become visible naturally as the nineteenth century wore on. See Briggs, *Victorian Things*, 114, on the United States and cheap spectacles.

other than liberating for women. The exploration of visibility in *The Bostonians*, however, is enmeshed in a critique of the collusions and conspiracies between seeing and being seen, performance, insincere productions of the self, publicity, and the tawdry world of a decaying lyceum culture which have the effect, in the main, of calling into question the terms of these liberatory imperatives.

From a narrow perspective on the issue of the oppression of women by men, *The Bostonians* stands or falls by whether or not readers agree with the narrator's claim that he or she is only the "reporter" of Basil Ransom's "angry" condemnations of what he sees as "a herd of vociferating women".[3] James' novels are dominated by the representation of women; and these women are, more often than not, vastly more responsive, sensitive, and pragmatic than the frequently feeble men who try to exercise power over them. This is certainly the case in *Daisy Miller*, where the desiccated narrator is unable to comprehend Daisy and her defiance of the stifling conventions of the expatriate community in Rome.

Yet James feared women writers. In one of his final assessments of George Sand, a writer he professed to admire, James praises her novels for being "beautiful, plentiful, and fluid", but he goes on to observe that "the sense of fluidity is fundamentally fatal to the sense of particular truth". Uppermost in James' numerous pieces on George Sand is a focus on "loquacity", "the laxity of the feminine intellect", and the "imagination" of women as being characterized by the "restless, nervous, and capricious".[4] In a similar vein, in the year that his first fiction was published, Miss Prescott is attacked for using "too many words" and for possessing "in excess", and with some uncertainty as to what or who is the possible fatality, "the fatal gift of fluency".[5] If George Eliot, in 1866, can be brought into James' pantheon by virtue of her "masculine comprehensiveness", by 1873 the "diffuseness" of *Middlemarch* as "too copious a dose of pure

---

[3] James, *The Bostonians*, 44.
[4] James, "George Sand" (1868), in *Literary Criticism: French Writers, Other European Writers, the Prefaces to the New York Edition*, New York: Library of America, 1984, II, 759, 721, 731, 699.
[5] James, review of *Azarian: An Episode* by Harriet Elizabeth Prescott, *North American Review*, XCVII (1863), in *Literary Criticism*, II, 610.

fiction" is his complaint.[6] Forced into acknowledging the success of writers such as Mrs Humphry Ward in 1892, James drifts into considering the "effective feminine voice" in general, only to vanquish it by organizing the noise of machinery and industrial production as his terms of reference. "No example would be more interesting" than "the way in which women, after prevailing for so many ages in our private history, have begun to be unchallenged contributors to our public. Very surely and not at all slowly the effective feminine voice makes its ingenious hum the very ground-tone of the uproar in which the conditions of its interference are discussed."[7]

Fluid, fertile women clearly threaten James in ways that go beyond the literary, and floods, general incontinence, and the impossibility of any form of containment inform all his judgments about their work. In the context of James' vitriolic observations on women's writing in general, it is not difficult to read *The Bostonians* as endorsing what can be read as the abduction and enslavement of Verena Tarrant.[8] "If he should become her husband he should know a way to strike her dumb" must be one of the most brutal phrases in the whole of James, and Olive rightly fears that Verena's mouth will be "stopped by a kiss". This allusion to *Much Ado about Nothing* ("Peace, I will stop your mouth. [*Kissing her*]") reminds us, as Tony Tanner has argued, that phallic pens are at war with women's voices in this novel.[9]

But Alfred Habegger sees both William Dean Howells and Henry James as "sissies" in a world of men, war, and business; and if this assessment is even partly right, the distance between Basil Ransom and Henry James is immense. For Habegger, James was suspended between a "man's world" and the "women's sphere".[10] James,

---

[6] James, review of *Felix Holt* (1866), in *Literary Criticism: Essays on Literature, American Writers, English Writers*, New York: Library of America, 1984, I, 911; James, review of *Middlemarch* (1873), in *Literary Criticism*, I, 965.

[7] James, "Mrs. Humphrey Ward" (1892), in *Literary Criticism*, I, 1371.

[8] According to the *Oxford English Dictionary*, "Basil" refers to the antidote for the basilisk's venom and in its modern French form, "basilic", both to the serpent and the plant: as Verena observes, "[we] might go round as poison and antidote!" (James, *The Bostonians*, 80). "Basil" is also the name of the "iron" or "fetter" used to manacle slaves.

[9] James, *The Bostonians*, 278, 119; Tony Tanner, *Scenes of Nature, Signs of Men*, Cambridge: Cambridge UP, 1987, 158-71.

[10] Alfred Habegger, *Gender, Fantasy, and Realism in American Literature*, New York: Columbia UP, 1982, 63.

however, abominated publicity, public spaces, and the world of men and business: visibility, for the most part gendered neuter in James, was one of his greatest horrors.[11] For *The Bostonians*, these issues are at least as significant as the cliché-ridden campaign (not, of course, to be confused with real campaigns) on behalf of women's rights mounted by a privileged Olive Chancellor entirely for self-serving purposes.

Seeing

Since Laura Mulvey's Lacanian analysis of film, the concept of the male gaze and its controlling power has become only too familiar.[12] Long before Lacan and Mulvey, however, James was no stranger to the "empire of the eye", and he had a much less abstract and far more physiological, corporeal, sense of vision than Jacques Lacan.[13] For an empirical philosopher such as John Locke, "impressions" were not abstract and insubstantial – they involved sensory disturbance and left palpable marks. John Carlos Rowe captures the essence of this, alerting us to some of the physical, metaphysical, and ideological elements involved:

> The "impression" as at once material and immaterial, as violent act and superficial glance, as fleeting moment and enduring mark (memory-trace), as noun that cannot suppress its verbal origin – this impression is the divided present and rhetorical catachresis in which language finds its own origin, even as it preserves this secret beneath the gaze of the eye and the voice of the I.[14]

James' backward reach is to the radical empiricism of John Locke, in what is also an affiliation with William James, to an idea of seeing as

---

[11] For a discussion of privacy and publicity in James, see Peter Rawlings, *Henry James and the Abuse of the Past*, Basingstoke: Palgrave Macmillan, 2005, Ch. 3.
[12] Laura Mulvey, "Visual Pleasures and Narrative Cinema", *Screen* XVI/3 (Autumn 1975), 6-18; Laura Mulvey, *Visual and Other Pleasures*, Bloomington: Indiana UP, 1989.
[13] Henry James "A Chain of Cities" (1874), in *Collected Travel Writings: The Continent*, New York: Library of America, 1993, 504; Jacques Lacan, *The Four Fundamental Concepts of Psycho-analysis*, trans. Alan Sheridan, ed. Jacques-Alain Miller, New York: Norton, 1977.
[14] John Carlos Rowe, *The Theoretical Dimensions of Henry James*, Madison: U of Wisconsin P, 1985, 193.

the process of making knowledge and truth, thereby, one of achieving control, mastery, and power.[15]

James devotes a lot of energy in *The Bostonians* to describing eyes. Basil Ransom's "magnificent eyes" are "dark, deep and glowing"; they are also "unremunerated" and "barbaric";[16] Olive Chancellor's are "extraordinary", and towards the end of the novel, we learn that they are "strange" and "green".[17] Mrs Farrinder has "large, cold, and quiet" eyes, and Dr Prance's "pupils" are "little, sharp, fixed".[18] If he engenders in his daughter "enthusiastic" eyes, Verena Tarrant's father possesses the peculiar ability "to look round at the company with all his teeth"; he "gaze[s] at the carpet with supernatural attention", "never" seeing "so much as when he had his eyes fixed on the cornice".[19] Selah Tarrant is a "mesmeric healer", as well as an incorrigible sponger, but Verena is much more under Olive's hypnotic control that she ever was under his. Olive has an extraordinary repertoire of ocular moves and many of them are palpable: she can bore "the carpet with her conscious eyes" and release ballistic "cold glare[s]".[20] Ransom feels "Olive's eyes receiving him" and Verena that "her friend's strange, uneasy eyes searched very far; a little more and they would go to the very bottom".[21]

The battle between Olive and Ransom for Verena is largely one about who shall control her visibility. Ransom's fluctuating yet strengthening influence over Verena is mapped in terms of the respective power he and Olive have over the novel's visual economy. Olive's high point appears to be in New York when, during Verena's speech, "the only thing wanting to her triumph was that [Ransom]

---

[15] "Truth *happens* to an idea. It *becomes* true, is *made* true by events in a world where "knowing … exists concretely" (William James, *Writings, 1902-1910*, New York: Library of America, 1987, 823, 898; emphasis in original).

[16] James, *The Bostonians*, 6, 181, 218.

[17] *Ibid.*, 17, 357.

[18] *Ibid.*, 27-28, 35-36.

[19] *Ibid.*, 46, 49, 103, 91.

[20] *Ibid.*, 58, 242.

[21] *Ibid.*, 237, 251. This is all consonant with "corpuscular" theories of vision. For Locke, sensory experience is constituted by particles of matter, the "thinking eternal being" is only "some certain system of matter" (John Locke, *An Essay Concerning Human Understanding* [1690], ed. Peter H. Nidditch, Oxford: Clarendon P, 1975, 627). See Laurens Laudan's article, "The Nature and Sources of Locke's Views on Hypotheses", *Journal of the History of Ideas*, XXVIII/2 (April-June 1967), 211-13, on Locke and corpuscular physics.

should have been placed in the line of her vision", so that she might enjoy what she mistakenly believes is "his embarrassment and confusion".[22] Increasingly, as Ransom gains in ascendancy, "fixed in the belief that the sex in general requires watching", Olive's "searching, accusing eyes" are more often than not "on the ground", as she rails against herself for being a "blind idiot".[23] By the close, shortly before Ransom "thrust[s] the hood of Verena's long cloak over her head, to conceal her face and identity", he sees with "astonishment" that the eyes that looked at him out of [Olive Chancellor's] scared, haggard face were ... eyes of tremendous entreaty".[24] It is in New York – as "His eyes came back to Verena's, the expressions of which had changed before they quitted them" – that Basil intensifies his campaign against Olive, and it is in Central Park that Verena "felt his eyes on her face – ever so close and fixed there": "Verena had been commended of old by Olive for her serenity while exposed to the gaze of hundreds; but a change had taken place, and she was not unable to endure the contemplation of an individual."[25]

In the broadest sense, the Central Park section of the novel is a "turning-point" for the hapless couple of Ransom and Verena:

> The truth had changed sides; that radiant image began to look at her from Basil Ransom's expressive eyes. She loved, she was in love – she felt it in every throb of her being. Instead of being constituted by nature for entertaining that sentiment in an exceptionally small degree ... she was framed, apparently, to allow it the largest range, the highest intensity. It was always passion, in fact; but now the object was other.[26]

I shall argue that four of the shaping elements in this passage can be located in Locke's *An Essay Concerning Human Understanding* and the empirical tradition it partly constitutes: the contingent nature of truth; its concept of personal identity; the power of sentiment (on which I shall concentrate); and the controlling paradigm of corporeality. I shall also consider a fifth element: the vital importance for Verena that she should suffer painfully by the end of the novel and

---

[22] James, *The Bostonians*, 230.
[23] *Ibid.*, 182, 218, 246.
[24] *Ibid.*, 389, 383.
[25] *Ibid.*, 234, 294.
[26] *Ibid.*, 332.

beyond. I shall return to this passage after considering empiricism more broadly in relation to James and Locke.

Jerome Huyler observes in his *Locke in America: The Moral Philosophy of the Founding Era* that for nearly a quarter century historical research has been effectively discounting the influence of John Locke on the "founding of the American republic"; and his book does much to rectify the problem.[27] Yet Huyler's exclusive emphasis is on the "social and political principles" in play. Like Barbara Arneil, whose *John Locke and America: The Defence of English Colonialism* appeared in the following year, Huyler has nothing to say about the impact of Locke on American aesthetics and philosophy.[28] Michael Bell, in his *Sentimentalism, Ethics and the Culture of Feeling* minimizes the importance of James' sentimental vocabulary in "The Art of Fiction" (and his contentions are very much my point of departure in this essay): "James' 'moral sense,' 'feeling,' and 'sensibility' embody the transformative assimilation of sentiment: while constituting a dense field of sentimental vocabulary, they are so altered as to hardly reveal this."[29]

Experience, observation, perception, and reflection are as much the defining characteristics of James' theory and practice of fiction as they are at the core of Locke's *Essay*. "Experience" and "empiricism", from the Greek *empeiria* (experience) are practically interchangeable; but I prefer "empiricism" for both Locke and James because of the roots of *empeiria*. The word literally means "in trial", which is highly appropriate, I think, to the experience of nearly all James' characters, and to James' affinities with various forms of his brother William's American pragmatism.[30] From the early sixteenth century on (according to the *Oxford English Dictionary*), an empiric in medicine

---

[27] Jerome Huyler, *Locke in America: The Moral Philosophy of the Founding Era*, Kansas City: Kansas UP, 1995, ix. John Henry Raleigh, in "Henry James: The Poetics of Empiricism", *PMLA*, LXVI/2 (March 1951), 107-23, acknowledges the importance of Locke for American culture and for Henry James' empiricism in particular.

[28] Barbara Arneil, *John Locke and America: The Defence of English Colonialism*, Oxford: Clarendon P, 1996.

[29] Michael Bell, *Sentimentalism, Ethics, and the Culture of Feeling*, Basingstoke: Palgrave Macmillan, 2000, 7; Henry James, "The Art of Fiction", *Longman's Magazine*, 4 (1884), in James, *Literary Criticism*, I, 44-65.

[30] Richard A. Hocks, *Henry James and Pragmatistic Thought: A Study in the Relationship between the Philosophy of William James and the Literary Art of Henry James*, Chapel Hill: North Carolina UP, 1974 offers a comprehensive account of the relationship between William James' pragmatism and his brother's fiction.

and science was an untrained practitioner, or quack. For James, living, or groping through the attempt – Strether's "very gropings would figure among his most interesting motions", as the Preface to *The Ambassadors* has it – is quackery in this strict, empirical, sense.[31] This is what unites, among others, Catherine Sloper, Verena Tarrant, Isabel Archer, Maisie, and Strether. In this context, *The Bostonians* is an attack on dogmatism anchored in specious authority (books, history, and the like) and on attempts to professionalize Verena on her journey from drawing room to music hall.[32]

Famously, perhaps by now notoriously, Locke asserted that the congenital mind is a "white Paper" and that all knowledge derives from experience.[33] There can be no experience without the senses, or sensations, for these convey external objects to the mind and become there the subjects of reflection. Locke defines consciousness as "the perception of what passes in a Man's own mind" and tentatively suggests that perception is the "first step and degree towards knowledge".[34] He is rather vague, in ways hardly unfamiliar to James, about the possibility and nature of subsequent steps. At the outset of his *Essay*, Locke declares that "our business here is not to know all things, but those which concern our conduct".[35] Locke's account of how we live and try to pursue knowledge is intensely physiological or corporeal: nerves are solid objects, and encounters with the external world involve movement and "vibration", a word to which James is addicted in *The Bostonians*. There are liberal allocations of this kind of language to Olive in particular: she "drew in her breath, for an instant, like a creature in pain; then, with her quavering voice, touched

---

[31] Preface to *The Ambassadors* (1909), in *Literary Criticism*, II, 1313.

[32] The "gas-lighted" drawing room in which Verena first performs has all the stark visibility of a "street-car", but it remains, nominally, a private space. In New York, at Mrs Burrage's, Ransom speculates on the extent to which this is a private or a public event, given the presence of a "platform": "The platform it evidently was to be – private if not public – since one was admitted by a ticket given away if not sold" (214). This intermediate space, where Verena looks increasingly like "a walking advertisement" (225), gives way to the Boston Music Hall, with its thronging crowd and all the paraphernalia of posters, photographs, and organ music. As Mrs Luna observes, Olive "has taken it to bring out Miss Tarrant before the general public" (318). Once with Ransom, Verena's only "platform" is to be "the dining-table itself", and he tells her "you shall mount on top of that" (337).

[33] Locke, *Concerning Human Understanding*, 104-105.

[34] *Ibid.*, 105, 149.

[35] *Ibid.*, 46.

with a vibration of anguish, she said: 'Oh, how can I ask you to give up?'"; Verena has a "vibrating voice", and "she seems to vibrate, to echo with every word".[36] Detecting these vibrations is always more important to Ransom than any sense he can impute to Verena's speeches: "After he had stood there a quarter of an hour he became conscious that he should not be able to repeat a word she had said; he had not definitely heeded it, and yet he had not lost a vibration of her voice." There is a fundamental distinction in the novel between what can be felt through the "inner sense" and what is available "through the impediment of mere dazzled vision".[37] Rescuing Verena from this "dazzle" and awakening her "inner sense" is the putative project of the novel.

In "The Art of Fiction", James' most significant account of experience, he is dismayed by, and yet fundamentally in agreement with, Walter Besant's injunction in his own *The Art of Fiction* that one should write from experience.[38] The problem is that Besant sees experience as finite and cognizable, whereas for James:

> [it] is never limited, and it is never complete; it is an immense sensibility, a kind of huge spider-web of the finest silken threads suspended in the chamber of consciousness, and catching every air-borne particle in its tissue. It is the very atmosphere of the mind; and when the mind is imaginative – much more when it happens to be that of a man of genius – it takes to itself the very hints of life, it converts the very pulses of the air into revelations.[39]

Nothing could be at a greater distance from Locke's *Essay*, it might be argued, than this passage, with its clear investment in Romantic notions of the imagination. But Locke set no limit on experience and would have scorned the idea that anything other than death can complete it. For James, as *The Bostonians* demonstrates, the eye and visual transactions in general are affairs of immense palpability, and embodied notions of sensibility are at the core of Locke's lexicon. What, though, about "silken threads" and "tissue", and the conversion of "the very pulses of the air into revelations"? This whimsical vocabulary seems utterly at odds with Locke's corporealism.

---

[36] James, *The Bostonians*, 71, 75, 189.
[37] *Ibid.*, 230.
[38] Walter Besant, *The Art of Fiction*, Boston: Cupples, Upham and Co., 1884, 15-20.
[39] James, "The Art of Fiction", 52.

But James' analysis of the consciousness, especially the artistic consciousness, can be situated comfortably in turn of the eighteenth-century physiological and biological treatises written in the empirical tradition. For the French biologist Xavier Bichat, life was a function of that tissue, organized in such a way as to resist dissolution and disintegration. James' "tissue", however ethereal it seems, is Bichat's stubborn primal life material, what he defines as any "agglomeration of cells".[40] The discourse of James' "The Art of Fiction" is organicist, rooted as it is in nineteenth-century biology, physiology, and cell theory. The analytical yield of all this is in the correspondences it allows us to perceive between texts, textures, weaving, and bodies. It is clear, then, that James' account of experience is as physiological as anything in Locke's *Essay*. James' map of experience, however, has its ultimate destination in the imagination; and we have been taught by William Blake and his followers that Locke's properties of the mind are "blankness, narrowness, and duskiness".[41] But on the question of the imagination and its limits, Locke argues that our experiences are transmitted through sensations to a mind that makes "new Compositions" and that these are "perfectly inexhaustible".[42] There are evident synergies between James' and Locke's account of experience and the imagination, and these extend to the metaphorical imaginary of each writer.

The tropes deployed by Locke to chart the relation between the mind and the world correspond closely with James' in his Preface to *The Portrait of a Lady*. James' "house of fiction", I would argue, was first conceived in Locke's *Essay*.[43] Locke argues that:

> ... external and internal Sensation, are the only passages that I can find, of knowledge, to the Understanding .... These alone ... are the windows by which light is let into this *dark Room*. For, methinks, the

---

[40] Marie François Xavier Bichat, quoted in François Jacob, *The Logic of Living Systems: A History of Heredity*, trans. Betty E. Spillmann, London: Allen Lane, 1974, 57.

[41] Syndy M. Conger, *Mary Wollstonecraft and the Language of Sensibility*, London and Toronto: Associated UP, 1994, xxxvi.

[42] Locke, *Concerning Human Understanding*, 168.

[43] Victoria Coulson, in her "Prisons, Palaces, and the Architecture of the Imagination", in *Palgrave Advances in Henry James Studies*, ed. Peter Rawlings, Basingstoke and New York: Palgrave Macmillan, 2007, 169-91, argues that, in James, "every house turns out to be a prison" (184). But without confinement there can be no art for James, and, for Locke, no life.

> *Understanding* is not much unlike a closet wholly shut from light, *with only some little openings left*, to let in external visible Resemblances, or *Ideas* of things, without.[44]

For James:

> The house of fiction has in short not one window, but a million ... every one of which has been pierced, or is still pierceable, in its vast front, by the need of the individual vision. These apertures, of dissimilar shape and size, hang so all together, over the human scene that we might have expected of them a greater sameness of report than we find. They are but windows at the best, mere holes in a dead wall. .... But they have this mark of their own that at each of them stands a figure with a pair of eyes ... they are, singly or together, as nothing without the posted presence of the watcher – without, in other words, the consciousness of the artist.[45]

If Locke is James' architect, the house seems to function quite differently. Locke's self appears to be the passive receiver of the light, whereas James' consciousness is somehow the animator of dead walls.

This reading, however, does no more than merely conform to post-Romantic expectations of what ought to be the incongruities between Locke and James. It entirely overlooks the fact that if, for James, each "pair of eyes" is a "unique instrument" resulting in different impressions, for Locke: "every thing does not hit alike upon every Man's imagination. We have our Understandings no less different than our Palates."[46] He later adds, in a resonantly enigmatic statement, that:

> Some Eyes want Spectacles to see things clearly and distinctly; but let not those who use them therefore say, no body can see clearly without them .... Everyone knows what best fits his own Sight. But let him not thence conclude all in the dark.[47]

Locke and James identify similar mechanisms and frameworks for experience, observation, perception, and the working of the imagination. But whereas James seems to celebrate immensity,

---

[44] Locke, *Concerning Human Understanding*, 162-63.
[45] Henry James, Preface to *Portrait of a Lady*, in *Literary Criticism*, I, 1075.
[46] Locke, *Concerning Human Understanding*, 8.
[47] *Ibid.*, 678.

boundlessness, and uniqueness, Locke sees such infinitudes (which he does not deny) as intensely dangerous. I would argue, however, that James' celebrations are frequently dark and desperate, and that Locke, more often than not, relishes the terrors of the immensity he specifies.

Reflections

Verena Tarrant spends most of her time in *The Bostonians* in forms of confinement not of her own making and in realms of visibility organized on her behalf. In Olive Chancellor's house, Ransom "has never felt himself in the presence of so much organized privacy".[48] Enclosed spaces, and how women in particular relate to them on a private-public axis, abound in the novel; and as with Locke's closet and James' house of fiction, they articulate and define agents and objects of visibility. From Ransom's perspective, the principal contrast is between the "forum" and the "fireplace" as spatializations of the public and the private, and he rejects Olive's view that "home-culture" is "perfectly compatible with the widest emancipation".[49] For Olive, emancipation involves an absence of form and a confused social economy. Verena makes a "scene" of the "mean little room in Monadnoc Place" where she has the "air of being a public character":

> There was indeed a sweet comicality in seeing this pretty girl sit there and, in answer to a casual, civil inquiry, drop into oratory as a natural thing. Had she forgotten where she was, and did she take him for a full house? She has the same turns and cadences, almost the same gestures, as if she had been on the platform.[50]

The miscegenation of public and private spaces, together with the hybrid subjectivity in which it results, is at odds with the "sublime economy of art" for James.[51]

"Where there is no law there is no freedom", proclaimed Locke, and James, like Ransom, believed not only that uncurbed desires for liberation and liberty were delusory, but that they entail a collapse of the regulations on which visibility depends.[52] If freedom can exist

---

[48] James, *The Bostonians*, 15.

[49] *Ibid.*, 79.

[50] *Ibid.*, 194-96.

[51] James, Preface to *The Spoils of Poynton* (1908), in *Literary Criticism*, II, 1139.

[52] Locke, "Second Treatise on Civil Government" (1690), in *Social Contract: Essays by Locke, Hume and Rousseau*, The World's Classics, ed. Sir Ernest Barker, London:

only in relation to law, then visibility is contingent on ways of seeing, forms of attention, what is excluded as well as included, and on the conventions we deploy individually and communally for filtering, ordering, and framing. James is to admire in *The American Scene* the "finer feeling for enclosure" in the South and finds himself "cold-bloodedly" preferring those aspects of the "great folly" of slavery that might have resulted in the retention of a "vision" of "a multitudinous complicated life" to hotels that signify only crassness and the taking of liberties.[53] It is not vacancy that this "ancient contemplative person" experiences as his "ship draws near" to the shores of America, but the "monstrous form of Democracy", and the "something deficient, absent" is the exclusion, the exclusiveness, on which his art has depended for its power.[54] Becoming visible is one thing, total visibility in the context of incontinent publicity is quite another, for indiscriminate seeing is no seeing at all. Locke's dark closet with the glimpses of light it allows, and the corresponding incarceration in a house of fiction posited by James, are acknowledgements of a perspectivism Verena encounters for the first time in Central Park.

"There is only seeing from a perspective", Nietzsche argues in *The Genealogy of Morals*, "only a knowing from a perspective".[55] In his *A Pluralistic Universe*, William James contends that the world of experience, the "world experienced", and the "field of consciousness" are identical with a perceiving self, a "body", which is "the storm centre, the origin of co-ordinates": "everything circles round it, and is felt from its point of view"; this world "comes at all times with our body at its centre, centre of vision, centre of action, centre of interest".[56] But "a pluralistic, restless universe", he states in *The Will to Believe* is one "in which no single point of view can ever take in the whole scene". "Goodness, badness, and obligation", he continues, "must be *realized* somewhere in order really to exist", and "their only

Oxford UP, 1947, 47. James does not limit this restriction to women in his fiction: this is also Strether's realization in *The Ambassadors* (1903).
[53] Henry James, *The American Scene* (1907), in *Collected Travel Writings: Great Britain and America*, New York: Library of America, 1993, 686-87.
[54] James, *The American Scene*, 401-402.
[55] Friedrich Nietzsche, *The Joyful Wisdom* (1882), trans. Thomas Common, in *The Complete Works of Friedrich Nietzsche*, ed. Oscar Levy, Edinburgh and London: T.N. Foulis, 1910, X, 152-53.
[56] William James, *A Pluralistic Universe* (1909), in *Writings, 1902-1910*, New York: Library of America, 1987, 803n.

habitat can be a mind which feels them"; "beyond the facts of [the individual's] own subjectivity there is nothing moral in the world".[57] As the tellingly entitled "On a Certain Blindness" has it, "neither the whole truth, nor the whole of good, is revealed to any one single observer, although each observer gains a partial superiority of insight from the peculiar position in which he stands".[58] Verena's aspiration "simply" for "freedom" and for the "lid to be taken off the box in which we have been kept for centuries" is aesthetically, socially, and philosophically untenable, not least because all seeing is partial, and however freely seen we want to be, we always have to be framed (as it were). What she has in effect constructed is a box with "glass sides", which Ransom seeks to smash and replace, unpromisingly, with "castles in the air".[59]

In effect, Verena is largely unconscious, and therefore without much of a personal identity, until the point at which she acknowledges, or reflects on, her sentiment of love – if not, as James has it in his notebook, her "sentiment of sex".[60] For Locke, and for James, feeling is a defining characteristic of the consciousness, or what it is to be human. Michael Bell, in a long tradition, regards eighteenth-century moral philosophers, such as Shaftesbury, Kames, Hume, Smith, and Hutcheson, as making some kind of "affective turn" by rejecting Locke's emphasis on reason. But Bell fails to give feeling, in all its guises, sufficient reach in Locke. For Locke, as for many subsequent philosophers, personal identity is a social business: consciousness and feeling are transitive, not intransitive states. Consciousness is consciousness of; feeling, feeling for. Until Verena begins to reflect on what Ransom tells her in Central Park, she has barely (if at all) reflected on anything. At one level, *The Bostonians* engages with the question of personal identity in relation to consciousness, and it does so not from the perspective of literary sentimentalism (which it parodies), but from that of the physiology and psychology of sentimentalism. There is nothing mysterious or mystical about Verena's sentiment for Basil. She is moved; but moved

---

[57] William James, *The Will to Believe* (1897), in *Writings 1878-1899*, New York: Library of America, 1992, 589, 600.

[58] William James, "On a Certain Blindness" (1896), in *Writings 1878-1899*, 860.

[59] James, *The Bostonians*, 232, 276, 318.

[60] Henry James, *The Complete Notebooks of Henry James*, eds Leon Edel and Lyall H. Powers, New York: Oxford UP, 1987, 20.

in Locke's sense. Her sentiment is physical, corporeal. But the metaphysics of identity, or of becoming visible, are necessarily inextricable from those of performance in *The Bostonians*.

In New York, Olive Chancellor finds herself walking "down the Fifth Avenue ... and after a while became conscious that she was approaching Washington Square".[61] At this point, Olive can be seen as merging momentarily with Dr Sloper in *Washington Square*, as she deliberates over the marital fate she might arrange for Verena by agreeing to a match with Burrage. There are parallels between Verena and Catherine Sloper in that both are used to explore the role of performance in the constitution of personal identity. By the end of *Washington Square*, Catherine is marooned on the sofa, where she becomes, like Lionel Trilling's Lady Bertram in Jane Austen's *Mansfield Park*, a proto-existentialist heroine who refuses to accept the "requirements of personality". In his account of *Mansfield Park*, Trilling represents Lady Bertram as the stubborn matter, or biological fact, that interrogates falsifying representation and, by extension, the trickery of realism.[62]

For Trilling, as for Jane Austen, novels, like the theater, offer "the experience of the diversification of the self"". Indeed, the amateur theatricals at the heart of *Mansfield Park*, like Verena's speechifying, dramatize this very issue. Trilling sees problems of representation as being at the centre of Jane Austen's concept of "personality" in *Mansfield Park*: the skill of representation, the appearance of sincerity being its principal achievement, allows the "personality" to develop from "character".[63] The personality is a theatrical event, whereas character is the refusal of such a performance. This disavowal of personality, the desire to revert to matter, or to the "biological fact" of the self (which Trilling equates with Freud's account of the "death instinct" in *Beyond Culture*), is one of our "secret inexpressible

---

[61] James, *The Bostonians*, 273.

[62] There has been a resurgence of interest in the work of Lionel Trilling's "after theory". See Peter Rawlings, *American Theorists of the Novel: Henry James, Lionel Trilling, Wayne C. Booth*, London: Routledge, 2006; *Lionel Trilling and the Critics: Opposing Selves*, ed. John Rodden, Lincoln: Nebraska UP, 1999; Harvey M. Teres, *Renewing the Left: Politics, Imagination, and the New York Intellectuals*, New York: Oxford UP, 1996.

[63] Lionel Trilling, *The Opposing Self: Nine Essays in Criticism*, Uniform Edition, New York and London: Harcourt Brace Jovanovich, 1955, 193, 202.

hopes".[64] Indolence, the refusal to act or become involved, amounts to a vigorously resistant selfhood which challenges simplistic divisions between the patriarchal, visible, and powerful on the one hand, and the feminine, domestic, and powerless on the other. Both Lady Bertram and Catherine Sloper have, in effect, understood the emphasis Hobbes places on performance and the self in *Leviathan*, and neither of them likes it:

> *Persona* in Latin signifies the *disguise*, or *outward appearance* of a man, counterfeited on the stage; and sometimes more particularly that part of it which disguiseth the face as a mask .... So that a *person*, is the same that an *actor* is, both on the stage and in common conversation; and to *personate*, is to *act*, or *represent*, himself, or another.[65]

Verena enters the novel as a Hobbesian person and leaves it as a Lockean human. But this transition cannot be, for we are in a novel by James, without its pain.

Ransom early observes that "there was a strange spontaneity in [Verena's] manner; and an air of artless enthusiasm. If she was theatrical, she was naturally theatrical".[66] As for her personal identity in relation to her corporeal self, her talent is only for "embodying a cause", and Ransom enquires of Miss Birdseye whether Verena consists "of nothing but her opinions".[67] In the Hobbesian tradition, Verena's appearances are not restricted to the public sphere: unlike Lord Mellifont, in "The Private Life", she also performs in private.[68] Her father wonders, for instance, whether he had better "take a hall right away ... or wait till she had made a few more appearances in private".[69] It is not until her conversation with Ransom in Central Park that Verena begins to develop a sense of normative, or conventional, privacy, and hence notions of interiority and consciousness. The patriarchal contours of this burgeoning sense of a privacy predicated

---

[64] Trilling, *Opposing Self*, 202.

[65] Thomas Hobbes, *Leviathan* (1658), ed. J.C.A. Gaskin, Oxford: Oxford UP, 1996, 106-107.

[66] James, *The Bostonians*, 46.

[67] *Ibid.*, 103, 190.

[68] James, "The Private Life" (1892), in *Complete Stories, 1892-1898*, New York: Library of America, 1996, 58-91.

[69] James, *The Bostonians*, 91.

on the ideology of the happy family are clear enough: "Both the nurse and her companion gazed fixedly, and it seemed to Ransom even sternly, at the striking couple on the bench; and meanwhile Verena, look[ed] with a quickened eye at the children (she adored children)." There is no doubt that Verena, previously enthralled by her father and Olive, is now under Ransom's "spell" as he projects "a light into [her] mind", but Verena is far from a passive player in all this, as Ransom, too, has "reflection[s] forced upon him".[70] In any event, Ransom's words in Central Park, "the most effective and penetrating he had uttered, had sunk into [Verena's] soul and worked and fermented there" as she inspects the sentiment (or feeling) of love.[71] What Ransom exploits (or benefits from), as the more concrete meaning of reflection as a "bending" or "turning" (*OED*) is mobilized, is the "generosity with which [Verena] would expose herself, give herself away, turn herself inside out, for the satisfaction of a person who would make demands on her".[72]

James engages both with the genre of sentimental fiction here and its initiations in Locke's *Essay*. Verena's "throb" is physical enough, and reminds us that to be sentimental in the original sense is to have located what Barker-Benfield calls the "material basis for consciousness" and the extent to which, as he goes on, sentiment and sensibility eventually became "identifiable with sexual characteristics".[73] When Verena sees herself reflected in Ransom's eye – that compound "radiant image" consists of Ransom's eyes, the "truth" she apprehends, and how she now perceives herself – the narrator informs us, pragmatically enough, that "the truth had changed sides". Verena substitutes a life-enabling image for the "reflection of ugly lecture-lamps" that characterizes Miss Birdseye's face.[74] Mobile truth can easily be associated with William James and Pragmatism, and with the Maisies and Strethers of James' fiction, but it is also, in ways largely unacknowledged, central to what Locke sees as the trial and error of experience. If a kind of so-whatness determines William

---

[70] *Ibid.*, 287-88, 285, 299.

[71] *Ibid.*, 331-32.

[72] *Ibid.*, 328.

[73] G.J. Barker-Benfield, *The Culture of Sensibility: Sex and Society in Eighteenth-century Britain*, Chicago: Chicago UP, 1992, xvii.

[74] James, *The Bostonians*, 332, 25.

James' sense of truth, rather than any absolute criteria, then the corresponding concept in Locke is "concernment".

Truth has to be tested in experience for Locke; but he fully acknowledges both the variability of individual experience and the peculiarity of any truth pertinent to it. For Locke, only what relates to (or is made to relate to) an experiencing subject can become consequential: "But where the Mind judges that the Proposition has concernment in it; where the Assent, or not Assenting is thought to draw consequences of Moment after it ... the Mind sets itself seriously to enquire, and examine the Probability."[75] The truth changes sides for Verena (as it does for Isabel Archer) once the isolating barrier of her own egotism, her "mania for producing herself personally", breaks down and as she realizes that her selfhood, or the reflection that constructs it at least, is other-directed, and contingent on a sentiment communally generated.[76] To see herself reflected is to encounter a reflection and to become, in turn, reflective. In the process she discovers a sentiment that qualifies her to enter social and human realms, as distinct from those of the puppet theaters and drawing room platforms to which Ransom has hitherto seen her as consigned.[77]

It is the mote of "something public" in the "eye" that Ransom and Verena remove in their ocular transaction.[78] Away from her father, and increasingly independent from Olive, Verena's "own springs" are "working" as she reacts on her reflections and reflects on her reactions: "Strange I call the nature of her reflections, for they softly battled with each other as she listened ... to his sweet, distinct voice ... which almost tickled her cheek and ear."[79] As Locke has it, "every Man is put under a necessity by his own constitution".[80] In New York Verena becomes nervous, and it is Ransom who makes her "nervous and restless". "'She said she was a little nervous'", reports Burrage to Olive, who observes in reply, "'It's the first time I have ever heard of that!'".[81] We need to recall, however, that for Locke "nervous" meant not some kind of neurasthenic weakness but, as the *OED* defines one

---

[75] Locke, *Concerning Human Understanding*, 717-18.

[76] James, *The Bostonians*, 214.

[77] Ransom sees Verena as an "inflated little figure ... whom you have invented and set on its feet, pulling strings" (*ibid.*, 293).

[78] *Ibid.*, 27-28.

[79] *Ibid.*, 147, 285.

[80] Locke, *Concerning Human Understanding*, 263.

[81] James, *The Bostonians*, 274.

contemporary meaning of the word, "sinewy, muscular, vigorous, and strong".

"Consciousness" and "conscience", interchangeable in the seventeenth and eighteenth centuries, derive from the Latin *conscius* and *conscientia*, both meaning "what we know, or share, with others": in this context, "individual consciousness" is an oxymoron. Feeling and consciousness are functions of and contingent on community, and it follows that since these define what it is to be human, an egotist can only be, in David Hume's terms in his *Enquiry Concerning the Principles of Morals*, a "monster".[82] No reflection is possible in a dark closet, or in the egotistical self; without reflection, there can be no knowledge, no consciousness, and no selfhood. But if experience is boundless, the self has to be bound; and raging everywhere in James, of course, is the epic battle between experience that can never be limited and the arresting imperatives of art. In any event, cloaked and abducted, Verena is comprehensively contained at the end of the novel.

"Tears", Barker-Benfield reminds us, "are the proper emblem of the literature of sensibility and sentiment", and James happily supplies them at the end of *The Bostonians*.[83] In doing so, he makes an empirical move, for tears and suffering are offered as essential elements of being human long before such novels as Susan Warner's *The Wide, Wide World* (1850) appeared. For Locke, the will is determined by the mind; and the mind is moved only by uneasiness and pain. Pain, unease, and dis-ease are as elemental to the deep structure of Puritan ways of taking on the world as they are at the centre of Cartesian and Lockean experiential formulations. For Locke, in ways reminiscent of Verena's visual disturbance in Central Park: "The Understanding, like the Eye, whilst it makes us see, and perceive all other Things, takes no notice of itself: And it requires art and pains to set it at a distance, and make it its own Object."[84] When "sensibility" entered English in the seventeenth century, it derived from the French *sensibilité*, which denoted not just, or even at all, the capacity to feel, but the capacity to feel pain. Locke holds, in a chapter

---

[82] David Hume, *Enquiry Concerning the Principles of Morals* (1777), in *Enquiries Concerning Human Understanding and Concerning the Principles of Morals*, ed. L.A. Selby-Bigge, 3rd edn, Oxford: Clarendon P, 1975, 235.

[83] Barker-Benfield, *Culture of Sensibility*, 7.

[84] Locke, *Concerning Human Understanding*, 43.

of the *Essay* entitled "Of Power", that "The chief if not the only spur
to humane Industry and Action is uneasiness" and that "where-ever
there is *uneasiness*, there is *desire*".[85] It is important to realize, then,
that the original meaning of "sensibility" is not just having the
capacity to feel, but the capacity to feel pain.

John Keats dwelt at length in an 1819 letter, as well he might have
done only two years before his own death, on the whole business of
"soul-making".[86] Unsurprisingly, given his critique of the deceptive
consolations of becoming visible, Trilling quotes this letter
approvingly in *Sincerity and Authenticity*: "In 1819 Keats said in one
of his most memorable letters, 'Do you not see how necessary a
World of Pains and troubles is to school an Intelligence and make it a
soul?,' that is to say, an ego or self which, as he puts it, is 'destined to
possess the sense of Identity'."[87] For James, then, visibility has its
penalties. The bleak reward, as Locke earlier recognized, is that
without unhappiness, there can be no desire, and unless there is pain,
there can be no consciousness.

---

[85] *Ibid.*, 230, 257.
[86] John Keats quoted in Trilling, *The Opposing Self*, 343.
[87] Lionel Trilling, *Sincerity and Authenticity*, London: Oxford UP, 1972, 166.

"THE TRUE AMERICAN WOMAN": NARCISSA OWEN'S EMBODIED NATIONAL NARRATIVE

KAREN L. KILCUP

Narcissa Owen's *Memoirs* commence not with the Dedication or Introduction, but with a 1906 photograph of Owen on her seventy-fifth birthday. An inhabitant of both the nineteenth and twentieth centuries, Owen wears a tastefully embroidered black dress suggesting an affluent woman of fashion, while her pleasantly direct expression, coupled with eyeglasses held gracefully but not casually in her right hand, proclaims a person of seriousness and intellect, capable of commanding both the drawing room and the classroom. Mother, housekeeper and impresario for her political son Robert, and unofficial spokesperson for educated, acculturated Cherokees, Owen projects a version of Cherokee, Southern, and American, history in her own embodiment. This essay explores Owen's negotiations of this embodiment across private and public spheres, and it will argue that her representations, both in images and words, undercut, unpack, and complicate gendered norms not only for Native American women, but for American women more generally.

Born in 1831 in Arkansas Indian Territory to a Scots-Irish mother and mixed-blood Cherokee father who died when she was only three years old, Owen encountered the Cherokee nation *in extremis* during the forced migration of the Trail of Tears in 1838-1839.[1] In her *Memoirs*, privately published in 1907, Owen suggests that her first sustained engagement with Cherokee culture occurred in 1880 when, following her son Robert Jr's government appointment, she moved to Oklahoma Indian Territory to teach music in the Cherokee Female Seminary. In her earlier years she was occupied by attaining the education appropriate for the daughter of an affluent, slaveholding

---

[1] Narcissa Owen, *A Cherokee Woman's America: Memoirs of Narcissa Owen, 1831-1907*, ed. Karen L. Kilcup, Gainesville: UP of Florida, 2005, 5-7. All subsequent references to the *Memoirs* in the text are to this edition.

family, marriage to railroad executive Robert Latham Owen, raising her two sons, heading volunteer work in Lynchburg, Virginia, during the Civil War, and then widowhood, financial trouble, and work as a private music teacher to send her sons to college. When Robert Jr's career advanced (he eventually became a US Senator) she returned with him to Washington, DC and resumed her role as a socialite and artist. As this sketch only intimates, Owen's public roles and occupations were numerous and many-faceted.[2]

For Owen, public and private spheres are always interconnected, in as much as her narrative depicts her guiltless freedom to circulate in various spaces. Whether this freedom derived from her Cherokee background, her fluid but fundamentally elite class status, her age, her education, or some combination of these and other factors is unclear; but no adequate conceptual framework exists to describe the variety of her experiences and of her performances of womanliness (or Cherokeeness, for that matter). Alison Piepmeier's charge resonates here: "What needs to be more fully articulated and explored [in studies of nineteenth-century womanhood] are the modalities of embodiment that make use of both public and private, that are neither fully victim nor agent, that – rather than being appropriate or deviant – are multiple, transitional, strategic, playful, contested."[3] In some sense, Owen provides a paradigmatic argument for readers' self-examination, since what has characteristically been perceived as contradictory behavior – that is, crossing boundaries between public and private – in Owen's case generates apparently little or no dissonance. We must ask, then, why do *we* see dissonance?

Although she often represents herself as a conventional Victorian American wife and mother, Owen repeatedly and deliberately juxtaposes and confuses "white" and "Indian", "savage" and "civilized", in the process necessarily challenging corporeal conventions. To be "out in public", according to Piepmeier, "suggests a body taking up space and moving through the world of commerce, government, or celebrity". In a nineteenth-century context, however,

---

[2] Deborah Cameron, in her essay "Theorizing the Female Voice in Public Contexts", in *Speaking Out: The Female Voice in Public Contexts*, ed. Judith Baxter, New York: Palgrave Macmillan, 2006, proposes a significant difference between a "public setting" and "the public sphere" (7), but for Owen even this distinction blurs.
[3] Alison Piepmeier, *Out in Public: Configurations of Women's Bodies in Nineteenth-century America*, Chapel Hill: U of North Carolina P, 2004, 2.

"the phrase may also suggest transgression or deviance".[4] Embodiment, whether literal or metaphorical, was a particular problem for both genteel Southern ladies and for Native American women in pre-twentieth-century America. The former's body provided one important ideological ground for the Civil War. As Stephanie McCurry argues, "It was the free (white) man's ability to claim a right of property in his wife's body – that is, exclusive sexual access – that distinguished him from a slave man or a dishonored one".[5] For Native women, who for white men represented both the virgin land and the libidinous woman of color, embodiment could represent another war zone. These perspectives were complicated for Owen by her Cherokee heritage, for Cherokee women had traditionally enjoyed positions of authority and visibility. Owen may have composed her *Memoirs* in part as a means of negotiating these contradictions: as recent critics have asserted, the print medium may have provided at least some women writers with "a kind of protected space where her actual physicality was masked", offering instead a "syncretic, multivalent embodiment" and "tools for negotiating and shaping ... [a] public corporeal presence".[6] Moreover, Owen's work intimates that self-representation can be variously encoded, including such nonlinguistic modes as photography, painting, and music.[7]

While appearing to conform both bodily and performatively to gendered norms dictating public and private behavior, Owen repeatedly, simultaneously, and often humorously affirms and defies corporeal conventions through what I will call "transitive discourse", which appears in the narrative's quirky shape, patchwork contents,

---

[4] *Ibid.*, 1.
[5] Stephanie McCurry, "'The Soldier's Wife': White Women, the State, and the Politics of Protection in the Confederacy", in *Women and the Unstable State in Nineteenth-century America*, eds Alison M. Parker and Stephanie Cole, College Station: Texas A&M UP, 2000, 19.
[6] Piepmeier, *Out in Public*, 175. For these optimistic views of print culture, Piepmeier cites Nina Baym, "Between Enlightenment and Victorian: Toward a Narrative of American Women Writers Writing History", *Critical Inquiry* XVII/4 (Summer 1991), 22-41, and Nicole Tonkovich, "Rhetorical Power in the Victorian Parlor: *Godey's Lady's Book* and the Gendering of Nineteenth-century Rhetoric", in *Oratorical Culture in Nineteenth-century America: Transformations in the Theory and Practice of Rhetoric*, eds Gregory Clark and S. Michael Halloran, Carbondale: Southern Illinois UP, 1991, 158-83.
[7] See Hertha D. Wong, *Sending My Heart Back Across the Years: Tradition and Innovation in Native American Autobiography*, New York: Oxford UP, 1992.

and fluctuating rhetoric. Mixing personal, family, second- and third-hand tribal history, and auto-ethnography,[8] with public events, gossipy anecdotes, personal adventures and family relationships, with high and low art, and with money, national shame, and national identity, she incorporates the functions of historian, performer, and visitor, as well as autobiographer. Juxtaposing rhetorical registers and subject matters, she opens a space for multiracial women in American history, literature, and art. She affirms women's agency and repudiates their victimization, and while contesting the equally debilitating images of the squaw and the Indian Princess, and revealing herself as mother, artist, teacher, craftswoman, socialite, and philanthropist, she also redefines American womanhood. Her image, and her model, was not available to everyone. She elides entirely a portrait of enslaved or freed women. The poor and working women in her account are objects of charity, though at one point she does suggest that through hard work and with assistance, poor women can become "ladies". Nevertheless, while often retaining her privilege, she reaches out to her readers, encouraging them through her example to become more visible in American culture and in the creation of national identity.

The first section of this essay provides a brief prehistory of embodiments, both literal and linguistically articulated, for American Indian women – the subjects to whom, in many cases, Owen is directly or indirectly replying. In the subsequent sections, emphasizing the "continual, productive tensions between dominant discourses and women's corporeal and discursive strategies",[9] I will take up Owen's responses to the following questions: what does it mean to be a citizen and patriot? What does it mean to be a heroine? What does it mean to be an artist? Her responses, and the overlapping roles that she performs in spheres that are almost never unambiguously public or private, unsettle, rather than settle these questions, complicating normative notions of gender, race, and ethnicity, and actively engaging her readers in a re-envisioning of what it means to be an American woman, "out in public".

---

[8] See Mary Louise Pratt, *Imperial Eyes: Travel Writing and Transculturation*, New York: Routledge, 1992.
[9] Piepmeier, *Out in Public*, 4.

Embodying foremothers

We can best appreciate Owen's self-representations, whether in photographs, narrative, or painting, by first looking back briefly to the representations of – and by – some of her Native predecessors. Early colonial discourse grounded itself in a forceful pictorial and linguistic image: Pocahontas.[10] Both mediator and object of desire, she calmed European fears of a savage continent by embodying security in a young, female form willing to risk death to save John Smith. Smith's elaborate narrative suggested that the New World was not only safe, it was alluring. In some sense, the story served as a promotional or marketing device.[11] Images of Pocahontas from the contact and colonial periods emphasize both her civilizability and her exotic desirability, portraying her alternatively in traditional English clothing clasping a fan, holding her scantily garbed body above Smith's endangered head, or kneeling before Christian baptism.[12] As we shall see, Owen speaks repeatedly to her own ultracivilized status and her Christian faith, thereby rejecting such eroticized images of Native women in particular and the subordinate status of women more generally.

In composing this representation of the Indian Princess, Europeans missed or elided the cultural background that led to Pocahontas' intercession with her father, Powhatan. Clara Sue Kidwell emphasizes American Indian women's traditional power and rejects the interpretation of romantic love superimposed on the Pocahontas narrative, concluding: "If indeed it happened at all, Pocahontas, a chief's daughter, probably saved John Smith to demonstrate her power as an emerging woman in Powhatan society – by adopting him."[13] Images of Pocahontas as alluring and susceptible to civilization miss the point entirely, mistranslating her actions within a Euro-American

---

[10] On Owen and Pocohontas, see Stephen Brandon, "'Mother of **U.S.** Senator an Indian Queen': Cultural challenge and appropriation in *The Memoirs of Narcissa Owen*", *Studies in American Indian Literatures*, XIII/2-3 (Autumn-Fall 2001), 15-17.

[11] See Annette Kolodny, *The Lay of the Land: Metaphor as Experience and History in American Life and Letters*, Chapel Hill: U of North Carolina P, 1975, 5.

[12] Images of Pocohontas have permeated American culture. For examples, see: http://xroads.virgina.edu/~CAP/PIX/pocahontas.gif; http://www.williamsburg private tours.com/pocohontas_saving_life3.jpg; http//:www.unvie.ac.at/Anglistik/easyrider/data/pages/Pocahontas/pocohontas.htm.

[13] Clara Sue Kidwell, "Restoring the Power of Thought Woman", in *Sisterhood Is Forever: A Woman's Anthology for a New Millennium*, ed. Robin Morgan, New York: Washington Square Press, 2003, 169-70.

framework that assumed women's subordination to men and their status as objects rather than agents. Even as they coded their own messages for different audiences with varying understandings of gender roles, American Indian women from Nancy Ward to Owen – and beyond – struggled with this problem of mistranslation, and sometimes willful mistranslation, especially in relation to momentous matters of war and peace.[14]

Peace was in short supply during the nineteenth century, at least as far as Native Americans were concerned. By the latter part of the century, the time of Owen's middle age (and after the death of her husband Robert in 1873), the war on Indians had assumed a different, more commercial form. Such forms included the widely distributed photographs of Edward Curtis, which in some ways connect to the literary movement of regionalism (and its commercial concomitant, tourism), as well as the Wild West show, which Buffalo Bill began in Omaha in 1883, precisely the same year that Sarah Winnemucca published *Life among the Piutes: Their Wrongs and Claims*.[15] Capitalizing on the public's fascination for (and guilt about) Native Americans, Winnemucca had since the late 1870s been lecturing about the federal government's shocking treatment of its Indian peoples, appearing clad in garments that invoked the image of Pocahontas, though they did not accurately represent traditional Paiute wear.[16] Much like those of her enslaved female counterparts, Winnemucca's 1883 narrative required paratextual framing – the apparatus of authenticity, beginning, most notably for our purposes, with her staged

---

[14] Beloved Woman Nancy Ward (*c.* 1738-c.1822) was an important participant in Cherokee negotiations with the federal government. For Ward's speech to US treaty commissioners, see Karen Kilcup, *Native American Women's Writing c.1800-1924: An Anthology*, Malden, MA: Blackwell, 2000, 27; for an analysis of the speech and that of Ward's respondents, see Karen Kilcup "'The art spirit remains to me to this day': Contexts, Contemporaries, and Narcissa Owen's Political Aesthetics", in Narcissa Owen's *Memoirs*, 5-7.

[15] Sarah Winnemucca, *Life among the Piutes: Their Wrongs and Claims*, Bishop, CA: Sierra Media, 1969.

[16] For a discussion of images of Native Americans in the late nineteenth and early twentieth centuries, see Rayna Green, "The Tribe Called Wannabee: Playing Indian in America and Europe", *Folklore*, LXXXXIX/1 (1988), 30-55. For a discussion of the Canadian Mohawk, E. Pauline Johnson's staging of identity, see Cari Carpenter, *Seeing Red: Anger, Femininity, and American Indians*, Columbus: Ohio State UP (forthcoming).

image and photographs, which were frequently pasted into copies of her book.[17]

Although Owen was working in Indian Territory as a music teacher when Winnemucca's book was published, it is not unreasonable to assume that, given the widespread popularity of the latter's volume and its relatively broad distribution, Owen would have seen both the book and an image of the author and would have read the testimonials to her civility and virtue that appeared in its appendix. If these testimonials, coupled with the photographs, advance the necessary vindication and authorization required of earlier enslaved women and of Winnemucca near the end of the century, it is not unreasonable to inquire, what happened between 1883 and 1907, when Owen's *Memoirs* were published? Do events in American history explain the absence in Owen's work of extra-authorial materials? Is Owen's own character the determinant, including her ability, but refusal, to pass as white? Does her marriage to Robert L. Owen inoculate her against charges of immorality? Does the probably private publication of her volume make the difference? Or does the transformation derive from some combination of these factors?

---

[17] In terms that echo Lydia Maria Child's Introduction to Harriet Jacobs' *Incidents in the Life of a Slave Girl* (1861), ed. Jean Fagan Yellin, Cambridge, MA: Harvard UP, 1987, Mary Mann's Editor's Preface both authenticates and authorizes Winnemucca's story. The volume's aim, Mann emphasizes, is *"to tell the truth"*, since "it is of the first importance to hear what only an Indian and an Indian woman can tell" (Mary Mann, Editor's Preface, in Winnemucca, *Life among the Piutes*, 3). On Winnemucca's self-presentation in photographs, see Joanna Cohan Scherer, "The Public Faces of Sarah Winnemucca", *Cultural Anthropology*, XIII/2 (May 1988), 178-204. Scherer underestimates Winnemucca's self-authorization and power in these images: in the most famous, Winnemucca stands facing the viewer and looking directly at the camera with a pleasant but strong expression. I am grateful to Carolyn Soriso of West Chester University for directing me to this article and for additional information about Winnemucca's photographs (Soriso, e-mail communication, 9 February 2007). For another important potential influence on Owen, see Alexia Kosmider's discussion of Cherokee author and editor, Ora Eddleman Reed: "Strike a Euro-American Pose: Ora Eddleman Reed's 'Types of Indian Girls'", *American Transcendental Quarterly*, XXII (1998), 109-31. Reed sought to counter absurd eastern notions of Indians and Indian territory generally, in part through the photographic feature, "Types of Indian Girls", which began in her periodical, *Twin Territories* in late 1898 and continued regularly until the magazine ceased publication in May 1904. Reed refers to Narcissa and Robert Owen Jr in her "Great Work of an Indian", *Sturm's Oklahoma Magazine*, II/6 (1906), 7-9.

Although it is impossible to be certain, the self-confidence expressed in the *Memoirs* coupled with the author's photographic and pictorial self-representations indicate that the issues that haloed texts like Winnemucca's were non-issues for Owen. Owen speaks back not only to the images of Indians constructed by whites but also, whether consciously or not, to earlier representations by Indian women themselves. Owen's frontispiece photograph, which we can compare not only with images of Winnemucca and Harriet Jacobs but also with that of Walt Whitman in *Leaves of Grass* (1855), resonates with ambiguity. If it symbolizes a necessary authorization (indicating that this writer is educated, elite, civilized), it also interrogates the notion of whiteness. Unlike the photos of Winnemucca or even of the light-skinned, respectable, and matronly Jacobs, Owen's photograph renders racial or ethnic categorization difficult – though her class status is abundantly clear, there is no question of transgression or the erotic deviance assumed for women of color. The power that the photograph embodies is clearly intentional, for the same power reappears in the photo accompanying a contemporaneous *New York Times* story about Owen, entitled "Mother of US Senator an Indian Queen". As Stephen Brandon points out, in the photograph we can readily see her as the "American Queen" that the title of the accompanying *New York Times* signals.[18] Certainly, like her younger Cherokee contemporary, Ora Eddleman Reed, she rebuts the conventional image of the Indian woman as a beast of burden.[19]

Owen's opening self-image inaugurates a transitive discourse – an associatively organized rhetorical elaboration that amalgamates registers, topics, and styles – in which, in Owen's case, the "Indian", the affluent Southern lady, and the American woman form a complicated combination. We might well see this image as a precursor to photographs of twentieth-century political wives such as Jacqueline Kennedy Onassis. Like Owen's pictorial self-representations, such images provoke the question, what does it mean to be "in politics"? Are politicians' wives – and sometimes sisters, daughters, and mothers – not also functioning in the public sphere?

---

[18] Brandon, "'Mother of U.S. Senator an Indian Queen'", 18.
[19] Kidwell, "Restoring the Power of Thought Woman", 165.

"Home at the Metropolitan": Owen as citizen and patriot
The narrative that follows Owen's photograph paints a multiple portrait of her identity as an American woman, depicting her as a socialite, certainly, but also as a woman of serious purpose and action, engaged in the public sphere of politics. Deborah Cameron's observation about the necessarily domestic content and context for female platform speakers is equally relevant for US women writers of Owen's period and background: "Female voices are most obviously unwelcome in contexts where the community's most cherished values are ritually and solemnly affirmed, using a formal or elevated register of language to discuss 'the great subjects' in a quasi-'sacred' institutional space – the parliamentary chamber, the courtroom, the church, the lecture hall, the men's house."[20] However, Owen enters these domains often, and often by the front door, both in her physical presence and through the proxy embodiment of her reminiscences.

Given the frequently oral quality of the *Memoirs*, Judith Mattson Bean's observations about women speakers provide another helpful framework for understanding Owen. Bean underscores the significance of topic and register for women speakers, and highlights "the relationship of the speaker to the audience in terms of identity factors such as race, gender, and class. If an audience has multiple identities or speech communities, a speaker may shift among registers in order to appeal to those differing groups."[21] Owen seems not to require an apology or authentication, but the Dedication, written as if she were speaking directly to some audience members, offers an explanation:

> To my children and to the Cherokees .... In this book I give you some stories of my Indian ancestors and their old traditions, which were given to me as a child. The promise to give this record of the past I have faithfully, lovingly, and with true pleasure made an effort to keep. (45)

Using an appropriate context and modest register for upper middle-class women, she affirms her family and Cherokee nation as her explicit audience and motive for speaking. As Elizabeth Wilkinson

---

[20] Cameron, "Theorizing the Female Voice in Public Contexts", 8.
[21] Judith Mattson Bean, "Gaining a Public Voice: A Historical Perspective on American Women's Public Speaking", in *Speaking Out: The Female Voice in Public Contexts*, 29.

has observed, however, this account would presumably be redundant for her Cherokee readers and listeners, who would already be familiar with the history that Owen relates.[22] Moreover, the publication of Owen's book, with photographs, suggests her ambition to reach a larger, multiethnic audience, not only in its own time but also in the future. This potentially multiple audience accounts for her diverse, public and private subject matter, and for her widely varying registers in the *Memoirs*, a profoundly political text whose transitive discourse situates individual, tribal, and US national concerns in conversation with one another.

In its more conversational moments, Owen's book simulates a visit with the reader (in terms suggested by Alison Easton elsewhere in this volume), to whom she relates a personal narrative that surprisingly often possesses national consequences. For example, one rather ponderously (and confusingly) genealogical section of the narrative details minutely her connections, through her husband's family, with General Washington, and her possession of Washington family "relics". Owen's ability to dispose of these relics intimates her own position as American royalty: "Not only relics of letters, but a number of pieces of cut glass, formerly belonging to General Washington, came to me, and, feeling that I was not a blood relative of Washington, I concluded to present most of the pieces I had to the United States Government and have them placed with the Washington relics at the National museum" (144-45). Mary Stuart Smith, Washington's relative and Owen's interlocutor, responds with gratitude – and an application form for the Daughters of the American Revolution. The **DAR** application is especially important: "In a culture that privileges primacy – especially in the period she was writing, the Colonial Revival – Owen asserts that her 'royal' family predates the Mayflower" through her ancestor, Queen Quatsis.[23] But she also affirms her connections to the founding fathers via her social link with Washington's descendant. This anecdote surfaces in an important section of the book's concluding chapter, in which Owen underscores

---

[22] Elizabeth Wilkinson, "'We Are Your Mothers': Cherokee Women's Voices for Land Preservation", paper delivered at the American Literature Association Convention, 25 May 2007. On the problems with Owen's historical accuracy and a discussion of the reasons behind her creative reconstruction of Cherokee culture, see Brandon, "'Mother of U.S. Senator an Indian Queen'".
[23] Kilcup, "Narcissa Owen's Political Aesthetics", 27.

her high place in Lynchburg society (142). Here Owen offers a confidential exchange with a reader who might be either family or stranger, as she cannily combines an intimate register that clashes with the national subject.

Owen simultaneously preserves her role in domestic space in this section, entitled "Home at the Metropolitan [Hotel]", while she affirms her participation in public life, both social and political. It is a short distance from the indoor social world (itself a mixture of public and private) composed of cordial letters and friendly visits, as well as of obituaries of friends and acquaintances, to the outdoor world of presidential parades (viewed discreetly from indoors). "At home" in the Metropolitan Hotel, whose very name figures serendipitously the overlapping of public with private, Owen stands at a liminal space as she describes McKinley's second inaugural parade. She reports on the crowd's approval of Robert E. Lee's nephew, Fitzhugh Lee ("there was a greater explosion of joy than when the new President passed in review"), deconstructing the concept of nation. Patriotism for the South competes with and blends with patriotism for the United States – Owen's alliances lean toward the former, as she suggests with the familiar reference to "Fitzhugh". Once again, register contends with substance.

Owen's talkative account of Roosevelt's inaugural parade underscores even more emphatically the rhetorical and substantive mixing endemic to her narrative and her identity:

> From the Riggs House I saw Theodore Roosevelt and the notables of the day with him in the last presidential procession. A new feature of the procession was the introduction of Indians, representing the wild tribes from the Western plains and Oklahoma. Decidedly the most artistically dressed American figures were the four Indian chiefs on horseback, dressed in their native costume, with their heads bedecked with their gorgeous war bonnets. These Indians seemed to form a body-guard for the President, following so closely in his wake. Artistically speaking, they were picturesque beyond expression. (146)

While remaining within an appropriate, patriotic domain and celebratory register for a woman of Owen's class and period, this description incorporates many moments of excess, coded principally in the description of the Indians. Significantly, they are "the most *artistically* dressed *American* figures … with their gorgeous *war* bonnets". More striking than the president himself, these *"chiefs"* bespeak a symbolic power ironically encoded in their imagined position as *"body-guards* for the President, following so closely in his wake". Recurring to the gender-appropriate domain of beauty, Owen twice cites their "artistically" appealing character. Like Owen herself, the chiefs conjure the Native Americanization of the East ("from the Western plains and Oklahoma"), in an inversion of the actual process of Euro-American conquest. The Riggs House, home of the Riggs Bank – the bank of Presidents and only one block from the White House – confirms Owen's, and Native America's, place at the heart of the capital. Here Owen's transitive discourse occurs not through rhetorical register but through the blending of images and the mixing of aesthetic and political domains.

In addition to the Riggs Bank, we can catalog many more of Owen's numerous references to the "quasi-'sacred' institutional spaces" and "great subjects" that Cameron emphasizes. Simultaneously "Cherokee" and "American", these political spaces are occupied by Owen's father, who is "the last hereditary chief" of the Cherokees, by her son Robert in his role as Indian Agent for the Five Civilized Tribes, by Owen's father's affiliation with President Jefferson in Chapter 3, and by her own connections, through her artwork, to the Jefferson family among others (48, 125-28, 77-78). Owen's discussion blends a familiar, intimate rhetorical register with the "great subjects" and "quasi-'sacred' institutional spaces", as she affirms her (and American women's) right both to these subjects and their own voices. Ultimately, Owen presents herself as both an American Queen – especially at the end of her book, when she is crowned May Queen by her fellows in the Bartlesville Tuesday Club – and as a modern version of the Cherokee Beloved Woman, a woman of extraordinary powers who, like Nancy Ward, could speak to her people, Cherokee and "American", through both her pictures and her "word pictures". With public and private subjects and rhetorical registers intertwined, she speaks in a variety of liminal spaces, not only to her own family and generation, but also to the multiple audiences of the future.

"'You are an angel'": Owen as heroine
Owen's images as an older woman contrast with her livelier early embodiments – her accounts of her heroic actions are among the

book's most entertaining narratives. Living in the Virginia countryside as a young wife and mother, she describes a swimming party in "Memories of Clinch River and Lynchburg". Again, her register is complex, alternating elevated description and personal anecdote. Owen carefully lays out the episode's context in both physical and, characteristically, aesthetic terms: "This home was a pleasant kind of wild, romantic place, with the river making a wide, grand circle around it. It was most picturesque, being very secluded, four or five miles from other settlements" (101).

On one occasion, young lady guests decide to "go bathing at a deep place in the river called the Cat-hole, where the water was very deep, though so limpid that ledges of stone could be seen almost across the river". When Owen arrives at the swimming hole, she quickly sees that two girls, who could not swim, were drowning, and she plunges in to save them:

Figure 11.1 Narcissa Owen, 75th birthday (1906) from *Memoirs of Narcissa Owen* (1907)

> I felt for the depth of the water, and I found it up to my mouth, but, fortunately for me and them, I extended my hand as far as possible and our fingers tipped and our hands clinched. Then their weight drew me over to them, in twelve feet of water. With only one hand to swim and two well-grown girls suspended from the other, I did the most vigorous swimming that woman ever did before or since.

Owen insists that no one should tell their mother, but her heroism is discovered, with the girls' mother announcing, "'Mrs. Owen, I know you are an angel! I know you are an angel!'", confirming Owen's appropriately feminine behavior, and both substantively and rhetorically returning us to the family sphere (102). Although she makes light of the episode to her interlocutor, describing herself as "rather a bad angel", she concludes, "I guess it is a good thing that there are times in our lives when emergencies arise that we have but one thought, and that an unreasoning impulse, as in this instance, to save life" (103). By constantly shifting registers, Owen manages to have it both ways – to represent herself as a powerful maternal (private) figure who is capable of masculine (public) heroism.

She reinforces this characterization with the subsequent story in which, faced with some rough, drunken men, she proves more than a match. Here Owen's power derives from her speaking authority, her verbal self-embodiment. After making a "drunken joke", one of the men follows her and her female companion threateningly; but, although Lucy nearly faints, Owen's response differs: "His impertinence made me so angry that I shook my riding whip in his face and gave him peremptory orders to march on. He saw how angry I was, and I don't know but that he thought I had a pistol." The danger is exacerbated, and her heroism enhanced, by their location in a "very narrow gorge, with just enough room for the road, with mountains on both sides of us". Owen's courageous command prompts the man to leave. She concludes the narrative by re-feminizing herself: "we went on over the bridge home, the house being in full view. The man then knew that we had some one to defend us and asked no more of our company" (104). Although Owen herself has provoked his departure, she reinscribes herself into a narrative of American middle-class femininity. Owen negotiates public power and femininity, again, as she safeguards her own and her friend's virtue, contesting the stereotype of Indian women as lascivious or sexually available.[24] Although her transitive discourse finally recapitulates her status as a vulnerable woman, the residue of her speaking power remains.

Owen's verbal heroism extends to her words' indirect power. When General David Hunter and the Union Army are preparing to attack Lynchburg in June 1864, Owen encounters two Union spies asking for food at her home, Point of Honor, though she claims that "they were dressed as Confederates, and their being spies never once entered my head". When they ask about Confederate forces in the area, Owen describes how

> I counted 20,000 fighters by way of comforting the supposed Confederates. I told them we would 'give the Yanks fits' in the

---

[24] Winnemucca writes about the sexual exploitation of Native women, in *Life among the Piutes*, 34, 37.

morning. When morning came, by sunrise Hunter's Army was in full retreat.

A number of years after the war, Owen learns from her housekeeper, Anna, that her father was a soldier in Hunter's forces. Owen's humor underscores the authority she claims, though delicately and inadvertently, over the Union army:

> 'Well,' I said, 'when at home you can give my *compliments* to your father and tell him that I am the very *lady* who told him when to run.' Anna gave him my message. He laughed, and said that he was one of the men to whom I had given supper on the evening mentioned. (113; emphases added)

Once again private affairs – feeding soldiers at her home – and the rhetoric of gentility converge with public matters, as Owen underscores her agency in national affairs and her unwitting, and therefore "feminine", heroism; her register of modesty, and the context-specific efficacy of her speech, gender her action as appropriate.[25]

Owen's public heroism reverberates in her story of organizing the sewing of uniforms for Confederate soldiers: "We made quantities of clothing, and were, of course, very proud of our work." But she undercuts this heroism with the humor of error, as her transitive discourse mixes national and domestic subjects. After the first company puts on their uniforms and their captain sends them to march in front of Owen's home "to show off their new uniforms":

> ... they marched up and down with the sleeves of their gray shirts flapping about five inches over their hands. They were ordered to ground arms, and stood waving their sleeves like the arms of windmills. There was nothing for us to do but to have all the shirts returned to the hall and proceed to shorten the sleeves.

---

[25] Other episodes depicting Owen's heroism relate to her role as an impromptu nurse during her time at the Cherokee Female Seminary (120-22) and her rescue of a friend whose dress had caught fire (90). In her emphasis on femininity, Owen may be deliberately contrasting herself to the unladylike and intentionally outspoken Winnemucca, who deliberately intervened in public affairs of war and peace.

This service to the Confederate nation (again, Owen depicts herself as a patriot) becomes unnecessary when the government assumes responsibility for production: "gradually they took charge of such things themselves, and by degrees the ladies retired from taking an active part in the work" (107). The ladies' work continues, however, with care for "the wives and children of the soldiers of Lynchburg", and Owen herself ultimately assumes responsibility for overseeing this charity work. This episode as a whole depicts her as being out in public but doing the feminine work of sewing and charitable visiting.

As Alison Easton's essay in this volume underscores, charitable visiting involved a complex and shifting relationship between public and private domains, although, as she also points out, historically, both social visiting and charitable visiting were regarded as public events, raising questions about knowledge, power, empathy, conciliation, social change and social cohesion. The relative status of visitor and visited is always at issue. The chatty tone and personal anecdotes in Owen's memoir inflect much of it with the feeling of a visit, but she describes a literal visit in "The King Story", when a soldier's widow falls gravely ill, and Owen decides to cut her hair and sells the resulting braids for "fifty dollars each in Confederate money". After Mrs King makes a dramatic and unexpected recovery, the proceeds enable the widow to travel to New England, work in the factories, and send her three children to school. In the triumphant conclusion, Mrs King and her daughter return to call on Owen and present her "with a box of a dozen spools of gorgeous-colored silk thread as a token of her gratitude, just like the true Irish heart in her. Jack and his brother were then young men and Dora was a young lady" (112). In this case, Owen moves from her own home through the public sphere and into another home – though, as an outsider, she carries with her the public responsibility of charity. But her efforts here go beyond the norm, representing a feminized but powerful and enabling kind of heroism, for she enables the recipients of her charity to rise in class status to near equals. Owen depicts herself throughout her narrative as a homely or inadvertent heroine, but a heroine who easily moves between public and private domains through transitive discourse occurring variously in intimate and detached rhetorical registers.

"On Pennsylvania Avenue": Owen as painter

Speaking to the Indian Princess myth and image, Owen's frontispiece photograph represents at one level a Native Americanization of the East, an inversion of the normal processes of civilization. In some sense she represents (embodies and advances) a bidirectional biracialization of America, by way of both her photographic and verbal images. Owen's paintings offer a similarly powerful reintegration of American culture. As a proxy for her own embodiment, "moving through the world of commerce, government, or celebrity", her portraits of Thomas Jefferson and his daughter, Martha Jefferson Randolph (Mrs Thomas Mann Randolph), and grandson, Thomas Jefferson Randolph, and of Jefferson's great-granddaughter and great-great-granddaughter and her children, cross the divides of ethnicity, class and era. Owen's description of how she completed her work is informative:

> I painted the portraits in my studio in the Corcoran Building, at the corner of Fifteenth street and Pennsylvania avenue, Washington, D.C. Those of Thomas Jefferson and of Mrs. Thomas Mann Randolph, who was Martha, his daughter, I copied from pictures in black and white from a book loaned me through the courtesy of the officer in charge of the Carnegie Library. The portraits of Thomas Jefferson Randolph and his daughter, Mrs. R.G.H. Kean, of Lynchburg, Virginia, were done from photos loaned me by Mrs. John S. Morris. Mrs. Morris and her daughters were the only living models that I had. (Mrs. Morris's two daughters are representatives of the sixth generation of the Jefferson family before referred to as being born at Monticello, my Indian Territory home.) (83)

The rhetoric here rewards scrutiny. The opening line assumes an assertive note with just an edge of defensiveness. The next sentence marries the same tone to a more personal one, courtesy of the reference to the "loan" from "the officer in charge of the Carnegie Library". The final two sentences move into a progressively more personal, even conversational register.

Not only does this short passage bear enormous symbolic weight, so do the paintings themselves. The first shows contemporaneous images of Jefferson and his daughter, both purportedly from 1803. Jefferson is portrayed with pen and paper, while Martha wears an elegant gown and has her hair arranged tastefully in soft curls around her face. Both are, of course, representations of representations, at least twice removed from their subjects. Perhaps most striking is Martha's relative importance; her much lighter image in the middle of the painting invites the reader to focus on her rather than on her more famous father. Even more peculiar is the depiction of Jefferson's grandson, taken from an 1875 photograph, in which he appears older than his grandfather and mother. The painting as a whole thus has the odd impact of a contemporary tabloid cover that assembles clearly disparate images, and it unsettles viewers' understanding of time. The second painting, of the women and girls, is much more homogeneous, though the image of Mrs Kean – also taken from a photograph – has the same kind of disjunctive temporal effect. Both paintings, however, amalgamate private and public dimensions both in the content of their images and the ways in which they are deployed by Owen. The first intrudes the more domestic image of Martha between those of her father and son, with the temporal disruption enhancing that intrusion. In constructing her images in this manner, Owen figures (whether consciously or not) the "transgression or deviance" of a female "body taking up space and moving through the world of commerce, government, or celebrity".[26]

More importantly, that the paintings were derived from images obtained from a descendant of Jefferson and that the girls were born at Monticello emphasizes Owen's American credentials and her personal relationship with American "royalty". The obsession that Owen shows with both social connections and genealogy throughout her book emerges in her insistence on the equality of her Cherokee and American associations, which range from Lynchburg to Indian Territory, which the audacious symbolism of naming her Indian Territory home Monticello underscores. Similarly, her meticulous documentation of the location of her studio in the nation's capitol not only establishes her credentials as an artist, but emphasizes her authority in representing the nation. Again Owen's transitive discourse carries her across social, political, and ethnic domains.

These domains are also intermingled in the use to which the paintings were put as Indian Territory exhibits in the 1904 St Louis Louisiana Exposition, which "was intended to honor Jefferson's memory and to commemorate his purchase of Louisiana and the Western country". Owen continues, "Wishing to do my part in

---

[26] Piepmeier, *Out in Public*, 1.

honoring him and at the same time to show the world that the Cherokees were a cultured and civilized people, I painted ... the portraits of six generations of his family, doing what honor I could to the Indian people and to Jefferson's merits as a great statesman" (82). As we have seen, however, Jefferson's statesmanship is less in evidence in the portraits than his role as the patriarch of a large – and increasingly female – family. Moreover, Owen contests the image of the savage explicitly, as we see here and in her response to a newspaper reporter's mischaracterization of her work, which she describes in "Modern Misrepresentation of the Indians": "The facts are the Indians of Indian Territory are civilized, educated, Christian people. I myself, the 'Cherokee 82 years old,' was born October 3, 1831, and my painting was not done in a teepee, but on Pennsylvania Avenue, in the Corcoran Building, opposite the Treasury, at Washington city" (133-34).[27] Unlike "uncivilized" people – including slaves and uneducated Indians[28] – she knows her own history and insists on its meaning: her place is at the heart of the nation, where she works in a private setting (her studio) on a project with public import.

As we have seen with the chiefs in the Presidential parades, this significant placement figures the centrality of both the Cherokee, and Native Americans more generally, to the nation – and, again significantly, implies a complicated relationship to the country's wealth, signified by her location "opposite the Treasury". Money, public money, is repeatedly Owen's subject, and she has no compunction about commenting caustically on "the world of commerce [and] government", however transgressive it might be to do so. At the same time that she highlights Robert's public involvement in the repayment of $5 million for their lands and articulates her own very public voice on the federal land grabs, she incorporates a photograph of Robert, as well as her husband and other son, William, along with one of her "Point of Honor" homes in Lynchburg – all proxy embodiments – underscoring the intimate connection between public and family life. By her example, she indicates that American women have not only the right but also the responsibility to speak about the national family, just as Nancy Ward had done before her in two national contexts, US and Cherokee.

---

[27] See Brandon, "'Mother of U.S. Senator an Indian Queen'", 14.

[28] Neither Winnemucca nor Jacobs, for example, can identify her date of birth with precision.

The photograph of her embroidery works across traditional aesthetic boundaries, explicitly challenging distinctions between high (or public) and domestic art. She confides how, on one visit to Baltimore, "I bought a fine supply of embroidery materials – chenille, zephyr worsted, foille la ciel, and silk floss – intending to make some very handsome work for an elegant parlor chair". Such creative work, she suggests in her *Memoirs*, can be as time-consuming as painting:

> When completed, I had put one month of *artistic* labor on the work, and it occurred to me that the work was too *valuable* to have it ruined by carelessness or rough usage. Not that I was unwilling to *honor* my friends with my best efforts, but to have my month's labor ruined was another thing … and the more I thought of it the more I was resolved to take care of my *beautiful* work. (115; emphases added)

After her widowhood, she framed the piece "as a kind of heirloom", hanging it on the dining-room wall. She confirms its value by loaning it "as a patriotic citizen" to an "exposition" sponsored by the Town Agricultural Society in Muskogee, where a visitor sought to buy it for seventy-five dollars. The provenance Owen gives (the work becomes a gift to her son Robert) also underscores its value forty years after its creation, as she describes it "still looking as much like a painting as ever" (116). Transgressing the boundaries between, and revaluing the hierarchies of, pictorial and linguistic art, Owen's transitive discourse erases disciplinary structures.

Finally as musician and music teacher Owen participates in another artistic endeavor that underscores her variable public presence. Before her marriage Owen worked in several schools as a music teacher, a profession that she is forced to resume after her husband's death. The location for this work resonates literally and symbolically. She boards with friends in the "*National* Hotel" in Norfolk, Virginia:

> Across the alley from [the hotel] they had rented a *private* house, which was *connected* by a *bridge* to the *hotel*. There Mr. and Mrs. Holt and all their family had their *private* rooms, and I had mine on the lower floor, directly under Mrs. Holt's *bed-room*, where my music pupils could come in from the *street* door without disturbing any one but myself. (117; emphases added)

Not only is the "private house" linked to the public hotel by a bridge, but also Owen's own quarters become the middle ground between "the street" and her own private rooms, as the literal, corporeal boundary is rendered essentially permeable.

Owen's audacity in recounting the life story of a woman who is not the great public man or hero – a story that nonetheless insists on herself figuring significantly in both American and Cherokee history, which she presents as intimately interconnected – asserts her "multiple, transitional, strategic, playful, contested" embodiments.[29] Far from the uncivilized portrait of the "squaw", Owen provides her readers with an image of an American Queen who is at once Cherokee, Southern, and fully American – and also emphatically feminine. Embodied in her images, her behavior, and her transitive discourse, her level of public visibility varies, but her assurance about her place remains steady. Recording more than a set of physical locations, Owen performs a subjectivity that shifts quickly and adeptly from one domain to another and often blends them substantively, generically, and rhetorically, without apparent effort or conflict, challenging her readers to reject self-limiting categorical thinking and to follow her example.

In describing a friend whose husband was bankrupted by his over-trusting nature, and that friend's strong character, Owen makes an observation that could as easily refer to herself: "The true American woman is ever equal to the demands of changed circumstances and a ready helper" (96). A final example performs and symbolizes the transitivity of Owen's experiences and of her representations of those experiences. Her volume concludes first, with a public, spoken thanks and blessing to the members of the Bartlesville Tuesday Club: "'May each of you in your turn meet with the same blessings of friendship you have showered on me.'" The second closing gesture ostensibly addresses the Tuesday Club members but reaches beyond them: "And I look forward with pleasure to our next meeting. God grant we may all be again at dear Monticello, May day, 1908" (155). Last but not least, she implicitly returns us with these words to the dedication and photo at the beginning, reiterating her signature and underscoring her invitation to her readers to return to Monticello, the home where America begins.

---

[29] Piepmeier, *Out in Public*, 2.

American Women Travelers
and the Material Feminine

Shirley Foster

In 1889, Nellie Bly (the pseudonym of Elizabeth Cochrane, later
Seaman), a reporter for Joseph Pulitzer's *New York World*, proposed
to her editor that in order to produce material for an article she should
attempt to travel round the world in less than Phileas Fogg's famous
eighty days. In response, the paper's business manager demurred, as
Bly describes in her account of her experiences:

> "It is impossible for you to do it," was the terrible verdict. "In the first
> place you are a woman and would need a protector, and even if it were
> possible for you to travel alone you would need to carry so much
> baggage that it would detain you in making rapid changes … no one
> but a man can do this." [1]

Determined upon her venture, Bly managed to persuade him that she
was well able to undertake the project and was eventually allowed to
go. The ways in which she overcame his objections will be discussed
later, but at this stage it is important to note that his reactions are
significant in two respects. First, they metonymically exemplify the
constraints faced by nineteenth-century American women who
attempted to challenge assumptions about what was proper or feasible
for them to do. Second, they succinctly reveal how in this period
"woman" was constructed or defined in terms of gender-specific
trappings (the baggage): womanhood was equated with a set of
material attachments, linked to corporeality, without which not only
was physical movement considered impossible, but the female being
was herself ontologically inconceivable.

By the last decades of the nineteenth century, as social historians
have pointed out, American women were gaining an increasing profile

---

[1] Nellie Bly, *Nellie Bly's Book*, New York: The Pictorial Weeklies Co., 1890, 2.

as claims for suffrage and higher education for women developed. Their growing mobility and visibility through the wider spheres of public life at home – political activity, reform movements, entry into the professions – extended even further in the case of those who, like Bly, sought to override gendered cultural expectations by traveling abroad. American women had, of course, been among the bands of travelers who had been crossing the Atlantic to see the Old World since the immediate post Civil War era (and even before), but as the century proceeded so they ventured further and further afield. Such undertakings, especially to little-known or dangerous regions, or involving unusual efforts, both challenged gender stereotypes and necessitated exposure beyond the traditional domestic sphere of femininity. In her recent study of how women "came out" in public in nineteenth-century America, Alison Piepmeier, arguing for wider scholarly exploration of "modalities of embodiment that make use of both public and private" instead of reliance on a simplistic binary approach, stresses the importance of the female body and its physical agency in this new visibility.[2] As she shows, the female body could be the site for challenges to the dominant discursive formulations of femininity, and thus the means of interpellating the categories of public and private: "the body can demonstrate and enact the fluidity of boundaries via its literal physical movements." Furthermore, as she notes, "the question becomes not whether women were public or private beings but how women gained access to the power and authority of the public world without becoming transgressive figures".[3]

Clearly, for women travelers in particular, the body, linked with its material accoutrements, has the kind of significance outlined by Piepmeier: it facilitates the desire for movement, expansion, and entry into unknown territories; it is also the signifier upon which are written the gender expectations and constraints of the cultural hegemony that have to be negotiated. The achievement of this kind of corporeal freedom for women, insertion into a new geographical space, is linked to issues of identity, both self and national. In the post Civil War period, foreign travel became for Americans an especially important context in which to re-affirm a sense of nationhood that had grown

---

[2] Alison Piepmeier, *Out in Public: Configurations of Women's Bodies in Nineteenth-century America*, Chapel Hill: U of North Carolina P, 2.
[3] *Ibid.*, 9.

fragile with the events of preceding years. If confrontations with Europe called up less than flattering reminders of what America had become, exploration to remoter areas could restore confidence in both self and country. Female travelers could, moreover, prove not only what women, but what American women, could do.

This political and nationalistic agenda is clearly – and somewhat bizarrely – illustrated by Fanny Bullock Workman (to be discussed in more detail later), the notable mountaineer, who included a photo of herself standing on a high plateau and reading a newspaper with the headline **VOTES FOR WOMEN** in her account of the Workmans' 1911-1912 expedition to the Siachen Glacier in the Eastern Karakoram.[4] As well as a statement of nationalistic feminism, this may have been a rejoinder to another well-known American female mountaineer, Annie Peck (with whom Workman crossed swords over altitude records), who, also in 1911, planted a pennant proclaiming "Votes for Woman" on Peru's second highest peak, Nevado Coropuna.

In her discussion of how nineteenth-century American women writers contributed to the creation of a national identity through their treatment of history, Nina Baym points out that "never before *in* history had women been given such opportunities to affect public life".[5] In this period, she argues, a "nationalist narrative" – one which saw America as the world's most advanced nation, driving towards the final achievement of the millennium – was developing. In this, women had a vital role to play in a variety of ways. Mary Suzanne Schriber, taking up Baym's argument, also notes that in the context of American exceptionalism and late nineteenth-century millennialism women were conceived as icons of national destiny; for them, a specifically American mission was imbricated in the act of travel, which itself helped to consolidate national identity. Moreover, since they carried the destiny of America and its millennial promise, they could thus insert themselves into history.[6] Their physical

---

[4] Intriguingly, there is no reference in the text to this picture: it is merely titled "On Silver Throne plateau at nearly 21,000 feet". See Fanny Bullock Workman and William Hunter Workman, *Two Summers in the Ice-wilds of Eastern Karakoram: The Exploration of Nineteen-hundred Square Miles of Mountain Glacier*, London: T. Fisher Unwin, 1917, facing 128.

[5] Nina Baym, *American Women Writers and the Work of History 1790-1860*, New Brunswick, NJ: Rutgers UP, 1995, 7.

[6] Mary Suzanne Schriber, *Writing Home: American Women Abroad, 1830-1920*, Charlottesville: UP of Virginia, 1997, Ch. 1.

achievements were paralleled by their contribution to their country's self-image.

Before presenting a more detailed discussion of the mutually revealing relationship between what will be referred to as "the material feminine", corporeal agency, and nineteenth-century travel, it might be helpful to consider the implications for this study of some recent theoretical work. Of course "material" itself has variable, even ambiguous, meaning. Judith Butler takes it to mean the materiality or matter of bodies, their physicality which "enacts an inchoate drama of sexual difference" and is governed by certain discursive practices and regulatory norms.[7] Susan Bordo, drawing on Marx and Foucault, suggests that "material" refers to the direct grip that culture has on bodies through the practices and bodily habits of everyday life.[8] Raia Prokhovnik also uses the term to mean the fleshly, the physical, as opposed to the subjective, the mind-affected character of the body.[9]

All these ideas are variously suggestive, and, keeping them in mind, this essay uses "material" to focus on those visible trappings attached (or assumed to be attached) to the female body that help to generate or at least modify its cultural and/or political significance. Butler, proposing the idea of a politically regulated "culturally constructed body", sees this body as a surface on which are inscribed the signifiers that produce gender identity. For her, "Such acts, gestures, enactments, generally construed, are *performative* in the sense that the essence or identity that they otherwise purport to express are *fabrications* manufactured and sustained through corporeal signs and other discursive means".[10] Bordo offers a similar view: "The body, as anthropologist Mary Douglas has argued, is a powerful symbolic form, a surface on which the central rules, hierarchies, and even metaphysical commitments of a culture are inscribed and thus reinforced through the concrete language of the body." Bordo also notes that certain features of nineteenth-century female dress, such as bustles and corsets, which accentuate the

---

[7] Judith Butler, *Gender Trouble: Feminism and the Subversion of Identity*, London: Routledge, 1993, 49.
[8] Susan Bordo, *Unbearable Weight: Feminism, Western Culture and the Body*, 2nd edn, Berkeley: U of California P, 2003, 33-36.
[9] Raia Prokhovnik, *Rational Woman: A Feminist Critique of Dichotomy*, 2nd edn, Manchester: Manchester UP, 2002, 153-56.
[10] Butler, *Gender Trouble*, 93, 136.

difference between the male and female forms, "reflected, in symbolic terms, the dualistic division of social and economic life into the clearly defined male and female spheres".[11] Other recent feminist criticism has reiterated that, as there is no such thing as the "natural" body, so gender itself, as reflected on the body, can be perceived as a social construct, ethnically coded and inscribed so as to reveal social, class and cultural values.[12]

It can be argued that the critics cited here are employing a metonymic discourse: although gender essentialism is sometimes implied, most of their propositions have primary relevance to middle-class women, whether or not this is overtly stated. Similarly, it will readily be recognized that in the following discussion the term "woman" is class and race specific; the ways in which gender is theorized and read here are always inflected by class and race ideologies. There are justifications for this. In the first place, the large majority of nineteenth-century and early twentieth-century female American travelers were white, middle- or upper middle-class, more or less financially secure, and well educated. Clearly, then, the cultural conditions that enabled their undertakings and produced their ensuing discourses were determined by their class and social positioning. Secondly, concepts of material femininity and corporeal agency have quite different implications with respect to, say, impoverished female mill workers or farm laborers of the period, than to a leisured and prosperous female bourgeoisie for whom self-presentation is intrinsic to the cultural milieu in which they move. Furthermore, ideas about the commodification of women raised here are largely applicable to those women who – as purchasers or recipients – have agency in the sphere of produced femininity. The discussion that follows is thus implicitly based on a non-universalizing apprehension of gender: middle-class is the silent qualifier in the analyses of femaleness.

In the "gender perilous" activity of travel for women, the body, then, is clearly an intrinsic element.[13] Travel not only involves physical movement into new and often contested spaces, but also foregrounds

---

[11] Bordo, *Unbearable Weight*, 165, 181.

[12] See Prokhovnik, *Rational Woman*, for a discussion of these points.

[13] The term "gender perilous" is developed by Jennifer Bernhardt Steadman in her PhD thesis, "Travel Writing and Resistance: A Feminist Reading of Travel Narratives by African-American and Euro-American Women", Emory University, 2000.

the links between gender and cultural expectations. Certain unwomanly exploits, for example, could be judged as deviant, written on to the female body through appearance (clothes, stance, and so on). But this identity, so produced, could be exploited by the subject so as simultaneously both to reinforce and challenge cultural hegemonies. Dress – one of the most obvious of the performative acts of the gendered body – is, of course, of central significance for nineteenth-century women travelers, and will feature largely in the following discussion. A humorous example of the way in which female clothing could be used so as to empower, while still conferring normality on the wearer, is offered by Mrs Algernon St Maur, an English traveler to the United States in the 1880s. St Maur records delightedly how the large pockets in her voluminous skirts enable her to hide a bag of peanuts, bought from a street stall in New York and disapproved of by her male companions as "the quintessence of vulgarity".[14] So beneath her surface respectability, she can indulge in illicit pleasures. This example also foregrounds how women travelers, like others of their sex who entered the public realm, were inevitably subjecting themselves to the male gaze, a gaze that identified and categorized them not only through their actions but through their appearance and accompanying cultural baggage. For such women, dress was especially gender defining: strategies for ease of mobility (such as wearing divided skirts or trousers to ride cross-saddle) came up against criteria of sexual appropriateness and propriety which could act as restrictions on freedom of movement as well as on self-image.

As has already been suggested, however, the constraints of gender-specific embodiment could become the means of empowerment when taken into the public arena.[15] By exploiting hegemonic images of womanhood, women who traveled in difficult or unusual regions could overcome these constraints while still apparently acknowledging their validity. Such a strategy, physically and visibly enacted in geographical movement, becomes even more evident in the women's descriptions of their exploits. "Performance", in Butler's

---

[14] Mrs Algernon [Susan] St Maur, *Impressions of a Tenderfoot During a Journey in Search of Sport in the Far West*, London: John Murray, 1890, 277.

[15] Mary P. Ryan, in *Women in Public: Between Banners and Ballots, 1825-1880*, Baltimore, PA: Johns Hopkins UP 1990, argues that as nineteenth-century American women entered the public realm, the maintenance of visible sexual difference became a means of ordering disordered or threatening circumstances, thus giving women a degree of control over their situation.

sense, is not confined to the corporeal sphere but operates, too, in the literary one, as the female traveler, the subject of her own narrative, constructs a textual self which both articulates personal desire and satisfies cultural norms. Such visibility in the literary arena also problematizes the notion of a public/private dichotomy and its relation to self-representation through the material feminine. As we have seen, Piepmeier argues that the boundaries between public and private are not fixed but fluid, with the female body an agent in this fluidity.[16]

It can be claimed that this dichotomy is further complicated in the context of the publicized written word. In the activity of travel, overt adherence to middle-class notions of female respectability and proper femininity – or, indeed, challenges to them – probably had little impact, for example, on the native peoples who accompanied expeditions and whose cultural conventions were very different from those of their Western employers. In contrast, the public gaze to which the woman traveler exposed herself through literary re-enactment, when she wrote of her experiences (and particularly when these were accompanied by illustrations of herself) was both critical and unavoidable. Deliberate subjection to the observation of a culturally congruent audience, an act of textual performance, also raises questions of intention. Had these moneyed, privileged middle-class women, whose social advantages enabled them to undertake daring and extraordinary projects, internalized the hegemonic ideologies of femininity through which they seem to be contextualizing themselves and their exploits? Or was it rather that when they entered the public worlds of journalism and popular authorship they strategically negotiated such ideologies in order to protect themselves against criticism as well as advertising their achievements? As will be shown, for the women discussed here, publishing the self only narrowed the line between subverting gender norms and adhering to them.

Nellie Bly's rejoinder to her male professional colleagues who were trying to thwart her project illustrates her triumphant resistance to restrictive male readings of women. Challengingly, she declares her intention, if they do decide to send a man instead of her, of finding another newspaper to sponsor her adventure – she will start the same day as he does and beat him. More pragmatically – and significantly

---

[16] Piepmeier, *Out in Public*, 9.

for this discussion – once she has won her challenge, she proves how she can pack everything she needs into one small bag:

> In [my bag] I was able to pack two traveling caps, three veils, a pair of slippers, a complete outfit of toilet articles, ink-stand, pens, pencils, and copy-paper, pins, needles and thread, a dressing gown, a tennis blazer, a small flask and drinking cup, several complete changes of underwear, a liberal supply of handkerchiefs and fresh ruchings and most bulky and uncompromising of all, a jar of cold cream to keep my face from chapping in the varied climates I should encounter.[17]

The operation itself, subverting the code of domestic/enclosed female space, directly refutes cultural assumptions about the expansive materiality of womanhood, as summed up in a later conversation Bly has with a young man on the way to China: "he told me that ... he had always killed the desire to love and marry because he never expected to find a woman who could travel without a number of trunks and bundles innumerable."[18]

More importantly, Bly's careful itemization of the contents of her single bag confronts her critics not by claiming that women should seek to avoid definition by materiality, but by proving that such materiality can be both gender-specific and empowering. By carrying the gendered private into the public space in which she desires to act, she is giving herself the freedom others are trying to deny her. She is also undercutting conventional associations between women and the body – women seen as dominated by corporeality and its demands – by, on the one hand, acknowledging this relationship, and, on the other, showing how it can be negotiated like any other aspect of the natural physical world. Thus Bly can be both the embodied and the disembodied woman, mistress of and not slave to her corporeality, which becomes a tool rather than an encumbrance in the public arena.

Had Bly set out on her venture eleven years later, she could have found her strategy recommended in Mary Cadwalader Jones' *European Travel for Women*, a guide book of notes and suggestions especially for women travelers. Warning women not to "try to drag about the huge arks with which some Americans still advertise their

---

[17] Bly, *Nellie Bly's Book*, 5.
[18] *Ibid.*, 30.

nationality",[19] Jones advises that, while it is "almost impossible to say how much or how little luggage you should take", "the only sensible thing to do ... is to choose among your belongings those which really add to your daily comfort, and then proceed to build a bag around them".[20] Although it is a case of the less the better, Jones, like Bly, foregrounds certain items as being indispensable for the traveler's comfort, including buttons, sewing-silks, elastic and a tape-measure. Therefore what might be considered the trivia of femininity become essential components in women's bodily negotiations of the foreign.

Bly's refutation of assumptions about the material feminine can be interestingly compared with those of her female rival in the round-the-world race, Elizabeth Bisland. Bisland, a journalist on *Cosmopolitan*, set out to compete against Bly on the urging of her editor who had heard of the challenge. She left the same day as Bly but failed to beat the latter's record of seventy-two days (she returned four days behind). In contrast to her rival, Bisland makes allegiance to the material feminine the reason why she cannot be ready in such a short time: "I was not prepared in the matter of appropriate garments for such an abrupt departure."[21] She takes much more luggage than Bly, and claims that she could easily have managed more. Yet in itemizing apparently trivial essentials, she too both guarantees her female "normality" and asserts her control over her own undertaking:

> Happily I took the precaution of carrying plenty of pins and hair-pins. I had had some previous experience with their vicious ways, and well knew in critical moments in foreign parts they would get up playful little games of hide-and-seek that would tend to undermine my temper, and the only sure preventive was to have geologic layers of them all through the trunk, so that a shaft might be hastily sunk through one's belongings at any moment with a serene certainty of striking rich deposits of both necessities of female existence.[22]

---

[19] Mary Cadwalader Jones, *European Travel for Women: Notes and Suggestions*, New York: Macmillan, 1900, 32. Jones was the sister-in-law of Edith Wharton, herself a much traveled woman.
[20] *Ibid.*, 35, 40.
[21] Elizabeth Bisland, *A Flying Trip Around the World in Seven Stages*, New York: Harpers, 1891, First Stage, 1.
[22] *Ibid.*, 2.

Through the ironic textual surface, Bisland is both mocking and validating gender-specific behavior. Her use of a pseudo-scientific metaphor, moreover, inserts herself into the world of male enterprise: her own bodily action of mining her luggage in order to regulate her female appearance empowers her as an explorer while still ensuring her feminine respectability.

Figure 12.1 Annie S. Peck in her mountaineering costume. Courtesy New York Public Library

Bly's and Bisland's insistence on their own femininity in the context of non-feminine enterprise is replicated by Annie S. Peck, one of the most famous turn-of-the-century American women mountaineers. To achieve her goals – including the ascent of the Matterhorn in 1895 (she was one of only three women to do this in the nineteenth century), and her triumphant accomplishment of the summit of Huascarán in Peru in 1908, after five previous attempts – Peck donned proto-masculine attire: knickerbockers and puttees, below a hip-length woolen tunic. She also rode astride, wearing a long overcoat opening to the waist so as to give the impression of a divided skirt, which, as she ironically observed, "I trust prevented my shocking the sensibilities of anyone".[23] The significance of this clothing, and Peck's self-presentation through it, will be discussed below. Here it is important to note that alongside this determined non-conformity Peck is also anxious to position herself within the arena of "normal" womanhood.

Describing her encampment on a glacier in a tiny tent (a private, enclosed, female space) she details her preparations for sleeping:

> To sit in cramped quarters with bundles and bags by my side, take off high laced boots, change stockings, get into Eskimo trousers, pull out

---

[23] From Annie Smith Peck, *A Search for the Apex of America*, 1911, quoted in Elizabeth Fagg Olds, *Women of the Four Winds*, Boston: Houghton Mifflin, 1985, 23.

and make use of my toilet articles, cold cream, Pond's extract, Japanese stoves, comb and braid my hair, when half dead with fatigue and stiff with cold, – well, it was the hardest kind of labor.[24]

Like Bly, Peck is here constructing a complex and deviant subject which both advertises difference and is accordant with cultural norms. The extraordinary courage and resilience which have enabled her to reach one of the highest peaks in the world are here shown as harnessed to equally gargantuan physical efforts to maintain her proper femininity in extremely adverse conditions. For her, "the hardest kind of labor" is not the enormous struggle to make the ascent, but the difficulty of changing clothes and anointing her face in a very small space. It is also worth noting that the specific detail given – cold cream and Pond's extract – reinforces her strategy of familiarization: apart from its taking place in a different environment, this, she insists, is any bourgeois woman's night-time routine as she sits at her dressing-table. Tempting though it might be to hear an ironic note in this passage, it offers itself far more as a conscious piece of textual self-presentation exploiting the images of womanhood available at this time. Peck's radical self-aggrandizement is rendered acceptable by her careful performance of feminine bodily ritual.

As has already been suggested, the most challenging disparity between conventional images of the female body and the exercise of corporeal freedom was felt by those women who undertook daring and demanding physical enterprises. At the end of the nineteenth century women's clothes regulated the visibility of that body and defined its parameters in ways that hindered adventurous activity. Long skirts, ridiculously tight waists that constrained breathing, and features that emphasized sexual allure rather than bodily capabilities were of little use to the female traveler. Some female travelers, like Peck, directly challenged cultural conventions by dressing in the garments that gave them the greatest ease of movement. Such garments, almost inevitably modeled on male attire, subjected the wearers to charges of gender insubordination. However much the chief consideration behind

---

[24] Peck, *A Search for the Apex of America*, quoted in Olds, *Women of the Four Winds*, 39-40. Peck wrote several articles about the ascent. One version of the account, differing slightly from this extract, is to be found in Annie Smith Peck, "A Woman in the Andes", *Harper's Monthly Magazine*, CXIV/679 (December 1906), 7-8.

women explorers' choice of costume was practicality, none of them could be unaware of the cultural implications of their choice.

One of the first American female mountaineers, Julia Archibald Holmes, who came from a family of anti-slavery and women's rights supporters, climbed Pikes Peak, New Mexico, in the company of three men, wearing an "American Costume", or bloomers, "the official uniform of suffragists in the 1850s".[25] Holmes noted that this outfit, consisting of a calico dress reaching just below the knees, calico trousers, boots and a hat, gave her the necessary freedom of movement. In advocating the usefulness of this outfit for her purpose, she was not only demonstrating her good sense but also making an overt political statement about the restrictions suffered by women in both physical and political terms. Significantly, she published an account of her feat in the *Sybil*, a feminist periodical of the day.[26]

Not all women could be as directly iconoclastic as this. As has been shown in the case of Peck, in order to deflect hostile criticism, the adoption of unconventional costume could necessitate explanation or apology, even forms of disguise. A notable example is that of Isabella Bird, the well-known British Victorian traveler. Bird's traveling costume became the subject of notorious exchange soon after she published the account of her trip to the Rocky Mountains. She, too, adapted her dress so as to combine comfort and gender propriety, but when *The Times* of 22 November 1879 wrote of her that "she donned masculine habiliments for greater convenience", she felt obliged in 1893 to append a Note to the second edition of *A Lady's Life in the Rocky Mountains*:

> For the benefit of other lady travelers, I wish to explain that my "Hawaiian riding dress" is the "American Lady's Mountain Dress," a half-fitting jacket, a short skirt reaching to the ankles, and full Turkish trousers gathered into frills which fall over the boot, – a thoroughly

---

[25] Janet Robertson, *The Magnificent Mountain Women: Adventures in the Colorado Rockies*, Lincoln: U of Nebraska P, 1990, 3. Holmes herself wrote to her mother that "in all probability I am the first woman who has ever stood upon the summit of this mountain" (quoted in Robertson, ibid., 6), and in fact it was seventeen years before any other woman climbed in the Rockies.

[26] Julia Archibald Holmes, "A Journey to Pikes Peak and New Mexico", *Sybil*, III/18 (1895), 521-31.

serviceable and feminine costume for mountaineering and other rough traveling in any part of the world. [27]

Her riposte to *The Times* is not only a declaration of her feminine respectability (accession to cultural norms), but also an assertion of her right to choose her own mode of dress, and, indeed, to recommend it to other women.

To prove her case, Bird appended a picture of herself in her traveling costume on the title page of her book. Such textual visibility is a strategy employed by many others, a means of self-representation which was both a defense and self-promotional. Workman's published photograph of herself in the Karakoram has already been referred to, an image with national, political, and gender implications. Peck also advertised her own non-conformity in the studio portrait she had taken of herself in her mountain gear. Curiously, in the portrait a large black moustache is shown painted on her face mask, a feature that she herself called "rather superfluous" but one which sharply exacerbates the gender reversal of her outfit.[28] Moreover, Peck became exposed to the public gaze as an icon of female achievement when the Singer sewing-machine company gave away a packet of pictures of her in her climbing gear with every machine sold. The image of the unconventional woman who has become a well-known figure is thus exploited to market an item which, though it revolutionized women's work in terms of time and effort, continued to validate the association between woman and the home. Peck's extraordinary achievements, though ostensibly celebrated, are here firmly placed in the domestic sphere, while at the same time the representation of her bold iconoclasm would surely have spoken positively to the largely female audience who viewed it.

Peck, of course, did not seek to be represented in this configuration, even though she would probably have been amused by it. Workman, on the other hand, was eager to establish her gender propriety in the context of her unwomanly activity. In contrast to Holmes and Peck, she – as committed a feminist as they were – chose

---

[27] Isabella Bird, *A Lady's Life in the Rocky Mountains* (1879), London: Virago, 1983, vii-viii. Later in the book, however, Bird does admit that when she gets nearer "civilization" (Denver), she puts on a long skirt and rides side-saddle instead of astride in "deference to prejudices" (177).

[28] Olds, *Women of the Four Winds*, 52.

not to use their mode of corporeal presentation in order to facilitate women's entry into a traditionally male world. For her, although the body was the agent by which she accomplished her extraordinary goals, it was not the overt signifier of gender iconoclasm.

Workman was certainly eager to insert herself into the public arena – to make herself and her undertakings visible. These undertakings were on a grand scale. She was born into a wealthy family, and married a prominent physician, William Hunter Workman, himself well-to-do. In 1888, he gave up his practice and the couple traveled until the outbreak of World War I, at first in Europe and then further afield. They climbed in France and Switzerland, cycled in Spain, Algeria, India, Ceylon, and Java, and, finally, between 1898 and 1912, climbed extensively in the Karakoram and Himalayan mountains. Although undoubtedly they experienced much physical hardship, their financial advantages gave them freedom from the kinds of difficulties and anxieties experienced by Peck: they employed large numbers of coolies and guides (though these were often unreliable), and, with a big caravan bearing all their camping equipment and food, they were able to concentrate on the business of conquering previously unexplored peaks. This nomadic life not only separated them from the traditional activities of their social class at home, but also, for Workman herself, eliminated the domestic responsibilities linked to womanhood. She was thus able to operate freely in a man's world, the only woman in the party and, theoretically at least, unconstrained by the codes of civilization. Blessed with an apparently cast-iron constitution, in addition to keeping up with the men, she also led some expeditions on her own.

Workman's means of making known her pioneering successes was textual self-advertisement. On the title pages of the books she co-authored with her husband, she lists the honors awarded to her during her career. At the beginning of their *Ice-bound Heights of the Mustagh*, for instance, ten of her honors are listed, including Grand Medalist of the Club Alpin Français, Fellow Royal Scottish Geographical Society, and Corresponding Member American Geographic Society.[29] (There are only four honors listed under William's name.) Within the texts themselves – which are, with one

---

[29] Fanny Bullock Workman and William Hunter Workman, *Ice-bound Heights of the Mustagh: An Account of Two Seasons of Pioneer Exploration and High Climbing in the Baltistan Himalaya*, London: Archibald Constable, 1908.

exception, narrated in the first person plural, with individual references to either author made in the third person – Fanny Workman also details her own particular triumphs. In *Ice-bound Heights*, she notes of one of her solo-led trips: "By this ascent she broke her previous altitude record for women of 21,000 feet a second time on this day, and this time by 1,568 feet." On the same page, a footnote adds: "She has since climbed to an altitude of 23,000 feet in the Nun Kan range, which places her with the small band of men who have reached a height of 23,000 feet", an achievement she records in the later *Peaks and Glaciers of Nun Kun*.[30]

In Part II of *Two Summers in the Ice-wilds of Eastern Karakoram* – which, unusually, was authored by her in the first person because she was the actual leader of this expedition – Workman calls attention to her own visual record of her achievements. Noting how she and her husband painted their initials on suitable rocks to mark their successful ascents, she illustrates this with a photograph of a rock face inscribed with F.B.W. and dated "AUG 25 1912".[31] Further, in a note at the end of the section, after acknowledging the achievement of other woman in the field, she concludes, "but no other has carried out the exploration and climbing of great glaciers and high peaks in Asia".[32] Even her final apologia at the end of *Two Summers in the Ice-wilds* conflates feminist politics and self-promotion:

> The object of placing my full name in connection with the expedition on the map, is not because I wish in any way to thrust myself forward, but solely that in the accomplishments of women, now and in the future, it should be known to them and stated in print that a woman was the initiator and special leader of this expedition …. at present, it behoves women, for the benefit of their sex, to put what they do, at least, on record. [33]

Given her extraordinary gender-challenging achievements, it may therefore seem anomalous that Workman eschewed any radicalism of dress. As pictures of her indicate, despite the obvious inconvenience, for many years she traveled in long skirts, with her ankles covered.

---

[30] *Ibid.*, 308-309; Fanny Bullock Workman and William Hunter Workman, *Peaks and Glaciers of Nun Kun*, London: Constable, 1909.
[31] Workman and Workman, *Two Summers in the Ice-wilds*, facing 216.
[32] *Ibid.*, 224.
[33] *Ibid.*, 284.

Only when she began the more arduous mountain expeditions did she make some compromises such as shorter, calf-length skirts, and puttees over her boots, but she still frequently wore a large-brimmed hat, sometimes with a veil, rather than the tight-fitting caps often worn by the men. Like other women explorers she exploited the visual in order to insert herself visually into the public arena. On cycling trips in North Africa and India, she posed for photographs, dressed in long-sleeved white blouses, neat ties, floor-length skirts, a hat, and sometimes a striped parasol.[34] In *Ice-bound Heights*, she and William are photographed as "The Leaders of the Expedition", and here she again appears in a small hat, a neat blouse with a necktie, and calf-length skirts. Workman's insistent conventionality in this respect may have been strategic, but it may have also had a more personal, ideological basis. While deploring the miserable position of women in Algerian Arab households, for instance, she notes that the woman hostess at one of the public houses they visit near Tunis was "not attired in the costume commonly worn by her sex, but in a complete man's suit of tightly-fitting white jean trousers, high gaiters and short sackcoat ... [a] cordial amazon in trousers".[35] If there is a note of admiration beneath the ostensible disapproval here, this is nevertheless not a path which Workman herself wished to follow.

This apparent conventionalism seems submissive to the model of woman as culturally constructed: Workman's advertised retention of female dress guarantees her femininity and shows that her extraordinary physical triumphs are wholly compatible with this femininity. It can also be seen as an enactment of agency, a declaration of female empowerment. To her female audience/readers, Workman shows the possibilities of the womanly body, even in the garments which appear unsuitable for her kind of activity; to her male audience/readers, she offers the assurance that she has not abandoned her sex and therefore does not ostensibly present a threat to gender binaries. It is also a demonstration that the ideological binaries of male/public, female/private are both inadequate and negotiable.

---

[34] This apparel is reminiscent of that of Mary Kingsley, the well-known English explorer of West Africa, who both in her written narrative and in photographs emphasizes the femininity of her outfit.
[35] Fanny Bullock Workman and William Hunter Workman, *Algerian Memories: A Bicycle Tour over the Atlas to the Sahara*, London: T. Fisher Unwin, 1895, 137, 139.

Workman has gained access to the power and authority of the public world without becoming a transgressive figure.[36]

Figure 12.2 Fanny Bullock Workman, from *Two Summers in the Ice-wilds of Eastern Karakoram* by Fanny Bullock Workman and William Hunter Workman (1917)

If Workman's climbing outfit articulated her adherence to conventional codes of femininity, it did so discreetly and without ostentation. A much more extreme display of the materiality of womanhood was made by May French-Sheldon, the wife of a wealthy American businessman, who was one of the first women to explore Africa. In 1891, at the age of forty-three, commanding a caravan of 138 porters (which included a few native women), she led an expedition into the Mount Kilimanjaro region of East Africa, which lasted three months and covered nearly a thousand miles.[37] Of central

---

[36] It is clear also that Workman wished to dissociate herself from more obviously feminist figures: her notorious challenge to Peck's claim that "I have the honor of breaking the world's record [of height climbed] for men as well as women" (Peck, "A Woman in the Andes", 187) was probably inspired partly by a wish to maintain her womanly difference, as well as by jealousy.

[37] Interestingly, although May French-Sheldon's ostensible purpose was anthropological investigation, she does not mention this until Ch. 3 of her book, *Sultan to Sultan: Adventures among the Masai and Other Tribes of East Africa* (1892), ed. Tracey Jean Boisseau, Manchester: Manchester UP, 1998. In the text, ethnographic detail is embedded in the narrative of exploration rather than added separately.

concern to her, as to other women explorers who had to negotiate with native, usually male, peoples, was how to act with authority and exercise control while at the same time making it evident that she had not relinquished her female affiliations.

Recognizing the importance of displaying the signifiers of gender affiliation, she chose to show herself not in an outfit symbolizing womanly submission and modesty but in one that exploited images of magnificence and hierarchy. To meet important chiefs or sultans, she donned an extravagant court dress of silver-trimmed white silk, bedecked with jewels, adding to this a tiara set on a long blonde wig. Significantly, like the other travelers discussed here, she used a picture of herself in her outfit as an illustration for her text. The ball gown and its accoutrements (symbols of culturally constructed womanhood, particularly associated with display and privilege) thus become here markers of both femaleness and power – French-Sheldon herself called it a dress suitable for a "white queen" and relished being given this title by the natives. She also enjoyed the authority it conferred upon her, as she notes of her encounter with one village prince:

Figure 12.3 May French-Sheldon, from *Sultan to Sultan: Adventures among the Masai and Other Tribes of East Africa* (1892)

> I held a full-dress reception, attired in my court gown and all the splendors of my jewel box and portable wardrobe. As usual, the function was a very distinguished social success, and exalted me far above mortals of common clay in the estimation of sultan, crown prince, courtiers, and plebeians.[38]

Whereas the material feminine of Bly, Bisland, and Peck implements images of domestic womanhood (creams, pins, and so on), that of French-Sheldon articulates a more public femaleness, in which gender is imbricated with class and race. Empowered by her

---

[38] *Ibid.*, 189.

whiteness and by the capitalist world behind her enterprise, she more blatantly exploits the gender-specific conventions of her own culture in order to facilitate her engagement with the sphere of colonialist enterprise (she and her husband were involved in various schemes of capitalist development in East Africa). At the same time, she insists on presenting herself in the role of normal womanhood and rejects the sartorial iconoclasm of cross-dressing. Noting that she always kept her skirts down to her feet when amidst her porters, she observes, "My woman's costume was never a hindrance to my progress, and I cannot conceive how masculine attire would have in any way been an advantage to me".[39] French-Sheldon's exaggerated, almost parodic gender affiliation, in the proto-colonialist context, additionally images woman as commodity, of particular significance in a period when wealthy American entrepreneurs visually advertised their successes by encouraging their women to dress as lavishly as possible. However she is exploiting this commodification (woman as sign) in order to enter the male-dominated world of trade and commerce, not only awing the native inhabitants with her appearance, but also using her jewels to gain concessions and favors.

Even more bizarrely, French-Sheldon also carried an Alpine stock displaying a blue pennant "emblazoned with the magic device, *noli me tangere*", which, she claimed "was much admired [by the natives] …. They innocently deemed it to be a badge of high rank, never having seen one before, hence inferred that I must be of supreme importance and possessed of limitless power."[40] In her construction of an inviolable yet sexually positioned personality, she was thus not only staging her own hero(ine)ism, but also attempting to forestall challenges to her dominance – an extraordinary gesture given the unlikelihood of her African audience's being able to understand her "magic emblem". At the same time, she played up the androgyny of her role: her extravagantly female costume also included a ceremonial sword and two loaded pistols (which she was quite ready to use). The name given to her by the natives – Bébé Bwana (woman master) – aptly signifies this fusion of male and female. She used the uncertainties it produced as a means of control, as her text makes clear: "The habit of regarding me as a man, and not being quite able to reconcile my office with that of a woman, was shown throughout my

---

[39] *Ibid.*, 244.
[40] *Ibid.*, 144.

safari by the men who were my personal *attachés*."[41] Here, the deliberate confusion of gender boundaries confers power and the chance to use it.

As has been suggested, intrinsic to this performative, masquerading aspect of feminine subjectivity are visible status and authority. French-Sheldon delights in recording how the sultans are fascinated by her long blonde hair, and notes that "my court gown was a source of endless admiration".[42] Beneath this somewhat brash self-aggrandizement lies French-Sheldon's recognition that her gender, advertised and linked to her economic and racial positioning, was her most powerful weapon in negotiating the difficulties and dangers of her expedition. It also, as Tracey Boisseau, the editor of her account, posits, may have had a wider purpose: "[French-Sheldon's] vivid descriptions of her costume and repetitive references to herself as a white queen in her written and verbal accounts suggest that this persona served as a device structuring her relations with European and American audiences as much as or more than African ones."[43]

Boisseau's commentary foregrounds the issue of the public gaze to which these female travelers were exposing themselves. It was suggested earlier that, rather than the act of travel itself, the audience who received the traveler's textual self-representation provided the real public arena. French-Sheldon, however, seems to be producing herself for two publics: the tribal peoples to whom she displays herself, and her readers. The former, she intended, would interpret her as a figure of power and a ruthless negotiator; the latter, she hoped, would read her as exemplary not only of colonial authority but also of extraordinary womanhood. Here, of course, questions about the degree of French-Sheldon's self-awareness need to be asked. Were the Africans really as impressed by her as she claims? Did they recognize the implicit racism embedded in her self-presentation? Was she deluding herself (and trying to delude her readers) about the successfulness of her strategies? Ultimately, perhaps, the public before whom she was performing was herself.[44]

---

[41] *Ibid.*, 211-12.

[42] *Ibid.*, 223.

[43] *Ibid.*, 8.

[44] French-Sheldon's insistent self-aggrandizement contrasts markedly with Mary Kingsley's ironic and self-deflationary account of herself in very similar situations.

For late nineteenth-century American women travelers, becoming visible entailed entering not only new physical and geographical realms, but also new socio-cultural ones that challenged their society's gender expectations and ideologies. Exploitation of the material feminine, as defined in this essay, became the means of negotiating these challenges, both enabling their undertakings and allowing them to remain within the bounds of hegemonic discourses of womanhood. Their recognition of how the private/domestic world of femininity can be taken into and used in the public worlds in which they moved, as adventurers and writers reproducing themselves in textual performance, makes them true innovators opening up new spaces for women.

PART III

BECOMING "MODERN"

GENDERING MODERNITY: FRANCES E. WILLARD'S POLITICS OF TECHNOLOGICAL SENTIMENTALITY

TIMOTHY A. HICKMAN

On 8 April 1883, Henry James famously explained his choice of subject for *The Bostonians* by recording in his notebooks that he wished to write a story that was both "very American" and "very characteristic of our social conditions". Upon reflection, James decided that "the situation of women, the decline of the sentiment of sex, the agitation on their behalf" was "the most salient and peculiar point in our social life".[1] For James, the changing relationship between (usually white and middle-class) women and men in late nineteenth-century America registered the historicity of his age. He marked the novelty of the present, that is, its specificity – its rootedness in time and place – by invoking women's politics as an indicator of the extent to which the world had changed, as a sign of the peculiarity of the present.

He was far from alone in this observation, and though *The Bostonians* is very critical of what he called "the agitation on their behalf", other texts were much less so. In *Women and Economics*, Charlotte Perkins Gilman agreed with James' observation, writing that a "greater and more important change than the world has ever seen, this slow emergence of the long subverted human female to full racial equality, has been going on about us full long enough to be observed".[2] Elizabeth Cady Stanton was among the most interested and articulate observers of that "slow emergence", writing in 1892

---

[1] Henry James (8 April 1883), rpt. in *The Complete Notebooks of Henry James*, eds F. O. Matthiessen and Kenneth B. Murdock, New York: Oxford UP, 1947, 47.
[2] Charlotte Perkins Gilman, "Women's Evolution from Economic Dependence", in *Women and Economics: A Study of the Economic Relations Between Men and Women as a Factor in Social Evolution*, excerpted in *Root of Bitterness: Documents of the Social History of American Women*, eds Nancy F. Cott, Jeanne Boydston and Molly Ladd-Taylor, Boston, MA: Northeastern UP, 2nd edn, 1996, 391.

that women now "fill the editor's and professor's chair, plead at the bar of justice, walk the wards of the hospital, speak from the pulpit and the platform". She explained that "such is the type of womanhood that an enlightened public sentiment welcomes today, and such the triumph of the facts of life over the false theories of the past".[3] But Frances E. Willard, president of the Women's Christian Temperance Union and the main subject of this essay, offered perhaps the most cogent elaboration of James' historical observation in a speech in 1888, "The Dawn of Woman's Day":

> In brief, the barriers that have hedged women into one pathway and men into another, altogether different, are growing thin, as physical strength plays a less determining part in our life drama. The gradual adjustment of every-day occupation, custom and law, to this new ideal, marks ours as a transition period. Those who have the most enlargement of opportunity to hope for from the change, will, in the nature of the case, move on most rapidly into the new conditions, and this helps to explain, I think, why women seem to be climbing more rapidly than men, to-day ... with souls more open to the [spiritual power] of the oncoming age.[4]

This dense passage will require considerable unpacking but, before that, we need to be very clear about the approach that all of these writers shared. In other words, we cannot begin to understand Willard's writing until we have examined a common rhetorical strategy that emphasized a perceived set of changes in middle-class women's lives as a means by which to establish the historical distinctiveness of late nineteenth-century American culture. In Willard's words, "this new ideal marks ours as a transition period". Therefore shifting gender roles could be imagined as emblematic of "transition", or as representative of historical change itself. For all of these writers, the perception of women's growing political and social power operated as a measure of the passage of time, as a way to distinguish the present from the past. They all shared a textual approach that produced, implicitly or explicitly, a sense of the past in order to assert a break with that past. As such, they participated in a

---

[3] Elizabeth Cady Stanton, "The Solitude of Self" (1892), in *The American Intellectual Tradition, 1865 to the Present*, eds David A. Hollinger and Charles Capper, 3rd edn, New York: Oxford UP, 2001, II, 52.
[4] Frances E. Willard, "The Dawn of Woman's Day", in *Root of Bitterness*, 403.

common but very effective narrative practice that helped to establish what they believed was the uniqueness of the period in which they lived. Perhaps more fundamentally, it was a strategy that separated the antiquated from the modern and thus helped to produce the sense of modernity itself.

This essay will examine that strategy, looking at a variety of texts in order to contextualize those written by Frances E. Willard. Willard, an academic turned political activist who led the Women's Christian Temperance Union from 1879 until her death in 1898, was a sentimental writer whose words offer plentiful evidence of her profoundly Christian world view, coupled with her strong commitment to the anti-alcohol cause. This combination of interests contributes to a popular view of her as an adherent to an older, womanist politics, rooted in an acceptance of the sentimental, domestic discourse that Barbara Welter identified in 1966 as a "cult of true womanhood" – that is, a middle-class depiction of women as pious, submissive, domestic and sexually pure.[5] Indeed, the WCTU's motto – "Home Protection" – is a clear illustration of the way that the older model empowered white, middle-class women's politics throughout the nineteenth century. As Willard stated in an 1888 speech, "society and government are two rainbows which interplay round a fountain, and that fountain is the home".[6]

Willard's WCTU, however, took on much more than temperance reform. Her "Do Everything" policy ensured that the WCTU would be nearly as interested in the politics of "the woman question" as it was with anti-alcohol measures. After looking at the late nineteenth-century intellectual context more broadly, this essay will explore the way that Frances E. Willard's writing, in a manner that is perhaps surprising for such a sentimental writer, used a technological metaphor in order to gender modernity as female, and to imagine it as an era of expanding opportunity for women. This made sense to Willard because she believed that modern transportation technology empowered women's mobility and enhanced their capacity to organize.

---

[5] Barbara Welter, "The Cult of True Womanhood: 1820-1860", *American Quarterly*, XVIII/2 (Summer 1966), 151-74.
[6] Willard, "The Dawn of Woman's Day", 403.

Modernity as cultural crisis

Before coming to Willard, however, we will need to look more closely at the broader context in which she was writing. The passages that I used to open this essay were redolent with the sense of what many historians have identified as a late nineteenth-century cultural crisis. All of those quoted above, despite their differences, wrote in ways that emphasized the present as a profound breaking away from the past. Many historians, perhaps beginning with Richard Hofstadter and his 1952 discussion of the "psychic crisis of the 1890s", have employed versions of the cultural crisis model to describe Gilded Age and Progressive Era culture.[7] In broad terms, the model generally holds that an important part of late nineteenth- and early twentieth-century cultural life involved a struggle to make human agency coherent in a period of rapid technological, economic, and political change.

This formulation has been controversial, both for its frequent focus on the intellectual elite and for what some scholars have argued is its tendency to forget that identity has always been under construction. From this latter perspective, formulations of cultural crisis as the

---

[7] Richard Hofstadter, *The Paranoid Style in American Politics and Other Essays*, London: Jonathan Cape, 1952, 148. Hofstadter used the phrase to think about the Spanish-American War. See also Robert H. Wiebe, *The Search for Order, 1877–1920*, New York: Hill and Wang, 1967; Henry F. May, *The End of American Innocence: A Study of the First Years of Our Own Time, 1912–1917*, New York: Alfred A. Knopf, 1959; Alan Trachtenberg, *The Incorporation of America: Culture and Society in the Gilded Age*, New York: Hill and Wang, 1982; Nancy F. Cott, *The Grounding of American Feminism*, New Haven, CT: Yale UP, 1987; James Livingston, *Pragmatism and the Political Economy of Cultural Revolution*, Chapel Hill: U of North Carolina P, 1994; and Clive Bush, *Halfway to Revolution: Investigation and Crisis in the Work of Henry Adams, William James, and Gertrude Stein*, New Haven, CT: Yale UP, 1991. Theoretical accounts of modernity abound, but a good start is Marshall Berman, *All That Is Solid Melts into Air: The Experience of Modernity*, New York: Penguin, 1988; Matei Calinescu, *Five Faces of Modernity: Modernism, Avant-garde, Decadence, Kitsch, Postmodernism*, Durham, NC: Duke UP, 1987; and Reinhart Kosselleck, *The Practice of Conceptual History: Timing History, Spacing Concepts*, trans. Todd Samuel Presner, Stanford, CA: Stanford UP, 2002. For more recent applications of and challenges to the crisis model that incorporate race, class and gender difference, see Gail Bederman, *Manliness and Civilization: A Cultural History of Gender and Race in the United States, 1880–1917*, Chicago: U of Chicago P, 1995; Elizabeth Grace Hale, *Making Whiteness: Southern Segregation, 1890–1940*, New York: Random House, 1999; and Robert G. Lee, *Orientals: Asian Americans in Popular Culture*, Philadelphia, PA: Temple UP, 1999. On the limitations of the crisis model, see especially Bederman, *Manliness and Civilization*, 11.

failure or disruption of the coherent assertion of self reify the concept of a stable, autonomous identity by suggesting that once, usually before industrialization and capitalism, we really were centered, independent, and rational subjects. Furthermore, such formulations tend to suggest that the immediately preceding period was one of stability and certainty, something hard to sustain in light of the massive upheavals capped by the Civil War, the abolition of slavery, and large-scale industrialization. Much of the recent scholarship suggests that the crisis model accepts precisely what it should question: the autonomous, rational subject.

But I suggest we need both of these approaches if we are to make sense of late nineteenth- and early twentieth-century culture. Recent cultural histories have shown that identity is always in construction and that the assertion of a stable subject is an ideological enterprise that often serves the interests of dominant social groups. But then again, cultural production in the Gilded Age and Progressive Era does seem to have been particularly occupied with the renegotiation of a destabilized sense of the self. "To immerse oneself in the documents of the period is gradually to come to recognize the depth of [these people's] sense of confusion and danger and to respect the historical specificity of their reported discomfort", according to the literary critic June Howard.[8] But we cannot, in Howard's words, hope to respect that specificity unless we place it alongside a kindred sense of confusion that has appeared at many other historical times and places. The profoundly disconcerting experience of historical change, the sense of crisis that typifies the culture of modernity, might be found in any number of texts, drawn from a variety of historical times and places. At the same time, the experience takes specific and novel forms that are particular to the time and place of their appearance.

In this sense, modernity is not to be found in a set of empirical factors like industrial capitalism, rationalized bureaucracies and representative democracy. It is rather an idea, a mode of historical consciousness. It is not a description of reality, but rather a way of valuing or defining "reality". It is an experience of the passage of time that has been persistent in the history of the West, but also very specific to its moment or moments of enunciation. It is as enduring as it is fleeting. Modernity is, therefore, a simultaneously particular, but

---

[8] June Howard, *Form and History in American Literary Naturalism*, Chapel Hill: U of North Carolina P, 1985, xi.

also a generalized experience of the passage of time. It is, therefore, very much a paradox.[9]

Matei Calinescu examined that paradox in *Five Faces of Modernity*, in which he traces the history of the concept of modernity from the coinage of the Latin word *modernus* in the fourth century of the common era.[10] He associated the term with a sense of the linear passage of time evident in early Christian eschatology, contrasting it with classical notions of time as a permanent cycle of old and new. Calinescu showed that a general sense of linear time has been central to Western intellectual and aesthetic culture, offering a means to assert the novelty of its own, particular historical present by positioning that present against a recent but now closed past, while also keeping an eye on a not yet realized future. The sense that we are hurtling along an arrow of time – the sense of *modernus* – has been reasserted under various names, in various guises, and with differing degrees of intensity for much of the intervening period. Renaissance, Enlightenment, Romanticism, historicism, modernity, and finally postmodernity are all names that have been deployed at times of particularly intense cultural ferment. Those attempts to assert the novelty of the present by naming it as a distinct moment have depended on comparisons with the past and future, seen as discrete periods that are nonetheless related to one another in varied and complex temporal narratives. Calinescu's study shows modernity to be a persistent historical condition. It offers a framework that might move scholarly practice away from debates over which period really was modern or whether there really was a crisis, to more productive attempts to describe the differing strategies and techniques that people have employed to produce and make evident the sense of modernity for themselves and their contemporaries.

This description of modernity as a mode of historical consciousness meets the demands of the more recent cultural history by admitting that people have faced challenges to the definition of the self in every historical epoch, but it does not surrender the specificity

---

[9] On the experience of modernity as a "paradoxical … unity of disunity", see Berman, *All That Is Solid*, 15. My sense of modernity, however, is closer to Jean-Francois Lyotard's description of postmodernity as the latest instance of modernity. See "Answer to the Question: What is Postmodernism?", in *The Postmodern Condition: A Report on Knowledge*, trans. Geoff Bennington and Brian Massumi, Manchester: Manchester UP, 1984, 71-82.

[10] Calinescu, *Five Faces of Modernity*, 1-92.

of a late nineteenth- and early twentieth-century "modern cultural crisis". Understanding the concept in this manner frees us from reductive empiricism, while simultaneously urging us to think about the similarities and differences in the multiple enunciations of modernity as an experience of the passage of time. In terms of Gilded Age and Progressive Era culture, it allows us to retain the sense of a modern cultural crisis while encouraging us to understand that crisis in its many inflections. Put another way, we are able to preserve a crisis of modernity without reducing that crisis to a single set of dominant texts if we recognize that not everyone understood or expressed the meaning of that crisis in the same way. Calinescu's formulation helps us to accommodate both the common condition as well as its specific iterations within the overarching framework of a "modern cultural crisis".

Many modernisms / many modernities

This brings us back to the passages that I opened with. As I noted, each of those fragments produced a sense of the past in order to posit a substantial break with that past, thus strengthening the description of the present as modern and the sense of modernity as crisis. Similar narrative strategies were common in late nineteenth-century writing, but not all writers identified changed gender relations as the definitive element of their era, nor did they agree on modernity's meaning. Highlighting technological change was a more common way to identify the present as a break from the past, but technology was an indicator whose mere deployment held nothing inherent that might anchor its meaning. Perhaps its most familiar and obvious iteration, at least in intellectual culture, aided the description of the modern cultural crisis as tragedy. Henry Adams, for instance, strikingly imagined in his 1907 autobiography how "he found himself lying in the Gallery of Machines at the Great Exposition of 1900, with his *historical neck broken* by the sudden irruption of forces totally new".[11] The consequence of a broken neck is, of course, paralysis, but the kind of paralysis that Adams suffered was a specifically historical paralysis – the incapacity to situate himself or his society within a coherent historical narrative. Further, Adams' inability to formulate a convincing history of the changes he saw around him was a

---

[11] Henry Adams, *The Education of Henry Adams: An Autobiography* (1907), ed. Ernest Samuels, Atlanta, GA: Houghton Mifflin, 1973, 382 (emphasis added).

consequence of "the sudden irruption of forces totally new". His historical consciousness was a casualty of the very history he had hoped to illuminate. Adams felt that "man had translated himself into a new universe which had no common scale of measurement with the old".[12]

Others also used modern technology to help define the rupture of present from past as tragedy. In his paradigmatic meditation on the modernity of the late nineteenth century, *A Connecticut Yankee in King Arthur's Court*, Mark Twain's lead character, Hank Morgan, explained that the tale's fictional seventh-century Britons "believed in enchantments":

> … nobody had any doubts; to doubt that a castle could be turned into a sty, and its occupants into hogs, would have been the same as my doubting, among Connecticut people, the actuality of the telephone and its wonders – and in both cases would be absolute proof of a diseased mind, an unsettled reason. Yes, Sandy was sane; that must be admitted. If I also would be sane – to Sandy – I must keep my superstitions about unenchanted and unmiraculous locomotives, balloons, and telephones to myself.[13]

In a manner very similar to Adams, Twain's text produced a sense of the historical incommensurability of the present to the past, and, also like Adams, he did so through the use of technology as an explanatory device. Twain's Arthurian England was utterly different from the United States of the late nineteenth century – something shown by a naïve medieval British belief in things patently absurd to a modern Connecticut person like Hank. Yet in the same ironic breath, Hank suggests that his fellow moderns' faith in late nineteenth-century technology was every bit as naïve as that of the Arthurians.

In Henry Adams' terms, the force which animated medieval society was religious faith, but Adams felt that the late nineteenth century was defined by an equally naïve credulity – faith in technology. Writing about himself in the third person, Adams confessed that he could find "no more relation … between the steam and the electric current than between the Cross and the cathedral. The forces were interchangeable if not reversible, but he could see only an

---

[12] *Ibid.*, 381.

[13] Mark Twain, *A Connecticut Yankee in King Arthur's Court* (1889), ed. Allison Ensor, New York: Norton Critical Edition, 1982, 105.

absolute *fiat* in electricity as in faith."[14] For both Adams and Twain, the present was utterly different from the past. But, at the same time, it was also absolutely identical to it. In either case, a coherent account of historical transformation was not possible, and they both showed this through the use of technological metaphor.

We can see the tragic aspect of this position very clearly in one of Dan Beard's illustrations for *A Connecticut Yankee in King Arthur's Court*. Beard drew a total of 221 illustrations for Twain's story, but Figure 13.1 offers the book's strongest image of late nineteenth-century modernity as cultural crisis:

'DELIRIUM, OF COURSE, BUT SO REAL!'

**Figure 13.1 Dan Beard, "Delirium, of Course, But SO Real",
from *A Connecticut Yankee in King Arthur's Court* (1888)**

The drawing illustrates events in the story's plot, but its depiction of the present as an irreversible breaking away from the past – of Hank and Sandy divided by a chasm that is guarded by scythe-wielding Father Time – is unmistakable. The image is unambiguously gendered, producing the present (which is slightly elevated) as male and the past as antiquated and female. Perhaps most disturbingly, the image of a baby on Sandy's lap suggests that the notion of a fertile, procreative marriage of past and present could be a product only of

---

[14] Adams, *Education of Henry Adams*, 381.

"delirium". Named "Hello Central" after a telephone operator's greeting, the baby is the love child of modern Hank and medieval Sandy. Her parentage and even her naming suggest that an unborn generation might bring a more humanized technology – if only modernity's rough edges might be rubbed smooth by the soft drag of the past. But in Beard's image, Time's heavy scythe has severed past from present, rejecting the comforting reassurance of organic historical descent. The simultaneous negation of the restorative aspect of both human and historical reproduction is perhaps the most powerfully unsettling element in this image. It depicts modernity as a tragedy of the highest magnitude.

These images were powerful, but probably the most popular iteration of modernity did not define its crisis as a tragedy, but rather as a triumph. In the same year that Twain published *Connecticut Yankee*, steel baron Andrew Carnegie published his famous article "Wealth" in the *North American Review*, and it is difficult to find a stronger statement of modernity as triumph. Carnegie was adamant about the present as a break from the past, and he measured the depth of that rupture by the yardstick of wealth. He explained that "the conditions of human life have not only been changed, but revolutionized within the past few hundred years .... The contrast between the palace of the millionaire and the cottage of the laborer with us to-day measures the change which has come with civilization." His valuation of the break was very different from the tragic visions of Twain and Adams. He wrote that "this change, however, is not to be deplored, but welcomed as highly beneficial". Driving his point home, he emphasized that "the 'good old times' were not good old times".[15]

But if Carnegie's appraisal of the break differed from what we have seen, then we also need to note the similar role of technology in his writing. He explained that:

> ... it is easy to see how the change has come. One illustration will serve for almost every phase of the cause. In the manufacture of products we have the whole story. It applies to all combinations of

---

[15] Andrew Carnegie, "Wealth", *North American Review*, CXLVIII/391 (June 1889), 653.

human industry, as stimulated and enlarged by the inventions of this scientific age.[16]

Carnegie's celebration of modernity as triumph is what we would expect from an immensely wealthy industrialist whose rags to riches story was the very paradigm of its genre. More important for this essay is his emphasis on technology, his claim that "the inventions of this scientific age" had created the wealth that marked the distance traveled between past and present. This helps to explain Carnegie's famous 1886 statement that "the old nations of the earth creep on at a snail's pace; the Republic thunders past with the rush of the express".[17]

We can further see this celebratory version of modernity in Figure 13.2, which offers a stark contrast with to Dan Beard's tragic illustration for *A Connecticut Yankee in King Arthur's Court*:

Figure 13.2 Frederick MacMonnies, *The Columbian Fountain* (1893)[18]

---

[16] *Ibid.*, 654.

[17] Andrew Carnegie, *Triumphant Democracy: or, 50 Years' March of the Republic*, London: Sampson Low, 1886, 1.

[18] Photograph reproduced from *The Dream City: A Portfolio of Photographic Views of the World's Columbian Exposition*, intro. Halsey C. Ives, St Louis, MO: Thompson Co., 1893-1894: available at the *World's Columbian Exposition of 1893* web site, Paul

Frederick MacMonnies' "Columbian Fountain" was among the centerpieces of Chicago's 1893 World's Columbian Exposition. From its central "court of honor" to its peripheral "midway plaissance", the exposition was an unrelenting hymn to the triumph of modernity. The MacMonnies fountain crystallized much of that message into one powerful image. It focused on transportation, as did much of the fair, showing Columbia perched high atop the ship of the republic, which is directed onward by "Fame" at the prow and driven by the combined energies of industry and the arts, represented by the female oarsmen on each side of the ship.

Figure 13.3 Detail from MacMonnies, *The Columbian Fountain* (1893)

Most importantly, we once again see an image of Father Time, but as Figure 13.3 makes clear, he now appears as a strong and reliable

V. Galvin Library Digital History Collection, Illinois Institute of Technology (http://columbus.gl.iit.edu/).

helmsman, using his scythe to steer the ship of state toward a secure future. The cherubs that surround the ship and lie in its wake – progeny, perhaps, of Time and Columbia – confirm the fertile productivity of America's dawning future. MacMonnies' use of neo-classical formal conventions to celebrate all things modern harmonized with the statue's substantive content, suggesting all-the-more powerfully that past and present could indeed be brought together in the service of a fruitful, dynamic and ever more industrious future.

If tragedy and triumph were two very different iterations of modernity as cultural crisis, then we must also acknowledge a third and final form. This middle position took on elements of both the triumphal and tragic, but cannot be fully accounted for by either of these. This third mode imagined modernity as opportunity and it was a form that appealed particularly to individuals and groups who had long been excluded from positions of social dominance, or even equality. For them, the social, economic and political transformation that defines the history of the late nineteenth century was certainly not tragic, but neither could it be seen as unadulterated triumph. At the conclusion of the Civil War, for instance, nearly four million African Americans had emancipated themselves from the bonds of slavery. This was certainly a radical rupture in a two-hundred-year North American history, but the freed people did not emerge into a world that welcomed them as equals. Especially after the end of federally imposed Reconstruction in 1877, racist hostility increased across the South as both the judgment of the courts and much of the white population turned ever further against them. Black writers were challenged to describe their world in ways that acknowledged the triumph of emancipation, but did not ignore the all-too-obvious reaction against their newly found freedom.

A frequent solution was to describe modernity as a period of only partial triumph, as a period of opportunity. In 1901, for instance, Booker T. Washington explained that he "used to cherish a feeling of ill will toward anyone who spoke in bitter terms against the Negro, or who advocated measures that tended to oppress the black man or take from him opportunities for growth". Like the writers we have already encountered, Washington used technological metaphor to help him explain that his animosity for those who resisted black emancipation had turned to pity. He declared that "one might as well try to stop the

progress of a mighty railroad train by throwing his body across the
track, as to try to stop the growth of the world in the direction of
giving mankind more intelligence, more culture, more skill, more
liberty, and in the direction of extending more sympathy and more
brotherly kindness".[19]

The sympathy and kindness that Washington hoped for was to be
extended towards African Americans, and this passage was meant to
explain its author's lack of enmity towards racists. Washington
accepted the fact that his society contained bigots who wished to turn
back the gains his people had made but he believed that it was a way
of thinking whose day had passed. For him, racism was a futile
attempt to turn back the clock and it would soon wither away,
especially when the white community realized the industrial
contributions made by his Tuskegee graduates. Of course, for the
conservative Washington, such arguments were sometimes used
against political activism and many disagreed with his belief in the
inevitability of a more egalitarian future, but for this essay what
matters is the way that the passage blends the sense of modernity as
triumph with a more temperate, tragic consciousness of modernity's
shortfalls, an awareness of the work yet to be done. It is also important
to note that Washington, like the others we have read, used modern
technology – the image of the railroad – to illustrate what he described
as a period of opportunity for African Americans.[20]

This third iteration of the cultural crisis of modernity, that is,
modernity as opportunity, is where Frances E. Willard's writing
registers most strongly. Middle-class women had also lived through
the vast changes of the late nineteenth century and many of those
women were involved in the temperance movement. At least a few
might have agreed when Willard explained what she thought these
changes meant for them. As we saw in the passage near the beginning
of this essay, she believed that "the barriers that have hedged women
into one pathway and men into another, altogether different, are
growing thin, as physical strength plays a less determining part in our

---

[19] Booker T. Washington, *Up from Slavery* (1901), ed. William L. Andrews, New
York: Norton Critical Edition, 1996, 93.

[20] This apparently paradoxical image, given the "separate but equal" accommodations
that invested railroad travel, like much of everyday life, in Washington's South,
should be understood within the context of Washington's covert financial support for
legal challenges to Jim Crow segregation laws. See Louis R. Harlan, "Booker T.
Washington in Biographical Perspective" (1970), rpt. in *Up from Slavery*, 204-19.

life drama", but this passage grows in significance when we place it into the context sketched above.

In the first instance, Willard notes the passing of the language of what she called "separate pathways" for men and women. Assessing the empirical validity of her claim is not a task for this essay, but considering its place in the textual production of a female modernity is. Willard quite clearly believed that women were empowered in an emerging world where physical strength played an ever-decreasing role in what she called "our life drama", and as we shall see, Willard, like most of the other writers we have encountered, believed that these new conditions were largely the product of technological change. Most importantly, however, Willard's interpretation of the new world produced by technological change was emphatically gendered. She wrote that "those who have the most enlargement of opportunity to hope for from the change, will, in the nature of the case, move on most rapidly into the new conditions, and this helps to explain, I think, why women seem to be climbing more rapidly than men, to-day".[21]

The politics of technological sentimentality

Willard's was a bold move, and following it adds an important element to our understanding of her writing. Declaring modernity female, and doing so by way of an argument grounded in a familiarity with the effects of modern technology, might seem to be surprising in a writer whose most obvious strategy was an appeal to the sentiment of Christian Motherhood. But according to the historian Ruth Oldenziel, "there is nothing inherently or naturally masculine about technology. The representation of men's native and women's exotic relationship with technology elaborates on a historical, if relatively recent and twentieth-century Western tendency to view technology as an exclusively masculine affair."[22] For Frances E. Willard, technology was certainly not an exclusively masculine affair – it empowered women. But to understand her logic, we need first to engage her sense of a woman's fundamental nature, and then turn to an examination of the ways in which that essence was enhanced by modern technology.

---

[21] Frances E. Willard, *How to Win: A Book for Girls* (1886), rpt. in *The Yellow Wallpaper*, ed. Bale Bauer, Boston, MA: Bedford Books, 1996, 110-19.
[22] Ruth Oldenziel, *Making Technology: Masculine Men, Women and Modern Machines in America, 1870-1945*, Amsterdam: Amsterdam UP, 1999, 10.

In 1888 Willard gave an address to the Chicago Woman's League entitled "The Dawn of Woman's Day". She began her talk with a prayer, and then declared that "mother-love works magic for humanity, but organized mother-love works miracles". This is a typically sentimental opening that appealed to then popular notions of social motherhood. But her concept of organization is more complex than it may at first appear. She goes on to explain that

> ... organization is the one great thought of Nature. It is the difference between chaos and order, it is the incessant occupation of God. But next to God, the greatest organizer is the mother.

On the surface, this looks like a standard appeal to women's domesticity, to household management skills, but it was not. This was a biological argument. Willard told her audience that "she who sends forth from the sanctuary of her own being a little child, has organized a great spiritual world, and set it moving in the orbit of unchanging law. Hence woman, by her organism, is the greatest organizer ever organized by the beneficent creator."[23]

Locating a woman's essence in reproductive biology was certainly not a move that was unique to Frances E. Willard. As Carroll Smith-Rosenberg has shown, the American Medical Association championed a similar argument, starting in the mid-nineteenth century.[24] But for Willard, unlike the physicians of the AMA, the potential to have a child was the source of a woman's strength, not the seat of fragility or dependence. It was, rather, the wellspring of what Willard argued was a woman's most distinctive and powerful attribute: the ability to organize. As she said above, "organized mother-love works miracles".

Willard's argument, however, was not limited by a too-literal biological determinism. She explained to her listeners that "I do not say 'all mothers,' because all women who are technically mothers are not 'mother hearted,' while many a woman is so, from whom the crisscross currents of the world have withheld her holiest crown".[25] Again, her sentimental appeal is clear and very powerful. Willard, quite conventionally, identifies Christian motherhood as the essence

---

[23] Willard, "Dawn of Woman's Day", 399.
[24] Caroll Smith-Rosenberg, "The Abortion Movement and the AMA, 1850-1880", in *Disorderly Conduct: Visions of Gender in Victorian America*, New York: Oxford UP, 1985, 217-44.
[25] Willard, "Dawn of Woman's Day", 400.

of the feminine, but now makes clear that the actual bearing of children was not required. "Mother heartedness" was primarily a spiritual calling, a sympathy – a sentiment – that transcended bodies and, as she stated earlier, connected women's agency to God's omnipotence. But, as we have seen, the most important single quality that she extracted from motherhood was the ability to organize.

The logical coherence that underlies this sentimental appeal is impressive. For many, the argument's irresistible conclusion was to join forces with the Women's Christian Temperance Union, an organization whose very existence served as an expression of Willard's notion of woman's essence. But a further corollary of the argument implied that anything which could support, strengthen and enhance this inborn capacity for organization must by definition encourage and empower women in the fulfillment of their deepest spiritual essence. Herein lay Willard's fondness for modern technology – by making physical strength irrelevant to modern lives, modern technology enhanced a woman's ability to communicate and to travel. Modern technology therefore fostered women's capacity to organize, affirming and empowering what Willard believed was the fundamental nature of woman.

She clarified this connection in an 1886 text called *How to Win: A Book for Girls*, writing that:

> In an age of brute force, the warrior galloping away to his adventures waved his mailed hand to the lady fair who was *enclosed* for safe keeping in *a grim castle* with moat and drawbridge. But to-day, when spirit force grows regnant, a woman can circumnavigate the globe alone, without danger of an uncivil word, much less of violence. We shall *never span a wider chasm* than this change implies. All our *inventions* have led up to it.[26]

Here, Willard followed what I have already established as a common means of marking a text as modern. Like all of the male writers we have so far encountered, her text projected an image of the past out of itself in order to establish a break from that past. Her medieval imagery, in fact, is not unlike that of *Connecticut Yankee*. As in Beard's visual image, Willard imagines the gulf between past and present as a "chasm", but unlike Sandy, the forlorn mother in Beard's

---

[26] Willard, *How to Win*, 110 (emphases added).

illustration, Willard's medieval woman "spans" the chasm, bridging time and space, as if to challenge Beard's gendering of late nineteenth-century modernity as masculine. In Willard's version, the antiquated past is gendered male, a period of "brute force", when a "lady fair" was clearly at a disadvantage because the world was unsafe. The consequence was the "enclosure" of women behind moat and drawbridge. Willard explained, however, that "all of our inventions" have led up to the temporal and spatial leap that the passage describes. It is precisely women's mobility – women's emergence out from the "grim castle" of the past – which proves that they have not been left behind, as in Beard's illustration, but have instead bridged the chasm and entered a world where "a woman can circumnavigate the globe alone".

In such a world, as Willard put it in her Chicago address, a home missionary woman "devoted to the Bohemians" might discover, by working with a foreign missionary woman, that "electricity and steel have shrunk the world till it is hardly bigger than an orange, [and] that the Bohemian beyond the sea needs looking after just as badly as his brother on this side".[27] In other words, modern technology could bring women together, helping them to realize their shared interests, and to recognize their common "mother-heartedness". As such, they might join forces in order to work the "miracles" which she believed would be the outcome of widespread organization.

She further developed this technological strand in *How to Win*, as she emphatically declared that the mission of the ideal woman was "**TO MAKE THE WHOLE WORLD HOMELIKE**". Again, such statements had a long history in nineteenth-century women's politics, but Willard went further than most, explaining that "a true woman carries home with her everywhere" and that "home's not merely four square walls". Once again, and most importantly, she employed technology as a metaphor to identify these new conditions as specific to her own historical present, to mark them as a departure from the past, to mark them as modern. She explained that people had once thought the contrary, that in the past they had believed that the home was indeed a sphere unto itself, and that one might as well throw away its household gods "as to carry away its weaving-loom and spinning-wheel", but the household survived, even as the "sewing-machine

---

[27] Willard, "Dawn of Woman's Day", 402.

took away much of its occupation".[28] Further, she showed the influence of another disciple of the libratory potential of modern technology, Edward Bellamy, when she wrote "indeed the next generation will no doubt turn the cook-stove out of doors, and the housekeeper, standing at the telephone, will order better cooked meals than almost any one has nowadays, sent from scientific caterers by pneumatic tubes, and the debris thereof returned to a general cleaning up establishment".[29] Again, Willard believed that technology had, and would continue, to release women from the conditions that had bound them to the home and set them on a "separate path", frustrating their "natural" and "God-given" ability to organize. She therefore and frequently referred to technological change in order to identify hers as a fundamentally changed and changing era – "a transition period" – and to construct modernity as an age of opportunity for women.

Finally, Willard's seldom read, penultimate book offers one last, and very clear, example of the role of modern technology in the thinking of this most sentimental of writers. In 1895 she published *A Wheel Within a Wheel, or, How I Learned to Ride the Bicycle*. After its introduction in 1886, the safety bicycle, that is a bicycle with two wheels the same size and pneumatic rubber tires, replaced the older and exceedingly masculine high wheelers. It quickly established itself amongst the most fashionable accessories of the late nineteenth century. Willard's decision to learn to ride one at what was then an elderly fifty-three years old was courageous, but it was also typical of a life that had been committed to what her texts helped to establish as an emergent female modernity that was often aided by women's improved mobility. She explained that "gradually, item by item, I learned the location of every screw and spring, spoke and tire, and every beam and bearing that went to make up [my bicycle]". This mechanical knowledge helped her to master the machine, which she

---

[28] This is a formulation that Elizabeth Cady Stanton would repeat in "The Solitude of Self", when she asked: "Is it then consistent to hold the developed woman of this day within the same narrow political limits as the dame with the spinning wheel and knitting needle occupied in the past? No, no! Machinery has taken the labors of woman as well as man on its tireless shoulders; the loom and the spinning wheel are but dreams of the past; the pen, the brush, the easel, the chisel, have taken their places, while the hopes and ambitions of women are essentially changed" (52).

[29] Willard, *How to Win*, 115.

named "Gladys", but more importantly, she "found a whole philosophy of life in the wooing and the winning of my bicycle".[30]

Unsurprisingly, this philosophy led to a perception of "the impetus that this uncompromising but fascinating and illimitably capable machine would give to [the] blessed 'woman question'". Indeed, Willard testified to her "love of acquiring" what she called a "new implement of power and literally putting it underfoot". She brought together many of the themes of this essay, writing that she "vainly thought that I had fought the antics of [my bicycle] as a sentry on duty away out on the extreme frontier of time".[31] To be fair, she referred here to her age, rather than to abstract notions of temporality and historical change. But I do not think that we would be doing violence to read this passage in the spirit of the technological vision that I have been discussing.

Frances Willard most definitely understood her era as a period of radical change. She imagined the present as a profound breaking away from the past, and that puts her writing squarely within the model of cultural crisis of late nineteenth- and early twentieth-century thought. But what draws my attention, and suggests important modifications to that older model is the way that this crisis resonates differently in her work than it does in writers who were often white, somehow privileged, and usually male. What I hope this essay has shown is that, depending on whose words we read, we receive an entirely different picture of the cultural landscape of turn-of-the-century America. Put another way, with each modernism that we engage, we encounter a different modernity. While many celebrated the crisis as triumph or mourned it as tragedy, Willard and others like her imagined it not as triumph, nor as tragedy, but rather as a moment of profound opportunity – as the opening of new horizons and the crossing of borders both spatial and temporal. Though the texts that we have engaged in this essay were very different in tone, audience and import, they all combined to help form a much broader discourse – the discourse of "modernity". Failing to recognize Frances E. Willard's politics of technological sentimentality as an important part of that discourse is to leave out one of its most popular, persuasive and

---

[30] Frances E. Willard, *A Wheel Within a Wheel: How I Learned to Ride the Bicycle with Some Reflections by the Way*, New York: Fleming H. Revell Company, 1895, 30-31.
[31] *Ibid.*, 43, 75, 51.

influential elements. It is also a failure to understand the rhetorical power of one of the period's most significant figures.

WOMEN, ANTI-IMPERIALISM, AND AMERICA'S CHRISTIAN MISSION ABROAD: THE IMPACT OF THE PHILIPPINE-AMERICAN WAR

SUSAN K. HARRIS

The USA's annexation of the Philippines in 1899 created a crisis for American women reformers in that the US practice of torturing Filipino insurgents and the pattern of openly racist policies in the treatment of civilians blatantly contradicted the rhetoric of Christian benevolence employed to rationalize colonial rule. For many activist women, these acts, and the spirit that motivated them, undermined the ideological basis of American women's own campaign for political and social equality. For half a century women – especially, though not exclusively, white Protestant women – had been arguing for entry to the workplace on the basis of their special ability to deliver Christian nurturance and benevolence, and by 1899, they had largely succeeded in certain professions. As Lori Ginzberg and others have shown, late nineteenth-century women's charity organizations sprang from the practice of home visiting among the poor, a system largely parish based and predicated on the assumption that God created inequality in order to encourage the haves to minister to the have-nots.[1] Late nineteenth-century administrators re-staged this scene, shifting controls from parish to municipality.

Nevertheless even the modern formulation rested in religious assumptions: Annie Fields, one of the originators of Boston's Organized Charities, notes in her manual *How to Help the Poor* that the mandate for charity derives from Christian principles, referring to Christ as "the Example from whom we receive our doctrine".[2] The successful professional woman at the turn into the twentieth century could think of herself both as an exemplary Christian and as an

---

[1] Lori Ginzberg, *Women and the Work of Benevolence: Morality, Politics, and Class in the Nineteenth-century United States*, New Haven: Yale UP, 1990, Ch. 2.
[2] Annie Fields, *How to Help the Poor*, Boston: Houghton Mifflin, 1884, 5.

exemplary citizen – giving evidence, not incidentally, that women deserved to win their long battle for the vote because they, even more than their male contemporaries, represented the fusion of religious and democratic ideals that many Americans figured as the generic national identity. But US conduct during the Philippine-American War not only exposed the principle of Christian benevolence as a front for capitalist aggression and racist exploitation, but also demonstrated that the much-vaunted US ideals of equality and citizenship were only false advertising. For the Protestant woman, whose professional identity was predicated on a fusion of Christian and US identities, this gave ample reason to feel ideologically vitiated. For what ends, then, was she devoting her energies to uplifting the poor, Americanizing the immigrant, or proposing strategies for legal reform? Could these be reconstrued as ends in themselves? In this essay I will consider how, contrary to prevailing scholarly opinion, American women not only voiced opposition to the Philippine-American War, but also how their protests indicated how deeply – and negatively – they were affected by the evidences of hypocrisy that the contrast between official rhetoric and news reports exposed. I will also suggest that this crisis precipitated a new level of civic engagement for women reformers, in which their demands for equality and civic participation were couched in Constitutional rather than religious terms.

Despite a flurry of memorial events in 1998 and 1999, the Spanish-American War, particularly that branch of it best known as the Philippine-American War, has a tenuous place in popular memory. The intervening century, which encompasses the cataclysmic experiences of two World Wars and dozens of smaller but bitter international conflicts, seems to have pushed the wars at the turn into the twentieth century into the corners of public consciousness. Yet in retrospect the events of 1898 and 1899 were seminal for subsequent US foreign engagements. Between April of 1898 and February of 1899 Spain lost the last of its overseas empire and the United States gained the first of its territories in locations far from its own borders. The repercussions of the United States' entry into the imperialist order could be felt not only in Spain, which still refers to the events as "el disastre", but also among the Concert of World Powers, the nations – Britain, Belgium, Germany, France, Austria, and Japan – which woke up to find a powerful new contender in the colonial game. Not insignificantly, US conduct during this war also resonated among Spain's former colonies – Cuba, Puerto Rico, Guam, and the Philippines – which first welcomed American interventions into their efforts to free themselves from Spanish domination and then found themselves having swapped one imperialist regime for another.

None of this went unobserved within the United States itself; in fact, the war stimulated great controversy. It also gave rise to an anti-imperialist movement that numbered among its members some of the best-known men of the time, from millionaire Andrew Carnegie to labor unionist Samuel Gompers, and from educator Felix Adler to humorist Mark Twain. Although they eventually lost out to the expansionist agenda, the anti-imperialists presented loud, clear, and – for many – convincing arguments about the dangers that annexation of Guam, Puerto Rico, and the Philippines posed for a nation that figured itself not only as Anglo-Saxon and republican, but also as a moral model for emerging nations. Controversies over this war were complex: both expansionists and anti-imperialists shared many of the same racial attitudes, and both used the narrative of America's moral mission to bolster their positions. Arguments for both sides illustrate the nexus of current opinion on class, race, and economic trajectories on the eve of the twentieth century.

The historiography of the war has, almost from the beginning, also constructed it as an intensely masculine endeavor. In part as a response to the image of Teddy Roosevelt and his Rough Riders, and in part because the Spanish-American War was seen as a way to finally reunite soldiers who had fought each other during the American Civil War, the wars of 1898 and 1899 have been portrayed not only as conducted by men but also commented on by an overwhelmingly male cast of characters. Women, Amy Kaplan has argued, stood in the background, implicitly supporting the war because the spirituality used to justify the materiality of their domestic realm was the same as the arguments used to justify the war: "the rhetoric of Manifest Destiny and that of domesticity share a vocabulary that turns imperial conquest into spiritual regeneration in order to efface internal conflict or external resistance in visions of geopolitical domination as global harmony."[3] Not only were women who supported the expansionists left in the background: until recently,

---

[3] Amy Kaplan, *The Anarchy of Empire in the Making of U.S. Culture*, Cambridge, MA: Harvard UP, 2002, 31.

it also appeared that few women played active roles in the anti-imperialist movement, a sharp difference from their presence during the Civil War. As a reflection of this prevailing assumption, few studies of the war, or collections of anti-imperialist writings, record a female presence. The major, and excellent, anthology of anti-imperialist writings edited by Philip Foner in the 1960s contains contributions from only half-a-dozen women – each represented by only one piece of writing. John Carlos Rowe's *Literary Culture and U.S. Imperialism from the Revolution to World War Two* mentions none in the period with which I am concerned. Responding to this apparent lacuna, Joan Waugh, who wrote a life of Josephine Shaw Lowell, one of the few female protestors whose name is well-recognized, suggests that the "emphasis on defining American manhood through patriotic symbols may explain the lack of women in leadership positions" – an anomaly, as she points out, during the Progressive period.[4]

The absence of women in anti-imperialism protest, however, seems more a matter of historiography than of history.[5] Ample evidence exists that women actively voiced their opposition to the war and, most importantly, to its aftermath. While expansionists used the rhetoric of American exceptionalism to justify intervention in Spanish colonial disputes, female anti-imperialists argued that the war had betrayed American religious and political ideals. They were particularly concerned that the United States had used religious arguments to support its invasion of foreign nations, and they were disturbed by reports of missionary complicity in torture. Although few of the explicitly anti-imperialist writings produced by women are fiction (like their male counterparts, female anti-imperialists primarily registered their protests through poetry, essays, speeches, and letters to

---

[4] Philip Foner and Richard C. Winchester, *The Anti-imperialist Reader: A Documentary History of Anti-imperialism in the United States*, 2 vols, New York: Holmes and Meier, 1986; John Carlos Rowe, *Literary Culture and U.S. Imperialism: From the Revolution to World War II*, New York: Oxford UP, 2000; Joan Waugh, *Unsentimental Reformer: The Life of Josephine Shaw Lowell*, Cambridge, MA: Harvard UP, 1997, 238.

[5] One of the best recent collections of women's anti-imperialist writings appeared on the website *Anti-imperialism in the United States* edited by Jim Zwick (http://www.boondocksnet.com). To my consternation, and certainly to that of other scholars, Google and Microsoft have forced Zwick to remove all textual matter from the site, consequently denying public access to arguably the best extant collection of American anti-imperialist writings at the turn into the twentieth century.

periodicals), other works of contemporary fiction by women – works not explicitly about the war or imperialism generally – did register doubts about America's Christian mission abroad. And it is this particular element of the anti-imperialist argument this essay focuses on.

Much of the protest against the war highlighted the complicity of American missionaries in the conquest and torture of Philippine nationals and, in a related move, missionary complicity in the mass killings of Chinese peasants during the Euro/Sino/American campaign to quell the Boxer Rebellion. Protestant Christianity, the bedrock both of American identity and numerous reform movements throughout the nineteenth century, and one of the justifications for American intervention into Catholic Spain's overseas empire, appeared in a very poor light when its representatives had the opportunity to wage their own war of overseas conquest. This was particularly troubling to American women, especially those who had justified their entry into the public realm by arguing that they were extending Christian domestic morality out of the house into the world. Many of the female anti-imperialists were also social activists, and their writings suggest that the debates over the war (which mixed racism, economic imperialism, political idealism, and Christian evangelicalism into one happy brew) may have precipitated a particularly acute identity crisis. Paradoxically, however, the crisis resulted in a new step into the public sphere. When American women expressed their anti-war sentiments in print, they demonstrated, to themselves as well as to their readers, that their voices would be an enduring element in the discursive arena.

Who were the women who protested, and what did they do when they were not engaged in the imperialism debate? Two women who are routinely mentioned in lists of anti-imperialists are Josephine Shaw Lowell and Jane Addams, both of whom were best known for their social work and philanthropy but whose public trajectory also prompted them to speak out on political issues. Lowell's life and work, especially, provides a nexus for examining the crisis posed by the US invasion of the Philippines. Josephine Shaw Lowell was born in 1843 and died in 1905. A native New Englander, Lowell was sister to Robert Gould Shaw (colonel of the fated Massachusetts 54th, a black regiment that was killed, to a man, at the assault on Fort Wagner during the Civil War). She was also the wife, albeit briefly, to Charles Russell Lowell of the New England Lowell clan. Charles too, died in the war, five weeks before the birth of their only child.

Coming to adulthood during the Civil War, and inheriting a legacy of social activism from her New England forebears, Josephine Shaw Lowell became a towering figure in the Charity Organization Society of New York City. Like most members of late nineteenth- and early twentieth-century charity organizations, Lowell's philosophy is vulnerable to a stringent critique for – among other things – its mangling of evolutionary ideas as it developed policies based on concepts of moral depravity and degeneration. However, as her biographer, Joan Waugh, the larger point is that Lowell was an extremely important figure in the development of nineteenth-century welfare.

She was also a pivotal figure in the Anti-Imperialist League. Ample evidence of Lowell's role can be found in the papers of Edward Ordway, Secretary of the league's New York branch. Held by the New York Public Library Research Division, Ordway's papers contain letters between Ordway and the men he recruited to publicize the League, such as Andrew Carnegie, Charles Eliot Norton, and Mark Twain. But Lowell's voice also sounds clearly throughout this correspondence, either in letters that she signed with her own name or in letters to Ordway telling him what he should say to the men he was attempting to enlist. Although she rarely made public speeches in her anti-imperialist guise – in part because of illness, and in part because she felt that the presence of a woman would hurt the cause – during the last five years of her life, Lowell not only agreed to let her name be used as a Vice President of the League, she also worked indefatigably to effect changes in Americans' understanding of how the move into imperialism betrayed the ideals for which she felt she had labored throughout her life. "No other nation has ever laid down the principle that all men are equal, or that governments derive their just powers from the governed or that taxation without representation is tyranny", she said in one of her rare public speeches: "To ignore these principles and deny them by their acts would not therefore scar the conscience of Englishmen, Frenchmen, or Germans, but it is impossible for us to do such things and preserve the moral qualities of which in past years we have been most proud."

As Waugh notes, Lowells' directives to Ordway are based upon her thirty-years experience working with men in the business and professional worlds. "Ask President [of Harvard] Eliot about enclosing Professor [William] James's letter", she instructed Ordway, "but don't send it to the Judges! They must have a very short letter and only the blank or they will throw the stuff away!"[6] When it became clear that the Republican Party emphatically embraced imperialism and that the League's radical stance would not make headway, Lowell and Ordway regrouped and formed the Filipino Progress Association in the hopes – again unrealized – that they could at least influence US conduct towards the people of the Philippines. Despite her own terminal illness, and the League's apparent failure, Lowell continued to support it, hoping that: "in the course of time both the two old inconsistent parties will disappear, and we shall have a real genuine struggle between democratic Democrats and plutocrats, the former defending human rights for all races, and the latter advocating the control of 'inferior' men, white, yellow, brown or black by the superior classes." "Until then", she continues:

> we need our little Leagues to keep the Filipinos in mind. I believe that, whatever protestation they have had so far against exploiters, and whatever decency the U.S. has shown in China and elsewhere has been due to the Anti-Imperialists, and that we cannot disband without immediate loss to the cause of justice and freedom.[7]

The point, as she had articulated it in her address to the anti-imperialism rally, was that the US had learned to use the rhetoric of rights in order to effect its own goals, but that the subjugated peoples had equally learned to resist them:

> The United States having obtained a foothold in a foreign country by professing friendship for the inhabitants, calls those inhabitants rebels because the people resist the invasion and try to defend their country. We direct our army to crush out all resistance. The Filipino people prefer death to subjugation, saying, as did Patrick Henry, the American patriot, 'Give me liberty or give me death'.[8]

---

[6] Waugh, *Unsentimental Reformer*, 236.
[7] Josephine Shaw Lowell, Letter, 22 September 1903, New York Public Library Manuscripts Collection. Ordway Collection, Box 1, Folder 1903.
[8] Waugh, *Unsentimental Reformer*, 236.

One consequence was a deep-felt sense of national shame: "We are forgiving the Filipinos, if they will give up all idea of independence", she wrote to Ordway on 5 July 1902, the day after Theodore Roosevelt (prematurely) proclaimed an official end to hostilities (though in fact hostilities continued for more than a decade), "[whereas] it is we who need forgiveness for invading their country".[9] Unlike many Americans, including many professed anti-imperialists, Lowell saw clearly the intersection of democratic ideals, racial ideologies, and nationalist prerogatives in the expansionist rhetoric used to justify annexation of the country and extermination of Filipinos who protested it.

The second well-known name here is Jane Addams, who was born in 1860 and died in 1935. Co-founder of Hull House, a prominent World War I anti-war activist, and winner of the 1931 Nobel Peace prize, Addams achieved legendary status for her career as a social worker in Chicago, but she was also a perceptive analyst of American life and an indefatigable reformer. Like Lowell, Addams broke with her former friend, Theodore Roosevelt over the Philippines and, also like Lowell, she supported William Jennings Bryan in the 1900 election. Again like Lowell, Addams had an official title in the movement – she served as a vice president of the National League from 1904-1919. In "Democracy or Militarism", written in 1899 in part to give voice to workingmen's viewpoints on the war, Addams notes that morality evolves with society, and declares that "patriotism" of the old order no longer can serve. Instead, she argues, it has become the case that "Unless the present situation extends our nationalism into internationalism, unless it has thrust forward our patriotism into humanitarianism we cannot meet it". Echoing prevailing disillusionment with American ideals, she quotes a speech made by Samuel Gompers, President of the American Federation of Labor, in which he claimed that "with the success of imperialism the decadence of our republic will have already set in", and she dismisses Rudyard Kipling's much-celebrated poem "The White Man's Burden" – which urged the US to bring the blessings of Western civilization to the Philippines by annexing them – with the comment that "With all [Kipling's] insight he has, over and over, failed to distinguish between

---

[9] Josephine Shaw Lowell, Letter, 5 July 1902, New York Public Library Manuscripts Collection. Ordway Collection, Box 1, Folder 1902.

war and imperialism on the one hand and the advance of civilization on the other". Having dismissed Kipling's arguments that Anglo-Saxons have a duty to uplift inferior peoples through a prolonged, hierarchical, colonial administration, she avers that Americans are imbued with a democratic idealism by "instinct". The question, she claimed, was what we would do in an international situation: "Do we mean to democratize the situation? ... Or are we going to weakly imitate the policy of other governments, which have never claimed a democratic basis?"[10]

Addams saw the common root of the problems of imperialism outside US borders and US government policies towards non-Anglo-Saxons within its own geopolitical domains as a failure of political and social vision. For her, the failure led to narrow conceptions of national identity and mission. "American conceptions of patriotism have moved, so to speak, from the New England village into huge cosmopolitan cities", she wrote in *Newer Ideals of Peace*, first published in 1907. Yet, she goes on to note, Americans "find themselves bewildered by the change and have ... failed to make the adjustment .... Unless our conception of patriotism is progressive, it cannot hope to embody the real affection and the real interest of the nation." And, she continues, moving from issues germane to American cities to issues concerning war, "We continue to found our patriotism upon war and to contrast conquest with nurture, militarism with industrialism, calling the latter passive and inert and the former active and aggressive, without really facing the situation as it exists". Like her friend William James, she also sought a "moral equivalent of war": "we come at last to the practical question as to how these substitutes for the war virtues may be found. How may we, the children of an industrial and commercial age, find the courage and sacrifice which belong to our industrialism."[11] And she concludes:

> Had our American ideals of patriotism and morality in international relations kept pace with our experience, had we followed up our wide commercial relations with an adequate ethical code, we can imagine a body of young Americans ... proudly declining commercial advantages founded upon forced military occupation and informing

---

[10] Jane Addams, "Democracy or Militarism", *The Chicago Liberty Meeting*, Liberty Tract No.1. Chicago: Central Anti-Imperialist League, 1899, n.p.
[11] Jane Addams, *Newer Ideals of Peace*, New York: Macmillan, 1907, 217.

their … government that … their ideals of patriotism and of genuine
government demanded the play of their moral prowess and their
constructive intelligence …. A different conduct is required from a
democracy than from the mere order-keeping, bridge-building, tax-
gathering Roman, or from the conscientious Briton carrying the
blessings of an established government and enlarged commerce to all
quarters of the globe.[12]

Addams thought in global terms; she saw that issues central to US
domestic conflicts were being mapped onto the new international
terrain, and she sought to reason her countrymen out of their errors
before the situation veered out of control.

The third prominent figure here is Mary Livermore. Former
abolitionist and suffragette, born in 1820 and by the time of the
Philippine-American War over eighty years old, Livermore came to
the Annual Meeting of the New England Anti-Imperialist League in
1903 because, she claimed:

I believe we are largely wrong – going astray in the principles of the
Republic through the delusion we have all been living in that America
is the Messiah of the race …. We have thought too highly of our
country. We have been too boastful of it. We have become too much
infected with the pride of it, and have thought we were better, a little
better, than the other nations.

But Livermore also adds that:

As for myself, I cannot do anything. Why, I am as badly off as the
Filipinos! I have for half a century been slowly, with a company of
other women, trying to obtain for women the rights which you want
for the Filipinos – the right to vote, to have a voice in representation,
and to effect something …. I ask that the Declaration of Independence
shall be exercised upon me and upon women generally …. Then, my
brothers, we could help you men.[13]

More than any of her younger colleagues, Livermore articulates the
dilemma of women trapped between their perception of political crisis

---

[12] *Ibid.*, 222.

[13] Mary A. Livermore, "Remarks at the Annual Meeting of the New England Anti-
Imperialist League", *Report of the Fifth Annual Meeting of the New England Anti-
Imperialist League*, Boston: New England Anti-Imperialist League, 1903.

– the failure of American ideals – and their own political impotence. Moreover her speech signals the imperative that women make the next move into full participation in the public sphere, freed from the shackles of a Christian domestic ideology that, while it had facilitated women's egress from the home in the mid-nineteenth century, by the 1890s had become a constraint rather than a facilitator.

Within the work of such prominent women as these, many with sterling histories as movers and shakers of the reform movement, who joined the anti-imperialist movement because they saw how badly the United States had failed its own ideals, a serious questioning of America's Christian mission abroad percolated through the sense of general disillusionment. Because so much of this questioning focused on missionary agencies, and because the missionary movement, like social reform, had been a major route for women seeking extra-domestic careers, questioning the movement in general in this way carried with it an implicit critique of women's roles. This questioning is evident in much of the protest literature of the period, both letters written to the editors of contemporary periodicals and poetry published in the same publications. These outlets constituted an important element of public sphere activity in a society where new communications technologies were quickly replacing the face-to-face conversations that geographical expansion had made impossible. Mass media, particularly newspapers and magazines, were instrumental here.

For instance, in 1899, in a letter to the editor of *City and State*, Caroline Pemberton engaged the religious issue by noting that the US was arming Philippine Muslims, whom she regarded as "heathen", against the Tagals, native Philippine Catholics who had fought the Spanish occupation and were now prepared to fight the Americans. Seeing the American Board of Foreign Missions – the chief Protestant evangelical organization in the area – as instigating a religious war, she begs "the honorable gentlemen who compose the American Board of Foreign Missions to permit me to remind [them] that the type of nineteenth century Christianity which civilizes from the mouths of cannon and Christianizes with the sword and torch need not shrink from employing the naked followers of Mohammed to carry the gospel of hate further into the hearts of our far-away 'subjects'". Accusing the American Board of adopting tactics of conversion-by-the-sword that the West has traditionally figured as Islamic, she claims that our own "battle-cry" had become "there is no God but our God, and McKinley is his prophet", and – in orthodox jeremiad style – she warns that "The path laid out for you to walk in has been trod before; it is the highway of nations that walked that way to their death and are now lying in the dust of their own ashes".[14]

In accusing the American Board of fomenting religious war, Pemberton opened the door for a full-fledged assault on America's Christian mission. Such an attack carried considerable significance for American women: not only had the missionary movement itself long been a staple of American Christian identity, large numbers of Protestant women supported it, either as participants or as donors. The Board's activities in the Philippines and in China, however, inspired increasing disillusionment with its aims and tactics. "White wing, white wing, / Lily of the air", sang the poet Katharine Lee Bates, author of "America the Beautiful":

> What word dost bring,
> On whose errand fare?
> Red word, red word,
> Snowy plumes abhor.
> I, Christ's own bird,
> Do the work of war.[15]

And again, in another poem, Bates posits England speaking to the United States, asking its former colony:

> What talk is thine of rebels? Didst thou turn,
> My very child, thy vaunted sword on me,
> To scoff to-day at patriot fires that burn
> In hearts unbound to thee,
> Flames of the Sunset Sea?[16]

Like their male counterparts, women protesters reveled in parodies of Kipling's poem "The White Man's Burden: To the U.S. on the

---

[14] Caroline Pemberton, "Arming Heathens Against Christians", *City and State*, VI, 25 June 1899, n.p.
[15] Katharine Lee Bates, "Pigeon Post", ll. 3-8, in *America the Beautiful and Other Poems*, New York: Thomas Y. Crowell, 1911, 28.
[16] "England to America", ll. 6-10 (*ibid.*, 27).

Annexation of the Philippines". Published on 4 February 1899, two days before the US Senate was scheduled to vote on annexation, "The White Man's Burden" was an explicit intervention into the US political process by a committed imperialist for whom British India epitomized the best of imperialist policies. The poem, universally quoted, was also universally satirized, among women as well as men. "Cling to the white man's burden", sang Virginia Butterfield that August, anticipating Ezra Pound as much as she satirized Kipling:

> The weight of dead men's rule,
> The corpse of Ancient Error,
> In garb of modern school.

And later prophesying that:

> Yours be the blame, if any;
> Yours be the wages won!
> Who sell the souls of many,
> To fill the purse of one.

And she concludes:

> Who cede, with pen and parchment,
> God's gifts to all the Race!
> Self-stripped of all His bounty,
> And doubting of His grace,
> Bear ye the white man's burden,
> With heavy hearts and loth;
> But loose the Free-man's guerdon –
> Ye cannot bear them both.[17]

Clearly, women as well as men participated in the anti-imperialist movement. For them, too, the US invasion of the Philippines posed a shock to a cultural identity predicated on descent from Protestant radicals who founded a nation dedicated to religious freedom and fair dealing with other nations. "Tortures of dearth and war our Fathers bore", protested poet Frances Bartlett:

---

[17] Virginia M. Butterfield, "Cling to the White Man's Burden", *The Public*, II, 19 August 1899, n.p.

To live, and serve their God, in liberty.
We lift His cross upon a far-off shore,
And 'neath its arms slay those who would be free.[18]

For Americans invested in this historical paradigm, the perception that
missionaries' much vaunted "benevolence" was a thin mask for
cultural imperialism brought the whole missionary endeavor into
doubt. "So, fellers, own up straight an' trew" concluded Aella Greene
in her dialect poem, "Them Fillerpeans",

> Thet ackshuns pruve you're greedy
> An' don't preten' your objec' is
> Befriendin' uv ther needy,
> Nor tell erbauout the isluns whare
> Your prairs an' teers air given
> Fer ederkatin' ignorance
> An' fittin' souls fer heaven![19]

As I suggested earlier, this sampling of women's protest literature
signals three major issues. First, it tells us that women participated
actively in the anti-war movement, especially through mass periodical
publication. Second, it shows us how deeply invested these women
had been in the narrative of Christian benevolence and how strongly
they reacted to the specter of that narrative's use to justify imperialist
aggression and torture. Third, it shows how the shock of that
recognition impelled women protestors into the next level of civic
participation – no longer justifying their activities by reference to a
now-debased Christian ideology, but rather justifying their
interventions on Constitutional grounds.

Having noted this move into the public sphere by way of periodical
publication, I want to expand on women's critique of the missionary
movement through examining a section from a novel, Kate Douglas
Wiggin's *Rebecca of Sunnybrook Farm*, published in 1903, and
through a short story, "Daughters of Zion" from *Rebecca of
Sunnybrook Farm*'s sequel, a volume entitled *New Chronicles of
Rebecca*, published in 1907. Although the *Rebecca* stories would
seem a most unlikely vehicle for missionary critique, in fact they

---

[18] Frances Bartlett, quoted in *Liberty Poems: Inspired by the Crisis of 1898-1900*,
Boston: James H. West, 1900, 99.
[19] Aella Greene, quoted in *Liberty Poems*, 46.

function much as *The Adventures of Huckleberry Finn* functioned in its critique of American racial attitudes: voicing social concerns through the perceptions of children rather than through direct narrative commentary.

Throughout most of the twentieth century, *Rebecca of Sunnybrook Farm* was marketed as a children's book, but in its own time it was regarded as general interest reading, a *Bildungsroman* set in a small town in Maine, and featuring a bright, lively, and very funny protagonist, Rebecca, aged ten or twelve when the novel opens, and a vivid cast of regional characters. The incident that concerns me here deals the visit of a missionary family, the Burches, to the town, with the purpose of reporting on their missionary activities and collecting money to continue them. The missionaries' effect on Rebecca is to fire her richly endowed but environmentally starved imagination with their tales of blue Syrian skies and brown Syrian natives. Wiggin's own position on the Burches' mission evinces some ambivalence, however, especially in her narrator's comment that Mr Burch's pitch to the townspeople "was much the usual sort of thing. Mr. Burch made impassioned appeals for the spreading of the gospel, and added his entreaties that all who were prevented from visiting in person the peoples who sat in darkness should contribute liberally to the support of others who could."[20]

The operative phrase here is "the peoples who sat in darkness" – a buzzword in turn of the nineteenth- into the twentieth-century anti-imperialist discourse that Wiggin's readers would not have missed. Originally a quotation from the Book of Matthew, this phrase, like Kipling's construction of "the white man's burden", had become a satiric leitmotif for those seeking to expose American religious hypocrisy in the Philippines. It had been used most famously two years earlier, by Mark Twain, whose virulently anti-imperialist essay, "To the Person Sitting in Darkness", had been widely reprinted. Wiggin and Samuel Clemens were friends – in a famous photograph, taken at his seventieth birthday party at Delmonico's, she sits to his left – so it is unlikely that her use of this phrase was accidental. In *Rebecca of Sunnybrook Farm* the implied critique – if that is what it is – is lightly given, however, detracting little if at all from the overall positive portrait of the missionary family.

---

[20] Kate Douglas Wiggin, *Rebecca of Sunnybrook Farm*, Boston, MA: Houghton, Mifflin, 1903, 128.

"Daughters of Zion", the story in the sequel collection, is more pointed. The plot involves Rebecca and her cohorts, under the encouragement of Mrs Burch, attempting to form a youth branch of the Maine Missionary Society. Patricia Hill, who has written on women's roles in the foreign mission movement, reads these episodes as evidence of the missionary movement's function as a place for women to realize their managerial potential, an argument supported by this story, in which the narrator informs us that Mrs Burch has encouraged Rebecca in the idea of becoming a missionary, "not, it is to be feared, because Rebecca showed any surplus of virtue or Christian grace, but because her gift of language, her tact and sympathy, and her musical talent seemed to fit her for the work".[21] One element to note here is the way the story suggests the possibility that managerial skills, a strong suit for Progressive Era women as they moved from the home to the workplace, are not only central to the missionizing project but also a possible threat to its purity – a valuation of skills over purpose. But the real emphasis of "Daughters of Zion" lies in its exposure of the missionaries' racial and cultural assumptions.

In the story, Wiggin's suggestion that the missionaries are both racist and imperialist shows through the girls' dialogue. In the following scene, they have just returned, defeated, from attempting to missionize a local curmudgeon, who has run them off his property. Back in their headquarters in the barn, they try to determine where they can apply their missionary energies next:

> "It must be nicer missionarying in those foreign places," said Persis, "because on 'Afric's shores and India's plains and other spots where Satan reigns' (that's father's favorite hymn) there's always a heathen bowing down to wood and stone. You can take away his idols if he'll let you and give him a Bible and the beginning's all made."

When one of the girls comments that foreigners are the easiest to convert, her friends take up the debate:

> "Haven't foreigners got any religion of their own?" inquired Persis curiously.

---

[21] Patricia R. Hill, *The World Their Household: The American Woman's Foreign Mission Movement and Cultural Transformation, 1870-1920*, Ann Arbor: U of Michigan P, 1985, 39.

"Ye-es, I s'pose so; kind of one; but foreigners' religions are never right – ours is the only good one." This was from Candace, the deacon's daughter.

"I do think it must be dreadful, being born with a religion and growing up with it, and then finding out it's no use and all your time wasted!" Here Rebecca sighed and chewed a straw, and looked troubled.

"Well, that's your punishment for being a heathen," retorted Candace.

"But I can't for the life of me see how you can help being a heathen if you're born in Africa," persisted Persis ....

"You can't." Rebecca was clear on this point. "I had that all out with Mrs. Burch when she was visiting .... She says they can't help being heathen but if there's a single mission station in the whole of Africa, they're accountable if they don't go there and get saved."

"Are there plenty of stages and railroads?" asked Alice; "because there must be dreadfully long distances, and what if they couldn't pay the fare?"[22]

After the whole project collapses, Rebecca sums up the enterprise:

Aunt Jane must write to Mrs. Burch that we don't want to be home missionaries. Perhaps we're not big enough, anyway. I'm perfectly certain it's nicer to convert people when they're yellow or brown or any color but white; and I believe it must be easier to save their souls than it is to make them go to meeting.[23]

Nowhere in either *Rebecca of Sunnybrook Farm* or its sequel is there mention of the Philippine-American War or of imperialism. Nevertheless I suggest that the fact that such passages could be published in 1903 and 1907 respectively is a sign that American women writers were not only questioning the missionary project themselves but confident that their readers were on the same wavelength. Kate Douglas Wiggin was a popular writer, one very mindful of her audience, and it is unlikely that she would go out of her way to assault their values.

"Daughters of Zion" presents a decided critique not only of missionaries' assumptions about the relationship of non-Christians to

---

[22] Kate Douglas Wiggin, "Daughters of Zion", in *New Chronicles of Rebecca*, Boston, MA: Houghton, Mifflin, 1907, 42.
[23] *Ibid.*, 57.

Christianity's imperial designs, but also about their implicit – or explicit – racism. Presented through the eyes of children, the missionary agenda is exposed for all its narrow-minded assumptions of cultural superiority. These assumptions, of course, are the same as those on which expansionists justified the war in the Philippines – the assumption, as President William McKinley articulated it, that it was Americans' duty "to educate the Filipinos, and uplift and civilize and Christianize them, and by God's grace do the very best we could by them".[24] In showing through the child's voice just how much Christian missionary practices rest on racist assumptions about people of color, Wiggin opens a space for serious questioning of the American Christian mission in the Philippines.

I think it is also important to note here that Wiggin's career began not in the literary arena, but in the pedagogical. Born in Maine, Kate Douglas moved to Santa Barbara, California, as an adolescent, and she trained in Los Angeles in the then-new pedagogy of the kindergarten movement, a recent import from Germany. Although her teaching career came to an end when she moved back east with her first husband, she continued to advise pre- and primary school teachers and to write on pedagogical subjects. Much of her fiction is created expressly for children.

This matters because it helps place Wiggin in the same frame as Addams, Lowell, and other late nineteenth-century women who began their careers in professions hospitable to women. Like charity and missionary work, early childhood education was an extension of the Christian woman's domestic realm, a justification for her move out of the private and into the public arena. As Catharine Beecher had claimed many years earlier, the justification for the female teacher was that she was admirably equipped to promulgate the Christian message. In moving from the classroom to an advisory position Wiggin joined the other women who created careers teaching others how to manage Christian benevolence. She became a type of the national Christian, administrative style. But "Daughters of Zion" also shows us Wiggin's progressive critique of the values underlying much of the rhetoric of Christian reform.

---

[24] General James Rusling, "Interview with President William McKinley", *The Christian Advocate*, 22 January 1903, 17.

Where this all brings us to is a question about the effect of the Spanish-American war on women whose careers had been predicated on their ability to enact the narrative of Christian benevolence and where their disillusionment took them in terms of civic engagements. I suggest that this crisis provided a turning point in American women's activist agendas: from here on, at least until the late twentieth century, the minority, not the majority, would call on Christian ideology to justify their pursuits. The rest would reformulate their philosophical underpinnings, following Addams' pragmatist leanings or, more frequently, reformulating the rationalist side of nationalist narratives to fit their needs. Once suffrage was granted in 1919, the Christian domesticity that justified activist women's initial forays into the public sphere could be reformulated as a female citizen's duty to expand the democratic privilege to all elements of the population. Moreover, the more women took part in public events, especially political events, the less they had to defend their rights to be there, providing yet more impetus for full civic participation. Beyond explicitly religious organizations (and even among them) female presence as organizers and administrators slowly became an established, secular, fact.

In this way the public controversy over means and ends precipitated by the Philippine-American war constituted a watershed in the professional history of American women. The Christian rhetoric used to justify the USA's entry onto the world stage as an imperialist power was quickly exposed as a sham, leading to widespread accusations of national hypocrisy and corresponding distrust of the motives of Christian evangelists. Evangelical organizations such as the American Board of Missionaries for Foreign Missions were forced to refocus their energies and repair their image. Meanwhile, American women found other ways to ease the transition from domesticity to the workforce, and American reformers in general turned to more secular models to justify their ends. Contrary to popular historiography, American women did participate in the anti-imperialist movement, voicing their discontent through poems, essays, and letters to periodical publications, and evidencing their disillusionment with the paradigm of American Imperial Christianity used to justify the war. One of the results of this general disillusionment was a shift in ideational direction among the organizers of American reform movements. Until the resurgence of faith-based charities encouraged by the Bush administration, Americans' rationale for government-sponsored reform efforts rested on ideals deriving from Constitutional principles rather than religious ones, giving American women a new, and secular, reason for continuing to develop their expertise as administrators, reformers, and political activists.

NOTES ON CONTRIBUTORS

MIA BAY is Associate Professor at Rutgers University and the Associate Director of the Rutgers Center for Race and Ethnicity for Historical Analysis. Her research interests center on African-American intellectual and cultural history. She is the author of two books: *The White Image in the Black Mind: African-American Ideas of White People 1830-1925* (Oxford University Press, 2000), and *To Tell the Truth Freely: The Life of Ida B. Wells* (Hill and Wang, 2009). She is currently completing a study of African-American views of Thomas Jefferson.

ANNE M. BOYLAN is Professor of History and Women's Studies at the University of Delaware and author of *Sunday School: The Formation of an American Institution, 1790-1880* (Yale University Press, 1988), and *The Origins of Women's Activism: New York and Boston, 1797-1840* (University of North Carolina Press, 2002). She is currently working on a documentary collection on the history of women's rights in the United States.

ALISON EASTON is Honorary Research Fellow at Lancaster University, UK, and formerly Senior Lecturer in English and co-director of its Institute for Women's Studies, and currently works on class/gender relations in nineteenth-century American literature. She is on the advisory boards of the Society for the Study of American Women Writers and the Nathaniel Hawthorne Society. Publications include *The Making of the Hawthorne Subject* (University of Missouri Press, 1996), the Penguin edition of Sarah Orne Jewett, *The Country of the Pointed Firs* (1996), and many other essays.

R.J. ELLIS is Professor of American and Canadian Studies, University of Birmingham. Recent publications include *Liar, Liar!: Jack Kerouac, Novelist* (Greenwich Exchange, 1999), *Harriet Wilson's* Our Nig*: A Cultural Biography* (Rodopi, 2003), an edition of Nan Green's memoir, *A Chronicle of Small Beer* (Trent Editions, 2004), and a website analysing illustrations to Stowe's *Uncle Tom's Cabin*. His specialisms center upon Beat writing and American women writers, and African-American writers of the nineteenth century. He is preparing a new edition of *Our Nig*, with Henry Louis Gates Jr.

JANET FLOYD is a Senior Lecturer at King's College London. Her interests are in nineteenth-century women's writing, the domestic and the American West. Her publications include *Writing the Pioneer Woman* (University of Missouri Press, 2002), and the co-edited essay collections, *Domestic Space: Reading the Nineteenth-century Interior* (Manchester University Press, 1999) and *The Recipe Reader: The Recipe in its Cultural Context* (Ashgate, 2003). She is currently at work on a monograph on mining and writing in the Gilded Age.

SHIRLEY FOSTER is a semi-retired Reader in English and American Literature at the University of Sheffield. Her main research interests are nineteenth-century English and American fiction, and travel literature. Her most recent publications include a co-edited anthology of women's travel writing, a literary life of Elizabeth Gaskell, an edition of Gaskell's *Mary Barton*, and articles on Gaskell's short stories and on Harriet Beecher Stowe in Europe. Forthcoming publications include an article on nineteenth-century American visitors to urban Britain.

SUSAN K. HARRIS is a Hall Distinguished Professor of American Literature at the University of Kansas. Her work on women writers includes *Nineteenth-century American Women's Novels: Inter-pretative Strategies* (Cambridge University Press, 1990, 2008) and *The Cultural Work of the Late Nineteenth-century Hostess* (Palgrave Macmillan, 2002). She is also a Mark Twain scholar. Currently, she is investigating the role of religion in US imperial discourse at the turn into the twentieth century.

TIMOTHY A. HICKMAN is a Senior Lecturer in History at Lancaster University. His research interests are in the cultural history of the Gilded Age and Progressive Era and the concept of modernity, particularly its textual enunciation as cultural crisis. He has published on the history of narcotic addiction and modernity in America, including his monograph on the subject, *The Secret Leprosy of*

Modern Days: Narcotic Addiction and Cultural Crisis in the United States, 1870-1920 (University of Massachusetts Press, 2007).

KAREN L. KILCUP is Professor of American Literature and Women's and Gender Studies at the University of North Carolina at Greensboro. She has broad research interests in nineteenth- and early twentieth-century American literatures. Her publications include major anthologies, recovery editions of women's writing and *Robert Frost and Feminine Literary Tradition* (University of Michigan Press, 1998). Her current monograph project is *Fallen Forests: Redeeming Nature in American Women's Writing*.

S.J. KLEINBERG is Professor of American History at Brunel University, London. She is a fellow of the Royal Society for the Arts and an Academy of Social Sciences Academician. Former editor of the *Journal of American Studies,* she is founding editor of a new journal, *History of Women in the Americas*, devoted to comparative and single nation histories of women in the northern and southern American hemisphere. Her major monographs include *Widows and Orphans First: The Family Economy and Social Welfare Policy, 1880-1939* (University of Illinois Press, 2006); *The Shadow of the Mills: Working-class Families in Pittsburgh, 1870-1907* (University of Pittsburgh Press, 1989); *Women in American Society, 1820-1920* (BAAS, 1990), and *Women in the United States, 1830-1945* (Macmillan, 1999). Edited publications include, with Eileen Boris and Vicki L. Ruiz, *The Practice of U.S. Women's History: Narratives, Intersections and Dialogues* (Rutgers University Press, 2007).

PETER RAWLINGS is Professor of English and American Literature and Head of the School of English and Drama at the University of the West of England, Bristol. His publications include *Henry James and the Abuse of the Past* (Palgrave Macmillan, 2005) and *American Theorists of the Novel: James, Trilling and Booth* (Routledge, 2006).

LINDSEY TRAUB, formerly Vice-President and College Lecturer in English, is now Emeritus Fellow of Lucy Cavendish College, University of Cambridge. She has published essays on Emerson, Henry James, George Eliot and various nineteenth-century American women writers, including Margaret Fuller and Louisa May Alcott. Her research interests also include nineteenth- and twentieth-century popular fiction.

MARGARET WALSH is Emeritus Professor of American Economic and Social History, University of Nottingham, Her main areas of research have been American business and transport history, the American West and American women's labor history. She has published, *Making Connections: The Long Distance Bus Industry in the USA* (Ashgate, 2000) and *The American West: Visions and Revisions* (Cambridge University Press, 2005). She guest-edited the gender issue of the *Journal of Transport History* (2002) and co-guest edited the gender and service sector edition of *Business History Review* (2008). She is currently working on a monograph on women and American automobility since 1945.

JANET ZANDY is Professor of English at Rochester Institute of Technology. Her edited books include *Calling Home: Working-class Women's Writings* (Rutgers University Press, 1990), *Liberating Memory: Our Work and Our Working-class Consciousness* (Rutgers University Press, 1995), *What We Hold in Common: An Introduction to Working-class Studies* (The Feminist Press, 2001), *American Working-class Literature*, co-edited with Nicholas Coles (Oxford University Press, 2007). Her book *Hands: Physical Labor, Class, and Cultural Work* (Rutgers University Press, 2004) received honorable mention for the American Studies Association's John Hope Franklin Prize. She was general editor of *Women Studies Quarterly* from 1997-2001. Her current research is on the vernacular of labor photography and photographic representations of workers.

SELECT BIBLIOGRAPHY

Abbate, Carolyn, "Opera; or the Envoicing of Women", in *Musicology and Difference: Gender and Sexuality in Music Scholarship*, ed. Ruth A. Solie, Berkeley: U of California P, 225-58.

Abbott, Edith, W*omen in Industry: A Study in American Economic History* (1910), North Stratford, NH: Ayer Reprint, 1969.

Adams Fields, Annie, *How to Help the Poor*, Boston: Houghton Mifflin, 1883.

Adams, Henry, *The Education of Henry Adams: An Autobiography* (1907), ed. Ernest Samuels, Atlanta, GA: Houghton Mifflin, 1973.

Addams, Jane, "Democracy or Militarism", *The Chicago Liberty Meeting*, Liberty Tract No.1. Chicago: Central Anti-Imperialist League, 1899.

Allcott, Louisa May, *An Old-fashioned Girl* (1870), New York: Puffin Books, 1991.

_____, Louisa May, *Little Women,* (1868), ed. Elaine Showalter, New York: Penguin Books, 1989.

_____, Louisa May, *Louisa May Alcott Unmasked: Collected Thrillers*, ed. Madeline Stern, Athens: U of Georgia P, 1995.

_____, Louisa May, *Moods* (1864), ed. with an introduction by Sarah Elbert, New Brunswick, NJ: Rutgers UP, 1991.

_____, Louisa May, *Work: A Story of Experience* (1873), ed. with an Introduction by Joy S. Kasson, New York: Penguin Books, 1994.

Allgor, Catherine, *Parlor Politics: In Which the Women of Washington Help Build a City and a Government*, Charlottesville: UP of Virginia, 2000.

Amott, Theresa L. and Julie A. Matthaei, *Race, Gender, and Work: A Multicultural Economic History of Women in the United States*, Boston, MA: South End Press, 1991.

Angelou, Maya, *I Know Why the Caged Bird Sings*, New York: Random House, 1969, 231.

Anzaldúa, Gloria, *Borderlands/La Frontera: The New Mestiza*, San Francisco, CA: Aunt Lute Books, 1987.

Apple, Michael W., in his *Ideology and Curriculum*, New York: Routledge, 1990.

Argersinger, Jo Ann, *Making the Amalgamated: Gender, Ethnicity and Class in the Baltimore Clothing Industry, 1899-1939*, Baltimore, MD: Johns Hopkins UP, 1999.

Armitage, Susan and Elizabeth Jameson, *The Women's West*, Norman: U of Oklahoma P, 1987.

Armstrong, Nancy, *Desire and Domestic Fiction: A Political History of the Novel*, Oxford: Oxford UP, 1987.

Arneil, Barbara, *John Locke and America: The Defence of English Colonialism*, Oxford: Clarendon P, 1996.

Arnesen, Eric, "American Workers and the Labor Movement in the Late Nineteenth Century", in *The Gilded Age: Essays on the Origins of Modern America*, ed. Charles W. Calhoun, Wilmington, DEL: Scholarly Resources, 1996, 37-57.

Aron, Cindy S., *Working at Play: A History of Vacations in the United States*, New York: Oxford UP, 1999.

Ashbaugh, Carolyn, *Lucy Parsons: American Revolutionary*, Chicago: Charles H. Kerr, 1976.

Attali, Jacques, *Noise: The Political Economy of Music*, trans. Brian Massumi, Minneapolis: U of Minnesota P, 1985.

Avallone, Charlene "Catharine Sedgwick and the Circles of New York", *Legacy*, XXIII/2 (2006), 115-31.

Bailin, Miriam, *The Sickroom in Victorian Fiction: The Art of Being Ill*, Cambridge: Cambridge UP, 1994.

Barker, Sir Ernest, ed., *Social Contract: Essays by Locke, Hume and Rousseau*, The World's Classics, ed. Sir Ernest Barker, London: Oxford UP, 1947.

Barker-Benfield, G.J., *The Culture of Sensibility: Sex and Society in Eighteenth-century Britain*, Chicago: Chicago UP, 1992.

Baron, Ava and Susan E. Clapp, "'If I didn't have my Sewing Machine…': Women and Sewing Machine Technology", in *A Needle, a Bobbin, a Strike: Women Needleworkers in America*, eds Joan M. Jensen and Sue Davidson, Philadelphia, PA: Temple UP, 1984, 20-59.

Bates, Katharine Lee, "Pigeon Post", ll. 3-8, in *America the Beautiful and Other Poems*, New York: Thomas Y. Crowell, 1911, 28.

Bay, Mia, *The White Image in the Black Mind: African American Ideas about White People, 1830-1925*, New York: Oxford UP, 2000.

Bay, Nina, *American Women Writers and the Work of History 1790-1860*, New Brunswick, NJ: Rutgers UP, 1995.

Baym, Nina, "Between Enlightenment and Victorian: Toward a Narrative of American Women Writers Writing History", *Critical Inquiry* XVII/4 (Summer 1991), 22-41.

_____, Nina, *American Women Writers and the Work of History, 1790-1860*, New Brunswick, NJ: Rutgers UP, 1995.

_____, Nina, *Woman's Fiction, A Guide to Novels by and about Women in America, 1820-70*, 2nd edn, Urbana: U of Illinois P, 1993.

Bean, Judith Mattson, "Gaining a Public Voice: A Historical Perspective on American Women's Public Speaking", in *Speaking Out: The Female Voice in Public Contexts*, ed. Judith Baxter, New York: Palgrave Macmillan, 2006, 21-39.

Bederman, Gail, *Manliness and Civilization: A Cultural History of Gender and Race in the United States, 1880–1917*, Chicago: U of Chicago P, 1995.

Bell, Michael, *Sentimentalism, Ethics, and the Culture of Feeling*, Basingstoke: Palgrave Macmillan, 2000.

Belsey, Catherine, *Critical Practice*, London: Methuen, 1980.

Bender, Daniel, *Sweated Work, Weak Bodies: Anti-Sweatshop Campaigns and Languages of Labor*, New Brunswick, NJ: Rutgers UP, 2004.

Berch Bettina, *The Endless Day: The Political Economy of Women and Work*, New York: Harcourt, Brace Jovanovitch, 1982.

Berger, John *Ways of Seeing,* Harmondsworth: Penguin, 1972.

Berman, Marshall, *All That Is Solid Melts into Air: The Experience of Modernity*, New York: Penguin, 1988.

Besant, Walter, *The Art of Fiction*, Boston: Cupples, Upham and Co., 1884.

Bird, Isabella, *A Lady's Life in the Rocky Mountains* (1879), London: Virago, 1983.

Bisland, Elizabeth, *A Flying Trip Around the World in Seven Stages*, New York: Harpers, 1891.

Blight, David, *Race and Reunion: The Civil War in American Memory*, Cambridge, MA: Harvard UP, 2001.

Bly, Nellie, *Nellie Bly's Book*, New York: The Pictorial Weeklies Co., 1890.

Bordin, Ruth, *Woman and Temperance: The Quest for Power and Liberty, 1873-1900*, Philadelphia, PA: Temple UP, 1981.

Bordo, Susan, *Unbearable Weight: Feminism, Western Culture and the Body*, 2nd edn, Berkeley: U of California P, 2003.

Boris, Eileen, *Home to Work: Motherhood and the Politics of Industrial Homework in the United States*, Cambridge: Cambridge UP, 1994.

Bose, Christine E., *Women in 1900: Gateway to the Political Economy of the 20th Century*, Philadelphia, PA: Temple UP, 2001.

Boydston, Jeanne, *Home and Work: Housework, Wages, and the Ideology of Labor in the Early Republic*, Oxford: Oxford UP, 1990.

Boylan, Anne M., *Sunday School: The Formation of an American Institution 1790-1880*, New Haven, CT: Yale UP, 1988.

_____, Anne M., *The Origins of Women's Activism: New York and Boston, 1797-1840*, Chapel Hill: U of North Carolina P, 2002.

Brandeis, Louis and Josephine Goldmark, *Women in Industry* (1908), New York: Arno Press, 1969.

Brandon, Betty, Virginia Bernhard, Elizabeth Fox-Genovese, Theda Perdue and Elizabeth Turner, *Hidden Histories of Women in the New South*, eds, Columbia: U of Missouri P, 1994.

Brandon, Stephen, "'Mother of U.S. Senator an Indian Queen': Cultural challenge and appropriation in *The Memoirs of Narcissa Owen*", *Studies in American Indian Literatures*, XIII/2-3 (Autumn-Fall 2001), 15-17.

Briggs, Asa, *Victorian Things*, Harmondsworth: Penguin, 1988.

Brodhead, Richard H., *Cultures of Letters: Scenes of Reading and Writing in Nineteenth-century America*, Chicago: U of Chicago P, 1993, 79-89.

Brown, Dona, *Inventing New England: Regional Tourism in the Nineteenth-century*, Washington, DC: Smithsonian Institute Press, 1995.

Brown, Hallie, *Homespun Heroines and Other Women of Distinction*, Xenia, OH: Aldine Publishing, 1926.

Brown, Kathleen, "The History of Women in the United States to 1865", in *Women's History in Global Perspective*, ed. Bonnie G. Smith, Urbana: U of Illinois P, 2005, II, 238-80.

Brown, William Wells, *The Rising Son; or, The Antecedents and Achievements of the Colored Race*, Boston: A.G. Crown, 1876.

Brundage, W. Fitzhugh, "'Woman's Hand and Heart and Deathless Love': White Women and the Commemorative Impulse in the New South", in *Monuments to the Lost Cause: Women, Art, and the Landscapes of Southern Memory*, eds Cynthia Mills and Pamela H. Simpson, Knoxville: U of Tennessee P, 2003.

_____, W. Fitzhugh, *The Southern Past: A Clash of Race and Memory*, Cambridge, MA: Harvard UP, 2005.

Buechler, Steven M., *The Transformation of the Woman Suffrage Movement: The Case of Illinois, 1850-1920*, New Brunswick, NJ: Rutgers UP, 1986.

Buhl, Mari Jo, *Women and American Socialism, 1870-1920*, Urbana: U of Illinois P, 1981.

Bush, Clive, *Halfway to Revolution: Investigation and Crisis in the Work of Henry Adams, William James, and Gertrude Stein*, New Haven, CT: Yale UP, 1991.

Bushman, Richard L., *The Refinement of America: Persons, Houses, Cities*, New York: Alfred A. Knopf, 1992.

Butler, Elizabeth B., *Women and the Trades: Pittsburgh 1907-1908*, New York: New York Charities Commission Committee, 1909.

Butler, Judith, *Gender Trouble: Feminism and the Subversion of Identity*, London: Routledge, 1993.

Butterfield, Virginia M., "Cling to the White Man's Burden", *The Public*, II, 19 August 1899, n.p.

Calinescu, Matei, *Five Faces of Modernity: Modernism, Avant-garde, Decadence, Kitsch, Postmodernism*, Durham, NC: Duke UP, 1987.

Cameron, Deborah, "Theorizing the Female Voice in Public Contexts", *Speaking Out: The Female Voice in Public Contexts*, ed. Judith Baxter, New York: Palgrave Macmillan, 2006, 3-20.

Carby, Hazel, "'On the Threshold of Woman's Era': Lynching, Empire, and Sexuality in Black Feminist Theory", in *"Race", Writing, and Difference*, ed. Henry Louis Gates, Jr., Chicago: U of Chicago P, 1995, 301-16.

_____, Hazel, *Reconstructing Womanhood: The Emergence of the Afro-American Woman Novelist*, New York: Oxford UP, 1987.

Carnegie, Andrew, "Wealth", *North American Review*, CXLVIII/391 (June 1889), 653-665.

_____, Andrew, *Triumphant Democracy: or, 50 Years' March of the Republic*, London: Sampson Low, 1886.

Carpenter, Cari, *Seeing Red: Anger, Femininity, and American Indians*, Columbus: Ohio State UP (forthcoming).

Carter, Paul A., *The Spiritual Crisis of the Gilded Age*, DeKalb: North Illinois UP, 1971.

Cartwright, Joseph, *The Triumph of Jim Crow: Tennessee Race Relations in the 1880s*, Memphis: U of Tennessee P, 1976.

Cather, Willa, "Three American Singers", *McClure's Magazine*, 42 (December 1913), 33-48.

_____, Willa, *The Song of the Lark* (1915), Oxford: Oxford UP, 2000.

Child, Lydia Maria, Introduction to Harriet Jacobs' *Incidents in the Life of a Slave Girl*, Boston: Published for the Author, 1861, 7-8.

Clark, Victor S., *History of Manufactures in the United States* (1916-28), 3 vols, New York: Peter Smith, 1949.

Clément, Catherine, *Opera, or the Undoing of Women*, trans. Betsy Wing, Minneapolis: U of Minnesota P, 1988.

Clement, Elizabeth, *Trick or Treat: Courting Couples, Charity Girls, Prostitutes and the Making of Modern Heterosexuality in New York City, 1900-1945*, Chapel Hill: U of North Carolina P, 2006.

Coburn, Carol K. and Martha Smith, *Spirited Lives: How Nuns Shaped Catholic Culture and American Life, 1836-1920*, Chapel Hill: U of North Carolina P, 1999.

Cohen, Miriam, *Workshop to Office: Two Generations of Italian Women in New York City, 1900-1950*, Ithaca, NY: Cornell UP, 1992.

Cohen, Patricia Cline, *The Murder of Helen Jewett*, New York: Random House, 1998.

Commons, John R., "The Sweating System in the Clothing Trades", in *Trade Unionism and Labor Problems*, ed. Commons, John R., Boston: Ginn and Co., 1905, 316-29.

Conger, Syndy M., *Mary Wollstonecraft and the Language of Sensibility*, London and Toronto: Associated UP, 1994.

Connor, Steven, *Dumbstruck: A Cultural History of Ventriloquism*, Oxford: Oxford UP, 2000.

Coontz, Stephanie, *The Social Origins of Private Life*, London: Verso, 1980.

Cooper, Anna Julia, *A Voice from the South*, Xenia, OH: The Aldine Printing House, 1892.

Cott, Nancy F., *The Bonds of Womanhood: "Women's Sphere" in New England, 1780-1835*, New Haven, CT: Yale UP, 1977.

_____, Nancy F., *The Grounding of American Feminism*, New Haven, CT: Yale UP, 1987.

_____, Nancy F., "'Giving Character to Our Whole Civil Polity': Marriage and the Public Order in the Late Nineteenth Century", in *U.S. History as Women's History: New Feminist Essays*, eds Linda K. Kerber, Alice Kessler-Harris, and Kathryn Kish Sklar, Chapel Hill; London: U of North Carolina P, 1995, 107-21.

Coulson, Victoria, "Prisons, Palaces, and the Architecture of the Imagination", in *Palgrave Advances in Henry James Studies*, ed. Peter Rawlings, Basingstoke and New York: Palgrave Macmillan, 2007, 169-91.

Cowan, Ruth Schwartz, *More Work for Mother: The Ironies of Household Technology from the Open Hearth to the Microwave*, New York: Basic Books, 1983.

Cowie, Jefferson, "A Century of Sweat: Subcontracting, Flexibility, and Consumption", *International Labor and Working Class History*, LXI/61 (April 2002), 128-40.

Cox, Karen L., *Dixie's Daughters: The United Daughters of the Confederacy and the Preservation of Confederate Culture*, Gainesville: UP of Florida, 2003.

Dallett Hemphill, C., *Bowing to Necessities: A History of Manners in America, 1620-1860*, New York: Oxford UP, 1999.

Daniel, Pete, *Breaking the Land: The Transformation of Cotton, Tobacco, and Rice Cultures Since 1880*, Urbana: U of Illinois P, 1985.

Davidson, Cathy N., "No More Separate Spheres!", *American Literature*, LXX/3 (September 1998), 443-63.

Davies, Gareth and Martha Derthick, "Race and Social Welfare Policy: The Social Security Act of 1935", *Political Science Quarterly*, CXII/2 (Summer 1997), 217-35.

Davis, Elizabeth Lindsay, *Lifting as They Climb*, Chicago: Race Relations Press, 1933.

Davis, Rebecca Harding, "The Wife's Story" (1864), rpt. in *Life in the Iron Mills and Other Stories*, ed. Tillie Olsen, New York: The Feminist Press, 1972, 177-222.

Deleuze, Gilles, *Dialogues II*, trans. Hugh Tomlinson, Barbara Habberjam and Eliot Ross, London: Continuum International, 2006.

DesJardins, Julie, *Women and the Historical Enterprise in America: Gender, Race, and the Politics of Memory, 1880-1945*, Chapel Hill: U of North Carolina P, 2003.

Deutsch, Sarah, *Women and the City: Gender, Space, and Power in Boston, 1870-1940*, New York: Oxford UP, 2000.

DeVault, Ileen A., *Sons and Daughters of Labor: Class and Clerical Work in Turn-of-the-century Pittsburgh*, Ithaca, NY: Cornell UP, 1990.

Dickens, Charles, *Martin Chuzzlewit* (1844), London: Wordsworth Editions, 1994, 678.

Dillon, Elizabeth Maddock, *The Gender of Freedom: Fictions of Liberalism and the Literary Public Sphere*, Stanford, CA: Stanford UP, 2004.

Donovan, Josephine, "Jewett on Race, Class, Ethnicity, and Imperialism: A Reply to Her Critics", *Colby Quarterly*, XXXVIII/4 (December 2002), 403-16.

Dornan, Inge and S.J. Kleinberg, "From Dawn to Dusk: Women's Work in the Antebellum Era", in *The Practice of U.S. Women's History: Narratives, Intersections, and Dialogues*, eds S.J. Kleinberg, Eileen Boris, and Vicki L. Ruiz, New Brunswick: Rutgers UP, 2007, 83-105.

Dublin, Thomas, *Women at Work: The Transformation of Work and Community in Lowell, Massachusetts, 1826-1860*, New York: Columbia UP, 1979.

DuBois, Ellen Carol, *Harriot Stanton Blatch and the Winning of Woman Suffrage*, New Haven, CT: Yale UP, 1997.

_____, Ellen Carol, *Woman Suffrage and Women's Rights*, New York: New York UP, 1998.

Dudden, Faye E., *Serving Women: Household Service in Nineteenth-century America*, Middletown, CT: Wesleyan UP, 1983.

Dunn, Lesley C. and Nancy A. Jones, *Embodied Voices: Representing Female Vocality in Western Culture*, Cambridge: Cambridge UP, 1994.

Easton, Alison, "Introduction: History and Utopia", in Sarah Orne Jewett, *The Country of the Pointed Firs and Other Stories*, ed. Alison Easton, Harmondsworth: Penguin, 1999, vii-xxii.

Easton, Barbara, "Industrialization and Femininity: A Case Study of Nineteenth-century New England", *Social Problems*, XXIII/4 (April 1976), 389-401.

Elbert. Monika M, *Separate Spheres No More: Gender Convergence in American Literature, 1830-1930*, Tuscaloosa: U of Alabama P, 2000.

Eliot, George, *Ermgart*, in *Jubal and Other Poems*, Edinburgh and London: Blackwood, 1870, 67-136.

Erenberg, Lewis, *Steppin' Out: New York Nightlife and the Transformation of American Culture, 1890-1930*, Westport, CT: Greenwood Press, 1981.

Evans, Sara, *Born for Liberty: A History of Women in America*, New York: Free Press, 1989.

Ewen, Elizabeth, *Immigrant Women in the Land of Dollars: Life and Culture on the Lower East Side, 1890-1925*, New York: Monthly Review Press, 1985.

Faner, Robert D., *Walt Whitman and Opera*, Philadelphia: U of Pennsylvania P, 1951.

Faue, Elizabeth, *Writing the Wrongs: Eva Valesh and the Rise of Labor Journalism*, Ithaca, NY: Cornell UP, 2002.

Fetherling, Dale, *Mother Jones: The Miners' Angel*, Carbondale: Southern Illinois UP, 1974.

Fields, Annie, *How to Help the Poor*, Boston: Houghton Mifflin, 1884.

Fink, Paula S., *Agrarian Women: Wives and Mothers in Rural Nebraska, 1880-1940*, Chapel Hill: U of North Carolina P, 1992.

Finley, Martha, *Elsie Dinsmore*, New York: Dodds, Mead, 1868.

Fite, Gilbert, *Cotton Fields No More: Southern Agriculture, 1865-1980*, Lexington: U of Kentucky P, 1984.

Fitzgerald, Maureen, *Habits of Compassion: Irish Catholic Nuns and the Origins of New York's Welfare System, 1830-1920*, Chapel Hill: U of North Carolina P, 2006.

Flexner, Eleanor, *Century of Struggle: The Woman's Rights Movement in the United States*, Cambridge, MA: Harvard UP, 1959.

Flynn, Elizabeth Gurley, "Memories of the Industrial Workers of the World", address to students at Northern Illinois University DeKalb, Illinois, 8 November 1962: http://www.geocities.com/CapitolHill/5202/rebelgirkl.html.

_____, Elizabeth Gurley, Paterson Strike Speech, New York Civic Club Forum, 31 January 1914: http://www.spartacus.schoolnet.co.uk/USA/flynn.htm.

_____, Elizabeth Gurley, *Rebel Girl: An Autobiography, My First Life (1906-1926)*, New York: International Publishers 1955.

_____, Elizabeth Gurley, *The Alderson Story: My Life as a Political Prisoner*, New York: International Publishers, 1963.

Flynn Baxandall, Rosalyn Gurley, *Words on Fire: The Life and Writing of Elizabeth Gurley Flynn*, New Brunswick, NJ: Rutgers UP, 1987.

Foner, Philip S. and Richard C. Winchester, *The Anti-imperialist Reader: A Documentary History of Anti-imperialism in the United States*, 2 vols, New York: Holmes and Meier, 1986.

_____, Philip S., ed., *Fellow Workers and Friends: I.W.W. Free-Speech Fights as Told by Participants*, Westport, CT: Greenwood Press 1981.

Foner, Philip S., ed., *Mother Jones Speaks: Collected Writings and Speeches*, New York: Monad, 1983.

Foote, Mary Hallock, "The Fate of a Voice" (1886), rpt. in *The Last Assembly Ball and the Fate of a Voice*, Boston and New York: Houghton, Mifflin, 1889, 215-75.

Ford, Ramona, "Native American Women: Changing Statuses, Changing Interpretations", in *Writing the Range: Race, Class, and Culture in the Women's West*, eds Susan Armitage and Elizabeth Jameson, Norman: U of Oklahoma P, 1997, 42-68.

Foster, Gaines, *Ghosts of the Confederacy: Defeat, the Lost Cause, and the Emergence of the New South*, New York: Oxford UP, 1987.

Fraser, Steven, "Combined and Uneven Development in the Men's Clothing Industry", *Business History Review*, LVII/4 (Winter 1983), 522-471.

Frederickson, George, *The Black Image in the White Mind: The Debate on Afro-American Character and Destiny, 1817-1914*, Hanover, CT: Wesleyan UP, 1987.

Freedman, Barbara, "Frame-up: Feminism, Psychoanalysis, Theatre", in *Performing Feminisms: Feminist Critical Theory and Theatre*, ed. Sue-Ellen Case, Baltimore, MD: Johns Hopkins P, 1990, 54-76.

French-Sheldon, May, *Sultan to Sultan: Adventures among the Masai and Other Tribes of East Africa* (1892), ed. Tracey Jean Boisseau, Manchester: Manchester UP, 1998.

Friedman-Kasaba, Kathie, *Memories of Migration: Gender, Ethnicity and Work in the Lives of Jewish and Italian Women in New York, 1870-1914*, Albany: State U of New York P, 1996.

Gamber, Wendy, *The Female Economy: The Millinery and Dressmaking Trades, 1860-1930*, Urbana: U of Illinois P, 1997.

Gardner, Sarah E., *Blood and Irony: Southern White Women's Narratives of the Civil War, 1861-1937*, Chapel Hill: U of North Carolina P, 2004.

Gatewood, William B., *Aristocrats of Color: The Black Elite, 1880-1920*, Bloomington: Indiana UP, 1990.

Giddings, Paula, *When and Where I Enter: The Impact of Black Women on Race and Sex in America*, New York: William Morrow, 1984.

Gilman, Charlotte Perkins, *Herland*, (1915), rpt. New York: Pantheon Books, 1979.

Gilmore, Glenda Elizabeth, *Gender and Jim Crow: Women and the Politics of White Supremacy in North Carolina, 1896-1920*, Chapel Hill: U of North Carolina P, 1996.

Ginzberg, Lori D., *Women and the Work of Benevolence: Morality, Politics, and Class in Nineteenth-century America*, New Haven, CT: Yale UP, 1990.

Glazener, Nancy, *Reading for Realism: The History of a U.S Literary Institution, 1850-1910*, Durham, NC: Duke UP, 1997.

Glen, Evelyn Nakano, *Unequal Freedom: How Race and Gender Shaped American Citizenship and Labor*, Cambridge, MA: Harvard UP, 2004.

Glenn, Susan A., *Daughters of the Shtetl: Life and Labor in the Immigrant Generation*, Ithaca, NY: Cornell UP, 1990.

Goldin, Claudia, *Understanding the Gender Gap: An Economic History of Women*, Oxford: Oxford UP, 1990.

Goldmark, Josephine, "Tenement Home Work and the Courts", *The Survey*, XXXV/21 (1916), 612-13.

Gollin. Rita K, *Annie Adams Fields: Woman of Letters*, Amherst: U of Massachusetts P, 2002.

Gordon, Wendy M., *Mill Girls and Strangers: Single Women's Independent Migration in England, Scotland, and the United States, 1850 -1881*, Albany: State U of New York P, 2002.

Gorn, Elliott J., *Mother Jones: The Most Dangerous Woman in America*, New York: Hill and Wang, 2001.

Green, Nancy L., "Fashion, Flexible Specialization and the Sweatshop: A Historical Problem", in *Sweatshop USA: The American Sweatshop: The Historical and Global Perspective*, eds Daniel E. Bender and Richard A. Greenwald, New York: Routledge, 2003, 37-55.

_____, Nancy L., *Ready-to-wear, Ready-to-work: A Century of Industry and Immigrants in Paris and New York*, Durham, NC: Duke UP, 1997, 137-60.

Green, Rayna, "The Tribe Called Wannabee: Playing Indian in America and Europe", *Folklore*, LXXXXIX/1 (1988), 30-55.

Greenwald, Richard, *The Triangle Fire, the Protocols of Peace and Industrial Democracy in Progressive Era New York*, Philadelphia, PA: Temple UP, 2005.

Grier, Katherine C., *Culture and Comfort: Parlor Making and Middle-class Identity, 1850-1930*, rev. edn, Washington, DC: Smithsonian Institution Press, 1988.

Grimke, Charlotte Forten, *The Journals of Charlotte Forten Grimke*, ed. Brenda Stevenson, New York: Oxford UP, 1988.

Gutiérrez, Ramon, *When Jesus Came, the Corn Mothers Went Away: Marriage, Sexuality and Power in New Mexico, 1500-1846*, Stanford, CA: Stanford UP, 1991.

Guy-Sheftall, Beverley, *Daughters of Sorrow: Attitudes Toward Black Women, 1880-1920*, New York: Carlson, 1990.

Haarsager, Sandra, *Organized Womanhood: Cultural Politics in the Pacific Northwest, 1840-1920*, Norman: U of Oklahoma P, 1997.

Habegger, Alfred, *Gender, Fantasy, and Realism in American Literature*, New York: Columbia UP, 1982.

Hale, Elizabeth Grace, *Making Whiteness: Southern Segregation, 1890–1940*, New York: Random House, 1999.

Hall, Jacqueline Dowd *et al.*, *Like a Family: The Making of a Southern Cotton Mill World*, Charlotte: U of North Carolina P, 1987.

Harding Davis, Rebecca, *Life in the Iron Mills; or, the Korl Woman*, with a biographical interpretation by Tillie Olsen, New York: The Feminist Press, 1972.

Harlan, Louis R., "Booker T. Washington in Biographical Perspective" (1970), rpt. in Booker T. Washington, *Up from Slavery* (1901), ed. William L. Andrews, New York: Norton Critical Edition, 1996, 204-19.

Harley, Sharon and Rosalyn Teborg-Penn, eds, *The Afro-American Woman: Struggles and Images*, Port Washington, NY: Kennikat Press, 1978.

Harper Cooley, Winifred, *The New Womanhood*, New York: Broadway Publishing Co., 1904.

Harper, Frances Ellen Watkins, "The Great Problem to be Solved" (1875), rpt. in *A Brighter Coming Day*, ed. Frances Smith Foster, New York: The Feminist Press, 1990, 219-222.

Harris, Sharon M., *Rebecca Harding Davis and American Realism*, Philadelphia: U of Pennsylvania P, 1991.

Harris, Susan K., *Nineteenth-century American Women's Novels: Interpretive Strategies*, Cambridge: Cambridge UP, 1990.

_____, Susan K., *The Cultural Work of the Late Nineteenth-century Hostess: Annie Adams Fields and Mary Gladstone Drew*, New York: Palgrave Macmillan, 2002.

Hart, Vivien, *Bound by our Constitution: Women, Workers, and the Minimum Wage*, Princeton, NJ: Princeton UP, 1994.

Hewitt, Martin, "District Visiting and the Constitution of Domestic Space in the Mid-nineteenth Century", in *Domestic Space: Reading the Nineteenth-century Interior*, 121-41.

_____, Nancy A., "Beyond the Search for Sisterhood: American Women's History in the 1990s", in *Unequal Sisters: A Multicultural Reader in U.S. Women's History*, eds Vicki L. Ruiz and Ellen Carol DuBois, New York: Routledge, 1990, 1-14.

Hewitt, Nancy A., *Women's Activism and Social Change: Rochester, New York, 1822-1872*, Ithaca, NY: Cornell UP, 1984.

Higginbotham, Evelyn, *Righteous Discontent: The Women's Movement in the Black Baptist Church, 1880-1920*, Cambridge, MA: Harvard UP, 1993.

Hill, Joseph A., *Women in Gainful Occupations: 1870-1920*, Washington, DC: US Bureau of the Census, Government Printing Office, 1929.

Hill, Patricia R., *The World Their Household: The American Woman's Foreign Mission Movement and Cultural Transformation, 1870-1920*, Ann Arbor: U of Michigan P, 1985.

Hine, Darlene Clark, "Rape and the Inner Lives of Black Women in the Middle West: Preliminary Thoughts on the Culture of Dissemblance", *Signs*, XIV/4 (Summer 1989), 912-920.

Hite, Molly, Introduction, in Emma Dunham Kelley, *Megda*, Schomburg Library Edition, New York: Oxford UP, 1988, xxvii-xxxvii.

Hobbes, Thomas, *Leviathan* (1658), ed. J.C.A. Gaskin, Oxford: Oxford UP, 1996.

Hocks, Richard A., *Henry James and Pragmatistic Thought: A Study in the Relationship between the Philosophy of William James and the Literary Art of Henry James*, Chapel Hill: North Carolina UP, 1974.

Hofstadter, Richard, *The Paranoid Style in American Politics and Other Essays*, London: Jonathan Cape, 1952.

Hoganson, Kristin L., *Fighting for American Manhood: How Gender Politics Provoked the Spanish-American and Philippine-American Wars*, New Haven, CT: Yale UP, 1998.

Holmes, Julia Archibald, "A Journey to Pikes Peak and New Mexico", *Sybil*, III/18 (1895), 521-31.

Hooks, Janet M., "Women's Occupations through Seven Decades", *Women's Bureau Bulletin*, No. 218, Washington, DC: US Department of Labor 1947, 52-62.

Howard, June, *Form and History in American Literary Naturalism*, Chapel Hill: U of North Carolina P, 1985.

_____, June, ed., *New Essays on "The Country of the Pointed Firs"*, Cambridge: Cambridge UP, 1994.

Huckle, Patricia, *Tish Sommers: Activist, and the Founding of the Older Women's League*, Knoxville: U of Tennessee P, 1991.

Huggins, Nathan Irvin, *Protestants against Poverty: Boston's Charities, 1870-1900*, Westport, CT: Greenwood Publishing, 1971.

Hull, Gloria T., Patricia Bell Scott, and Barbara Smith, eds, *All the Women Are White, All the Men Are Black, but Some of Us Are Brave: Black Women's Studies*, Old Westbury, NY: Feminist Press, 1981.

Hume, David, *Enquiries Concerning Human Understanding and Concerning the Principles of Morals*, ed. L.A. Selby-Bigge, 3rd edn, Oxford: Clarendon P, 1975.

Hunter, Tera W., *To 'Joy My Freedom: Southern Black Women's Lives and Labors after the Civil War*, Cambridge, MA: Harvard UP, 1997.

Hutcheon, Linda and Michael Hutcheon, *Opera: Desire, Disease and Death*, Lincoln: U of Nebraska P, 1996.

Huyler, Jerome, *Locke in America: The Moral Philosophy of the Founding Era*, Kansas City: Kansas UP, 1995. Raleigh, John Henry, "Henry James: The Poetics of Empiricism", *PMLA*, LXVI/2 (March 1951), 107-23.

Jackson, Holly, "Mistaken Identity: What if a Novelist Celebrated as a Pioneer of African-American Women's Literature Turned Out Not to Be Black At All?", *The Boston Globe*, 20 February 2005: http://www.boston.com/news/globe/ideas/articles/2005/02/20/mistaken_identity/.

Jacob, François, *The Logic of Living Systems: A History of Heredity*, trans. Betty E. Spillmann, London: Allen Lane, 1974.

Jacobs Bromberg, Joan, *The Body Project: An International History of American Girls*, New York: Random House, 1997.

James, Henry, *The Bostonians* (1886), Harmondsworth: Penguin, 1978.

_____, Henry, *Complete Notebooks of Henry James*, eds Leon Edel and Lyall H. Powers, New York: Oxford UP, 1987.

_____, Henry, *Collected Travel Writings: Great Britain and America*, New York: Library of America, 1993.

_____, Henry, *Collected Travel Writings: The Continent*, New York: Library of America, 1993.

_____, Henry, *Complete Stories, 1892-1898*, New York: Library of America, 1996.

_____, Henry, *Literary Criticism: French Writers, Other European Writers, the Prefaces to the New York Edition*, New York: Library of America, 1984.

_____, Henry, *The Complete Notebooks of Henry James*, eds F. O. Matthiessen and Kenneth B. Murdock, New York: Oxford UP, 1947.

_____, Henry, *What Maisie Knew*, Chicago: Herbert S. Stone and Co., 1897.

James, William, *Writings 1878-1899*, New York: Library of America, 1992.

_____, William, *Writings, 1902-1910*, New York: Library of America, 1987.

Janiewski, Delores E., *Sisterhood Denied: Race, Gender, and Class in a New South Community*, Philadelphia, PA: Temple UP, 1985.

Janney, Caroline E., "'To Honor Her Noble Sons': The Ladies Memorial Association of Petersburg, 1866-1912", in *Virginia's Civil War*, eds Peter Wallenstein and Bertram Wyatt-Brown, Charlottesville: U of Virginia P, 2005, 256-69.

_____, Joan M., "The Great Uprising in Rochester", in *A Needle, a Bobbin, a Strike: Women Needleworkers in America*, eds Joan M. Jensen and Sue Davidson, Philadelphia, PA: Temple UP, 1984, 94-113.

_____, Joan M., "The Great Uprisings: 1900-1920", in *A Needle, a Bobbin, a Strike: Women Needleworkers in America*, eds Joan M. Jensen and Sue Davidson, Philadelphia, PA: Temple UP, 1984, 83-93.

_____, Joan, *Loosening the Bonds: Mid-Atlantic Farm Women, 1750-1850*, New Haven, CT: Yale UP, 1986.

Johns, Elizabeth, *Thomas Eakins: The Heroism of Modern Life*, Princeton, NJ: Princeton UP, 1983.

Johnson, Joan Marie, "'Ye Gave Them a Stone': African American Women's Clubs, the Frederick Douglass Home, and the Black Mammy Monument", *Journal of Women's History*, XVII/1 (Spring 2005), 63-75.

_____, Joan Marie, *Southern Ladies, New Women: Race, Region, and Clubwomen in South Carolina, 1890-1930*, Gainesville: UP of Florida, 2004.

Johnson, Sarah A., "The Consumption of Middle Class American Women's Clothing through Mail Order Catalogues, 1850 to 1900", PhD diss., University of Brighton, 2003.

Jones, Jacqueline L., *Labor of Love, Labor of Sorrow: Black Women, Work, and the Family from Slavery to the Present*, New York: Basic Books, 1985.

Jones, Mary Cadwalader, *European Travel for Women: Notes and Suggestions*, New York: Macmillan, 1900.

Jones, Mother, "Civilization in Southern Mills", *International Socialist Review*, March 1901.

_____, Mother, *Autobiography of Mother Jones* (1925), Chicago: Arno, 1969.

Jordan, Winthrop, *White Over Black: American Attitudes toward the Negro, 1550-1812*, Chapel Hill: U of North Carolina P, 1968.

Jualynne, Dodson, E., *Engendering Church: Women, Power, and the AME Church*, New York: Rowman and Littlefield, 2002.

Judd, Richard W. Edwin A. Churchill, and Joel W. Eastman, eds, *Maine: The Pine Tree State from Prehistory to the Present*, Orono: U of Maine P, 1995.

Kaplan, Amy *The Anarchy of Empire in the Making of U.S. Culture*, Cambridge, MA: Harvard UP, 2002.

Kasson, John T., *Rudeness and Civility: Manners in Nineteenth-century Urban America*, New York: Hill and Wang, 1990.

Katz, Michael B., *In the Shadow of the Poorhouse: A Social History of Welfare in America* (1986), 10th Anniversary edition, New York: Basic Books, 1996.

Katzman, David, *Seven Days a Week: Women and Domestic Service in Industrializing America*, New York: Oxford UP, 1978.

Kelley, Emma Dunham, *Megda*, Boston: James H. Earle, 1891.

Kelley-Hawkins, Emma Dunham, *Four Girls at Cottage City* (1895), Boston: James H. Earle, 1898.

Kelley, Mary, "Beyond the Boundaries", *Journal of the Early Republic*, XXI/1 (Spring 2001), 73-78.

Kerber, Linda K., "Separate Spheres, Female Worlds, Woman's Place: The Rhetoric of Women's History", *Journal of American History*, LXXV/1 (June 1988), 9-39.

Kessler-Harris, Alice, "Designing Women and Old Fools: The Construction of the Social Security Amendments of 1939", in *U.S. History as Women's History: New Feminist Essays*, eds Linda K. Kerber, Alice Kessler-Harris, and Kathryn Kish Sklar, Chapel Hill: U of North Carolina P, 1995, 87-106.

_____, Alice, *Gender and Labor History*, Urbana: U of Illinois P, 2007.

_____, Alice, "Organizing the Unorganizable: Three Jewish Women and their Union", *Labor History*, XVII/1 (Winter 1976), 2-23.

_____, Alice, *In Pursuit of Equity: Women, Men, and the Quest for Economic Citizenship in 20th-century America*, New York: Oxford UP, 2001.

_____, Alice, *Out to Work: A History of Wage-earning Women in the United States*, New York: Oxford UP, 1982.

Kidwell, Clara Sue, "Restoring the Power of Thought Woman", in *Sisterhood Is Forever: A Woman's Anthology for a New Millennium*, ed. Robin Morgan, New York: Washington Square Press, 2003, 169-70.

Kidwell, Claudia B. and Margaret C. Christman, *Suiting Everyone: The Democratization of Clothing in America*, Washington DC: Smithsonian Institution P, 1974, 19-64.

Kilcup, Karen, "'The art spirit remains to me to this day': Contexts, Contemporaries, and Narcissa Owen's Political Aesthetics", in Narcissa Owen, *A Cherokee Woman's America: Memoirs of Narcissa Owen, 1831-1907*, ed. Karen L. Kilcup, Gainesville: UP of Florida, 2005, 1-44.

_____, Karen, *Native American Women's Writing c.1800-1924: An Anthology*, Malden, MA: Blackwell, 2000.

Klassen, Paula E., "The Robes of Womanhood: Dress and Authenticity among African-American Methodist Women in the Nineteenth-century", *Religion and American Culture*, XIV/1 (Winter 2004), 39-82.

Klein, Sarah, "Bringing up Jo: *Little Women*, Female Rhetorical Activity and the Nineteenth-century American Conduct Book Tradition", in *Domestic Goddesses*, ed. Kim Wells: http://www.womenwriters.net/domesticgoddess/klein alcott.htm.

Kleinberg, S.J., "Children's and Mothers' Employment in Three Eastern Cities", *Social Science History*, XXIX/1 (Spring 2005), 45-76.

_____, S.J. "Gendered Space: Housing, Privacy and Domesticity in the Nineteenth-century United States", in *Domestic Space: Reading the Nineteenth-century Interior*, eds Inga Bryden and Janet Floyd, Manchester: Manchester UP, 1999, 142-54.

_____, S.J., "Seeking the Meaning of Life: The Pittsburgh Survey and the Family", in *The Pittsburgh Survey Revisited*, eds Maurine Greenwald and Margo Anderson, Pittsburgh, PA: U of Pittsburgh P, 1996, 88-105.

_____, S.J., "Technology and Women's Work: The Lives of Working-Class Women, Pittsburgh, 1870-1900", *Labor History*, XVII (Winter 1976), 58-72.

_____, S.J., *Widows and Orphans First: The Family Economy and Social Welfare Policy, 1880-1939*, Urbana: U of Illinois P, 2006.

Kolodny, Annette, *The Lay of the Land: Metaphor as Experience and History in American Life and Letters*, Chapel Hill: U of North Carolina P, 1975.

Kosmider, Alexia, "Strike a Euro-American Pose: Ora Eddleman Reed's 'Types of Indian Girls'", *American Transcendental Quarterly*, XXII (1998), 109-31.

Kosselleck, Reinhart, *The Practice of Conceptual History: Timing History, Spacing Concepts*, trans. Todd Samuel Presner, Stanford, CA: Stanford UP, 2002.

Kuhn, Anne L., *The Mother's Role in Childhood Education: New England Concepts, 1830-1860*, New Haven, CT: Yale UP, 1947.

Lacan, Jacques, *The Four Fundamental Concepts of Psycho-analysis*, trans. Alan Sheridan, ed. Jacques-Alain Miller, New York: Norton, 1977.

Larkin, Jack, *The Reshaping of Everyday Life, 1790-1840*, New York: Harper Row, 1988.

Laudan, Laurens, "The Nature and Sources of Locke's Views on Hypotheses", *Journal of the History of Ideas*, XXVIII/2 (April-June 1967), 211-23.

Lebsock, Suzanne, *The Free Women of Petersburg: Status and Culture in a Southern Town, 1784-1860*, New York: W.W. Norton, 1985.

Lee, Robert G., *Orientals: Asian Americans in Popular Culture*, Philadelphia, PA: Temple UP, 1999.

Leppart, Richard, *The Sight of Sound: Music, Representation and the History of the Body*, Berkeley: U of California P, 1993.

_____, Gerda, *Black Women in White America: A Documentary History*, New York: Pantheon, 1972.

Lerner, Gerda, "The Lady and the Mill Girl", *Mid-Continent American Studies Journal*, X/1 (Spring 1969), 5-14.

Levine, Louis, *The Women's Garment Workers: A History of the International Ladies Garment Workers' Union*, New York: B.W. Huebsch, 1924.

Levine, Louis, *The Women's Garment Workers: A History of the International Ladies Garment Workers' Union*, New York: B.W. Huebsch, 1924.

Liberty Poems: Inspired by the Crisis of 1898-1900, Boston: James H. West, 1900.

Liebhold, Peter, and Harry R. Rubenstein, "Bringing Sweatshops in the Museum", in *Sweatshop USA: The American Sweatshop: The Historical and Global Perspective*, eds Daniel E. Bender and Richard A. Greenwald, New York: Routledge, 2003, 57-73.

Link, William A., *The Paradox of Southern Progressivism, 1880-1930*, Chapel Hill: U of North Carolina P, 1999.

Litwack, Leon, *Trouble in Mind*, New York: Vintage, 1999.

Livermore, Mary A., "Remarks at the Annual Meeting of the New England Anti-Imperialist League", *Report of the Fifth Annual Meeting of the New England Anti-Imperialist League*, Boston: New England Anti-Imperialist League, 1903.

Livingston, James, *Pragmatism and the Political Economy of Cultural Revolution*, Chapel Hill: U of North Carolina P, 1994.

Locke, John, *An Essay Concerning Human Understanding* [1690], ed. Peter H. Nidditch, Oxford: Clarendon P, 1975.

Lowenthal, David, *The Past Is a Foreign Country*, New York: Cambridge UP, 1985, 263-88.

Lucy Parsons Project, The, http://www.lucyparsonsproject.org.

Lyotard, Jean-Francois, *The Postmodern Condition: A Report on Knowledge*, trans. Geoff Bennington and Brian Massumi, Manchester: Manchester UP, 1984.

MacCabe, Colin, "Realism and the Cinema: Notes on Some Brechtian Theses", *Screen*, XVII/3 (Autumn 1976), 7-27.

Mack, Kenneth W., "Law, Society, Identity and the Making of the Jim Crow South: Travel and Segregation on Tennessee Railroads, 1875-1905", *Law and Social Inquiry*, XXIV/4 (Fall 1999), 377-409.

MacLeitch, Gail, "'Your Women Are of No Small Consequence': Native American Women, Gender, and Early American History", in *The Practice of U.S. Women's History: Narratives, Intersections, and Dialogues*, in S.J. Kleinberg, Eileen Boris, and Vicki L. Ruiz, New Brunswick: Rutgers UP, 2007, 30-49.

Mahood, Linda, *Policing Gender, Class and Family: Britain, 1850-1940*, London: U College London P, 1995.

Mann, Mary, Editor's Preface, in Sarah Winnemucca, *Life among the Piutes: Their Wrongs and Claims*, Bishop, CA: Sierra Media, 1969, 3.

Massachusetts Bureau of Statistics and Amy Hewes, *Industrial Homework in Massachusetts*, Boston, MA: Women's Educational and Industrial Union, 1915.

Materson, Lisa Gail, "Respectable Partisans: African American Women in Electoral Politics, 1877 to 1896", PhD diss., University of California at Los Angeles, 2000.

Mauss, Marcel, *The Gift: The Form and Reason for Exchange in Archaic Societies*, trans. W.D. Halls, London: Routledge, 1990.

May, Henry F., *The End of American Innocence: A Study of the First Years of Our Own Time, 1912–1917*, New York: Alfred A. Knopf, 1959.

McCammon, Holly J. and Karen E. Campbell, "How Women Won the Vote in the West: The Political Successes of State Suffrage Movements, 1869-1919", *Gender and Society*, XV/1 (February 2001), 55-82.

_____, Holly J., Karen E. Campbell, Ellen M. Granberg and Christine Mowery, "How Movements Win: Gendered Opportunity Structures and U.S. Women Suffrage Movements, 1866 to 1919", *American Sociological Review*, LXVI/1 (February 2001), 49-70.

McCarthy, Kathleen D., ed., *Lady Bountiful Revisited: Women, Philanthropy, and Power*, New Brunswick, NJ: Rutgers UP, 1990.

McCurry, Stephanie, "'The Soldier's Wife': White Women, the State, and the Politics of Protection in the Confederacy", in *Women and the Unstable State in Nineteenth-century America*, eds Alison M. Parker and Stephanie Cole, College Station: Texas A&M UP, 2000, 15-36.

McDowell, Deborah M., Introduction, in Emma Dunham Kelley-Hawkins, *Four Girls at Cottage City*, ed. McDowell, Deborah E., Schomburg Library Edition, New York: Oxford UP, 1988, xxvii-xxxviii.

McElya, Micki, "Commemorating the Color Line: The National Mammy Monument Controversy of the 1920s", in *Monuments to the Lost Cause: Women, Art, and the Landscapes of Southern Memory*, eds Cynthia Mills and Simpson, Pamela H., Knoxville: U of Tennessee P, 2003, 203-18.

McGovern, James R., "The American Woman's Pre-World War I Freedom in Manners and Morals", *Journal of American History*, LV/2 (September 1968), 315-333.

McLemee, Scott, "In Black and White", *Inside Higher Education*, 1 March 2005, 7.

McMurray, Linda O., *To Keep the Waters Troubled: The Life of Ida B. Wells*, New York: Oxford UP, 1998.

Mead, Rebecca J., *How the Vote Was Won: Woman Suffrage in the Western United States, 1868-1914*, New York: New York UP, 2004.

Meyerowitz, Joanne J., *Women Adrift: Independent Wage Earners in Chicago, 1880-1930*, Chicago: U of Chicago P, 1988.

Mills, Cynthia, "Gratitude and Gender Wars: Monuments to the Women of the Sixties", in *Monuments to the Lost Cause: Women, Art, and the Landscapes of*

Southern Memory, eds Cynthia Mills and Pamela H. Simpson, Knoxville: U of Tennessee P, 2003, 183-200.

Morgan, Francesca, *Women and Patriotism in Jim Crow America*, Chapel Hill: U of North Carolina P, 2005, 19-55. Evelyn Brooks Higginbotham, *Righteous Discontent: The Women's Movement in the Black Baptist Church, 1880-1920*, Cambridge, MA: Harvard UP, 1993, 150-64.

Morgan, Jennifer L., *Laboring Women: Reproduction and Gender in New World Slavery*, Philadelphia, PA: U of Pennsylvania P, 2004.

Morrison, Toni, *Playing in the Dark: Whiteness and the Literary Imagination*, Cambridge, MA: Harvard UP, 1992.

Morton, Patricia, *Disfigured Images: The Historical Assault on Afro-American Women*, New York: Praeger, 1991.

Moses, William Jeremiah, *The Golden Age of Black Nationalism, 1850-1925*, Hamden, CT: Archon Books, 1978.

Mulvey, Laura, "Visual Pleasures and Narrative Cinema", *Screen* XVI/3 (Autumn 1975), 6-18.

_____, Laura, *Visual and Other Pleasures*, Bloomington: Indiana UP, 1989.

Muncy, Robyn, *Creating a Female Dominion in American Reform, 1890-1935*, New York: Oxford UP, 1991.

Neverdon-Morton, Cynthia, *African American Women of the South and the Advancement of the Race, 1895-1925*, Knoxville: U of Tennessee P, 1989.

New York State, *Preliminary Report of the Factory Investigating Commission*, Albany: Arcus Co., I, 1912.

_____, *Second Report of the Factory Investigating Commission*, Albany, NY: J.B. Lyon Co., 1913.

Newman, Louise Michele, "Laying Claim to Difference: Ideologies of Race and Gender in the U.S. Women's Movement, 1870-1920", Ph.D. diss., Brown U, 1992.

Nietzsche, Friedrich, *The Complete Works of Friedrich Nietzsche*, ed. Oscar Levy, Edinburgh and London: T.N. Foulis, 1910.

Nieves, Angela David, "'We Gave Our Hearts and Lives to It': African-American Women Reformers, Industrial Education, and the Monuments of Nation-building in the Post-Reconstruction South, 1877-1938", PhD diss., Cornell University, 2001.

Nissenbaum, Stephen, *The Battle for Christmas*, New York: Alfred A. Knopf, 1996, 8-10, 62-63, 82-84.

Oldencrantz, Louise C., *Italian Women in Industry: A Study of Conditions in New York City*, New York: Russell Sage Foundation, 1919.

Oldenziel, Ruth, *Making Technology: Masculine Men, Women and Modern Machines in America, 1870-1945*, Amsterdam: Amsterdam UP, 1999.

Olds, Elizabeth Fagg, *Women of the Four Winds*, Boston: Houghton Mifflin, 1985.

Orleck, Annelise, *Common Sense and a Little Fire: Women and Working-Class Politics in the United States, 1900-1965*, Chapel Hill: U of North Carolina P, 1995.

Oshinsky, David M., *Worse than Slavery: Parchman Farm and the Ordeal of Jim Crow Justice*, New York: Free Press, 1997.

Owen, Narcissa, *A Cherokee Woman's America: Memoirs of Narcissa Owen, 1831-1907*, ed. Karen L. Kilcup, Gainesville: UP of Florida, 2005.

"Pansy" [Isabella Macdonald Alden], *Esther Reid* (1870), London: Thomas Nelson and Sons, 1901.

_____, *Four Girls at Chautauqua*, New York: Lothrop Publishing, 1876.

_____, *The Chautauqua Girls at Home*, New York: Lothrop Publishing, 1877.

Pateman, Carole, *The Disorder of Women: Democracy, Feminism and Political Theory*, Cambridge: Polity Press, 1989.

Patterson, Martha H., *Beyond the Gibson Girls: Reimagining the American New Woman*, Urbana: U of Illinois P, 2005.

Peck, Annie Smith, "A Woman in the Andes", *Harper's Monthly Magazine*, CXIV/679 (December 1906), 7-8.

Peiss, Kathy, *Cheap Amusements: Working Women and Leisure in Turn-of-the-century New York*, Philadelphia, PA: Temple UP, 1986.

_____, Kathy, *Hope in a Jar: The Making of America's Beauty Culture*, New York: Metropolitan Books, 1988.

Pemberton, Caroline, "Arming Heathens Against Christians", *City and State*, VI, 25 June 1899, n.p.

Perdue, Theda, *Cherokee Women: Gender and Culture Change*, 1700-1835, Lincoln: U of Nebraska P, 1998.

Perkins, Gilman, Charlotte, "Women's evolution from economic dependence" (1898), excerpted in Nancy F. Cott, Jeanne Boydston and Molly Ladd-Taylor, eds, *"Root of Bitterness: Documents of the Social History of American Women*, Boston, MA: Northeastern UP, 2nd edn, 1996, 391-395.

Pessen, Edward, *Riches, Class, and Power before the Civil War*, Lexington, MA: D.C. Heath, 1973.

Peterson, Carla L., *Doers of the Word: African-American Women Speakers and Writers in the North, 1830-1880*, New York: Oxford UP, 1995.

Picker, John M., *Victorian Soundscapes*, Oxford: Oxford UP, 2003.

Piepmeier Alison, *Out in Public: Configurations of Women's Bodies in Nineteenth-century America*, Chapel Hill: U of North Carolina P, 2004.

Pierce, Bessie Louise, *Public Opinion and the Teaching of History in the United States*, New York: Alfred A. Knopf, 1926.

Pope, Jesse E., *The Clothing Industry in New York*, New York: Columbia UP, 1905.

Porritt, Annie G., *Laws Affecting Women and Children in the Suffrage and Non-suffrage States*, New York: National Woman Suffrage Publishing Company, 1917.

Porter Benson, Susan, *Counter Cultures: Saleswomen, Managers, and Customers in American Department Stores, 1890 -1920*, Urbana: U of Illinois P, 1988.

Pratt, Mary Louise, *Imperial Eyes: Studies in Travel Writing and Transculturation*, London: Routledge, 1992.

Prokhovnik, Raia, *Rational Woman: A Feminist Critique of Dichotomy*, 2nd edn, Manchester: Manchester UP, 2002.

Pryse, Marjorie, "Sex, Class, and 'Category Crisis': Reading Jewett's Transitivity", *American Literature*, LXX/3 (September 1998), 517-49.

Rawlings, Peter, *American Theorists of the Novel: Henry James, Lionel Trilling, Wayne C. Booth*, London: Routledge, 2006.

_____, Peter, *Henry James and the Abuse of the Past*, Basingstoke: Palgrave Macmillan, 2005.

Reed, Ora Eddleman, "Great Work of an Indian", *Sturm's Oklahoma Magazine*, II/6 (1906), 7-9.

Reverby, Susan, *Ordered to Care: The Dilemma of American Nursing, 1850-1945*, Cambridge: Cambridge UP, 1987.

Richter, Amy G., *Home on the Rails: Women, Railroads and the Rise of Public Domesticity*, Chapel Hill: U of North Carolina P, 2005.

Riis, Jacob, *How the Other Half Lives: Studies among the Tenements of New York* (1901), New York: Dover Publications, 1971.

Riis, Thomas L., "Concert Singers, Prima Donnas and Entertainers: The Changing Status of Black Women Vocalists in Nineteenth-century America", in *Music and Culture in America, 1861-1918*, ed. Michael Saffle, New York: Garland, 1998, 53-78.

Robertson, Janet, *The Magnificent Mountain Women: Adventures in the Colorado Rockies*, Lincoln: U of Nebraska P, 1990.

Rodden, John, ed., *Lionel Trilling and the Critics: Opposing Selves*, Lincoln: Nebraska UP, 1999.

Roman, Judith A., *Annie Adams Fields: The Spirit of Charles Street*, Bloomington: Indiana UP, 1990.

Rotella, Elyce, *From Home to Office: U.S. Women at Work, 1870-1930*, Ann Arbor: U of Michigan P, 1981.

Rowe, John Carlos, *Literary Culture and U.S. Imperialism: From the Revolution to World War II*, New York: Oxford UP, 2000.

_____, John Carlos, *The Theoretical Dimensions of Henry James*, Madison: U of Wisconsin P, 1985.

Ruffin, Josephine, "Address of Josephine Ruffin, President of the Conference", *The Women's Era*, 2 (August 1895), 14.

Ruiz, Vicki L., *From Out of the Shadows: Mexican Women in Twentieth-century America*, New York: Oxford UP, 1998.

Rury, John L., *Education and Women's Work: Female Schooling and the Division of Labor in Urban America, 1870-1930*, Albany: State U of New York P, 1991.

Rusling, General James, "Interview with President William McKinley", *The Christian Advocate*, 22 January 1903, 17.

Ryan, Mary P., *Civic Wars: Democracy and Public Life in the American City during the Nineteenth Century*, Berkeley: U of California P, 1997.

_____, Mary P. *Women in Public: Between Banners and Ballots, 1825-1880*, Baltimore, MD: Johns Hopkins UP, 1990.

Sarah Orne Jewett Text Project, Terry Heller, ed., http://www.public.coe.edu/~theller/soj/sj-index.htm

Savage, Kirk, *Standing Soldiers, Kneeling Slaves: Race, War, and Monument in Nineteenth-century America*, Princeton, NJ: Princeton UP, 1997.

Schechter, Patricia Ann, *Ida B. Wells-Barnett and American Reform, 1880-1930*, Chapel Hill: U of North Carolina P, 2001.

_____, Patricia, "Unsettled Business: Ida B. Wells Against Lynching, or How Anti-lynching Got Its Gender", in *Under the Sentence of Death: Lynching in the South*, ed. W. Fitzhugh Brundage, Chapel Hill: U of North Carolina P, 1997.

Scherer, Joanna Cohan, "The Public Faces of Sarah Winnemucca", *Cultural Anthropology*, XIII/2 (May 1988), 178-204.

Schofield, Ann, "The Uprising of the 20,000: The Making of a Labor Legend", in *A Needle, a Bobbin, a Strike: Women Needleworkers in America*, eds Joan M. Jensen and Sue Davidson, Philadelphia, PA: Temple UP, 1984, 167-82.

Schriber, Mary Suzanne, *Writing Home: American Women Abroad, 1830-1920*, Charlottesville: UP of Virginia, 1997.

Scott, Anne Firor, *The Southern Lady: From Pedestal to Politics, 1830-1930*, Chicago: U of Chicago P, 1970.

_____, Anne Firor and Andrew Mackay Scott, *One Half the People: The Fight for Woman Suffrage*, Urbana: U of Illinois P, 1982.

Scott, Joan W., and Debra Keates, *Going Public: Feminism and the Shifting Boundaries of the Private Sphere*, Urbana: U of Illinois P, 2004.

Sergeant, Elizabeth S., "Toilers of the Tenements: Where the Beautiful Things of the Great Shops Are Made", *McClure's Magazine*, XXXV (July 1910), 231-41.

Sewell, Jessica Ellen, "Gendering the Spaces of Modernity: Women and Public Space in San Francisco, 1890-1915", PhD diss., University of California at Berkeley, 2000.

Shannon, Robert T., *Report of Cases Argued and Determined in the Supreme Court of Tennessee*, Louisville, TN: Fetter Law Book Co., 1902.

Sherman, Sarah Way, "Party Out of Bounds: Gender and Cass in Jewett's 'The Best China Saucer'", in *Jewett and Her Contemporaries: Reshaping the Canon*, eds Karen L. Kilcup and Thomas S. Edwards, Gainesville: UP of Florida, 1999, 223-48.

Sims, Anastatia, *The Power of Femininity in the New South: Women's Organizations and Politics in North Carolina, 1880-1930*, Columbia: U of South Carolina P, 1997.

Skocpol, Theda, *Protecting Soldiers and Mothers: The Political Origins of Social Policy in the United States*, Cambridge, MA: Harvard UP, 1992.

Small, Christopher, *Musicking: The Meanings of Performing and Listening*, Hanover, CT: UP of New England, 1998.

Smith-Rosenberg, Caroll, "The Abortion Movement and the AMA, 1850-1880", in *Disorderly Conduct: Visions of Gender in Victorian America*, New York: Oxford UP, 1985, 217-44.

_____, Caroll, "The Female World of Love and Ritual: Relations between Women in Nineteenth-century America", *Signs: A Journal of Women in Culture and Society*, I/1 (Autumn 1975), 1-29.

Solomon, Barbara Miller, *In the Company of Educated Women: A History of Women and Higher Education in America*, New Haven, CT: Yale UP, 1985.

Sommer, Doris, *Bilingual Aesthetics: A New Sentimental Education*, Durham, NC: Duke UP, 2004.

Sorenson, Mark W., *Ahead of Their Time: A Brief History of Woman Suffrage in Illinois*, Springfield: Illinois State Archives, 2001.

Spain, Daphne, *How Women Saved the City*, Minneapolis: U of Minnesota P, 2001.

St Maur, Mrs Algernon [Susan], *Impressions of a Tenderfoot During a Journey in Search of Sport in the Far West*, London: John Murray, 1890.

_____, Christine, *City of Women: Sex and Class in New York City, 1789-1860*, New York: Knopf, 1986.

Stansell, Christine, "The Origins of the Sweatshop: Women and Early Industrialization in New York City", in *Working Class America: Essays on Labor, Community and American Society*, eds Michael H. Frisch and Daniel J. Walkowitz, Urbana: U of Illinois P, 1983, 78-103.

Statistical History of the United States: From Colonial Times to the Present, 1976, intro. by Ben J. Wattenberg, New York: Basic Books 1976.

Stanton, Elizabeth Cady, "The Solitude of Self" (1892), in *The American Intellectual Tradition, 1865 to the Present*, eds David A. Hollinger and Charles Capper, 3rd edn, New York: Oxford UP, 2001, II, 48-53.

Steadman, Jennifer Bernhardt, "Travel Writing and Resistance: A Feminist Reading of Travel Narratives by African-American and Euro-American Women", PhD diss., Emory University, 2000.

Sutherland, Daniel E., *Americans and Their Servants: Domestic Service in the United States from 1800 to 1920*, Baton Rouge: Louisiana State UP, 1981.

Tanner, Tony, *Scenes of Nature, Signs of Men*, Cambridge: Cambridge UP, 1987.

Tate, Claudia, *Domestic Allegories of Political Desire: The Black Heroine's Text at the Turn of the Century*, New York: Oxford UP, 1996;

_____, Claudia, *Psychoanalysis and Black Novels: Desire and the Protocols of Race*, New York: Oxford UP, 1998.

Tayleur, Eleanor, "The Negro Woman: 1. Social and Moral Decadence", *The Outlook*, LXXIV (10 January 1904), 266-71.

Teachout, Woden Sorrow, "Forging Memory: Hereditary Societies, Patriotism, and the American Past, 1876-1898", PhD diss., Harvard University, 2003, 139-74.

Terborg-Penn, Rosalyn, "Discrimination Against Afro-American Women in the Women's Movement, 1830-1920", in *The Black Woman Cross-culturally*, ed. Filomina Chioma Steady, Cambridge, MA: Schenkeman Co., 1981, 310-15.

Teres, Harvey M., *Renewing the Left: Politics, Imagination, and the New York Intellectuals*, New York: Oxford UP, 1996.

Tholfsen, Trygve R., "Moral Education in the Victorian Sunday School", *History of Education Quarterly*, XX/4 (Winter 1980), 77-99.

Thurner, Manuela, "'Better Citizens without the Ballot': American Antisuffrage Women and Their Rationale during the Progressive Era", *Journal of Women's History*, V/1 (Spring 1993), 33-60.

Tolnay, Stewart E., *The Bottom Rung: African American Family Life on Southern Farms*, Urbana: U of Illinois P, 1999.

Tompkins, Jane, *Sensational Designs: The Cultural Work of American Fiction, 1790-1860*, New York: Oxford UP, 1985.

Tonkovich, Nicole, "Rhetorical Power in the Victorian Parlor: *Godey's Lady's Book* and the Gendering of Nineteenth-century Rhetoric", in *Oratorical Culture in Nineteenth-century America: Transformations in the Theory and Practice of Rhetoric*, eds Gregory Clark and S. Michael Halloran, Carbondale: Southern Illinois UP, 1991, 158-83.

Trachtenberg, Alan, *The Incorporation of America: Culture and Society in the Gilded Age*, New York: Hill and Wang, 1982.

Trilling, Lionel, *Sincerity and Authenticity*, London: Oxford UP, 1972.

_____, Lionel, *The Opposing Self: Nine Essays in Criticism*, Uniform Edition, New York and London: Harcourt Brace Jovanovich, 1955.

Twain, Mark, *A Connecticut Yankee in King Arthur's Court* (1889), ed. Allison Ensor, New York: Norton Critical Edition, 1982.

United States Congress, *Economic Security Act: Hearings Before the Committee on Ways and Means, House of Representatives, 74th Congress, First Session on H.R. 4120, A Bill to Alleviate the Hazards of Old Age, Unemployment, Illness, and Dependency, to Establish a Social Insurance Board in the Department of Labor, to Raise Revenue, and for Other Purposes*, Washington, DC: Government Printing Office, 1935.

United States Department of Commerce and Labor, Bureau of the Census, *Statistics of Women at Work: Based on Unpublished Information Derived from the Schedules of the Twelfth Census, 1900*, Washington, DC: Government Printing Office, 1907.

US Bureau of Census, 1902, *Statistical Atlas, Twelfth Census of the United States, 1900*, Washington, DC: US Government Printing Office, 1902.

US Congress, Senate, "Clothing Manufacturing", in *Reports of the Immigration Commission: Immigrants in Industries*, XI, pt 6, 61 Cong. 2 Sess., Report 633, 1911, 253-661.

_____, Senate, "Report on the Condition of Women and Child Wage Earners in the United States", in *History of Women in Industry in the United States*, IX, 61 Cong. 2 Sess. Report 645, 1910, 143-44.

Van Kleeck, Mary, *Artificial Flower Makers*, New York: Russell Sage Foundation, 1913.

Walker, Alice, *The Color Purple*, New York: Harcourt, Brace, Jovanovich, 1982.

Wallace, Michael, "Visiting the Past: History Museums in the United States", in *Presenting the Past: Essays on History and the Public*, eds Susan Porter Benson, Steven Brier, and Roy Rosenzweig, Philadelphia, PA: Temple UP, 1986, 137-61.

Walsh, Mary Roth, *Doctors Wanted: No Women Need Apply*, New Haven, CT: Yale UP, 1977.

Washington, Booker T., *Up from Slavery* (1901), ed. William L. Andrews, New York: Norton Critical Edition, 1996.

Watson, Elizabeth C., "Home Work in the Tenements", *The Survey*, XXV/19 (1911), 772-81.

Waugh, Joan, *Unsentimental Reformer: The Life of Josephine Shaw Lowell*, Cambridge, MA: Harvard UP, 1997.

Weiler, N. Sue, "The Uprising in Chicago: The Men's Garment Workers Strike, 1910-1911", in *A Needle, a Bobbin, a Strike: Women Needleworkers in America*, eds Joan M. Jensen and Sue Davidson, Philadelphia, PA: Temple UP, 1984, 114-39.

Weiner, Lynn Y., *From Working Girl to Working Mother: The Female Labor Force in the United States, 1920-1980*, Chapel Hill: U of North Carolina P, 1985.

Welke, Barbara, *Recasting American Liberty: Gender, Race and Railroad Revolution, 1865-1920*, Cambridge: Cambridge UP, 2001.

Welke, Barbara Y., "When All the Women Were White and All the Blacks Were Men: Gender, Race, Class, and the Road to Plessy, 1855-1914", *Law and History Review*, XIII/2 (Autumn 1995), 261-316.

Wells, Ida B., "Southern Horrors" (1892), rpt. in *Southern Horrors and Other Writings: The Anti-lynching Campaign of Ida B. Wells, 1892-1900*, ed. Jacqueline Jones Royster, Boston: Bedford Books, 1997, 50-63.

＿＿＿, Ida B., *Crusade for Justice: The Autobiography of Ida B. Wells*, ed. A. Duster, Chicago: U of Chicago P, 1970.

＿＿＿, Ida B., *The Memphis Diary of Ida B. Wells*, ed. Miriam DeCosta-Willis, Boston: Beacon Press.

Welter, Barbara, "The Cult of True Womanhood, 1820-1860", *American Quarterly*, XVIII/2 (Summer 1966), 151-74.

Wertheimer, Barbara M., *We Were There: The Story of Working Women in America*, New York: Pantheon Books, 1977.

White, Deborah Gray *Ar'n't I a Woman? Female Slaves in the Plantation South*, New York: Norton, 1984.

Wiebe, Robert H., *The Search for Order, 1877–1920*, New York: Hill and Wang, 1967,

Wiener, Marli, *Mistresses and Slaves: Plantation Women in South Carolina, 1830-1880*, Urbana: U of Illinois P, 1998.

Wiggin, Kate Douglas, "Daughters of Zion", in *New Chronicles of Rebecca*, Boston, MA: Houghton, Mifflin, 1907.

＿＿＿, Kate Douglas, *Rebecca of Sunnybrook Farm*, Boston, MA: Houghton, Mifflin, 1903.

Wiggins, Lida Keck, "Ohio's Madonna of the Trail", *Ohio History*, XLI, 1932, 161-66.

Willar, Frances E. d, "The Dawn of Woman's Day", in Nancy F. Cott, Jeanne Boydston and Molly Ladd-Taylor, eds, "*Root of Bitterness: Documents of the Social History of American Women*, Boston, MA: Northeastern UP, 2nd edn, 1996, 399-405.

Willard, Frances E., *A Wheel Within a Wheel: How I Learned to Ride the Bicycle with Some Reflections by the Way*, New York: Fleming H. Revell Company, 1895.

＿＿＿, Frances E., *How to Win: A Book for Girls* (1886), rpt. in Charlotte Perkins Gilman, *The Yellow Wallpaper*, ed. Bale Bauer, Boston, MA: Bedford Books, 1996, 110-19.

Willet, Mabel Hurt, *The Employment of Women in the Clothing Trade*, New York: Columbia UP, 1902.

Williams, Heather Andrea, *Self-taught: African American Education in Slavery and Freedom*, Chapel Hill: U of North Carolina P, 2005.

Wilson Logan, Shirley, "'What Are We Worth': Anna Julia Cooper Defines Black Women's Work at the Dawn of the Twentieth Century", in *Sister Circle: Black Women and Work*, ed. Sharon Harley, New Brunswick, NJ: Rutgers UP, 2002, 146-63.

Winnemucca, Sarah, *Life among the Piutes: Their Wrongs and Claims*, Bishop, CA: Sierra Media, 1969.

Wisner, Benjamin B., *Memoirs of the Late Mrs Susan Huntington of Boston, Massachusetts*, Boston, MA: Crocker and Brewster, 1836.

Woloch, Nancy, *Muller vs. Oregon: A Brief History with Documents*, Boston, MA: Bedford Books of St Martin's Press, 1996.

_____, Nancy, *Women and the American Experience*, third edn, New York: McGraw-Hill, 2000.

Wong, Hertha D., *Sending My Heart Back Across the Years: Tradition and Innovation in Native American Autobiography*, New York: Oxford UP, 1992.

Wood, Elizabeth, "Sapphonics", in *Queering the Pitch: The New Gay and Lesbian Musicology*, eds Philip Brett, Wood, Elizabeth, and Gary C. Thomas, London: Routledge, 27-66.

Wood, Sharon E., *The Freedom of the Streets: Work, Citizenship, and Sexuality in a Gilded Age City*, Chapel Hill: U of North Carolina P, 2005.

Workman, Fanny Bullock, and William Hunter Workman, *Algerian Memories: A Bicycle Tour over the Atlas to the Sahara*, London: T. Fisher Unwin, 1895.

_____, Fanny Bullock, and William Hunter Workman, *Ice-bound Heights of the Mustagh: An Account of Two Seasons of Pioneer Exploration and High Climbing in the Baltistan Himalaya*, London: Archibald Constable, 1908.

_____, Fanny Bullock, and William Hunter Workman, *Peaks and Glaciers of Nun Kun*, London: Constable, 1909.

_____, Fanny Bullock, and William Hunter Workman, *Two Summers in the Ice-wilds of Eastern Karakoram: The Exploration of Nineteen-hundred Square Miles of Mountain Glacier*, London: T. Fisher Unwin, 1917.

Zandy, Janet, *Hands: Physical Labor, Class, and Cultural Work*, New Brunswick, NJ: Rutgers UP, 2004.

INDEX

Editor: John V. Knapp
Publisher: Northern Illinois University

Style

A quarterly journal of
aesthetics, poetics, stylistics,
and literary criticism

Next in *Style*

Temporal Paradoxes in Fiction and Stylistics in American Literatures
Volume 43, Number 2, Summer 2009

Marie-Laure Ryan. "Temporal Paradoxes in Narrative"

Mark Edleman Boren. "Abortographism and the Weapon of Sympathy in Charles Brockden Brown's *Edgar Huntly; Or, Memoirs of A Sleepwalker*"

Robert E. Kohn. "Pynchon's Trasition from Ethos-based Postmodernism to Late-Postmodern Stylistics"

Roi Tartakovsky. "E. E. Cummings's Parentheses: Punctuation as Poetic Device"

Julian Wolfreys. "Everyday Modernities"

Information on Subscriptions and Sales

Style is now accepting new subscriptions and renewals to Volume 43 (2009):

Institutions $60; Individuals $40; Students $23; *all add $6 for foreign postage*

Current single numbers $18; add $2 for foreign postage

Attention Librarians and Collectors: Back volumes of *Style* may be purchased at $12 per volume for volumes 1-16 (plus $6 per volume for foreign postage) or at $180 for all 16 volumes (plus $20 for domestic postage and $30 for foreign postage). Volumes 17 to the present volume may be purchased at $60 per volume. Add $8 per volume for foreign postage. Inquire for single issue prices. Address orders to the Managing Editor, *Style*, Department of English, Northern Illinois University, DeKalb, Illinois 60115-2863.

❑ Please enter my subscription to *Style* for Volume 43 (2009)

Please make checks payable to *Style* in U.S. dollars and send to: *Style*, Department of English, Northern Illinois University, DeKalb, IL 60115-2863.

Name_____Address _____

City _____ State _____ Zip _____

My check in the amount of $_____ is enclosed.

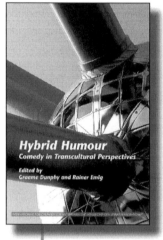